The Spectre of State Capitalism

CRITICAL FRONTIERS OF THEORY, RESEARCH, AND POLICY IN INTERNATIONAL DEVELOPMENT STUDIES

Series Editors

The contemporary world is characterized by massive wealth alongside widespread poverty, inequality, and environmental destruction—all bound up through class, race, and gender dynamics of inequality and oppression.

Critical Frontiers of Theory, Research, and Policy in International Development Studies, the official book series of the Development Studies Association of the UK, was established to contribute to critical thinking about local, national, and global processes of structural transformation. The series publishes cutting-edge monographs that promote critical development studies as an interdisciplinary and applied field and shape the theory, practice, and teaching of international development for a new generation of scholars, students, and practitioners. As the series evolves, we wish to publish a diverse and inclusive range of authors whose work engages in critical, multidisciplinary, decolonial, and methodologically plural development studies.

RECENTLY PUBLISHED IN THE SERIES

Disrupted Development in the Congo
The Fragile Foundations of the African Mining Consensus
Ben Radley

Politics and the Urban Frontier
Transformation and Divergence in Late Urbanizing East Africa
Tom Goodfellow

Equity, Evaluation, and International Cooperation
In Pursuit of Proximate Peers in an African City
Gabriella Y. Carolini

They Eat Our Sweat
Transport Labor, Corruption, and Everyday Survival in Urban Nigeria
Daniel E. Agbiboa

The Spectre of State Capitalism

Ilias Alami and Adam D. Dixon

OXFORD
UNIVERSITY PRESS

OXFORD
UNIVERSITY PRESS

Great Clarendon Street, Oxford, OX2 6DP,
United Kingdom

Oxford University Press is a department of the University of Oxford.
It furthers the University's objective of excellence in research, scholarship,
and education by publishing worldwide. Oxford is a registered trade mark of
Oxford University Press in the UK and in certain other countries

Published in the United States of America by Oxford University Press
198 Madison Avenue, New York, NY 10016, United States of America

British Library Cataloguing in Publication Data
Data available

Library of Congress Control Number: 2024932605

ISBN 9780198925194

DOI: 10.1093/9780198925224.001.0001

Printed and bound by
CPI Group (UK) Ltd, Croydon, CR0 4YY

For

Nejma and Amina

Olga, Fay, and Juno

Preface

This is not a book about China, Indonesia, Singapore, Russia, or any of the national or regional social formations often considered as representative of the new state capitalism in academic writings and political commentary. Our prime concerns and purpose in this book are different. We aim to address what we think are some of the main theoretical and political problems raised by the contemporary advent of state capitalism: why does state capitalism ascend? how does it ascend? why now? with what implications? how to explain its institutional diversity? what is the relationship between contemporary state capitalism and broader patterns of uneven development, such as neoliberalization, financialization, and the internationalization of production? How does it relate to secular capitalist trends of economic stagnation and the centralization and concentration of capital?

Providing definitive and exhaustive answers to these questions would be an enormously complex effort, and a task certainly too much to handle for a single monograph in a satisfactory way. Our aim is therefore more modest. Grappling with these questions and tackling head on some of the conceptual conundrums associated with them—such as establishing a sound distinction between the capitalist state and state capitalism; defining the spatialities and temporalities of the phenomenon (i.e. locating, spatializing, and periodizing state capitalism); and avoiding the pitfalls of Eurocentrism in theorizing—are means through which we aim to bring analytical clarity to the rapidly expanding and dynamic field of state capitalism studies and push it into novel, exciting directions.

Thus, our intervention is programmatic, and the book gives pride of place to questions of epistemology and the work of theoretical reconstruction and conceptual development. If much of the theoretical heavy lifting is concentrated in the early chapters, we also weave theory and empirics throughout the book. We use a wealth of economic indicators and data points as well as plenty of examples and illustrative case studies. Where relevant, we also make use of our own empirical research conducted in the scope of the European Research Council-funded *SWFsEUROPE* project on the global political economy of sovereign wealth funds. This included repeated interactions with sovereign fund managers at international summits, conferences, workshops, and other professional events over the past five plus years. We also conducted fieldwork in Senegal and Kenya in November and December 2021 on the growing entanglement of new national development strategies and foreign state-capital hybrids. Our analysis is also informed by the excellent research conducted by other *SWFsEUROPE* researchers (notably Milan Babic's work on foreign state-led investment and Imogen T. Liu's research on the transnationalization of Chinese state-owned capital) and by collaborations with colleagues based in the Netherlands, Canada, China, Germany, South Korea, the United Kingdom, the United States, Australia, and elsewhere. If this book is a synthesis of research work conducted over the last half-decade on state capitalism, it also draws upon arguments and reflections on recent changes in state-capital relations that we developed in the context of other research projects (see Clark, Dixon, and Monk 2013; Dixon 2014; Alami 2019).

The book is not presented as in-depth country case studies, as is often typical of the literature on state capitalism. Rather, the originality of the book lies in its broader perspective, with chapters contrasting and bringing into dialogue the experience of various social formations (e.g., including the 'usual suspects' like China, Brazil, Indonesia, and Singapore, but others too, such as the United States, the European Union, Senegal, Morocco, and other developing economies) and institutional and political forms (e.g., sovereign wealth funds, state-owned enterprises, policy banks, techno-industrial policy). To be clear, we are less interested in individual state trajectories than we are with their imbrication, co-constitution, and participation in the broader historic arc of state intervention we call the new state capitalism. As we compare and contrast these experiences, we critically explore the theoretical and political questions raised earlier.

We pay attention to material, discursive, and ideological dimensions. *Material*, in the sense that we situate the rise of present-day state capitalism within broader material processes, such as those related to the historic development and self-transformation of global capitalism. This includes mutations in the spheres of production, circulation, distribution of value, the continuation of accumulation in the face of market saturation and intensified competition, and geographical trends such as the unfolding of a new international division of labour and the unprecedented centralization and concentration of capital on a planetary scale. We emphasize in particular the emergence of a new geographical pattern of global capital accumulation since the 2000s, characterized by a secular shift in the centre of gravity of the world economy from the North Atlantic to the Pacific Rim and the turbulent geoeconomic and geopolitical reordering which accompany this shift, including, inter alia, the changing role of state power in the territorial organization of the planetary circuits of capital, mutations in the construction and expression of political authority in and through capitalist markets, new antagonisms between and within various segments of capital, intra-capitalist class conflicts, and the destabilization of the Global North/South axis. These material transformations, interests, and power struggles are shaping the polymorphism of the new state capitalism (its highly heterogenous institutional landscapes and configurations of state-capital relations across the spaces of the world economy).

Our analysis also foregrounds the *discursive* elements of the new state capitalism, or how it operates as a powerful set of discourses and representations. There has been a pronounced tendency to portray the rise of state capitalism as a new 'global drama' in world politics: we are told that state capitalism is a fast-emerging alternative economic model, constituting a monolithic threat to Western powers and the Western-dominated liberal world order, in a sort of grand strategic stand-off which constitutes the defining issue of our time. This discursive frame is not only severely limited in its capacity to grasp the extent of current state transformations. It also reproduces extremely problematic Eurocentric imaginaries: a vile, authoritarian state capitalism, largely a product of the East, threatening a more virtuous liberal-democratic form of free-market capitalism allegedly prevailing in the West. This straightforward message exists in some form in the current proliferation of business press op-eds, think-tank reports, national industrial strategies, monopolies commission statements, foreign policy documents, and so on. It allows simultaneously casting doubt on the legitimacy of non-Western actors while legitimating renewed state action by advanced capitalist states. In this book, we problematize this rhetorical weaponization of state capitalism as a form of geopolitical discourse, expose its underlying power relations, and unpack its material effects on competition and capitalist restructuring.

Relatedly, we question the common sense that is currently being forged by Western economic and political elites as to what counts (and does not) as state capitalist, and the political motivations and normative views about state/markets that undergird this power-laden epistemic act, which brings us to the significance of *ideology*. The rise of present-day state capitalism is triggering turbulent ideological adjustment concerning the place of the state in the economy and society, rapid redefinitions of what is considered the legitimate scope of state intervention, and new understandings of what counts as an appropriate separation between the public and the private spheres. We are particularly interested in unpacking how particular discourses about the public/private boundary are transformed into orthodoxies which legitimate some specific forms of state intervention and negate the political legitimacy of others. The question of state ownership neatly encapsulates these concerns. State ownership was largely considered an illegitimate form of state intervention by the (neo)liberal policy establishment in the 1980s and 1990s. As we are entering a sort of 'new state capitalist normal'—characterized notably by a vast expansion of the mass of capital controlled by states since the early 2000s and more visible modalities of statism—there has been a precarious (yet noticeable and significant) shift towards a certain re-legitimation and limited embrace of state ownership, even within these orthodox policymaking circles. As we show in this book, this ideological adjustment is ridden with contradictions and shaped by antagonistic interests. Besides, this is not so much a relaxation of the liberal stance on state ownership (even less so a move away from it) than as a mutation of it, one that allows preserving and reaffirming a clear-cut separation between the economic and the political under a new guise, and one that simultaneously (supposedly) establishes a clear distinction between liberal and illiberal forms of state-capital hybrids. Importantly, these mutations are happening against the backdrop of a crisis of liberal reason and resilient ('zombie' or 'mutant') neoliberalism creating complex and unstable ideological configurations.

Ilias Alami and Adam D. Dixon
Cambridge and Edinburgh, December 2023

Acknowledgements

This work began from a simple question posed in the autumn of 2018: what is state capitalism? Since then, we have been fortunate to test our ideas and claims with many interlocutors and collaborators. Special mention goes to Imogen T. Liu and Milan Babić, who were members of the *SWFsEUROPE* project and with whom we edited a special issue of the journal *Contemporary Politics* on state capitalism. Their collaboration early on was crucial for setting the case for how to approach the *problématique* of the new state capitalism. Emma Mawdsley deserves special mention for her collaboration on a paper published in Antipode on state capitalism and global development. Heather Whiteside and Jamie Peck also deserve special mention for their collaboration on co-editing a tripartite special issue on state capitalism in *Environment and Planning A: Economy and Space*, where our work was graciously applied and advanced in new empirical and theoretical ways. In addition, we would like to thank, Greig Charnock, Nick Jepson, Nana de Graaff, Dariusz Wójcik, Gordon Clark, Seth Schindler, Steve Rolf, Callum Ward, Jack Copley, Alexis Moraitis, Jack Taggart, Brett Christophers, Malcolm Fairbrother, Jeffrey Henderson, the participants in the Value-Form reading group, and the members of the Second Cold War Observatory. All views expressed herein are our own.

Various aspects and arguments of this book were presented at the following events and conferences, where we benefitted from the generous engagement of audience members: the Centre for Economic and Regional Studies, Institute of World Economics, Budapest, Hungary, the Université de Genève, the American Association of Geographers annual meeting, the Goldsmiths University of London, Goethe University Frankfurt, Umeå University, London School of Economics, European International Studies Association, Sciences Po Paris, the Global Conference on Economic Geography, the Open University UK, the Society for the Advancement of Socio-Economics, the International Karl Polanyi Conference, the China in Europe Research Network (CHERN), Manchester University, and the International Initiative for Promoting Political Economy.

Ilias Alami is grateful to the Department of Society Studies at Maastricht University, the Centre d'Études Européennes at Sciences Po, MaxPo Paris, and the Uppsala University Department of Human Geography for hosting him during part of the writing of this book. Adam Dixon would like to acknowledge the support of the Faculty of Arts and Social Sciences at Maastricht University and the Globalization, Transnationalism, and Development research programme for hosting the *SWFsEUROPE* project and to the Edinburgh Business School at Heriot-Watt University and Adam Smith's Panmure House for providing the time and space to complete the research and manuscript. This work was supported generously by the Marie Skłodowska–Curie Actions (grant agreement no.101024448) and by the European Research Council (grant agreement no. 758430) under the European Union's Horizon 2020 research and programme innovation.

Some of the chapters of this book draw, in part, upon previously published open access papers. Here we would also acknowledge the permission of publishers to use portions of these papers and essays:

Sage for:

Alami, I., and A. D. Dixon. 2020. State capitalism(s) redux? Theories, tensions, controversies. *Competition & Change* 24 (1): 70–94.

Alami, I., and A. D. Dixon. 2023. Uneven and combined state capitalism. *Environment and Planning A: Economy and Space* 55(1): 72–99.

Taylor & Francis for:

Alami, I., and A. Dixon. 2022. 'Expropriation of capitalist by state capitalist': Organizational change and the centralization of capital as state property. *Economic Geography* 98(4): 303–326; and Alami, I., M. Babic, A. D. Dixon, and I. T. Liu. 2022. Special issue introduction: what is the new state capitalism? *Contemporary Politics* 28(3): 245–263.

Elsevier for:

Alami, I., and A. D. Dixon. 2020. The strange geographies of the 'new' state capitalism. *Political Geography* 82: 102237.

Wiley for:

Alami, I., A. D. Dixon, and E. Mawdsley. 2021. State Capitalism and the New Global D/development Regime. *Antipode* 53 (5): 1294–1318.

Contents

List of Figures and Tables xiv
List of Abbreviations xv

1. State Capitalism(s) Redux? 1

2. Theories, Tensions, Controversies 23

3. The *Problématique* of State Capitalism 50

4. Rooting State Capitalism in the Churn of Uneven Development 77

5. State Capitalism Begets State Capitalism: On Combination and Political Multiplicity 112

6. Expropriation of Capitalist by *State* Capitalist: Centralizing Capital as State Property 141

7. The Rhetorical Weaponization of the New State Capitalism 171

8. Liberal Anxieties and Ideological Adjustment in Global Development 199

9. Conclusion: A Spectre Haunting Capitalism? 230

References 254
Index 280

List of Figures and Tables

Figures

1.1 The new state capitalism as an object of inquiry 14
3.1 The new state capitalism as object of inquiry and analytical construct 54
4.1 Material determinations of contemporary state capitalism 88
6.1 Explanatory model of organizational change 156

Tables

2.1 Mapping of the state capitalism literature 39
3.1 An alternative conceptual framework and research agenda for the study of contemporary state capitalism 74
4.1 Mapping state capitalist impulses 108
6.1 Explaining the contemporary rise of state-capital hybrids 151

List of Abbreviations

AI	artificial intelligence
BRI	Belt and Road Initiative
BRICS	Brazil, Russia, India, China, and South Africa
CAI	Comprehensive Agreement on Investment
CC	comparative capitalism
CCTV	closed-circuit television
CME	coordinated-market economy
DNA	Deoxyribonucleic acid
EU	European Union
EV	electric vehicle
FDI	foreign direct investment
FONSIS	Fonds Souverain d'Investissements Stratégiques
G-20	Group of 20
GDP	gross domestic product
GPE	global political economy
IDFC	International Development Finance Corporation
IMF	International Monetary Fund
IPE	international political economy
IPOs	initial public offerings
IRA	Inflation Reduction Act
iSOEF	Integrated State-Owned Enterprises Framework
LME	liberal-market economy
M&A	mergers and acquisitions
NATO	North Atlantic Treaty Organization
OECD	Organization for Economic Cooperation and Development
PPIAF	Public-Private Infrastructure Advisory Facility
PT	Partido dos Trabalhadores
R&D	research and development
SASAC	State-owned Assets Supervision and Administration Commission
SMEs	small and medium-sized enterprises
SOE	state-owned enterprise
SWFs	sovereign wealth fund
U&CD	uneven and combined development
UNCTAD	United Nations Conference on Trade and Development
WTO	World Trade Organization
ZTE	Zhongxing Telecommunications Equipment

1
State Capitalism(s) Redux?

As the world stumbles from crisis to crisis, *Leviathan* is back. Among financial analysts, business journalists, liberal commentators, and other pundits, the state is touted as both the saviour and the gravedigger of the capitalist economy.[1] It is simultaneously portrayed as all-powerful, encroaching on private property and sacrificing personal liberty, and too weak, lacking capacity to even secure the freedom of individuals, the wellbeing of populations, and a stable business environment. The source of this ambivalence may well reside in the contradictory role of the state in capitalist society. As Geoff Mann puts it: 'Capitalist modernity, in fact, is and always has been Keynesian on the inside, as it were—the call for the state when disorder looms or revolution threatens has always been an option, one that, like a panic button, is essential even when we never use it' (Mann 2017, xi). The reassuring presence of state intervention is not only required in crisis conditions. More generally, the state embodies 'market police', 'a market constituting and preserving power', which enables and facilitates the economy (Bonefeld 2017, 50–51).

For political economy in all its variants, from classical liberalism to developmentalism and neoliberalism, the question is therefore not whether the state should intervene or not. Rather, 'the issue is the purpose and method, the objective and aim of intervention' (Bonefeld 2017, 22). Indeed, state intervention is never unproblematic, inasmuch as capitalism, at least in its liberal form, is predicated upon a formal and institutionalized separation of economic and political power. The recent ambivalence concerning the 'return' of the state, may well be an acute but all-in-all univocal manifestation of this deep, congenital anxiety at the heart of liberal capitalist modernity concerning the scope and modalities of state power.

Yet there may be more to this quandary at the current historical moment. Indeed, liberal circles are agitated by another sort of angst which compounds hesitations and concerns regarding the current extent of state intervention. There are recurring calls for governments in western Europe, North America,

[1] https://www.bloomberg.com/opinion/articles/2020-03-17/coronavirus-will-revive-an-all-powerful-state.

The Spectre of State Capitalism. Ilias Alami and Adam D. Dixon, Oxford University Press.
 DOI: 10.1093/9780198925224.003.0001

and Australia to expand support to business activity in order to compete with Asian rivals where states intervene extensively in favour of 'their' firms. Emulating these state-led models of capitalism is thus depicted as a matter of economic necessity. It is, however, simultaneously portrayed as setting Western liberal capitalist economies on a dangerous path, one that leads away from the free-market doctrine that has allegedly defined their activity and economic success for decades.[2] We therefore find ourselves in the paradoxical situation where insistent demands for expanded state action are accompanied by laments that creeping statism (due to the policy response to the COVID-19 pandemic and other crises, heightened competition with Asian contenders, and industrial policy initiatives to address climate change) is already leading us to the perilous path of *state capitalism*. For instance, a Deutsche Bank research brief released during the COVID-19 pandemic bemoaned that renewed societal support for a strong role in the economy was dangerously pushing Germany 'on its way to state capitalism'. According to the brief's author, the Chief German Macroeconomist, 'It's quite grotesque indeed: while Germany is admired by other countries for its handling of the corona crisis, we are once again—in typical German style—chewing over everything real or imagined that doesn't work or didn't work even before the crisis.'[3] More recently, *The Wall Street Journal* offered a scathing critique of the policy orientation of the US President Biden administration, which combines an explicit embrace of industrial policy and ambitious spending plans: by 'adopting the Chinese government investment model' (which *The Wall Street Journal* considers to be 'broken'), Bidenomics is walking into the 'trap of state capitalism'.[4]

It is tempting to dismiss altogether these contradictory arguments based on their evident misreading of economic history and misunderstanding of the role of the state in capitalist society. This is a mistake. We submit that this cognitive dissonance expresses a particular set of contradictions characteristic of our current capitalist epoch. These contradictory demands about the extension of state prerogatives at home in response to the perceived threat of increasing foreign state-supported economic activities reveal a great deal about the competitive mechanisms of emulation through which the state's role as promoter, supervisor, and owner of capital is currently rapidly expanding across the world economy. They point to

[2] See, for example, https://www.wsj.com/articles/western-economies-embrace-state-intervention-emulating-asia-11604574001.

[3] https://www.dbresearch.com/servlet/reweb2.ReWEB?rwsite=RPS_EN-PROD&rwobj=ReDisplay.Start.class&document=PROD0000000000506968#_ftnref1.

[4] https://www.wsj.com/articles/bidens-march-to-state-capitalism-white-house-government-election-china-ce22b035?mod=article_inline.

interconnections, inter-referentiality, and combination in the emergence of new repertoires of state intervention. They also suggest that this global process of reconfiguration in the forms and modalities of state action is fraught with geopolitical tensions and accompanied by a profound crisis of liberal reason. In other words, they tell us something fundamental about our current global *state capitalist* predicament.

In this book, we treat these anxieties as highly suggestive of a set of *processes*, *interconnections* and *relations* which have been underappreciated in the literature on 'the new state capitalism'. The current proliferation of social scientific signifiers old and new, such as 'geoeconomic world order', 'national-populist economic policymaking', 'techno-nationalism', 'political capitalism', 'post-neoliberal statism', to name but a few, both testify to turbulent material transformations in the modalities of state intervention, and to the vitality of scholarly attempts at theorizing them (Milanović 2019; Gerbaudo 2021). Arguably, none of these terms embodies this intellectual effervescence more than the 'new state capitalism', a rubric which has gained increasing traction across the social sciences as well as in business and political commentary to register the more visible role of the state in capitalist economy and society.

This categorical label indexes an extremely wide constellation of political and institutional forms, including sovereign wealth funds, state enterprises, state-controlled pension funds, state asset management companies, national policy and development banks, and other state-sponsored economic vehicles; models of post-developmentalism, post-neoliberalism, and resource-nationalism; capitalism(s) in emerging economies such as China, Russia, Turkey, Indonesia, Singapore, or Hungary; the renewal of techno-industrial and neo-mercantilist policies, a renewed interest in development plans and spatial development strategies, and many more. If the 1990s and 2000s were the decades of 'globalization' and 'neoliberalism'/'financialization' (respectively), state capitalism may well be emerging as one of the most popular social-scientific signifiers of the 2010s–2020s.

Vicissitudes and Ambivalences in State Capitalism Studies

Despite (or perhaps due to) its popularity, state capitalism as a categorical label is far from perfect. This may explain why a great deal of confusion continues to cloud the debates as to the nature and implications of the phenomenon. Indeed, it seems to be turning into the shorthand-du-jour for anything involving the intervention of the state, raising concerns about the analytical power of the term. Hence, its capaciousness has been negotiated at the expense of its analytical expedience. We will discuss this at length throughout the book, and particularly in the next chapter. Of course, this is not specific to state capitalism. Many popular buzzwords like globalization, neoliberalism, and financialization have exhibited similar problems. There are, however, specificities to state capitalism which may render its validity as a representational category even more dubious. For one, it is at least 120 years old. Indeed, Sperber (2019, 101) locates 'the origins of the notion in the closing years of the 19th century'. This is potentially problematic inasmuch as understanding political economic transformation—particularly as they unfold before our eyes—through old vocabularies poses inevitable risks and limitations, such as making it hard to see what is new and specific about the present era.

These risks are compounded by the fact that the term, throughout its long history, has been associated with a great diversity of political-economic configurations and social formations, from Nazi Germany to East Asian developmentalism, post-independence Algeria, Brazil and Turkey under military dictatorship, West European and Nordic welfare states, the Soviet Union, and many more. It has also been deployed to refer to very different subject-areas and objects of inquiry, from war planning and the interaction between the state and large private monopolies to development strategies in the Third World. Through these associations, it has acquired a certain geopolitical and ideological flavour, so to speak, particularly within liberal circles. Ironically, the remarkable intellectual trajectory of the term and the richness of the debates it has sparked throughout the twentieth century have been almost entirely neglected by contemporary scholarly discussions on state capitalism, and some of these negative connotations have stuck. This is apparent in the current rhetorical weaponization of the term by Western business and state actors (e.g., Bremmer 2010). Indeed, we show in the book that state capitalism is increasingly deployed in corporate and policymaking circles as a form of geopolitical discourse: castigating a 'rogue' state capitalism (typically associated with emerging economies such as China and Russia) discursively enables Western business and state elites to justify tougher policy stances in areas such as foreign policy, trade, technology, and investment regulation towards increasingly capable and assertive non-Western contenders.

Furthermore, in our experience researching and writing on state capitalism, presenting our work, organizing conference panels, issuing call for papers, submitting articles for peer-review, and editing special issues and a blog series, we have realized that state capitalism tends to elicit paradoxical responses among social scientists and political analysts, which it is worth briefly addressing before we proceed.

On the one hand, some completely reject the category state capitalism (and the associated research agenda), in an almost knee-jerk reaction, on the basis that the term is often used as a buzzword with little (if any) explanatory or analytical power. It is also argued that the category state capitalism is conceptually misleading insofar as it tends to obfuscate the historical fact that capitalism is always 'statist' to some extent, or that the state is *always there* in capitalism.[5] In short, all capitalism is state capitalism *to some extent* (see Whiteside 2022). While we agree in general with this statement, we contend that this need not lead to a dismissal of the category state capitalism. Acknowledging the pervasive and extensive role of the state throughout the history of capitalism does not necessarily imply rejecting a programme of research into contemporary configurations in which the extent of such a role is particularly substantial.

The use of qualifiers such as 'new' or 'return' (e.g., 'the return of state capitalism', 'the rise of the new state capitalism', and so on), which is common in the literature, further complicates matters. Indeed, one may argue that many of the main political and institutional forms that state capitalism studies have been concerned with—sovereign wealth funds, state enterprises, development banks, and the like—have a very long history (perhaps as old as capitalism itself), and in fact have never left. What is more visible now, for whatever reason, might have been there, more or less under the radar, all along. Things like sovereign funds, often presented as paradigmatic of the new state capitalism, have many historical antecedents, such as the widespread use of stabilization funds in the 1930s (Braunstein 2014). Hybrid entities blending public and private power—such as 'company-states' (e.g., the Dutch East India Company) and corporatized forms of government—have played a fundamental role in the making of global capitalism (Stern 2011; Phillips and Sharman 2020). Large state sectors have also existed in many different historical and geographical contexts, including in post-1945 western Europe (Aharoni 2018). Succinctly put, the *new* state capitalism may not be so new after all. We certainly agree with this yet disagree that this implies dismissing the category. On the contrary, we make the case in the book for carefully identifying the concrete *temporal and spatial parameters* of current instantiations of state capitalism.

Similarly, one may argue that recent studies of state capitalism have been underpinned by a set of questionable dichotomies, such as state versus

[5] See Alami (2021) for a critical engagement with this view from a state-theoretical perspective.

market, commercial versus (geo)political logics, liberal versus illiberal, and democratic versus authoritarian (Hameiri, Jones, and Heathershaw 2019; Alami, Dixon, Gonzalez-Vicente, et al. 2021). Again, we would not disagree with this, but brushing off state capitalism on these grounds would be tantamount to throwing out the baby with the bathwater. Indeed, we strive to demonstrate in this book that it is both possible, and highly generative, to grapple with these rigid binary constructions by problematizing them. Destabilizing the assumptions and taken-for-granted ideas which have largely framed the field thus far is a productive way to probe into current forms of reassertion of state authority and changing configurations of state and corporate power.

On the other hand, there is a tendency (which really is the flipside of the knee-jerk rejection) among some social scientists and political economists to uncritically embrace state capitalism as an umbrella term and apply it to an extremely wide range of social phenomena, whose sole common ground is that they somehow involve the state. Anything related to the state's role in economy and society then becomes a case of state capitalism. We see this largesse (or generosity), ubiquity, and flexibility of state capitalism as a potential source of generative tension, one that can lead to creative uses of the term and innovative cross-disciplinary research. Nevertheless, this productive ambiguity must not lead to an inflation of meanings or an over-stretching of the rubric's realms of application, otherwise state capitalism may lose its substance, analytical purchase, and scientific and political relevance. There is also the risk that state capitalism research becomes a mere exercise in labelling any discernible modality of state intervention as state capitalist, rather than a coherent and structured field of social scientific inquiry aimed at theory-building (Whiteside, Alami, Dixon, and Peck 2023).

In short, the source of the ambivalence in the recent reception and proliferation of the usage of the term resides in serious issues of conceptual definition, which have led to significant theoretical and methodological difficulties. Does this mean that we should abandon state capitalism? Our answer is no.

A Case for the 'New' State Capitalism

We refuse to do away with state capitalism as a rubric, field of scholarly inquiry, and research programme. Despite significant limitations, which we explore at length in this book, an extremely lively and promising pluri-disciplinary research agenda has coalesced around the rubric state capitalism, demonstrating its potential for focusing scholarly efforts on an important set of transformations in the morphology of present-day capitalism, and particularly on the *changing role of the state*, and the drastic reconfiguration and expansion of its role as *promoter, supervisor, and owner of capital*. As such, we contend that state capitalism deserves the attention of political economists, economic and political geographers, political scientists, international business and strategic management analysts, development studies scholars, and other social scientists. While we are fully aware that, as Joshua Clover eloquently puts it, 'only at one's peril does one make strong claims about a historical period while still within it' (2016, 130), we argue in this book that we are currently witnessing a *historic arc in the trajectories of state intervention*.

Indeed, new global landscapes of state intervention have gradually emerged at the turn of the millennium and consolidated in the post-2008 global financial crisis environment. Governments across the world have increased their role as promoter, supervisor, and owner of capital by expanding and experimenting with several political, organizational, and institutional forms. While we are wary that 'measuring' state activism is a notoriously difficult task (Peck 2021), a few key data points may be useful to illustrate the magnitude of this expansion and convince the reader of its significance. Consider the following.

We have seen a multiplication and expansion of state-owned and state-controlled corporate entities, or what we call 'state-capital hybrids' (a concept we fully flesh out and put to work in Chapter 6). State-owned investment funds, often referred to as sovereign wealth funds (SWFs), have grown in size and number. According to the Sovereign Wealth Fund Institute, there are now 176 SWFs, which is more than six times as many as there were 20 years ago.[6] The assets controlled by these funds ballooned from less than $1 trillion in 2000 to more than $11.8 trillion in 2023, which is more than hedge funds and private equity firms combined. SWFs are a heterogeneous group, not least in terms of size. Some, like the SWFs of Norway and China, control assets upwards of $1 trillion, whereas others manage less than $1 billion. SWFs are also diverse in terms of their missions and organizational arrangements, including different missions, mandates, and investment objectives. Some funds invest domestically with a longer-term orientation and developmental objectives (such as industrial upgrading and infrastructural development, or providing patient capital for domestic firms), while others aim to maximize risk-adjusted returns like conventional portfolio investors

[6] https://www.swfinstitute.org/fund-rankings/sovereign-wealth-fund.

(Dixon 2017). This diversity notwithstanding, they collectively represent a new class of institutional investor. SWFs have become at once important components of national development plans and global financial markets, investing in some of the world's largest companies and partnering with other institutional funds.

State-owned enterprises (SOEs) have experienced a concomitant expansion. After theorists of the firm and neoliberals alike had predicted their death in the 1980s–90s (Peng, Bruton, Stan, and Huang 2016), they have re-emerged in re-constituted form across the world economy. There are new ways of governing them, with novel hybrid structures of ownership, control, and management, which hardly resemble the 'old' model of SOE—wholly owned by the state and acting as an extension of public bureaucracy (Musacchio and Lazzarini 2014). New models are characterized by partial state ownership (Cuervo-Cazurra 2018), where nearly 60 per cent of the largest state enterprises have a mix of public and private owners (IMF 2020, 49). With assets worth $45 trillion (equivalent to half of global GDP) which is up from about $13 trillion in 2000, 'the share of state-owned enterprises among the world's 2000 largest firms doubled to 20 percent over the last two decades' (IMF 2020, 5–6). According to the OECD, half of the top ten non-financial firms as measured by revenue are SOEs. In 2021, SOEs made up 132 of the world's 500 largest companies—up from thirty-two just two decades ago.[7] SOEs now dwarf even the largest privately owned transnational corporations, with Saudi Aramco currently leading the list with a market value of $2.084 trillion. These new SOEs are a diversified group in terms of size, complexity, structures of ownership, sectors of operation (from energy to mining, agro-chemicals, construction, utilities, communications, transports, aluminium, steel, aerospace, and semiconductors) and the functions they perform for 'their' government. According to some estimates, SOEs account for about 13–22 per cent of global market capitalization.[8] They now constitute a major force of transnationalizing capital, actively participating in cross-border mergers and acquisitions, cross-listing of shares, international portfolio investment, and foreign direct investment (Babic, Garcia-Bernardo, and Heemskerk 2020). Many have become key players in global corporate debt markets, successfully competing on the world market, and performing as efficiently as private

[7] https://oecdonthelevel.com/2022/02/01/state-owned-enterprises-are-on-the-rise-should-we-worry/.

[8] https://www.worldbank.org/en/events/2021/06/14/listing-state-owned-enterprises-in-emerging-and-developing-economies.

firms in some sectors (Musacchio and Lazzarini 2014; Cuervo-Cazurra 2018).

National development and policy banks have also returned to fashion, vastly expanding their loan portfolio and financial capacities in both developed and developing economies. There are now more than 900 worldwide, controlling assets worth $49 trillion (Marois 2021). They have been increasingly used to achieve a variety of objectives (such as maintaining financial stability, funding infrastructure, and providing 'patient capital' for development projects and key domestic firms) in developing, emerging, and advanced capitalist economies (Griffith-Jones and Ocampo 2018; Mertens, Thiemann, and Volberding 2021). Some have become so large that their loan portfolio and financial capacities now dwarf the volume of lending of the World Bank and regional multilateral development banks (Kring and Gallagher 2019).

While there is no doubt that China weighs heavily in the statistics and data points we provided so far, a vast body of academic and policy-oriented scholarship (not least reports by the International Monetary Fund, the World Bank, the United Nations Conference on Trade and Development, the Organisation for Economic Co-operation and Development, the G-20, and other global governance institutions) shows that this expansion is irreducible to the rise of China. It is also not reducible to the 'rise' of the BRICS and other emerging capitalist economies (Babic 2021; Kim 2021). These various state-capital hybrids (SWFs, SOEs, development banks) originate from countries across the income spectrum and from diverse types of political regimes, and their presence is highly significant in OECD countries too. They are often remarkably outward-oriented, and/or are increasingly integrated into global circuits of capital, including global networks of production, trade, finance, infrastructure, and corporate ownership, and actively participate in foreign listing, international portfolio investment, and overseas mergers and acquisitions (Haberly and Wójcik 2017; Lim 2018; Babic, Garcia-Bernardo, and Heemskerk 2020; IMF 2020; Alami, Dixon, and Mawdsley 2021; Werner 2021; McGregor and Coe 2022). Put differently, state-capital hybrids now constitute *major engines of global capitalism.*

Over the same period, techno-industrial policy and national development plans have expanded (in dialectical combination with the expansion of state-capital hybrids documented above), taken more assertive modalities, and made themselves more present in landscapes of policymaking across the North/South divide. A (pre-pandemic) UNCTAD World Investment Report notes that:

> [i]n the decade since the global financial crisis, the number of countries adopting national industrial development strategies has increased dramatically. The rate of adoption of both formal industrial policies and individual policy measures targeted at industrial sectors appears to be at an all-time high.
>
> **(UNCTAD 2018, 128–129)**

Elsewhere, it adds that 'national development strategies' have 'regained legitimacy' (UNCTAD 2018, 130). A recent study finds that '[t]he number of countries with a national development plan has more than doubled, from about 62 in 2006 to 134 in 2018' (Chimhowu, Hulme, and Munro 2019, 76). This proliferation of industrial policies and development plans has coincided with a renewal of interest in state-led spatial planning and the state-coordinated expansion of infrastructure, both of which had lost legitimacy during the 1980s–90s (Schindler and Kanai 2021). Indeed, one area where state-capital hybrids have been particularly successful is infrastructure investment and project implementation, including in sectors such as rail and road transport, ports, airports, water, mining, and energy. A report co-authored by the World Bank and the Public-Private Infrastructure Advisory Facility (PPIAF) notes that 83 per cent of investments in infrastructure projects in 2017 were sponsored by government-sponsored entities and SOEs in developing countries (World Bank-PPIAF 2017).

The increasing prevalence of these various modalities of state ownership and state activism is all the more significant when considered in the context of more muscular and aggressive forms of neo-mercantilism and 'economic nationalism', a general policy orientation where appeals to national identity fundamentally frame economic policymaking (Helleiner and Pickel 2005; Helleiner 2021). Economic nationalism encompasses a wide diversity of doctrines, practices, and policies, which, as a whole, have gained in political salience since the 2000s, and particularly in the aftermath of the 2008 global financial crisis, in a turbulent geopolitical context characterized by intensified competition in trade, investment and technology. In this context, techno-industrial development, innovation policy, and neo-mercantilist measures (including trade and investment restrictions, such as bans on foreign technologies, export controls, financial sanctions, etc.) have been increasingly linked to notions of national security and geoeconomic statecraft. Russia's war of aggression in Ukraine and the deterioration of Sino–US relations have only accelerated these developments over the past few years. Some go as far as to claim that this signals the transition to a new geoeconomic world order, characterized by the 'securitisation of economic policy' and 'weaponized interdependence' (Farrell and Newman 2019; Roberts, Choer Moraes, and Ferguson 2019).

Whether these claims are correct or not, it is clear that the automation, robotization, and digitalization of large-scale industry, the growing importance of monopoly control of intangible assets, and the increasing salience of logistics in global capitalism (Cowen 2014; Chua, Danyluk, Cowen, and Khalili 2018; Arboleda 2020; Durand and Milberg 2020) have prompted states to develop new forms of intervention and modalities of government-business cooperation. The objective is to foster the 'strategic coupling' of their domestic firms with global value chains, and to compete in sectors at the technological and productivity frontier of the fourth industrial revolution (5G technology, big data, the internet of things, artificial intelligence, advanced robotics, renewables and green mobility, and the like) (Yeung 2016; Thurbon and Weiss 2021; Werner 2021). Recent examples include the increasingly ambitious state-led plans to incentivize investment in the design and manufacturing of next-generation semiconductors—including the United States CHIPS and Science Act, the European Chips Act, South Korea's K-Chips Act, Made in China 2025, France's Electronique 2030, Germany's Industrial Strategy 2030, and similar schemes in Taiwan, Japan, and other technologically advanced capitalist economies. Moreover, matters of spatial planning, logistical connection, and infrastructure financing (at home as well as in other countries) have acquired an increasingly strong strategic and geoeconomic dimension (Kanai and Schindler 2019; Anguelov 2021; Schindler, Alami, and Jepson 2022).

In sum, what we have seen is, on the one hand, a multiplication of state-capital hybrids (including sovereign wealth funds, state enterprises, policy and development banks) and a geographical expansion of their control over resources and markets, and on the other, the concomitant development of more assertive and muscular forms of statism (encompassing techno-industrial policy, spatial development strategies, economic nationalism, and trade and investment restrictions).[9] This *combined* movement has unfolded across extremely diverse geographical, political, and ideological contexts, and it has been deeply implicated in various political economic projects, including (but not limited to): the rise of Chinese capitalism under the aegis of its party-state (Zhang and Peck 2016; Lim 2019); in Central Asia, the development of patrimonial forms of capitalism dependent

[9] The analytical distinction we are drawing here between state-capital hybrids and statism is inspired by Sperber (2019, 112–113). We fully flesh out this conceptual apparatus in Chapters 3.

on rents from oil and gas exports in Russia and Kazakhstan (Spechler, Ahrens, and Hoen 2017; Åslund 2019; Viktorov and Abramov 2022); in Central and Eastern Europe, the emergence of state-led illiberal regimes in countries like Hungary, Serbia, and Poland (Shields 2021; Rogers 2022; Karas 2022); in the Middle East and North Africa, the reconfiguration of the Arab Gulf economies and their particularly entangled combinations of state and capital (Hanieh 2018), the large state-owned sectors of countries like Egypt, Jordan, and Algeria, the development of an authoritarian political economy in Turkey (Öniş 2019; Kutlay 2020; Altınörs and Akçay 2022) and of an 'innovation' state in Israel (Maggor 2021); the precarious consolidation of extractivist-redistributive regimes in Latin America (Brazil during the Workers' Party period, Ecuador, Bolivia, and Venezuela) and in Africa (Zambia, Rwanda, or Ethiopia) (Behuria 2018; Jepson 2020); developmentalist 'resource nationalisms' in Malaysia (Lebdioui 2022) and Indonesia (Warburton 2018; Kim 2019a, 2019b); in western Europe, the revival of techno-nationalism, extensive support to national champions, and development banking; in the United States, a newfound appetite for state intervention and financial sanctions in the context of the 'Second Cold War' with China (Baltz 2022). Add to this the fact that public spending is currently at historically unprecedented levels (global averages),[10] and that central banks have been playing an increasingly crucial role in supporting economies worldwide. In other words, the recent upward trajectory of state-capital hybrids and muscular forms of statism is a *global* phenomenon.

Let us clarify at the outset that by *global*, we certainly do not mean that the rise of state capitalism is undifferentiated, nor that every country or region is equally concerned or affected. In fact, we argue at length in this book that these transformations in the repertoires of state action have happened unevenly across territorial borders, depending on a state's position in international and regional divisions of labour and in a world market structured by highly unequal geopolitical relations. Our point is that the recent upward trajectory of state-capital hybrids and muscular forms of statism testifies to the aggregate expansion of the state's role as promoter, supervisor, and owner of capital *across the spaces of the world capitalist economy*. This expansion must therefore be explained and theorized as a process which is global in *scope* (and, as we will see, global in *nature*), which is precisely our objective in this book.

[10] https://www.imf.org/external/datamapper/exp@FPP/USA/FRA/JPN/GBR/SWE/ESP/ITA/ZAF/IND.

Why Refer to This as State Capitalism?

A number of objections can be raised at this point. Why would sovereign funds, state enterprises, industrial policy, spatial development strategies, and other modalities of state intervention deserve the moniker state capitalism? Insofar as there are already rigorous terms and bundles of concepts which have been specifically developed for the study of these individual political, institutional, and organizational forms, why add a nebulous category to the mix? In other words, and linking back to some of the conceptual and definitional problems raised earlier in this introduction, what is the added value of labelling them as state capitalist?

Our response is that the added value of the category state capitalism resides precisely in that it calls for an understanding of the recent upward trajectory of these various political and institutional forms (including sovereign wealth funds, policy and development banks, state enterprises, techno-industrial policy, spatial development strategies, and economic nationalism) *together* and in *relation* to each other in a *co-constitutive* movement. Thus, in our conceptualization, state capitalism concerns the *aggregate* expansion of these political and institutional forms as a *world-historical totality*.

For us, what is both new and significant is not necessarily the increasing prevalence (or at least growing visibility) of these institutional forms and state transformations taken individually, independently, and in isolation from each other, but their *joint* and *concurrent expansion* at the current historical juncture. This is the specific phenomenon that warrants critical investigation, problematization, and rigorous theorization. In short, our contention is that state capitalism studies must aim to render amenable to analysis and critique the historic arc in the trajectories of state intervention documented earlier, and characterized by the co-development and mutual constitution of muscular forms of statism and the expansion of state-capital hybrids (Figure 1.1). One of our objectives in this book is to make the case for putting this object of inquiry at the core of the research efforts of state capitalism studies, and more broadly, political economy. We argue that this may go a long way towards providing the field of state capitalism studies with some structure and coherence, which is arguably necessary for it to become something more than a buzzword. We do not aim to bring an end to definitional debates, which are often highly productive. Rather, our hope is that, equipped with this common, basic understanding of the main objective of its research efforts, the field's eclecticism in the theories and methods it employs can be leveraged as a source of generative

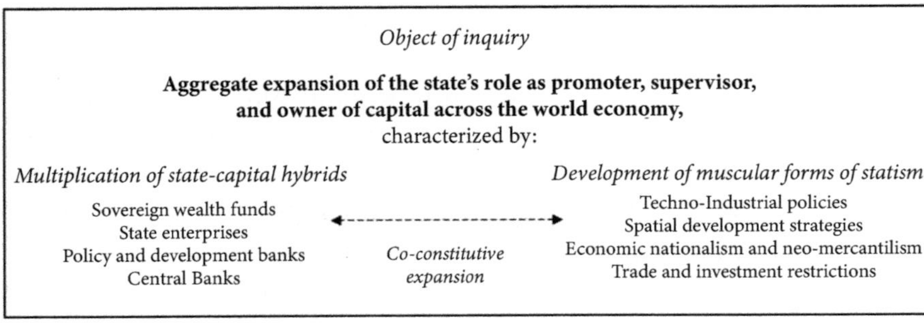

Figure 1.1 The new state capitalism as an object of inquiry

tension and channelled towards a cumulative and collective theory-building endeavour.

In making this argument, we call for modes of analysis which foreground the interrelations between repertoires of state intervention and situate them within broader capitalist dynamics. Let us circle back to the liberal anxieties with which we opened this introductory chapter. Recall that financial analysts, business journalists, liberal commentators, and other pundits are increasingly pressing their governments to expand state prerogatives in order to compete with (and even emulate) economic and geopolitical competitors. Recall also that the various forms of support that these competitors provide to business activity is evoked to justify tougher policy stances in areas such as foreign policy, trade, technology, and investment regulation. Our point, then, is that we must be particularly attentive to such mechanisms of inter-referentiality and combination in the making of state capitalism. As such, we propose a *relational* perspective to the study of state capitalism, one that aims at capturing the dialectical and cumulative unfolding of different modalities of state intervention across space, scale, and time, by tracing the various forms of interconnections between them. This, we argue in this book, is fundamental to grasping the inner nature of the new state capitalism as a variegated, world-historical phenomenon, and to reinvigorating systemic explanations for its rise and significance across the spaces of the world capitalist economy.

A Note on the Title of This Book

Before we present the structure of the book, let us briefly comment on its title, and in particular our choice of the word *spectre* to refer to state capitalism. It is an allusion to the ways in which liberal commentators evoke state capitalism as a ghost-like, disquieting figure casting its shadow on the world liberal order, acting as the organizing principle of geopolitical relations, and increasingly shaping the contours of the global economy. Needless to say, we strongly believe that moving away from such alarmist and anxiogenic narratives of global confrontation and exposing their underlying power relations is crucial for both scholarly and political reasons.

However, we do believe that the state transformations we study in this book are *potentially* epoch-defining. This is not only because of the breadth and scope of the recent upward and combined trajectories of state-capital hybrids and muscular forms of statism. It is also not simply because, in an age of pandemics and catastrophic climate heating, the state's expanded role as promoter, supervisor, and owner of capital may well be here to stay. The argument we develop in the book is rather that the reconfiguration of the global 'state–capital nexus' (van Apeldoorn, de Graaff, and Overbeek 2012) currently unfolding is not merely a historically contingent form of reconstruction of the modalities of intervention of the capitalist state. It is structured by deep-seated, secular transformations in the materiality of global capitalism. This may well point to a deeper transformation in the form of the state and its relation to capital, which may in turn imprint the future of capitalism with a distinctly new flavour. Our use of the conditional here is deliberate. None of this is predetermined and will depend on future political economic developments. There is an irreducible and radical openness to patterns of capitalist development and state trajectories, although this openness is not unstructured (Smith 2017). For these reasons, we argue, contemporary state capitalism deserves the qualifier of spectre. We return to this more speculative and forward-looking aspect of our argument in the concluding chapter of the book.

At the risk of drawing an artificial boundary between normative and scientific analysis, let us also be clear that this book is emphatically not about assessing the desirability of the expansion of the state's role as promoter, supervisor, and owner of capital. Nor are we in the business of drawing and policing boundaries between modalities of state intervention considered appropriate and illegitimate ones. This book is about carefully documenting the profound state transformations unfolding before our eyes and developing tools to robustly explain them. We see the state as contradictory and fraught with conflicts, insofar as it is the political form of antagonistic social relations (Bonefeld 2017). As such, the transformations that it experiences often simultaneously open up possibilities for some social actors while closing down opportunities for others, a process which is of course profoundly shaped by various lines of social division and exclusion (class, North/South, race, gender, sexuality, and so on). This is to say that speaking of the undesirability (or, on the contrary, the progressive potential) of state capitalism as if it were a monolithic force makes little sense to us. We return to these reflections in the conclusion.

Argument and Chapter Outline

The book is comprised of eight chapters in addition to this introduction. Chapter 2 critically reviews the theories, tensions, and controversies surrounding the study of state capitalism. To the students, researchers, and practitioners who are new to the field, this chapter will provide a useful overview and introduction of recent scholarship and debates on the new state capitalism. We frame this around a basic question: how has the 'new' state capitalism been theorized and explained? In exploring this question, we synthesize and critique the key arguments, as well as surprising silences and omissions, in four bodies of literature: strategic management, comparative capitalism, development studies, and global political economy. We note difficulties in theorizing how state capitalism differs from other forms of capitalism, as well as problematic geographical assumptions concerning the nature and scale of state capitalism. Explanations tend to focus on the rise of a nationally scaled and relatively coherent variant of capitalism. While such arguments are not necessarily wrong, these assumptions about the spatialities of the new state capitalism restrict readings of its rise and significance. Importantly, they leave little appreciation for the various forms of interconnections, inter-referentiality, and combination that may exist between the new repertoires of state intervention across the territorial borders of nation-states. They also preclude a reflection on the historic development and self-transformation of global capitalism, such as planetary mutations in the spheres of production, circulation, and distribution of value. As argued in subsequent chapters, these questions are fundamental for understanding contemporary state capitalism. This points to the need for an explicitly geographical approach, one that allows probing into the multiple spatialities (beyond nation-state centric territoriality) and temporalities (beyond that of catch-up development and crises) at the core of contemporary state capitalism.

In an effort to break the analytical impasse discussed in Chapter 2, we make the case in Chapter 3 for state capitalism not as a rigid category of analysis but as a means of problematizing and critically interrogating the current aggregate expansion of the state's role as promoter, supervisor, and owner of capital across the spaces of the world capitalist economy. We call this the *problématique* of state capitalism, which we propose to bring into conversation, epistemologically and methodologically, with the notion of uneven and combined development (e.g., Dunford and Liu 2017; Peck 2019). Our objective in this chapter is not to merely add a geographical twist to state capitalism studies. Rather, we show that this conceptual move enables a major geographical reorientation in the study of the new state capitalism in at least three ways. First, we submit that state capitalism must not be seen as an anomaly or a deviance from liberal, market-based capitalism, but as a particular modality of expression of the capitalist state, including in its liberal form. State capitalism is an *immanent potentiality*, an impulse which is contained in the form of the capitalist state and built into its DNA. This allows us redirecting characterization efforts away from constructing ideal-typical models of state capitalism juxtaposed to other (conventional) varieties of capitalism, and towards identifying the circumstances and conditions in which this potentiality is *actualized*, as well as its concrete *temporal and spatial parameters*. In other words, state capitalism must be defined with reference to concrete historical-geographical capitalist transformations, and in relation to inherited geographies of state intervention into social and economic processes. Second, the coming into being of state capitalism must not be explained by resorting to mechanical-abstract metaphors, such as the negation of an abstract model of free-market capitalism, a Polanyian pendulum (i.e., a counter-movement of the state somehow automatically following a period of market expansion), or axiomatic and historically indeterminate laws of peripheral catch-up development. Rather, we must locate state capitalist impulses within a set of determinate processes and social relations pertaining to the historical development and geographical remaking of global capitalism. Third, our proposed approach redefines the nature of comparative work away from an exercise in identifying the institutional contours of neatly demarcated territories categorized as state capitalist, and towards relational-comparative work consisting in tracing difference in connection, interdependencies, and co-evolution between different instantiations and repertoires of state action (Hart 2018; Sparke 2020). This, we argue, is essential to grasping the inner nature of the new state capitalism as a variegated, world-historical totality, and capturing the dialectical and cumulative unfolding of different modalities of state intervention across space, scale, and time. We call this 'uneven and combined state capitalism'. As a word of caution, Chapters 2 and 3 are conceptually dense and offer a deep dive into contemporary state capitalism debates and state-theoretical considerations. Readers who are not interested in these questions and who would rather jump right into our analysis of the morphology of the state in present-day capitalism may want to skip these chapters, and start at Chapter 4.

Chapter 4 puts our 'uneven and combined state capitalism' approach to work and offers a geographic reconstruction of the contemporary advent of state capitalism. We identify the determinate processes and relations pertaining to the historical development and geographical remaking of late capitalism which underpin the recent aggregate expansion of the state's role as promoter, supervisor, and owner of capital. We foreground two world-historical economic mutations in particular: one the one hand, the emergence of a more complex constellation of 'old' and 'new' international divisions of labour; and on the other, deep-seated tendencies towards economic stagnation, industrial overcapacity, and an intensification of international competition across a wide range of economic sectors. We show in the chapter that these phenomena have had multifaceted ramifications in terms of the temporal and geographical dynamics of value production, circulation, and distribution, and in terms of corporate strategies. Far from being passive observers, states have been directly implicated in these transformations. They have aided, accompanied, and occasionally expedited them by deploying a range of instruments, policies, regulations, and other modes of economic practice, in the context of their role as promoters of capital accumulation. As they have done so, states have themselves experienced a process of restructuring, involving profound transformations in pre-existing landscapes of state intervention, a rearticulation of the relations between states and the circuits of capital, shifting boundaries between the state and civil society, and a dramatic expansion of their role as promoter of capital accumulation, direct owner of capital, and investor-shareholder. We argue that this is precisely the phenomenon that is now increasingly being referred to as the 'new' state capitalism. In short, present-day state capitalism must be understood as a process of self-transformation of capitalist states as they have politically mediated these global (but regionally uneven) secular mutations. The chapter goes on to offer a panorama of this polymorphous process of state restructuring since the turn of the millennium, and particularly in the post-2008 global financial crisis environment. We identify four tendencies, which we call the 'productivist', 'absorptive', 'stabilizing', and 'disciplinary' state capitalist impulses. We illustrate each of these tendencies by focusing empirically on a variety of political, organizational, and institutional forms: techno-industrial and innovation policy, sovereign wealth funds, state enterprises, development and policy banks, international development agencies, spatial planning strategies, the state-led construction of large-scale infrastructure and logistical networks, and trade and investment restrictions.

In Chapter 5, we complement and enrich the theorization of the contemporary advent of state capitalism developed in Chapter 4. We explore the constitutive and catalytic role of combination and political multiplicity in shaping the development of state capitalism. Simply put, multiple states interact with each other as they politically mediate the churn of uneven development, and these relations and connections have causal significance in the rise of state capitalism. The various repertoires of state intervention that make up contemporary state capitalism develop in dynamic, inter-referential, and combinatorial forms, resulting in cumulative effects, which themselves produce further extensions of state prerogatives. Indeed, a particular form of state activism in a specific location may have cascading impacts and ricocheting effects across geographic space, including in non-adjacent locations and faraway places, insofar as they spark a policy response on the part of states which are directly affected. Effects may be less direct (but no less significant) when a particular modality of state intervention in one place transforms economic conditions and sociopolitical relations elsewhere, in turn prompting other states to react to this new context by developing novel prerogatives, capacities, institutional forms, and modes of economic practice. Relational co-constitution therefore shapes the form and outcome of emerging state capitalist landscapes. We substantiate this by argument by tracing three types of mechanism which have powerfully contributed to the cumulative unfolding of the landscapes of state capitalism: (1) competitive emulation in the context of geoeconomic and geopolitical rivalry; (2) peer group learning and mimetic behaviour; (3) enabling and mutual reinforcement. The chapter unpacks the catalytic effects of these mechanisms by analysing at a wide array of examples: the unfolding tech war between the US and China, the global green subsidies race, finance for infrastructure development in the Global South, cross-border finance management in developing and emerging economies, sovereign funds and industrial policy plans in Central Asia and Africa, digital authoritarian practices, state-owned investment in real estate and urban contexts, and green hydrogen strategies. These various cases illustrate that state capitalism tends to develop in a spiral-like movement, with self-reinforcing state transformations expanding geographically and across policy domains. We call this the 'spiral of state capitalism'.

Chapter 6 then zooms in on the paradigmatic organizational forms of the new state capitalism: state enterprises, sovereign funds and other state-capital hybrids. How can we explain their global rise and organizational transformation into increasingly sophisticated and globally competitive forms? Why do they increasingly emulate the practices and organizational goals of comparable private-sector entities, adopt the techniques of modern finance, resort to mixed-ownership, and extend their operations across geographic space? After critically engaging with arguments which emphasize the role of firm strategies, developmentalist logics, financialized norms, and Polanyian double movements, we develop an explanatory model of organizational change grounded in historical-geographical materialism and economic geographies of the firm. The expansion of state ownership (the role of states as owners) examined in the previous chapter created the conditions for a massive round of centralization of capital as state property (the mass of capital controlled by states) since the early 2000s. This historically unprecedented phenomenon is arguably the elephant in the room of state capitalism studies. The modern, marketized, globally spread state-capital hybrid emerged as an 'organizational fix' to mediate the geographical contradictions and imperatives associated with this process. Purposive organizational adaption consisted in developing new skills, operational capabilities, and mixed-ownership structures in order to leverage the financial system, allow for the development of *liquid forms of state property*, and facilitate the expansion of the latter into global circuits of capital.

Chapter 7 explores the importance of geopolitical discourse and in particular the rhetorical weaponization of the new state capitalism. We draw upon critical geopolitics to examine the context of wider geopolitical and geoeconomic shifts in which the social construction of the contemporary geo-category 'state capitalism' has happened in academic, policy-making, and popular analyses. We contend that, on the one hand, the emerging new spatiality of the global economy (as discussed at length in Chapter 4), and on the other, the parallel development of new geopolitical rivalries manifesting most notably around China and the United States, but also the uneasy position of the EU in this new geopolitical environment, have prompted the need for new discursive frames and geopolitical lines of reasoning. We scrutinize how the category state capitalism operates as a form of geopolitical knowledge in this new global context, that is, how it projects meaning and identity across space, and how it relates to other geopolitical meta-narratives. It does so by reinstituting a simple narrative of competition between two easily identifiable protagonists—(Western) democratic free-market capitalism and its deviant 'other', (Eastern) authoritarian state capitalism—and by reactivating older geopolitical grand narratives, such as the Cold War. This imaginary is saturated with notions of hostility, danger, competition, but also deviance and abnormality, which portray non-West political economies as a threat to global security and liberal world order. We then trace out some of the discursive effects that are produced by the mobilization of these discourses and imaginaries in two policy areas: (1) diplomacy and foreign policy; and

(2) trade, technology, competition regulation, and investment screening. We develop the argument that the category state capitalism is rapidly entering the main political lexicon in these two policy areas. This in turn discursively enables Western business and state actors to politically justify tougher policy stances vis-à-vis what they refer to as 'rogue' state capitalist countries and firms.

Chapter 8 then turns to a reflection on the ideological dimensions of contemporary state capitalism. We show that the rise of state capitalism is triggering complex ideological adjustments, focusing in particular on official discourses, practices, and agendas of global Development.[11] Empirically, our analysis relies upon a close reading of research and policy documents recently released by multilateral and supranational development actors such as the International Monetary Fund, the World Bank, the Organization for Economic Co-operation and Development, the United Nations Conference on Trade and Development, and the G-20. We show that these liberal regulative agencies are increasingly taking stock of the presence of state capitalism in global geographies of production, development finance, infrastructure, and policymaking, and have reluctantly acknowledged some of its developmental successes. This is prompting them to react and adapt to this new 'state capitalist normal'. So far this has taken the form of a *strategic discursive and ideological adjustment* involving a certain re-legitimation of the place of the state in Development, and a limited embrace of its role as promoter, supervisor, and owner of capital. We see the articulation of this new vision of the state in Development, not only as an attempt from these actors to remain relevant in a rapidly changing world, but as playing a fundamentally political role: it is an attempt at minimizing the multiple risks and dangers that are perceived to be associated with the current rise of state capitalism. This includes minimizing the potential for the political 'use' of state-capital hybrids, which would risk creating a further (geo)politicization of economic relations and a spiral of protectionism, or what the IMF now refers to as 'geoeconomic fragmentation', particularly in the tense geopolitical context. This also includes controlling the proliferation of state-capital hybrids and making sure that they assume liberal forms (especially in developing countries). Finally, this involves ensuring that their increasing cross-border activities create the least frictions possible in the global circuits of trade, production, and finance, and do not disrupt the competitive operations of the law of value.

[11] Here we refer to Gillian Hart's (2010) distinction between 'big D' Development and 'little d' capitalist development. 'Big D' Development refers to projects of political and economic transformation in the global South. By contrast, 'small d' development refers to the crisis-ridden expansion of capitalism as an economic system.

Put differently, we see the discursive re-legitimation of the state in Development, and its limited embrace of state-capital hybrids, as a way of addressing liberal anxieties regarding the direction in which the political form of global capital accumulation may be heading (the unchecked proliferation of state-capital hybrids possibly blunting competition, politicizing economic relations, and intensifying geoeconomic tensions), in order to preserve and further enshrine the centrality of market regulation in Development in an age of rising state capitalism and turbulent geopolitical reordering.

In recapping the key arguments of the book, the conclusion emphasizes our contribution to state capitalism debates and related literatures, from materialist state theory to the international political economy of state transformations, and the role of the state in global production and financial networks. We discuss directions for future research on state capitalism and raise a number of open questions (concerning the temporalities and permanence of the transformations analysed in the book, and their potential to durably transform the state and usher a new phase of global capital accumulation). Finally, we close the book by asking: *how* will state capitalism shape our near future? In this response to this core question, we offer a series of tentative thoughts, provisional arguments, and speculative hypotheses. We identify the seeds of possible future transformations contained within our state capitalist present, which we discuss with respect to neoliberalism, climate change, the future of capitalism as a mode of production, and progressive politics.

2

Theories, Tensions, Controversies

In the face of wide-ranging transformations in the modalities of state intervention (such as those documented in the previous chapter), social scientists, political commentators, and geopolitical analysts have argued that we are currently witnessing a resurgence of state capitalism under a new form. However, despite the widespread mobilization of the concept state capitalism for both categorization and explanation, there is neither consensus about what it exactly means, nor about its implications. Scholars have deployed the concept (and cognates) to designate a national variant of capitalism (Nölke, ten Brink, Claar, and May 2015), a new brand of SOE and/or state-sponsored investment fund (Lyons 2007; Musacchio and Lazzarini 2014), a particular type of state–business relation (Zhang and Whitley 2013; Nölke 2014), a threat or an alternative to (Western-dominated) (neo)liberal capitalism (Bremmer 2010; McNally 2012), a reconfiguration of the global 'state–capital nexus' (van Apeldoorn, de Graaff, and Overbeek 2012), the use of market mechanisms for the promotion of geoeconomic and geopolitical goals (e.g., Kurlantzick 2016), and 'an economic system in which the state uses various tools for proactive intervention in economic production and the functioning of markets' (Wright, Wood, Musacchio, et al. 2021, 2). Hence, the term not only lacks a unified definition, it refers to an extremely wide array of practices, policy instruments and vehicles, institutional forms, relations, and networks that involve the state to different degrees and at a variety of levels, time frames, and scales. While this proliferation of competing definitions and loose conceptualizations is not necessarily problematic, it nonetheless warrants a heightened level of reflexive scrutiny.

This chapter critically engages with the theories, tensions, and controversies surrounding the study of state capitalism. We frame our analysis around a simple question: how has the new state capitalism been theorized and explained? In exploring this question, we synthesize and critique the key arguments in three bodies of literature: strategic management, comparative capitalism, and global political economy. We focus in particular on the arguments that scholars across these bodies of literature have made concerning the specific properties and novel features of the new state capitalism, its

The Spectre of State Capitalism. Ilias Alami and Adam D. Dixon, Oxford University Press.
 DOI: 10.1093/9780198925224.003.0002

drivers of emergence, its location, its polymorphous character, its outward orientation, and its relation to the Western-dominated liberal capitalist world order.

We note that the loose, if not imprecise, conceptualizations of the category have allowed it to become some sort of 'banner to unite under' for a number of commentators with extremely different theoretical outlooks, methods, and objects of inquiry, which we welcome. Indeed, it has opened the *possibility* for a critical dialogue that could lead to a more holistic account of the changing role of the capitalist state at the current historical juncture. Nevertheless, we raise concerns about the concept's analytical value. This is an issue we briefly mentioned in the introduction in our comments on the current state of state capitalism studies, but now fully explore in its theoretical and epistemological dimensions. There have been, in particular, difficulties theorizing how state capitalism differs from other forms of capitalism, as well as problematic geographical assumptions concerning the nature and scale of state capitalism. These have significantly hampered efforts at explaining the rise and significance of present-day state capitalism, and in some cases led to analytical impasses as well as surprising silences and omissions.

Managing State Capitalism

In the strategic management, international business, and comparative corporate governance literature, state capitalism is seen as a particular *organizational and governance form* in emerging and transition economies. Hence, it is worth clarifying that debates in this literature are actually not about capitalism (understood as an historically specific mode of production). Rather, they are concerned with firms where the state plays a strategic management role, or put differently, in state ownership or control of capital. Management scholars argue that there has been a transformation of the 'well-known model of state capitalism'—by which they refer to wholly owned state-owned enterprises (SOEs) 'as extensions of the public bureaucracy'—into 'new models' (Musacchio and Lazzarini 2014).

What is fundamentally new about those models is that 'since the late 20th century ... [state versus private] ownership boundaries are not fixed' (Peng, Bruton, Stan, and Huang 2016, 298). SOEs have become 'hybrid organizations' (Bruton, Peng, Ahlstrom, et al. 2015), where states own majority or minority equity positions in firms, or what has been termed 'partial state ownership' (Inoue, Lazzarini, and Musacchio 2013). Moreover, various 'marketized' forms of state ownership and control (Li, Cui, and Lu 2017) have gained in importance, such as state-owned holding companies, SWFs, state-controlled pension funds and life insurance funds, national development banks, the provision of strategic support to private firms using subsidized credit and/or other forms of support and protection to stimulate new firm capabilities and upgrading, and the facilitation of merger and acquisitions in strategic sectors. In short, the 'new form' of state capitalism is characterized by 'market orientation' and by 'increasing globalization' (Grosman, Okhmatovskiy, and Wright 2016, 202). Management scholars suggest that those various forms of state-controlled and state-directed capital deserve attention because they are 'thriving' not only in their home countries but also in the global economy where they are 'taking center stage' (Musacchio, Lazzarini, and Aguilera 2015).

Indeed, one of the main concerns of this literature is to explain 'the *centrality* and *longevity* of SOEs as an organizational form in the global economy' (Peng, Bruton, Stan, and Huang 2016, 312, emphasis added), as illustrated by the various data points mentioned in the introductory chapter of this book. Management scholars consider this a new research puzzle, insofar as the literature previously assumed SOEs as *temporary* organizational forms (Grosman, Okhmatovskiy, and Wright 2016). From that conventional perspective, SOEs are relics of central planning destined to be privatized as countries liberalize and transition to modern market economies. Hence, the central research question: 'what contributes to their ability to survive and, in some cases, prosper?' (Bruton et al. 2015, 93).

The second main research puzzle is to explain how SOEs are performing at least equal to, if not better, than private companies. Again, what must be emphasized is that the conventional management literature on SOEs predicts that the latter will, as Musacchio, Lazzarini, and Aguilera (2015, 116) remark, 'underperform their private counterparts *under almost any circumstance*'. This is due to what the literature calls 'the liabilities of "stateness"', which broadly refers to how 'dysfunctional political interference' negatively affects firm-level economic performance (Megginson and Netter 2001; Megginson 2017; for surveys on the performance and efficiency costs of state ownership, see Estrin, Hanousek, and Svejnar 2009). The key concern is with the *economic performance at the firm level* of various types of organizational and governance arrangements involving state ownership or control.

Importantly, this is also what frames the interest of the management literature in diversity/variety. The literature is concerned with three types of diversity: (1) various forms of state ownership/control (or what is sometimes termed 'organizational diversity'), (2) different outcomes in terms of firm performance, strategy, and organizational effectiveness, and (3) different country-level institutional arrangements. Though it is important to underline that, in contrast with the comparative capitalism literature examined in the next section, country-level institutional diversity is only examined inasmuch as it affects the previous two types of diversity. For instance, Musacchio, Lazzarini, and Aguilera (2015, 116) seek to 'identify the institutional conditions that will affect the performance of each type of state capitalism'; Bruton et al. (2015) examine how (national) institutions affect the systems of governance, and hence the incentives that board members and executives face; and Meyer and Peng (2016, 6) argue that '[w]ith respect to state ownership, differences in political systems translate into substantive differences in the objectives, governance structures, and top management team composition in SOEs'. The cognate field of international business follows a similar approach: it is concerned with 'how organizational diversity of emerging economy SOEs derived from macro-institutional reforms [encompassing administrative and fiscal decentralization, privatization, market liberalization, and industrial restructuring] can extensively impact their overseas venturing strategies' (Li, Cui, and Lu 2017, 998).

Overall, this literature is concerned with how variegated institutional change is 'a driving component of SOE strategy [encompassing institutional logics and strategic objectives, capabilities and patterns of resource allocation, and internal organizational dynamics] in emerging economies' (Li, Cui, and Lu 2017, 998). It explains diversity as follows: institutional variety at national and local level leads to organizational diversity of SOEs at field-level, which in turn lead to differing firm-level strategies (for instance in terms of overseas investment). Moreover, while this literature provides excellent 'thick' descriptions of the evolution and path-dependency of state control in particular countries, it is little concerned with theorizing the reinvention of state-owned capital, its nature, and the extent of its diversity beyond firm-level and across national contexts.

A Critical Assessment

These debates in the management literature, particularly the most recent, have made important contributions to the study of state capitalism inasmuch as they challenge the stereotypical view (prevalent in the wider management discipline) that the performance of SOEs is tendentially bad; and they draw attention to the role of country-level institutional diversity in the emergence of various forms of state capital and different strategic, performance, and organizational outcomes at the firm-level. Nevertheless, the literature has at least five limitations.

First, it under-theorizes the relationship between the state and SOEs. It tends to take for granted that the influence of state bureaucrats and politicians is a source of 'dysfunctional political interference' in state-controlled firms. This ontological view, and the broader normative stance about the public–private divide in which it is grounded (the public as a source of interference, the private as a source of economic efficiency), is problematic, because it leaves little room for scenarios where firms are efficient in economic terms and simultaneously perform functions that further the strategic interests of state actors. It also precludes considerations of (geo)economic and (geo)political strategies that involve both private and public actors.

Second, the literature tends to conceive of the scope and motives for state action in narrow terms. For instance, Musacchio and Lazzarini (2014, chapter 3) explain in their influential account that they firmly ground their arguments about state capitalism in three fundamental logics for state intervention: fixing market failures, providing social goods, and industrial policy. While this is of course a legitimate theoretical decision, this is nonetheless a restricted understanding of state capitalism. Those three logics, as important as they are, only cover a fraction of the multifaceted role of the state in capital accumulation and capitalist society. Reducing the polymorphism of state intervention to those three logics leaves the strategic management literature inadequately equipped to grasp a great deal of phenomena deeply entangled with state capitalism, many of which will be further commented upon throughout this book, and in particular in Chapter 4, such as the role of state capitalism in reconfiguring economic and political sovereignty, in negotiating neoliberalization, financialization, and globalization, in mediating geopolitical competition between different states, or in disciplining labour and containing domestic political antagonism.

The third limitation is that while the literature convincingly shows that new governance and organizational forms have indeed emerged, such as the listing of large SOEs on stock exchanges, the professionalization of their management, the adding of boards of directors with independent members, and a certain budgetary autonomy (Musacchio and Lazzarini 2014, 48); it has been less successful in explaining the emergence of such new organizational forms in the context of wider dynamics of global capital accumulation, notably in the context of a historically unprecedented round of concentration and centralization of capital, much of which is landing in the controlling hands of states. We return to this important topic in Chapter 6.

Fourth, by primarily locating state capitalism in emerging and transition economies phenomenon, the literature paints an incomplete (if not misleading) picture about the geographies of state capitalism: as Babic, Fichtner, and Heemskerk (2017, 35) note, 'the TSOE [transnational state-owned enterprises] phenomenon clearly goes beyond emerging markets and is prevalent in the industrialized West as well', such as in France, Germany, Japan, and elsewhere (see also Kim 2022). Similarly, Haberly and Wójcik (2017, 252) argue that the 'state capitalist [corporate ownership] network sprawl, has increasingly spread beyond commodity exporters and developing countries, to larger developed countries with historically strong interventionist streaks'. According to the OECD own dataset, SOEs in the OECD area are valued at over two trillion USD and employ over six million people. They are also largely concentrated in critical sectors on which large parts of the private economy depend.[1]

Finally, there is also a tendency in some (but not all) of this literature to use state capitalism as a self-explanatory category, resulting in circulatory forms of reasoning. For instance, the vast presence of SOEs has been explained by the alleged dominance of the logic of state capitalism in a particular space of accumulation (e.g., 'there are a lot of SOEs in China because China has a state capitalist system'), while the very presence of these SOEs has been said to signal the prevalence of a state capitalist logic in such space (e.g., 'there are a lot of SOEs in China, therefore China is a state capitalist economy'). This confusion of state capitalism as *explanandum* and *explanans* results in assuming away what needs explaining.

Comparative (State) Capitalisms

In early variants of Comparative Capitalism (CC) scholarship, the state's role was given limited analytical treatment and taken for granted, save for some specific variants. For instance, Whitley (1999, 2000) identified a 'state-organized business system', while Schmidt (2002, 2003) argued that 'state capitalism', epitomized by French *dirigisme d'état*, is a third European variety of capitalism alongside the coordinated-market economy (CME) and liberal-market economy (LME) ideal-types. While extensions have since been made to the frameworks to better account for the importance of the state (e.g., Hancké, Rhodes, and Thatcher 2007; Schmidt 2009), there is still a widespread sense, including among some of the key proponents of

[1] https://www.oecd.org/corporate/oecd-dataset-size-composition-soe-sectors.htm.

those approaches, that the role and diversity of state intervention are still underplayed in the CC scholarship (e.g., Witt and Redding 2013; Zhang and Whitley 2013; Wilkinson, Wood, and Deeg 2014). This has of course become more obvious given the recently more visible role of the state *everywhere*, but also because the literature has considerably extended its geographical scope, from a rather narrow focus on Western Europe, North America, and Japan, to Asia, Central and Eastern Europe, and Latin America. What clearly appeared from this 'globalization' of the field (and from the inclusion of more countries in its typologies) is that the CC scholarship did not capture well the role of the state and its various forms of intervention in spaces beyond Europe and in national economies that diverged from the two central CME/LME ideal-typical varieties of capitalism (Carney and Witt 2014).

To correct this myopia, a number of CC scholars strive to identify and outline the institutional contours of national varieties of capitalism that are *state-led*. This has consisted in analytically constructing one or several models of state-led varieties of capitalism (cf. Nölke, ten Brink, May, and Claar 2019; and Petry, Koddenbrock, and Nölke 2023 for some of the finest proposals). 'Real' cases (read, national political economies) are then confronted with these analytical constructs, in order to gain a deeper understanding of capitalist diversity. Despite considerable diversity in how the models are constructed (based on inductive or deductive methods), the analytical process remains essentially the same, which is that the models of state capitalism are set in contradistinction to other national varieties of (*non* 'state-led') capitalism.

Mainly three factors linked to the form and role of the state are included as institutional dimensions in the process of categorization of state capitalist diversity: (1) the nature and extent of state intervention (from direct involvement in production and investment to the less direct promotion of specific sectors); (2) the nature of state–business relations (particularly the network of governance arrangements that link the state to private sectors actors, such as policy networks, business associations, deliberation councils and interpersonal relationships); (3) the type of state (i.e., is the state considered characterized by more 'developmental', 'predatory', 'regulatory', or 'welfare' elements?).

For instance, Walter and Zhang (2012) identify a state-led variety of capitalism in Asia, in which they include China and Malaysia, featuring strong state intervention (large industrial output produced by SOEs, large government investment) and tight state control of business and labour organizations. The typology of Asian business systems proposed by Witt and Redding (2013), though ultimately rejecting the validity of a state-led capitalist variety (more on this below), also includes a categorization of the state in the countries studied (following the four ideal types previously mentioned). Carney and Witt (2014) offer yet another typology of Asian business systems, in which a state-led variant of capitalism mixes both predatory and developmental state elements, and includes countries such as Malaysia, Thailand, China, India (the more developmental ones), and Vietnam, the Philippines, Laos, Indonesia (the more predatory ones). Using a similar typology, Fainshmidt, Judge, Aguilera, and Smith (2018, 316) claim to have identified a variant of capitalism where 'the state takes an active and direct role in the economic ordering of society. In these systems, political networks often serve as the mechanism through which economic activity is coordinated. These networks tend to monopolize and sustain power, introducing predatory elements to the state.' They find that countries as diverse as Pakistan, Russia, Venezuela, China, Vietnam, Indonesia, Malaysia, India, Argentina, Mongolia, Belarus, Sri Lanka, Thailand, Philippines, and Bangladesh belong to this state-capitalism variant. For those authors, state-led capitalism *exists beyond Asia*. Nevertheless, other CC studies challenge the argument that economies across geographical regions belong to the same state-led variety of capitalism (e.g., Witt and Redding 2013; Witt, Kabbach de Castro, Amaeshi, et al. 2018).

While many of the above-mentioned studies (and much of the CC literature) are mostly concerned with comparing country-level institutional diversity in a static manner (often using modelling and cluster analysis), a number of studies consider how various institutional forms of strong state intervention have changed over time. For example, Zhang and Whitley (2013) look at how patterns of institutional change and economic governance arrangements have evolved in varieties of East Asian capitalism between the 1980s and the 1990s–2000s. They argue that Japan, Taiwan, Thailand, and Malaysia faced common 'external pressures' (growing global capital and product market integration and intensifying political pressures from Western governments and multinational institutions) which contributed to '[eroding] direct state intervention in the economy and weakened state-controlled institutions through which economic activity was governed' (Zhang and Whitley 2013, 322). Nevertheless, those common pressures did not shape institutional change evenly across East Asian economies. This is because those pressures were mediated by 'the interest and power configuration of dominant coalitions, particularly the number and variety of different socio-economic actors represented in the coalition, such as big business in different sectors, SMEs, landlords, farmers and labor' (2013, 323). According to Zhang and Whitley, of the two East Asian economies considered state-led in the 1980s (Malaysia and Taiwan), only Malaysia remained so in the 2000s (Taiwan became a 'co-governed' variety of capitalism, characterized by reduced state intervention). This is an important argument to explain the uneven persistence of the state-led variety of capitalism over time.

Finally, an influential strand of CC research, that draws upon international political economy and international business, proposes to characterize state capitalism explicitly in terms of *its form of external integration in the global political economy*, or what is referred to as the 'transnational embeddedness' of state capitalism (Nölke, ten Brink, Claar, and May 2015, 542). For the key proponents of this argument, the 'state-permeated' variety of capitalism—which is 'typical for large emerging markets' such as Brazil, India, and China—is not only defined by 'dense informal relationships between public authorities and major domestic corporations, which function as the central coordination mechanism of the economic system' (Nölke 2014, 79–80), as much of the CC literature argues. State-permeated capitalism is also characterized by both a 'deep immersion' in international trade and global production networks and by a 'policy of selective and phased integration into the global economy' (Ten Brink 2013; Nölke, ten Brink, Claar, and May 2015, 542), including the strategic use of inward and outward foreign investment, and various forms of support to 'their' emerging transnational corporations. Importantly, the strong role of the state in those economies is seen as an attempt at orchestrating 'catch-up' development. Indeed, it is intimately linked to their *timing* of insertion into the global economy. In other words, these authors ground their analysis of state-permeated capitalism in (neo-)Listian theories of the developmental state and in Gershenkron's theory of late development (McNally 2012; Nölke 2014, 4).

What distinguishes 'state capitalism 3.0' from 'previous waves of state capitalism' is that 'third-generation late developers' are not coherently directed by a central planning body, and they use sophisticated policies not simply to shield themselves from global competition in a protectionist fashion but to improve their relative position in the world economy (McNally 2012, 755; Nölke 2014, 89).

A Critical Assessment

The renewal of interest within the CC scholarship in the role of the state in (re)producing capitalist institutional diversity is welcome. This literature has contributed significantly to the study of state capitalism in three ways. First, it demonstrates that various state institutions and modalities of intervention shape and are shaped by national variants of capitalism. Second, it highlights the importance of examining state–business relations and (formal and informal) networks in the study of state capitalism and has provided a more nuanced and sophisticated picture in that regard than the strategic management literature discussed earlier. Third, it shows the crucial role that ideas and conflicts between various interests play in the persistence of strong state intervention (albeit in changing forms) in relation with globalization pressures. This is an important argument to understand the diversity of state capitalism, and its reproduction (or not) over time. Nonetheless, this literature has several shortcomings.

As previously discussed, the CC field has reacted to its previous lack of attention to the state in two ways, and reached diametrically opposite conclusions, both of which are problematic in our view. On the one hand, commentators have upheld the validity of the category state(-led, -permeated) capitalism, and have fleshed out what are deemed to be its key institutional features. However, this has proved to be a particularly thorny exercise, and commentators tend to disagree over the *specific* institutional contours of state capitalism. The issue is not so much the dissensus. Although, the debates about what institutions and forms of intervention to include (or not) and about how to measure/quantify features such as 'strong state intervention' are potentially endless (the proliferation of typologies attests to that). Consequently, one wonders about the potential of this analytical strategy in yielding fresh insights into the nature of state capitalism. Moreover, a relatively small methodological difference in the institutional characterization of state capitalism as an *ideal type* (or in the institutional variables used to perform a cluster analysis) may result in significant changes in the categorization of national economies as state capitalist. This may depict very different pictures of where *actually existing* state capitalism is located in the world economy, from an exclusively Chinese or East Asian phenomenon, to a state-led variety distributed across emerging economies, or across entire regions and continents. In short, a small change in what CC scholars look at might lead to a *dramatic shift in the geographies of state capitalism*. This has major implications for how we understand state capitalism, its nature, and drivers.

This leads us to the second claim by some CC scholars, which has been to reject altogether the categorical validity of state capitalism on the basis that the state plays a pervasive role in most, if not all, of the national economies investigated. This position can be summed up as *strong capitalist states everywhere, state capitalism nowhere*, as Witt, Kabbach de Castro, Amaeshi, et al. (2018) argue. This conclusion is equally problematic for at least two reasons. First, it does not allow moving beyond the (somewhat trivial) statement that 'the state matters', and it does not say much if anything about the recently more visible role of the state. Second, it eludes the question of explaining why the role of the state is so variegated across the world capitalist economy. Indeed, and perhaps ironically given the focus of the CC field on institutional diversity, by emphasizing commonality (the strong role of the state), this conclusion dilutes diversity. Overall, both conclusions remain wanting, and arguably reflect the analytical impasse that the field has reached in the study of state capitalism.

Furthermore, if the CC literature has done a good job at explaining the *maintenance* or *persistence* of state capitalism in the face of pressures emanating from globalization, it does not say much about its *resurgence*, *renewal*, and *reinvention*. In particular, and with some important exceptions (e.g., Nölke, ten Brink, Claar, and May 2015; Nölke, ten Brink, May, and Claar 2019), it has done little to explain the transnational dimensions of state capitalism, or how state capitalism itself has been a driving force of globalizing capital (via foreign investment, cross-listing of shares, M&A, transnational networks of elites, etc.). This is highly unfortunate, given that those transnationalizing tendencies are identified across the social sciences as the single most important features about the new form of state capitalism, that is, what makes it distinctively different from previous forms, or periods, of state capitalism.

There are additional ways in which the analytical outlook of the CC literature is problematic in state capitalism studies. Not only is it inadequately equipped to capture the various forms of interconnections, interreferentiality, and combination between repertoires of state intervention across the territorial borders of nation-states (as discussed later on in this chapter), it also almost invariably leads to rigid analytical constructs. There is of course room for debates surrounding the exact institutional contours of state capitalism(s), just like there is scope for considering hybridity (i.e., real cases exhibiting features of both state-led and other variants of capitalism). Nonetheless, this approach is largely a double exercise in boundary-making, consisting in drawing lines of distinction between types of capitalisms, and in placing real cases within the confines of thereby established ideal-types. Setting aside for now the question of the frame of reference used for the construction of varieties of state capitalism (or what is considered the norm against which such varieties are derived), our point here is that such an approach necessarily relies upon rigid and static analytical constructs of state capitalism as a set of specific institutions, modalities of state intervention, governance arrangements, or combination thereof. This restricts discussions of state capitalism in two ways: what to include (or not) in this list, and the extent to which nation-states fit ideal-type varieties of state capitalism (or not). As we argue below, it is virtually impossible to answer such questions without fetishizing some specific institutions and forms of intervention at the expense of others that might be less visible but equally important. This also forecloses the possibility that the manifest institutional and political forms of state capitalism in one place could be significantly different than in another.

State Capital in the Global Political Economy

The contribution of global political economy (GPE) (or international political economy, IPE) research on state capitalism is somewhat heterogeneous. While it is clear that management scholars are mostly interested in state-owned or state-controlled capital, and that the CC literature is concerned with (national) state-led varieties of capitalism, state capitalism in GPE covers a highly diverse range of research topics and objects of inquiry. We identify four (overlapping) themes that cover the main contributions of the field.

First, GPE scholars have discussed the implications of state capitalism as a source of cross-border finance, and particularly, a source of patient capital. For instance, Kaplan (2021) argues that the longer-term horizons of Chinese state-to-state lending provides more fiscal space to Latin American debtors than when they borrow from financial markets, thereby affecting their policy choices. For Kaplan, this has the potential to trigger a move away from the more traditional (Western) market-centric governance of sovereign borrowing. Critical scholars are more sceptical: for Gonzalez-Vicente (2017), state capitalism as a source of finance and investment is unlikely to significantly alter South-South relations. Taylor (2014, 354) argues similarly that 'state capitalism as exported to Africa serves the class interests of externally oriented fractions with aspirations to become internationally competitive, accumulate mega-profits and entrench their domestic positions'. The question of state capitalism as a source of finance is not reserved to the developing world. Thatcher and Vlandas (2022, 2016) show how both state and private actors in Germany and France have actively sought to attract investment from SWFs. Indeed, Asian and Middle Eastern SWFs helped recapitalize distressed banks and automotive firms in the West in the post-2008 crisis environment (Haberly 2014, 2011). This also increased the participation of state-controlled capital in the global network of corporate ownership and control (Haberly and Wójcik 2017).

Second, GPE scholars have studied state capitalism in light of the reconfiguration of the state under conditions of globalization and financialization in order to achieve developmental objectives, maintain state sovereignty, and preserve existing domestic political orders. For instance, Nem Singh and Chen (2018) show how the internationalization and upgrading of SOEs allowed designing new developmental policies across the developing world. SWFs can play a developmental role (when used to invest in 'strategic' sectors, firms, or projects) but can also be used as state instruments to retain sovereignty at home, or extend it abroad (Dixon and Monk 2012). For Carney (2015, 2018) and Huat (2016), the rise and persistence of state capitalism (under the shape of SOEs) can be explained by its 'stabilizing role' in the face of financial globalization. By addressing macroeconomic and financial volatility and protecting from 'political challengers' who may benefit from financial globalization, state capitalism contributes to regime maintenance and the preservation of domestic political orders. Haberly and Wójcik (2017, 258) suggest interpreting the new state capitalism as 'politically-mediated Polanyian double-movements of marketization and societal-protection, surrounding the advance of neoliberalism and globalization'. This has given rise to what Haberly and Wójcik call 'a market-conforming, financial-return oriented state capitalist paradigm [...] not as a reaction to neoliberalism and globalization, but rather as a means for sustaining them' (2017, 251).

The Amsterdam School of critical IPE argues similarly that the current crisis of global capitalism has triggered a 'reconfiguration of the global state-capital nexus', marked by 'the combination of a "return of the state" with a continued deepening of the process of capitalist transnationalization and globalization' (van Apeldoorn, de Graaff, and Overbeek 2012, 472–473). In the West, the crisis has forced the state to take on an extraordinary role in order to protect the interests of capital in general, though this has so far not led 'to any durable statist direction of the market' but rather to an instrumentalization of the crisis to promote further neoliberalization (2012, 478–479). Across the Global South, the particular configuration of the state–capital nexus corresponds to a statist version of capitalism (involving both rentier and developmentalist strategies) in which the state plays a particularly important role in directing capital accumulation. In both the West and the Global South, they argue, the reconfiguration of the state–capital nexus is geared towards deepening commodification of labour and nature.

Third, GPE commentators have explored the interplay of statist and commercial strategies in the internationalization (or transnationalization) of state capitalism, via SWFs and state asset management bodies, SOEs' outward FDI, M&A, and equity investment, and the creation of 'national champions'. The key issue here is the following: are the going-abroad strategies of state capitalism *more* driven by state (geo)political interests, such as the acquisition of key resources and the expansion of statecraft, or by profit-maximization? Empirically, contributors have sought to answer this question by focusing on state-owned capital invested overseas in a number of strategic sectors such as natural resources and energy. A much-debated case is that of the oil industry. Meckling, Kong, and Madan (2015, 1161) identify three types of perspective on the matter. Scholars often close to Western corporate and policy-making circles have articulated the first type of perspective. It contends from a realist standpoint that the going-abroad strategies of state capitalism (largely seen as an emerging market phenomenon) are 'a product of statecraft' (e.g., Bremmer 2010; Kurlantzick 2016). National oil companies are typically seen as 'arms of state power'. This is generally perceived as a threat (for a number of reasons detailed below), and those accounts are often characterized by an alarmist and anxiogenic tone.

The second type of approach claims, on the contrary, that when going abroad, national oil companies are 'commercially minded', and that 'governments follow firms more than they lead their internationalization' (Meckling, Kong, and Madan 2015, 1162; e.g., Steinfeld 2010; Victor, Hults, and Thurber 2012). The third type of perspective provides a more nuanced account. For example, Meckling, Kong, and Madan (2015) argue that the internationalization of Indian and Chinese national oil companies is neither primarily state-driven nor market-driven; rather, it follows a 'hybrid' pattern characterized by 'the co-existence of cooperation and conflict between increasingly entrepreneurial, profit-driven national oil companies pulling to global markets and partially supportive and interventionist home governments' (2015, 1160).

Similarly, for de Graaff and van Apeldoorn (2018, 121), Chinese energy SOEs perform a 'dual role, adhering to commercial principles abroad (e.g., prioritizing profit-making) but retaining the responsibilities of a state-owned company at home (e.g., prioritizing energy security and social stability)' (see also de Graaff 2012). This constitutes 'the essentially contradictory nature of Chinese transnationalizing state-directed capital' (de Graaff and van Apeldoorn 2018, 121). Jones and Zou (2017) explore the case study of a Chinese SOE investing in hydropower energy in Myanmar. For them, the analytical distinction between state-driven or market-driven internationalization is problematic, both empirically (they find evidence for both theses), and theoretically, because it relies on a poor conceptualization of the relationship between the state and SOEs. Their key argument is that Chinese SOEs have 'considerable power and autonomy to pursue profit-making activities and are very weakly regulated', due to the dispersal of power and authority to diverse, cross-cutting state apparatuses that are unevenly fragmented, decentralized, and internationalized (Jones and Zou 2017, 755). Nevertheless, parts of the state also 'strive to control SOE activities where their interests are at stake. Thus, party-state/SOE relations are best understood in terms of an evolving struggle within a transformed, multilevel governance structure' (2017, 755; see also Jones and Hameiri 2021).

Fourth, GPE scholars have debated the relation between the rise of state capitalism and the future of the (Western-dominated) liberal economic order and the global hegemony of neoliberalism. The Chinese model is often the key concern here. Here again, a number of general perspectives can be identified. The first one sees the resurgence of state capitalism, and especially its Chinese instantiation, as a threat to the 'free market' and liberal democracy. For instance, Bremmer (2010) contends that state capitalism is quite simply antithetical to Western liberal capitalism and seriously risks impairing the smooth functioning of markets. In an influential book on contemporary state capitalism, Kurlantzick (2016) provides a slightly more nuanced account and makes a distinction between authoritarian 'types' of state capitalism (China, Russia, Egypt, Vietnam) and more democratic ones (Brazil, Indonesia, etc.). In his view, the former 'could undermine the best aspects of free-market capitalism—innovation, entrepreneurship, individualism, and democracy', while the latter 'could coexist with individuals' economic and political freedoms' (2016, 11–12). Furthermore, while acknowledging that 'some of the modern state capitalists [...]—Singapore and Malaysia come to mind—are important pillars of the world trading system, generally follow its rules, and—in the case of Singapore—have been leading advocates for expanding free trade globally and in Asia' (2016, 11–12), Kurlantzick still argues that overall state capitalism 'presents a real potential alternative to the free-market model, and as an alternative it presents serious threats to political and economic stability around the world', inasmuch as 'these countries will provide much of the world's growth over the coming decades, and so will command ever-larger power in international institutions' (2016, 23).

Another set of GPE scholars also emphasize the potential of state capitalism in reshaping the liberal order, though importantly, this is not necessarily perceived as a threat. For example, for Nölke, ten Brink, Claar, and May (2015), the liberal order is unlikely to deepen—rather, it will be increasingly influenced by the state-permeated model prevalent in large emerging economies (see previous section on CC). The 'common economic institutions shared by this group' have the potential to become a 'State Capitalist Consensus', which could replace the 'Post-Washington Consensus' (2015, 540–541). Besides, the 'foreign economic strategies' of state-permeated economies are already 'facilitating such a process' (2015, 541). McNally (2013) makes a similar argument: 'the refurbished state capitalisms of emerging market economies, especially from China ... seems to be producing a truly monumental alternate model of [neoliberal market] capitalism' (2013, 37). In contrast with Nölke and co-writers, the primary distinction with neoliberal market capitalism does not reside so much in a set of common economic institutions than in their 'considerable distrust of markets and full-out economic liberalization', their 'pragmatic use of markets', and in their shared 'strong belief in the potential benefits of state power, a belief that undergirds their economic management philosophies' (McNally 2013, 38–39). For McNally (2013, 43–44), 'the possibility of a struggle between the established Washington Consensus and refurbished state capitalisms has become quite prominent', though he emphasizes that 'refurbished state capitalisms are deeply enmeshed in the global political economy and their practitioners own immense amounts of global financial assets, most significantly U.S. treasury debt. Both models of capitalism are thus simultaneously co-dependent and in competition.'

The possibility that co-dependence and competition will lead to a scenario of 'co-existence' of the Western liberal capitalist model and the Chinese state capitalist model is envisaged by de Graaff and van Apeldoorn (2018), who argue that each could 'maintain their own distinct political and economic system, both systems being—in different ways—part of and compatible with a capitalist and globally interlinked world economy. In this hybrid scenario China retains a relatively autonomous trajectory, partially adapting to the rules of the game of the liberal order, but at the same time holding on to distinctive aspects of its state–society model and foreign policy orientation' (2018, 115). In another article, they further contend that the rise of state capitalism outside the Western core is leading towards 'an increasingly multipolar order' and might 'force a more active role of the state in the West' (van Apeldoorn, de Graaff, and Overbeek 2012, 482). More recently, they argued that we are witnessing 'a relative convergence' between the roles that the Chinese and US state play 'inasmuch as the still strongly market-directing Chinese state also has at the same time come to embrace a global market-creating role, while the US is now also showing signs of a stronger emphasis on market-direction' (van Apeldoorn and de Graaff 2022, 306). Table 2.1 summarizes the key insights of our analysis thus far.

Silences, Omissions, and Conceptual Issues

In this section we look further into three critical issues: (1) the 'missing link' of a theory of the capitalist state, (2) the time horizons of state capitalism, or the question of 'periodization', (3) spatial-territorial considerations, or

	Main objects of enquiry	Key concerns	Diversity	Geography
Strategic management	State capitalism as an organizational and governance form	The emergence new organizational and governance forms	Various forms of state ownership and control (organizational diversity)	Emerging and transition economies
	A focus on the firm level (mainly SOEs)	The longevity, centrality, and internationalization of state capitalism in the global political economy	Firm performance and strategy	
Comparative capitalism	State capitalism as a national variety of capitalism/business system	Identification of the institutional contours of state capitalism as an ideal-type	Country-level institutional diversity	China, Asia, the BRICS (depending on authors)
	A viable alternative to CME/LME variants of capitalism?	State–business relations and informal networks between public and private actors	One variety of state capitalism? Several varieties?	
	Adaptation of national varieties of state capitalism in the face of globalization	Its form of external integration in the global political economy		
Global political economy	State capitalism as an actor in global finance	State-to-state lending and SWFs as sources of patient capital	A more diverse global financial architecture	Sources of surplus from Asia and the Middle East, investing in the rest of the world
	State capitalism and state sovereignty	SWFs and SOEs as new developmental instruments, as tools for regime maintenance, and as devices for expanding sovereignty abroad	Different state capitalist strategies in the face of financialization and globalization yield variegated outcomes	Global South, Asian authoritarian regimes
	Interplay of statist and commercial strategies in the transnationalization of state capitalism	Is the process driven by (geo)political interests or profit-maximization?	Diversity as a result of economic and/or geopolitical competition	China/Russia
	State capitalism as the rise of an alternative model of capitalism	Implications for the future of the (Western-dominated) liberal economic order and the global hegemony of neoliberalism	A more diverse world order, or what one characterized by conflict between two blocs	East versus West, or some form of complementarity (depending on authors)

Source: Authors.

the question of 'locating' state capitalism. Our argument is that many of the analytical limitations and shortcomings previously discussed actually result from an incomplete or unsatisfactory engagement with these three deeply entangled issues. This has hampered the ability of the field of state capitalism studies to substantiate some of its core claims concerning the emergence of new global landscapes of state intervention. Tackling these three critical issues head on is key to unleashing the general potential of state capitalism as both a social scientific category and a lens for analysis, and this will be the explicit objective of the conceptual framework we develop in Chapter 3 and deploy in the remainder of the book.

The 'Missing Link': A Robust Theory of the State

As we have seen, much of the literature uses state capitalism as a heuristic device to broadly refer to configurations of capitalism where the state plays a particularly *strong* role in organizing the economy and society, in supervising and administering capital accumulation, or in directly owning and controlling capital. If this conceptualization appears to be clear and straightforward, it pivots on a particularly thorny issue: what does *strong* actually mean? What is the backdrop against which the strong role is assessed (whether quantitatively or qualitatively) and following what criteria or standard of comparison? With some creative exceptions (e.g., Kim 2022), it is fair to say that state capitalism studies as a whole have lacked a thorough and self-reflexive engagement with these fundamental questions.

We contend that there is quite simply no way of rigorously defining what is meant by a strong role of the state without establishing in the first place what is the general role of the state in capitalist society. In other words, what are the essential features and basic functions that *all states must perform*? Only on this basis can there be a reflection on the specific conditions, characteristics, and implications of an extraordinarily strong role of the state. Hence, we argue that if state capitalism is to be useful as a representational category, it must be clear from the outset that *state capitalism* is not synonymous with the *capitalist state*. This simple distinction may sound trivial. Yet, it is a crucial theoretical question, which may well be at the core of many analytical challenges, difficulties, and impasses that the field of state capitalism studies has experienced so far, and which requires engagement with theories of the socially necessary role of the state in capitalist society. Nevertheless, with very few exceptions (e.g., van Apeldoorn, de Graaff, and

Overbeek 2012; van Apeldoorn and de Graaff 2022), the field has suffered from a lack of robust engagement with state theory, perhaps ironically, given its self-defined object of study. In the next chapter, we will firmly ground our conceptualization of state capitalism in state theory. For now, let us substantiate our claim about the need for a robust theory of the capitalist state by highlighting some of the issues the absence of such a theory might raise.

It has become commonplace in state capitalism studies to label particular institutions (e.g., strong ties between states and capital markets) (Petry 2020), modalities of state intervention (e.g., direct state support to 'national champions') (Lin and Milhaupt 2013), and organizational forms (e.g., state-owned enterprises or sovereign wealth funds) (Clark, Dixon, and Monk 2013) as state capitalist. This is not to say that these things do not deserve to be categorized as state capitalist (in fact, as argued in the introductory chapter, our concern in this book is precisely with the joint and concurrent expansion of many of these political and organizational forms at the current historical juncture). Rather, we want to point to the need for deeper reflection as to why certain repertoires of state intervention are unproblematically accepted as state capitalist, while others (perhaps equally significant) are rarely characterized as such.

Relatedly, state capitalism research has tended to exhibit a bias for the study of particular forms of intervention (such as SOEs, SWFs, and development banks) at the expense of others. The American military-industrial complex, for example, is rarely referred to as an instantiation of state capitalism, despite its extraordinary significance for both the trajectories of American capitalism and global political economy. Quantitative easing and other central bank interventions are another case in point. These forms of state action have recently been instrumental in maintaining global capitalism on life support. Yet quantitative easing and other central bank interventions rarely seem to qualify as state capitalist. Our point is not necessarily that phenomena like quantitative easing or military-industrial complexes would necessarily deserve to be labelled as such. Rather, it is that the field of state capitalism studies would benefit from greater self-reflexivity with respect to such methodological and theoretical choices. Assuming that the presence of particular institutions or forms of intervention attests to a strong role of the state, if not grounded in an overall theory of the state, constantly run the risk of fetishizing such institutions and forms of intervention at the expense of others that might be less visible but equally important (for instance, the 'hidden' industrial policy in the United States, Block 2008; Wade 2012; Baltz 2022). Moreover, fetishizing specific institutions or governance arrangements might be particularly problematic inasmuch as the function of institutions does not necessarily follow from their form. In fact, institutional function is often variable and context dependent (Dixon 2014; Ho 2018). This results in difficulties identifying the specific features and unique elements of state capitalism, in contrast with other forms of capitalism.

Other students of state capitalism have attempted to define the strong role of the state by quantifying it. For instance, Kurlantzick identifies

> state capitalists as countries whose government has an ownership stake in or significant influence over more than one-third of the five hundred largest companies, by revenue, in that country.... Below this one-third level of government ownership of companies by revenue, the economy is still determined primarily by the market, even though the state may play a significant role.
>
> **(2016, 9)**

Here we are not opposed to the attempt at quantification per se; rather, we are sceptical of the ad hoc construction of indicators to measure and quantify the role of the state in the economy without grounding in any theoretical basis. The choice of the above threshold, for instance, seems arbitrary (see also Peck 2021). Another problem stemming from this lack of theoretical grounding is that there has been a tendency in the field to construct (discursively and analytically) state capitalism as an abnormal form of capitalism, which somehow suggests that the state is relatively absent or passive in *normal* configurations of capitalism. Needless to say, this position is untenable.

By contrast, van Apeldoorn, de Graaff, and Overbeek (2012) and van Apeldoorn and De Graaff (2022) examine the recent resurgence of state activism in light of a historical materialist theory of the state. This theoretical grounding emphasizes that that political and economic power are always entangled and affords nuance to the claim that the state is 'returning'. Indeed, the state has never left, even in the spaces of the world economy that have experienced the deepest rounds of neoliberalization and apparent state rollback, and even in spaces often labelled as liberal market economies. Thus, the lesson, or challenge, for state capitalism studies is to account for both the permanent and pervasive role and functions of the state in capitalist society (in enforcing the rule of law and property rights, managing labour and land-nature, regulating money and finance, etc.) *and* for the recent historic arc in the trajectories of state intervention. This leads us to the essential—and intimately related—issue of periodization.

On the Time Horizons of State Capitalism: The Question of Periodization

Looking at the state in capitalism from an historical perspective, we are faced with two outstanding facts: first, the remarkable historical continuity of its pervasive role; second, its conspicuously changing character, in terms of the scope and depth of state intervention, but also, more broadly speaking, in terms of the shifting boundary between public and private spheres and the breadth of the tasks it has performed throughout the historical development of capitalism. This underlines the importance of clearly delineating the time horizons of state capitalism. In short, what exactly is *new* about the new state capitalism? This is particularly important given how much the literature relies on notions of 'novelty', 'return', and 'reinvention'. Our contention is that a thoroughly defined periodization is necessary to substantiate the claim of historical novelty, and to clearly identify the specific properties and drivers of emergence of present-day state capitalism.

Here our argument is not that the state capitalism literature does not provide any periodization—several contributors actually provide very comprehensive ones. Let us consider two examples. The historically attuned account offered by Musacchio and Lazzarini (2014, chapter 2) is useful in showing how state ownership has changed since the late nineteenth century. Their periodization covers almost all the historical geographies of capitalism, from state ownership of infrastructure in the colonies, to the planned economy of the Soviet Union, large-scale nationalizations in the West after the Second World War, and so on. Nölke (2014, introductory chapter) suggests a periodization underpinned by a different principle. He identifies three waves of 'successful' catch-up capitalist development, each corresponding to a period of state capitalism: (1) Germany and Japan (in late nineteenth century); (2) the New Deal in the United States, German and Italian Fascism, Stalinism, the Swedish Model, and East Asian developmentalism (from the 1930s to the rise of neoliberalism in the 1980s); (3) state capitalism 3.0 in emerging economies in the contemporary period.

The historical depth of these two accounts at periodization is admirable, yet they also point to significant difficulties and limitations in how the field of state capitalism studies has attempted to delineate the time horizons of state capitalism. Here we identify a clear paradox. On the one hand, the literature as a whole tends to treat state capitalism as a sort of extraordinary, exceptional, if not abnormal phenomenon. On the other, the more historically attuned studies such as the ones just discussed cover extremely large chunks of history and point at the many historical antecedents of the organizational and political forms considered new in much of the literature. This strongly suggests that state capitalism may actually be the historical norm more than an exception. If that is the case, what does this mean for theorizing state capitalism in its current modalities? If state capitalism is a permanent feature of capitalism, how analytically useful is the concept in making sense of current trajectories of state intervention? Indeed, wide-ranging periodizations, while providing historical depth to the concept, stretch its boundaries so much that it risks diluting its analytical purchase ('everything becomes an instantiation of state capitalism'). An added difficulty in attempts at periodizing state capitalism is that what may be considered state capitalism in one historical-geographical context may pass as ordinary and inconspicuous in another.

To move past these impasses, we reframe the problem of the periodization of state capitalism. In the remainder of this book, we aim to periodize not on the basis of specific organizational forms (e.g., economic entities, institutions, governance, legal arrangements, etc.) or the specific objectives they aim to achieve (e.g., catch-up development, fixing market failures, delivering public goods), but on the basis of their embedding in planetary dynamics of capitalist restructuring. What this means is that we are not interested in identifying the historical antecedents of, say, sovereign wealth funds or development banks, the large presence of which would indicate the existence of previous 'waves' or 'brands' of state capitalism. This has been comprehensively done already by some of the studies earlier mentioned, inviting interesting reflections on the ways in which past instantiations of state capitalism materially and ideologically inhabit the present. Rather, we propose to firmly situate what we call contemporary state capitalist *impulses* (notably the combined expansion of state-capital hybrids and of muscular forms of statism) within the historical development and geographical remaking of global capitalism.

The added value of this approach, we show in the remainder of the book, is that it allows developing a more nuanced understanding of the temporalities of present-day state capitalism, one that is attentive to both contingent and structural factors. The literature has shed light on the role of the 2008 global financial crisis in sparking a strong (conjunctural) response from the state. Some commentators have also considered this renewal of state activism against the backdrop of more long-term tendencies, in Polanyian fashion. For instance, Dolfsma and Grosman (2019) interpret contemporary state capitalism as a Polanyian countermovement against 'too much' neoliberal globalization and its crises. Boyer (2020) sees the current rise of what he calls *capitalisme à impulsion étatique* (capitalism with a state impulse) as a state-led attempt at reasserting national sovereignty against the forces of transnational capitalist globalization. Without discounting these arguments, our point here is that their emphasis on a particular type of cyclical temporality (i.e., a counter-movement of the state somehow automatically following a period of market expansion) is not particularly well suited to capture long-term, secular capitalist tendencies—including trends of economic stagnation, the centralization and concentration of capital, the internationalization of production—which have profoundly altered the scope and modalities of state intervention over the past twenty years or so. Paying careful attention to these historical transformations in global capitalism is essential to better understanding the temporalities of present-day state capitalism, as well as its spatialities. Which leads us to our third critical issue.

Locating State Capitalism: Territorial and Geographical Considerations

Our critical survey of the literature shows the importance of geographical considerations in making sense of state capitalism in at least two respects. First, there are different views on *where* state capitalism is geographically located: in China, Asia, emerging and transition economies, and Middle Eastern oil-exporting countries. Others argue that varieties exist across regions. Second, many contributors emphasize the transnationalizing dimensions of state capitalism. Nevertheless, we note that the field of state capitalism studies as a whole has tended, at least until recently, to exhibit an under-developed sense of space, and some of its core geographical assumptions concerning the nature, scale, and spatial organization of state capitalism have led to restricted and potentially misleading reading of its contemporary advent.

We have seen that much of the literature consists in outlining the institutional contours of state capitalism. Entire nation-states or blocs of nation-states are then positioned in this category. Here the framework of assumptions concerning spatial organization is that state capitalism is *primarily* contained within neatly demarcated national territories. State capitalism exists, including in the geographical sense, alongside other varieties of (non-state) capitalism (e.g., Fainshmidt, Judge, Aguilera, and Smith 2018; Nölke, ten Brink, May, and Claar 2019). It may make incursions in other territories, such as when it exports state-owned capital or competes abroad over access to markets or sources of raw materials, but it is primarily a national creature and a product of domestic social forces. For example, Kurlantzick contends that 'the most autocratic and powerful state capitalists will use their state companies as de facto weapons of war, creating serious conflict in some of the most strategically important places on earth' (2016, 25). When the focus is not on entire nation-states but on specific organizational forms, such as SWFs and SOEs, these are nonetheless seen as the causal result of domestic structures and conflicts (e.g., Nölke 2014; Li, Cui, and Lu 2017; Braunstein 2019). State-owned firms may well be taking centre stage in global markets, but they remain creatures of their 'home countries'.

Thus, there is a strong bias in the literature towards methodological nationalism, where state capitalism is seen as primarily determined at the national level. This has profound implications, including a tendency to see geographic space as a mere container of relatively coherent models of state capitalism, or as a passive terrain of competition between such models and other forms of state capitalism. This geographic 'anaemia' (a term we further discuss below) can take different forms. Spechler et al. (2017, 2), for example, contend that 'the obvious contrast to state-capitalism is free-market capitalism', with either of these models prevailing in discrete geographic spaces. Approaches to state capitalism inspired by the developmental state literature tend to fall in a similar 'territorial trap' (Agnew 1994), whereby the national territory is reified as a container of state capitalist models and construed as the main unit of analysis. For instance, in their study of emerging markets state enterprises, Nem Singh and Chen (2018, 1091) argue that the decision to retain them and support their developmental roles is influenced by 'a country's model of development based on state capitalism'. The approaches to state capitalism prevalent in international business and strategic management likewise exhibit an underdeveloped sense of space. According to prominent contributors to this literature, the geographic nature and spatial variegation of SOEs have been systematically understudied, leading to a neglect of place-based contextual elements and spatial relations in structuring strategic decisions and firm operations across territorial borders (Deng, Delios, and Peng 2020).

As a result of these geographical assumptions concerning the nature and scale of state capitalism, the extant literature offers a restricted and potentially misleading reading of its contemporary advent. To be clear, this is not to say that national-domestic factors do not matter in the rise of state capitalism. They obviously do. This is also not to say that the field has been entirely unable to look at scales beyond the national. Our argument is rather that most approaches in state capitalism studies are 'geographically anaemic', meaning 'firstly, that they are framed at an inappropriate geographical scale; and secondly, that in conjunction with this framing, they conspicuously disregard certain vital geographical trends in recent capitalist history' (Christophers 2012, 272).[2]

Consider for instance the question *why* does state capitalism ascend? Due to their core geographical assumptions, state capitalism studies have provided restricted responses to this question: the development of state capitalism has been largely interpreted as the rise of a nationally scaled and a relatively coherent variant of capitalism. As it grows in significance on the international stage (via the internationalization of its firms, extending loans and investing abroad, etc.), it increasingly competes with other varieties of capitalism, both for access to global markets and as a model, distinct from (neo)liberal capitalism, for other countries to emulate. Politically, what is at stake is the sustainability of the new models of state capitalism (Nölke et al. 2019), or the extent to which these constitute a threat for the smooth functioning of markets and the liberal world order (Bremmer 2010). Anaemic geographical imaginaries are evident in the narratives of a confrontation between rival political-economic models which pervade the literature. For example, Kurlantzick (2016, 23) argues that 'state capitalism usually offers a vision of the future that is more protectionist, more dangerous to global security and global prosperity, and more threatening to political freedom than the alternative of free-market capitalism' (see also Bremmer 2010). The problem with such geographical imaginaries is not only that they locate the abnormality or exceptionalism of state capitalism outside of the Western core of the world economy, thereby reproducing orientalist tropes, and misleadingly reduce the question of contemporary state capitalism to a geopolitical clash between two easily identifiable protagonists—(Western) democratic free-market capitalism and its deviant state capitalist (eastern) 'other' (a warlike discursive frame which we already mentioned in the introductory chapter, and will scrutinize at length in Chapter 7). They are also poorly equipped to grasp the extent of current state transformations unfolding across the spaces of the world capitalist economy, including in states which assume liberal forms (Babic 2021; Kim 2022). This contributes to the relative incapacity in the study of state capitalism to even *see* state capitalism in advanced capitalist economies, which is a major hurdle to elucidating the phenomenon in both its globality and its totality.

Consider also the question of the polymorphism of the new state capitalism. The remarkable diversity in the institutional landscapes of state capitalism is of course acknowledged in the literature, but as a result of

[2] Christophers is referring here to studies of financialization. We argue that his remark equally applies to state capitalism studies.

its methodological nationalism, is largely seen as a product of national-domestic political economic contingent factors. As previously mentioned, this leaves little appreciation for the various forms of interconnections, inter-referentiality, and combination that may exist between repertoires of state intervention across the territorial borders of nation-states. Yet there is ample evidence that these relations are fundamental to the recent upward trajectories of state intervention and their institutional diversity, as we will see in detail in Chapters 4 and 5. Let us take two examples to illustrate this argument. The first one is that of the recent creation of state investment funds in Western economies such as Ireland, France, and Italy (and see Dixon 2017; Mertens and Thiemann 2018). This development is directly related to the growing volumes of state-controlled investments from the Middle East and China invested in those economies, insofar as the Irish, French, and Italian state investment funds aim at channelling these investments to key sectors. Similarly, the renewal of state activism in Brazil during the rule of the Workers' Party was intimately connected to state-led capital accumulation, rapid industrialization, and sprawling urbanization in China, and the boom in primary commodity prices that this generated from the early 2000s to the mid-2010. Indeed, the extraordinary large rents from commodity exports flowing into Brazil provided the material basis for renewal of state activism in the economy.

State capitalism studies have also experienced difficulties grasping spatial practices and strategies at a variety of scales that cut across the national, as well as their interconnection. For instance, the relation between the regional and the transnational remains underexplored, although there are clear signs that it can be highly significant. Indeed, much of the state support to the internationalization of Chinese SOEs is provided by municipal and provincial states, often in partial autonomy from the central government (see Gu et al. 2016). The national state remains of course a key site in the political geographies of state capitalism, but the literature can benefit from a deeper sensitivity to the multi-scalar relations that contribute to the reconfiguration of economic territory and sovereignty via diverse state-capitalist strategies and practices. A number of GPE contributors have gone some way in this direction when considering the fragmentation of the state and the question of multi-level governance (e.g., Gu et al. 2016; Jones and Zou 2017).

Finally, the anaemic geographies of state capitalism studies have precluded a reflection on the historic development and self-transformation of global capitalism, such as planetary mutations in the spheres of production, circulation, distribution of value, the continuation of accumulation in the face of market saturation and overproduction, and geographical trends such as the unfolding of a new international division of labour and the historically unprecedented centralization and concentration of capital. As we show in this book, these questions are fundamental for understanding contemporary state capitalism. This points to the need for an explicitly geographical approach, one that allows probing into the multiple spatialities (beyond nation-state centric territoriality) and temporalities (beyond that of catch-up development and crises) at the core of contemporary state capitalism.

Conclusions

Debating state capitalism is not new. There have been previous rounds of academic debates about state capitalism, each at historical junctures characterized by deep capitalist crises and renewed state activism from the end of the nineteenth century to the 1970s and 1980s (see Sperber 2019 for an excellent intellectual-historical overview), not unlike the contemporary conjuncture. State capitalism as a research agenda and field of study in its current form has provided valuable insights into an extremely wide array of spatially diverse practices, policy instruments and vehicles, institutional forms, governance arrangements, and networks that involve the state to different degrees and at a variety of levels, time frames, and geographical scales. As such, it has contributed to our understanding of the present polymorphism of state intervention across the world capitalist economy. Furthermore, the term's capaciousness and its wide circulation have allowed state capitalism to become some sort of 'banner to unite under' for a number of commentators with extremely different theoretical outlooks, methods, and—perhaps more importantly—objects of inquiry.

Nevertheless, this emerging field of research has experienced conceptual difficulties, which have significantly hampered efforts at explaining the rise and significance of present-day state capitalism. We argued in this chapter that this is due to an incomplete or unsatisfactory engagement with three deeply entangled issues: (1) the 'missing link' of a theory of the capitalist state, (2) the time horizons of state capitalism, or the question of 'periodization', (3) spatial-territorial considerations, or the question of 'locating' state capitalism. In the next chapter, we develop a conceptual framework and associated programmatic reorientation of state capitalism studies, with the explicit aim of tackling head on these critical issues.

3

The *Problématique* of State Capitalism

As argued in the previous chapter and in this book's introduction, the field of state capitalism studies has so far faced serious conceptual issues, which have in turn led to analytical impasses and surprising silences and omissions. These have limited the concept's analytical purchase and rigour, as well as the development of state capitalism as a coherent field of social scientific inquiry, ultimately hampering efforts at explaining the rise and significance of the historic arc in the trajectories of state intervention that we are currently witnessing. Before we go any further in our analysis, we must aim to resolve some of these conceptual and analytical problems. The task of this chapter is therefore one of theoretical reconstruction and conceptual development.

Our main contention is that unleashing the generative potential of state capitalism as both a social scientific category and a lens for analysis requires *three conceptual moves*. First, it requires rethinking how we even conceive of state capitalism as a representational category. We make the case not to use state capitalism as a static analytical construct (such as the rigid models often used in the literature), but as a set of critical interrogations concerning the changing role of the state. We show how conceiving state capitalism as a research puzzle rather than a turnkey category ready to be deployed in empirical research can help us address the series of theoretical, political, and geographical conundrums raised by the present upward trajectory in the repertoires of state intervention. Second, unleashing the productive potential of state capitalism requires that we firmly locate it within a set of logical relations with other fundamental political economic categories, such as the capitalist state and capital accumulation. Instead of juxtaposing state capitalism to other varieties of capitalism (presumed to be more conventional), we must clearly articulate how the category relates to the capitalist state. For this, a solid grounding in materialist state theory is crucial. Third, bolstering the analytical purchase of the category state capitalism demands a keener attention to the spatialities and temporalities at the core of the current aggregate expansion of the state's role as promoter, supervisor, and owner of capital across the spaces of the world capitalist economy. Our objective is not to

The Spectre of State Capitalism. Ilias Alami and Adam D. Dixon, Oxford University Press.
 DOI: 10.1093/9780198925224.003.0003

merely add a geographical twist to state capitalism studies as a means to remedy their 'anaemic geographies' (which we have established in the previous chapter). Rather, our argument is that bringing state capitalism into conversation, epistemologically and methodologically, with the notion of uneven and combined development, enables a major conceptual and programmatic reorientation of the field. We call this 'uneven and combined *state capitalist* development'.

From a Rigid Model to a Flexible *Problématique*

As we have seen, state capitalism is notoriously difficult to define, and there are multiple questions raised by the concept and its many meanings, such as, how to define it and characterize it with respect to other forms of capitalism (without the 'state' qualifier), why and how does state capitalism manifest itself, with what implications, and how to explain its institutional diversity. We have also raised concerns, in the introduction and previous chapter, about how the field as a whole tends to address these questions, that is, by setting up rigid models, or by means of static categorical constructions. Consider, for instance, how the state capitalism literature often structures its arguments and analyses around clear-cut binaries, such as, inter alia, states versus markets, national versus transnational, public versus private, (geo)politics versus commercial logics, liberal versus illiberal, democratic versus authoritarian, rent-seeking versus profit-seeking objectives, and so forth. Attempting to address the aforementioned questions about state capitalism in such dichotomous terms will necessarily give rise to many of the conceptual issues and analytical pitfalls we have pointed at earlier in this book, insofar as they are a source of foreclosed conclusions. What if, instead of reinforcing these rigid binary constructions (and establishing new ones, such as state capitalism versus liberal-market capitalism), we actually deploy state capitalism as a means to challenge and problematize them? What if destabilizing the familiar dichotomies which have entrapped the field is actually what makes the rubric state capitalism intellectually stimulating and a useful analytical tool to probe into current rearticulations of state intervention? In this section, we argue that this invites a rethink of what state capitalism is as a representational category, in a way that allows (and encourages) greater self-reflexivity in the use of the rubric and the various dichotomies the field of state capitalism studies often relies upon and (sometimes uncritically) reinforces. We draw upon two important set of contributions.

First, we take inspiration from the work of economic geographer Jamie Peck, and in particular, his reflections on thinking through (and with) categories such as neoliberalism (2013) and capitalism (2019b, 2021). Reflecting on the utility of the category capitalism and responding to one prominent recent critique, Peck (2019b, 1194) makes the case for:

> mobilis[ing] relatively plastic categories of analysis, not rigid ones that beg binary answers (capitalism, yes or no); plastic categories held in constant dialogue (and tension) with empirical inquiries that call upon them as sensitizing devices (or maps) and not as a source of foreclosed conclusions. Awkward, orthogonal, and contradictory cases, like 'capitalism(s),' consequently become especially attractive, and potentially productive, as theory-shaping sites.

Heeding Peck's advice, we propose to introduce some level of 'plasticity' in our use of the category state capitalism. This does not need to imply sacrificing academic rigor. On the contrary, as we argue below, this plasticity is crucial if we want the concept to gain analytical and empirical clout. Thus, we treat state capitalism as a flexible category that eschews simple binary oppositions (e.g., state capitalism versus liberal capitalism, or geopolitics versus profit motives) and their resulting dichotomous answers. In other words, we do not reduce state capitalism to the question 'state capitalism, yes or no'. Similarly, we do not limit state capitalism to a box-ticking exercise (or the idea that the presence of a certain type of state institution or instrument would signal the existence of a state capitalist system). We also do not engage in the construction of 'ideal types', wherein state capitalism is set in contradistinction to other varieties of capitalism, such as liberal market-based economies, purported to be more ordinary (as is common in the Comparative Capitalism tradition; see previous chapter). Hence, we construe state capitalism not as a static categorical construct or rigidly defined model, but as a flexible means of problematizing and critically interrogating the object of inquiry which we have delineated in the introduction of this book, that is, the current aggregate expansion of the state's role as promoter, supervisor, and owner of capital across the spaces of the world capitalist economy. In other words, more than a fully formed concept or rigidly defined model we see state capitalism as a 'sensitizing device' to help us address the series of theoretical, political, and, as we will see, geographical conundrums raised by this upward trajectory in the repertoires of state intervention. This is what we call the *problématique* of the new state capitalism.

Second, to further specify how this *problématique* can help us critically interrogate this upward trajectory in the repertoires of state intervention, we turn to Nathan Sperber's (2019a, 2019b) intellectual-historical survey of previous strands of writings on state capitalism during the first three-quarters of the twentieth century. Importantly, Sperber underlines the originality and diversity of these rich contributions, notably those entertaining deep connections to the historical materialist tradition, from writings on state-monopoly capitalism to scholarship on state capitalism in the Third World. Sperber calls for recovering their legacy and intellectual contribution, which has been largely neglected in more recent waves of writings on state capitalism. He shows that in these various strands of reflection, 'state capitalism served not so much as a single signifier ... than as a terrain for interrogating the system-wide implications of concrete entanglements between the state and economic life' and as 'a site of reflections on the relations entertained by the state with capitalist forms' (Sperber 2019a, 101, 111). This speaks to our understanding of state capitalism as a *problématique*. Furthermore, Sperber notes (2019a, 119, our emphasis) that these writings

> grappled with the *system-wide attributes of state capitalism*, in terms of *state-owned capital* and of *public–private relations*, and in terms of the overall balance of power between the *state qua accumulator* and private capital owners. Despite the absence of definitional and conceptual consistency throughout this Marxist-inspired literature, for much of the 20th century theories of state capitalism thus displayed a generative capacity for interrogating the *fundamental macro-institutions of politicised capitalist landscapes*.

Bringing these insights to bear on the morphology of present-day capitalism allows us to further flesh out our *problématique* of the new state capitalism: if, as argued and documented in the introductory chapter of this book, the current aggregate expansion of the state's role as promoter, supervisor, and owner of capital is characterized by the co-development of muscular forms of statism (encompassing industrial policy, spatial development strategies, economic nationalism, trade and investment restrictions) and the multiplication and growing significance of state-capital hybrids (including sovereign wealth funds, state enterprises, policy and development banks, central banks), then the *problématique* of state capitalism is about critically interrogating the role that this historic arc in the trajectories of state intervention plays in the (geo)political re-organization of global capitalism. Moreover, it is about reflecting on what passes as the *ordinary* role of the state in economy and society, and on what is considered the *normal* separation between the state *qua* public and the private spheres of economic activity. It is therefore also about historicizing the politicized character of some of these emerging landscapes of state intervention and re-articulations of state-capital relations. In a nutshell, our contention is that wrestling with these interrogations while destabilizing the problematic familiar dichotomies which have entrapped the field of state capitalism studies is precisely what makes the *problématique* of state capitalism both challenging and generative. Our argument so far is represented visually in Figure 3.1.

Now, as should be clear from the above, the *problématique* of the new state capitalism enables us to reconceive efforts to characterize state capitalism. Insofar as it is fundamentally concerned with processes of state transformation and their embedding in the development of global capitalism, the *problématique* allows us to move towards a more dynamic understanding of state capitalism, one that refuses to construe state capitalism as an abnormal configuration of capitalism, and which is more sensitive to its mutations over time. This way, we break away from tendencies (common in the field of contemporary state capitalism studies) to exceptionalize state capitalism. These tendencies, often resulting from static categorization methods, are questionable at best. Indeed, we know that the perimeter, depth, and modalities of state action have varied considerably throughout the historical

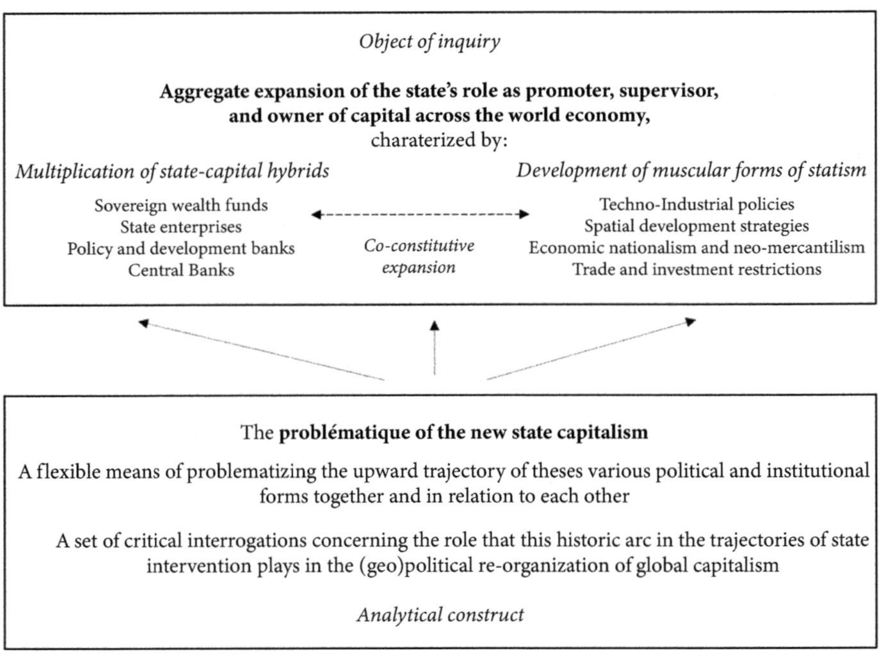

Figure 3.1 The new state capitalism as object of inquiry and analytical construct

geographies of capitalism. This historical record is evidence of the capitalist state's remarkable ability to reinvent its modalities of intervention, at times greatly expanding its prerogatives. We also know that what may be considered state capitalism in one historical-geographical context may pass as ordinary and inconspicuous in another. Furthermore, historic instances of state capitalism have taken highly diverse political, institutional, and organizational forms. Consequently, for us, exceptionalizing state capitalism, whether in historical or ontological terms, is a mistake. What is required instead is a conceptualization of state capitalism that can account for this remarkable dynamism and diversity in the modalities of state intervention, while establishing a clear link and conceptual distinction between state capitalism and the *capitalist state*. This brings us to our second argument and conceptual move in this chapter.

Locating *State Capitalist Impulses* in the Form of the Capitalist State

Unleashing the generative potential of state capitalism as a rubric of analysis requires that we firmly locate it within a set of logical relations with other fundamental political economic categories, such as the capitalist state and capital accumulation. For this, we must turn to materialist state theory, which we can broadly define as a diverse set of theoretical propositions concerning the role, class character, and form of the state in capitalist society (Barrow 1993; Clarke 1991). In firmly grounding our *problématique* of the new state capitalism in a sustained engagement with materialist state theory, we now directly address what we have identified in the previous chapter as a major issue in state capitalism studies, which is that it has suffered from a lack of a robust theory of the state. Thus, by engaging with state theory, we not only aim to remedy the analytical and conceptual difficulties that the field has faced as a result of this lack, we also explicitly aim to situate analyses of contemporary state capitalism within a rich tradition of debates that have long problematized the relations between states and markets, from the influential contributions of Ralph Miliband (1969) and Nicos Poulantzas (1973) to the 'state-derivation' debate (Agnoli and Brückner 1968; Hirsch and Viertel 1977), the social-democratic theories of the state of Habermas (1988) and Offe (1972), Bob Jessop's 'strategic relational' approach (2002), neo-Gramscian perspectives (Shields 2012; Bieler and Morton 2018) and the 'Murdoch School' (e.g., Chacko and Jayasuriya 2018; Hameiri, Jones, and Heathershaw 2019). These various strands of writing on the state hold considerable potential, largely untapped so far, in theorizing state capitalism both historically and in its contemporary manifestations. And, conversely, we would argue that the *problématique* of state capitalism offers a fruitful epistemic angle to further develop and refine theories of the nature and class character of the capitalist state (see Alami 2021).

Our starting point is a fairly simple proposition, yet with significant theoretical implications: the capitalist state must be seen as *logically prior* to state capitalism. This means that the two categories do not operate at the same level of abstraction. This allows us to clear out a common misunderstanding. Recall that, as discussed in the introductory chapter of this book, some sceptics tend to reject the category state capitalism on the basis that capitalism is always statist to some extent, that states and capitalist markets are always mutually constituted, and therefore, that 'all capitalism is state capitalism'. Put differently, they see state capitalism as some sort of pleonasm, or bogus category, which must therefore be dismissed. Now, such reasoning is only valid if the two levels of abstraction (that of state capitalism and that of the capitalist state) are conflated. However, if, as we suggest, the capitalist state is conceived as logically prior to state capitalism, then acknowledging the pervasive role of the state in capitalism does not invalidate the category state capitalism and is not an argument in favour of its dismissal. Rather, this encourages us to locate our conceptualization of state capitalism within the broader context of the state's pervasive role in capitalism. Therefore, before we attempt to outline the contours of state capitalism, we must first firmly establish the place and role of the state in capitalist society.

In doing so, we will aim to avoid two problems. First, there is a tendency in some corners of the state capitalism literature (notably within the disciplines of strategic management and international business) to conceive of the state as a set of individualized social actors, such as bureaucrats, politicians, and other state representatives acting as managers or sitting on the board of directors of state enterprises and sovereign wealth funds. The problem with seeing the state through the lens of state personnel is that, simply put, the state does things in capitalism which cannot be grasped by exclusively focusing on the individualized actions of state representatives and the personal connections between bureaucrats, state managers, and economic elites. As we will see shortly, the state is an incredibly complex entity which plays a multifaceted role in capitalist economy and society, which is irreducible to individualized actions, and is traversed by profound contradictions. This must be taken into consideration when theorizing state capitalism. Second, when conceptualizing the state, we want to avoid relying on any form of state–market dichotomic model, which have proved to be so problematic in contemporary state capitalism studies. Positing states and markets as separate spheres of social existence which exist in autonomy, 'relative', 'embedded', or otherwise (as variously put in the developmental state and other social scientific literatures) is an obstacle to grasping complex articulations of public–private relations and the various institutional, legal, political and territorial forms which mediate them. By contrast, we will aim to develop a conceptualization of states and markets that emphasize their inner connections as differentiated moments of the same social totality, that is, the social relations constituting capitalist society.

In this book, our understanding of the state is informed by a particular tradition of writings on the state grounded in the critique of political economy, notably the work of Simon Clarke (1991), John Holloway (1991), Peter Burnham (1996), and Werner Bonefeld (2017). In particular, we draw upon their conceptualization of the state as the political form of the social relations that constitute capitalist society (Clarke 1991; Bonefeld 2014, 2017). As discussed below, we also bring a spatial and scalar sensitivity to this strand of writings by enriching and complementing it with insights from the literature on state spatialities and state rescaling as developed in economic and political geography (e.g., Brenner et al. 2003; Gough 2004; Peck 2004; Brenner 2009). These writings in the tradition of the critique of political economy underline that while the state appears as an independent political form, formally separated from the economic sphere, standing 'above' civil society, and acting as the neutral guarantor of general societal interest, its material reproduction is bound up with the expanded reproduction of capitalist social relations (Clarke 1991; Bonefeld 2014). The state therefore strives to secure the conditions for sustained capital accumulation. Now, the exact modalities according to which it does so, besides enforcing the rule of law and property rights, are always historically and geographically specific. In fact, as intimated earlier, these have greatly varied throughout the historical geographies of capitalism. Think about, for instance, the various institutions, instruments, policies, regulations, prerogatives, and other modes of economic practice which states have historically developed in order to 'intervene' in economic and social life, notably to manage and facilitate the reproduction of labour power, nature/land, and money in ways consistent with expanded capitalist reproduction (de Brunhoff 1981; Smith 1984/2008; Parenti 2015). Consider, also, the extent to which some of the main characteristics and spatial parameters of statehood, such as political authority, territory, and economic sovereignty, have been reconfigured in the process (Arrighi 1994; Agnew 2017).

What this means is that the capitalist state cannot be defined in the abstract as a set of functions or basic acts of economic coordination that it must perform (Clarke 1991). Defining the state in such a way would imply a lapse into the type of fetishism of certain state prerogatives and institutions which we criticized in the previous chapter. This would also introduce a degree of functionalism in our understanding of the state that is unwarranted. As Tony Smith (2017, 184) reminds us: 'State policies are radically indeterminate', in the sense that they can take an indeterminate plurality of possible paths, albeit broadly consistent with capital accumulation. Indeed, he adds, 'this radical indeterminateness of the capitalist state is not unrestricted' (2017, 190), meaning that the state cannot systematically implement reforms that would rupture the social relations that constitute capitalist market societies without dismantling itself or sabotaging its own reproduction. The radical open-endedness of the *content* of state action (what it does and how it does it) is therefore determined by its *form* (i.e., its social constitution as the political form of capitalist social relations, which material reproduction is bound up with the expanded reproduction of the latter).

The state, then, cannot be defined in the abstract as a set of functions or basic acts of economic coordination that it must perform because it has no existence outside of the concrete institutional developments of the state apparatus, the activities of state agents, and other forms of state power, which are an expression of the historical-geographical development of social relations (Holloway 1991). What we can do, however, is define the general role of the state in an essentially 'negative' manner: the state strives to overcome the various obstacles and blockages to capital accumulation (Burnham 1996). Importantly, the state's room of manoeuvre for securing conditions for accumulation is restricted by and subordinated to the conditions imposed by the movement of expanded capitalist reproduction as a whole, and it is conditioned by a context of interstate competition (Clarke 1992; Holloway 1994). It is therefore caught up in the following contradictory spatial-territorial imperatives: states interact with each other as they attempt to foster global capital accumulation (which is beneficial to all states) while simultaneously competing to improve their respective position in a highly uneven and hierarchical world market and attract capital in their own domestic territory (Burnham 1996).

We will return to this crucial point repeatedly throughout the book. For now, the argument is that, from the perspective developed here, there is absolutely no antithesis between a strong state and market freedom. Quite the contrary, as Bonefeld (2010, 17) puts it, 'not only does the free market require the strong, market-facilitating state, but it is also dependent on the state as the coercive force of that freedom'. Now, this is not to portray the state as an all-powerful social actor. Although it concentrates tremendous social and material power, which it can exert in a range of ways from waging war and policing territorial borders to expropriating property, confiscating wealth, and redistributing social resources, the actions of the state are generally driven by precarious attempts to manage the crisis-ridden dynamics of capital accumulation and contain the antagonism of capitalist social relations. Through this process, it does not solve the contradictions that stem from capitalist reproduction, let alone crises. While the state can certainly design elaborate strategies and courses of action in the short and medium run, and sometimes even longer-term development plans,[1] state action is generally much more ad hoc, haphazard, and driven by trial-and-error and 'fail-forward' than it is about the implementation of stable, coherent, and consistent developmental visions.

This is because the state is caught up in a series of contradictions with profound political implications for governance and policymaking. Jack Copley and Alexis Moraitis (2021) call this the 'politics of governing alienation': the state is simultaneously pulled in opposing directions by contradictory imperatives, notably, on the one hand, the forces and disciplines of world market competition, and on the other, the need to appease domestic constituencies (with antagonistic class interests) and secure political legitimacy at home. In aiming to reconcile these contradictory imperatives, and in dealing with their consequences—from economic dislocations to political instability—the state is more akin to a firefighter than it is to a great planner and visionary. As Erik Swyngedouw (1992, 45) explains, at any given point, landscapes of state intervention as well as their spatial expressions must 'not be conceived as intentionally and a priori designed in order to produce particular forms of political-economic coherence'. Rather, they result from messy, crisis-driven state attempts at capturing, temporarily suspending, or spatially displacing various blockages to capital accumulation, social conflicts of various forms, and capitalist contradictions.

Nonetheless, as the state strives to do so, it may very well drastically enhance the perimeter and scope of its interventions into social and economic processes, adopt new prerogatives and capacities (and/or restructure existing ones), and develop new targets and strategies. In more concrete

[1] One may think here of historical examples such as Hamiltonian developmentalism in the United States, Meiji-era Japanese state-led industrialization, the East Asian and Latin American 'classical' developmental states, state-driven modernization in Germany under Bismack, French *dirigisme d'état*, contemporary Chinese 'party-state' capitalism, and many others. See Ernest Ming-Tak Leung (2021) for an excellent intellectual history of some of these instances.

terms, this can take a great diversity of modalities of expression, including the state deepening and extending its influence over non-state economic actors and entities, and shaping the circuits of capital via instruments such as taxation, fiscal transfers, regulations, economic planning, techno-industrial policy, public procurement at preferential prices, investment in infrastructure, currency manipulation, and so on. Following Sperber (2019a, 112–113), we refer to this as 'statism'. These are a set of powerful tools through which the state may regulate, create, or destroy capitalist markets, influence the pace of scientific and technological development across sectors and industries, boost the competitiveness of private capitals operating in its territory or abroad, and shape how surplus value is extracted and the conditions of its circulation and appropriation. Combined with the repressive arm of the state, these statist policy tools may also be deployed to manage the flow of the labour force as well as govern the workers and populations rendered surplus to the immediate needs of capital for waged labour (Bernards and Soederberg 2021).

Moreover, as part of its attempt to remove obstacles to accumulation, the state may decide to directly own and control capitalist production and assets, by creating state enterprises and other forms of corporate entities which are separate from the government but at least partially owned or controlled by the state. We refer to these as 'state-capital hybrids'. State-capital hybrids enable the state to accumulate capital in its own right, notably where private capital could not, or would not, invest. This could be because investing in particular sectors of production or regions may be perceived as too risky, or because the average rate of profit in this particular sector is lower than elsewhere, rendering it unattractive. This could also be because profitable production in this particular sector requires an extremely large upfront investment in fixed capital, which private firms fail to amass on their own; or because of specific sectoral features, such as a tendency for 'natural' monopolies or oligopolies to emerge. In these cases, the state itself can either centralize capital to the scale required and directly invest it, or it can inject state-owned capital to complement private capital. Alternatively, the state may assume (which is to say, socialize) some of the risks associated with the investment, and/or directly produce and deliver the goods and services itself. This has typically been the case in sectors such as infrastructure, public works, and public utilities (water, electricity, and information and communications). This is important insofar as the state provision of a highly efficient network of connective infrastructure can facilitate the mobility of labour, capital, technology, and knowledge, thereby playing a crucial role in reducing the socially necessary labour-time involved in the production of commodities, and the socially necessary turnover time involved in realizing the surplus value embodied in these commodities by selling them on the market at a profit.

The state can also assume direct ownership and control of productive capacities in the context of its broader effort to catalyse industrial capital accumulation and/or to diversify the industrial base in its territory. The delivery of industrial inputs priced below prices of production are means through which the state, via state enterprises, can channel surplus value (produced from their own process of exploitation) to industrial capitals in targeted sectors.[2] Furthermore, the state may assume direct ownership and control of productive capacities as a result of its intervention to bail out financially distressed firms, either by injecting capital and taking ownership, or by overseeing takeovers and merger and acquisitions by other private capitals. Finally, the state may secure and retain control over productive capacities in sectors considered geo-strategic, such as defence and energy, where coordinated production under the aegis of the state is seen as a matter of national security.

As the reader will have noticed, many of these modalities of state intervention are precisely what commentators describe as state capitalism. In fact, we ourselves proposed earlier to characterize present-day state capitalism as the combined expansion of statism (encompassing industrial policy, spatial development strategies, economic nationalism, trade and investment restrictions) and state-capital hybrids (including sovereign wealth funds, state enterprises, policy and development banks, central banks). But our point is this: none of the above evinces an abnormal transformation of the state. These are fully compatible with the ordinary operations of a state in a capitalistically constituted society, or, more accurately, its *form-determined* operations. Put differently, as part of its normal functioning and constant restructuring to deal with the vagaries of capital accumulation, the capitalist state may very well (and it repeatedly has in the past) dramatically bolster its role as promoter, supervisor, regulator, guarantor, and direct owner of capital. What this means is that state capitalism must not be seen as an anomaly or a deviance from liberal, market-based capitalism (or, for that matter, any sort of capitalism without the 'state' qualifier). It is not an irregular deviation of the capitalist state from its form and determinations. Rather, we contend

[2] This transfer of surplus-value can act as a subsidy, either allowing backward capitals to continue valorizing at the average rate of profit (which, without the subsidy, would be driven out of the market by competitors with superior technological endowment and labour productivity), or allowing cutting-edge capitals to realize an abnormal profit (that is, a profit rate above the average rate of profit prevailing in their sector).

that state capitalism must be seen as a particular modality of expression of the capitalist state, including in its liberal form. In short, state capitalism is an *immanent potentiality*, an impulse which is contained in the form of the capitalist state and built into its DNA.

Now, none of this is to say that state capitalism does not matter. On the contrary, what we call 'state capitalist impulses', especially when they develop in combinatorial forms (as we will see throughout the book), can result in profound transformations in pre-existing landscapes of state intervention, a rearticulation and rescaling of the relations between states and the circuits of capital, and shifting boundaries between the state and civil society (Brenner et al. 2003; Gough 2004; Peck 2004). All of these may in turn have profound implications for world politics. Equipped with this robust understanding of the relationship between state capitalism and the capitalist state, we can now refine our *problématique* of the new state capitalism.

Remember that we argued earlier that the *problématique* of state capitalism invites reflection as to the norms (and their momentary solidification into orthodoxies) that establish a clear separation between the state qua public and the private spheres of economic activity. We can now add that what must be the object of our attention is the dynamic process through which state capitalist impulses lead to the *politicization* of certain landscapes of state intervention and to the redefinition of said norms. Indeed, at times where state capitalist impulses have ostensible implications for the circuits of capital, the balance of power between and within classes, and in terms of geoeconomic force fields (as it is the case at the current historical juncture), such norms will appear to be suddenly challenged or even crumbling, notably from the standpoint of state and business actors who either stand to lose from such reconfigurations, or who anxiously perceive that they are. There is a politics of anxiety here, associated with the real or imagined consequences of contemporary state capitalist impulses. For example, much ink has been recently spilled, both in academic and policymaking circles, over the extent to which the increasingly transnational operations of sovereign funds and state enterprises are distorting markets, generating unfair competitive advantages over private firms, and even constituting a threat to global security and the international world order (cf. Bremmer 2010; Kurlantzick 2016). This speaks to the liberal apprehension with which we opened the introductory chapter, and to which we will return later in this book. For now, our point is that state capitalist impulses are accompanied by struggles over the political legitimacy of emerging state capitalist landscapes and their ramifications (as well as, more specifically, particular forms of statism and state-capital hybrids), and over the political-economic normativities defining the relation between the economic and the political (cf. Meulbroek 2023).

Importantly, these material struggles are expressed in the realms of public discourse and ideology, as we will see in Chapters 7 and 8. They take place at home (at a range of scales, from central to local levels of government) between various social actors with divergent interests due to their class positions, but also in the more immediate sense of how they relate to emergent landscapes of state intervention, in the context of intertwined financial, economic, political, environmental, and health crises. There are multiple stakes involved in these domestic struggles, including which individual firms or segments of capital will directly benefit or loose from renewed state activism,[3] while preventing that the latter becomes the object of popular demands, as we have recently seen with recent movements for re-municipalization (Paul and Cumbers 2023), calls for 'People's Quantitative Easing' (Coppola 2019), radical versions of Green New Deals (Aronoff et al. 2019), and vast democratic state ownership (Lawrence and Hanna 2020). Indeed, capitalist elites are aware that ostensibly strong forms of state intervention, notably those that appear to blur the lines between public and private spheres, risk setting up dangerous precedents, in that they open up space for demands to harness the powers of the state towards different aims, such as the de-commodification and democratization of economic life (Burnham 2011). Redrawing strict boundaries between the economic and the political is a way of preventing such politicization, notably by defining which modalities of state intervention are legitimate, and which are not.

These legitimacy struggles take place transnationally as well, where they involve competing states and the various capitals they represent in the context of turbulent geopolitical reordering, including the rise of China as a hegemonic challenger, and a partial breakdown of the North/South axis which has structured much of the thinking and practice in world politics over the past 80 years (Alami, Dixon, Gonzalez-Vicente, et al. 2022). What is at stake here is a battle over what forms of statism and state-capital hybrids are considered legitimate and compatible with the (still dominant but increasingly in crisis) Western-dominated liberal system of market-centric governance. For non-Western contenders, this is about carving out space in this system and perhaps, at times, challenging some of its parameters. For the more established (advanced capitalist) actors, this is about simultaneously

[3] See, for example, Wood, Onali, Grosman, and Haider (2023) on the UK governments' response to the COVID-19 pandemic and the sectional and private interests benefitting from it; and Germann (2022) on the different views of various fractions of capital and social interests with respect to the current remaking of the German state.

casting doubt on the legitimacy of the landscapes of intervention deployed by these challengers, while legitimating renewed state action on their part.

In our view, then, the *problématique* of state capitalism is not so much about studying capitalist configurations which are assumed to be politicized a priori (and distinct from allegedly non-politicized ones), as the literature tends to do. Rather, in line with the case for plastic and flexible forms of theorization that me made earlier, it is about interrogating why and how certain landscapes of state intervention and state–capital relations *become* politicized, notably when state capitalist impulses are perceived to be challenging established lines of division between and within states, classes, and sections of capital. Thus, we see politicization as a set of dynamic and conflictual processes involving a range of legitimacy struggles concerning the appropriate scope and form of state intervention. State capitalist impulses and their spatial expressions are both the catalyser and terrain of such struggles.

Furthermore, our conceptualization of state capitalist impulses as an immanent potentiality contained in the form of the capitalist state allows us to rethink how we approach the question of state capitalism at the current historical juncture. From this perspective, what is at stake in the contemporary rise of state capitalism is not so much the growing assertiveness of a nationally scaled and relatively coherent variant of capitalism. Rather, we suggest that characterizing state capitalism requires identifying the circumstances and conditions in which this potentiality is *actualized* as well as its concrete *temporal and spatial parameters*. Indeed, if, as argued earlier, the state is the political form of capitalist social relations, then it follows that its restructuring and transformations—including the state capitalist impulse—must be grasped as a moment of the dynamic process of capital valorization, a process which unfolds unevenly in time and space. As Brenner, Jessop, Jones, and MacLeod (2003, 10) remind us, 'state spatial strategies must be viewed as historically specific practices through which state institutions attempt to adjust to the constantly changing geoeconomic and geopolitical conditions in which they operate: their modalities, targets, and effects evolve qualitatively during the history of capitalist development'. Characterization efforts must therefore be focused on both the spatiality and temporality of the capitalist transformations politically mediated by the state, and on the reconfiguration of the landscapes of state intervention that such process of political mediation involves (Alami 2021).

In other words, there can be no analytically useful definition of state capitalism in logical abstraction from the determinate material process of uneven capitalist development. State capitalism must always be defined, characterized, and explained with reference to concrete historical-geographical capitalist transformations, in relation to inherited landscapes of state intervention into social and economic processes, and with reference to specific processes of politicization. This brings us back to the argument made in the previous chapter about the need for an explicitly geographical approach, one that allows probing into the multiple spatialities and temporalities at the core of contemporary state capitalism. For this, we turn to recent elaborations on the concept of uneven and combined development.

Uneven and Combined State Capitalism

Our third argument and conceptual move in this chapter consists in bringing the concept of uneven and combined development (U&CD) front and centre to the *problématique* of state capitalism, as a means to probe into the spatialities and temporalities at the core of the current aggregate expansion of the state's role as promoter, supervisor, and owner of capital across the spaces of the world capitalist economy. In this book, we conceive of U&CD as a research agenda and a methodological predisposition (rather than a unified theory or approach) drawing attention to the unstable and multi-scalar geographical remaking of capitalism (Peck 2019a; Rolf 2021). According to Dunford and Liu (2017, 69), U&CD

> interprets dynamic historical change and comparative geographical differentiation in terms of the co-existence of tendencies towards differentiation and equalization of the conditions of production, consumption, distribution and exchange, deriving from capital accumulation and political multiplicity.

Political multiplicity refers to the co-existence and simultaneity of a plurality of social formations (with idiosyncratic histories and state capacities), enmeshed in asymmetrical economic, political, and military relations, which evolve by interacting with each other, producing 'hybrid effects and non-linear outcomes—whether these outcomes are new social forms or unique historical events' (Rosenberg, Zarakol, Blagden, et al. 2022, 295). The concept of U&CD has experienced a certain renewal of interest in the field of international relations and historical sociology over the past twenty years (Rosenberg 2022), and more recently in economic geography (Hudson 2016; Dunford and Liu 2017; Peck 2019a) and global political economy (Antunes de Oliveira, Germann, and Rolf 2023). Its merits and weaknesses have been hotly debated. It is therefore important to specify at the outset how we use it in this book.

Importantly, in bringing this notion into the study of state capitalism, we are careful not to conflate 'the *fact* of U&CD as a *theory* of U&CD' (Rioux 2015, 508; Charnock and Starosta 2018, 325). This means that we do not attribute explanatory power to U&CD. Thus, our approach differs from theorists who root their understanding of U&CD in the 'international' (conceived as both a social dimension and geographical scale) in order to explain the causal significance of the coexistence and interaction of multiple societies (see, e.g., Rosenberg 2013). Similarly, we do not conceive U&CD as a 'general abstraction'—a claim about the plural nature of social development across human history (Rosenberg 2022). We largely share the scepticism which has been voiced concerning such transhistorical conceptions of U&CD, notably their lack of explanatory power (they often take for granted that which needs to be theorized) and their tendency to see unevenness as an abstract condition rather than the determinate geographical manifestation of concrete processes of capitalist accumulation and restructuring (cf. Ashman 2009; Kiely 2012; Rioux 2015; Charnock and Starosta 2018).

More concretely, for us, U&CD is not the answer to the question of 'why and how state capitalist development is uneven and combined'. Rather, the *fact* of uneven and combined state capitalism is precisely what must be elucidated: why and how has there been an aggregate expansion of the state's role as promoter, supervisor, and owner of capital across the spaces of the world capitalist economy, characterized by the combined expansion of state-capital hybrids and of muscular forms of statism? How does this result from the historical developmental trajectory and geographical remaking of global capitalism? How do uneven landscapes of state capitalism result from various forms of interdependence, co-development, and combination between diverse repertoires of state intervention?

In developing the notion of uneven and combined state capitalist development, we follow Greig Charnock and Guido Starosta (2018) whose substantive theorization of uneven development is grounded in the critique of political economy (see Iñigo Carrera 2008). For Charnock and Starosta (2018, 325),

> the key to providing something like a 'unified field theory' of uneven development is dialectically rooted in the intrinsic material unity between human beings and nature, and the socially mediated character of that unity (hence between productive forces, social relations of production, and their actualization in and through the conscious practice of individuals). In other words, we want to put labour, and its historically changing forms of existence, at the centre of the theorization and analysis of uneven international development.

Charnock and Starosta (2018, 327) thus conceive of the substantive social content of uneven geographical capitalist development as rooted in the material process Marx calls the 'real subsumption of labour to capital'. By contrast with formal subsumption, where the labour process is merely controlled and dominated by capital in order to extract 'absolute' surplus value, real subsumption involves the complete reorganization of the labour process (in its social and technical aspects) by capital, notably through the use of science, technology, and machinery to increase labour productivity, in order to maximize the systematic extraction of 'relative' surplus value. More precisely for our purpose, this means that the determinants of the expansion of present-day state capitalism must be sought in the historical-geographical transformations in the material forms of production of (relative) surplus value on a world scale. This is important insofar as labour has been conspicuously absent from the contemporary field of state capitalism studies, but also because, as we will see, focusing on labour allows shedding light on a range of capitalist transformations which have not been brought to bear thus far on state capitalism debates, such as the automation, robotization, and digitalization of large-scale industry and questions of 'secular economic stagnation'.

Furthermore, in accordance with this focus on global labour transformations, our unit of analysis cannot be any of the ones conventionally used in the state capitalism literature, i.e., a specific type of state-capital hybrids, (say, Brazilian state enterprises, Singaporean sovereign funds, or Indonesian policy banks), an individual country (e.g., France, Egypt, China, or South Korea), or a state-led national variety of capitalism (in the BRICS, East Asia, or elsewhere). Rather, we start from the accumulation of capital as a *global process* which formal unity finds expression in changing constellations of the international division of labour (Charnock and Starosta 2016). These changing constellations in turn lead to uneven spatial differentiation, which is manifest in variegated socio-technical conditions of capitalist development across various scales. We will aim to locate in Chapters 4 and 5 the role of the combined expansion of state-capital hybrids and of muscular forms of statism in changing constellations of international divisions of labour and associated patterns of geographically uneven development. Indeed, while state capitalist impulses may unfold at a multiplicity of scales, we argue that we must conceive of their geographical horizon as global. As such, we offer an alternative to the methodological nationalism and other forms of territorial traps that pervade studies of state capitalism. Our key argument is, however, not simply that U&CD provides an antidote to the anaemic geographies of state capitalism and to the literature's unsatisfactory treatment of the temporalities of contemporary state capitalism. We contend that the notion of U&CD (and the set of critical interrogations which it raises concerning the how and why of uneven and combined development) enable a major geographical reorientation in the study of the new state capitalism in at least four ways.

First, the coming into being of state capitalism must not be explained by resorting to mechanical-abstract metaphors, such as the negation of an abstract model of free-market capitalism, a Polanyian pendulum (i.e., a counter-movement of the state somehow automatically following a period of market expansion), a Smithian seesawing motion (i.e., the rhythms of state intervention inexorably accompanying the geographical ebb and flow of capital), or axiomatic and historically indeterminate laws of peripheral catch-up development. What is required instead, is a characterization of state capitalism's rise in its concrete historical and geographical fullness. If, as argued earlier, state capitalism is a potentiality contained in the form of the capitalist state, then the question we must answer is what are the historically specific generative processes and relations leading to the actualization and concretization of this potentiality? Here the methodological principles of U&CD encourage us to carefully think through this question in relation to *time*. This need not involve a form of periodization which conceives of capitalist history as a succession of neatly demarcated 'blocs' of time, with, for instance, state capitalism succeeding previous stages of capitalism (such as liberal, Keynesian, developmental, neoliberal, or financialized capitalisms, each corresponding to paradigmatic modalities of state intervention and institutional forms), or with the 'new' state capitalism replacing previous waves of state capitalism. Rather, we mean locating contemporary state capitalist impulses (notably the combined expansion of state-capital hybrids and of muscular forms of statism) within a set of determinate processes and social relations pertaining to the historical development and geographical remaking of global capitalism.

Importantly, these determinate processes and social relations can have multiple and overlapping temporalities. Take for example, exceptional state responses to crisis-events such as financial crises and pandemics. Although, in some cases, these may drag on in time and become more permanent (such as the central bank provision of liquidity to the financial system), the time horizons of these state interventions are usually relatively short in comparison to other modalities of state power, such as those that are rolled-out to facilitate specific class-political projects of elite reproduction (think of the decades-long transformations of the Chinese state to enable the consolidation of the rule of the Chinese Communist Party). Similarly, compare and contrast the time frames of the forms of state activism made possible in many resource-rich countries by the 2000–2014 'commodity super-cycle', to the temporalities of the processes of state restructuring which have mediated longer-term capitalist trends such as the internationalization of production and the financialization of capital accumulation.[4] Our argument here is not simply that scrutinizing the different temporalities of state capitalist impulses is essential to understanding their historical specificity, as well as that of the new state capitalism as a world-historical totality. It is also, crucially, that thinking state capitalism in relation to time, as we will do throughout this book, requires theorizing the *synchronicity* of state capitalist impulses. This means explaining their simultaneous occurrence—some state capitalist impulses appear significantly related to each other, while others seem to have less discernible connections—by revealing the generative processes and relations underpinning them. This also means showing how synchronicity itself can become a causal factor in the further development of state capitalist impulses, as we elaborate below when we discuss the question of political multiplicity and combination, as well as in Chapter 5. Moreover, we argue that linking state capitalist impulses to wider processes that, on the surface, appear separate from them—such as mutations in the spheres of production, circulation, distribution of value, the continuation of accumulation in the face of market saturation and overproduction, and geographical trends such as the unfolding of a new international division of labour and the unprecedented centralization and concentration of capital on a planetary scale—is a necessary step in clearly specifying what is qualitatively new about the new state capitalism, and for substantiating claims about the historically novel character of the current upward trajectory in the repertoires of state intervention.

Our second point is that our *problématique* of uneven and combined state capitalism, by encouraging us to probe into question of space and uneven development, also reframes the question of political and institutional diversity. As noted earlier in the book, contemporary landscapes of state capitalism are characterized by great diversity in at least two respects. On the one hand, both state-capital hybrids and muscular modalities of statism have developed under a wide range of forms. For instance, far from constituting the rise of a single organizational form, contemporary state-owned enterprises feature highly diverse structures of ownership, governance, and management. They also significantly differ in terms of size, complexity, sector of operation, and

[4] Let us note in passing that, overall, state capitalism studies have done a good job looking at short-term temporalities (such as those associated with crises) as well as more medium-term ones (e.g., various catch-up development projects), but have been less concerned, if at all, with longer-term temporalities, notably those related to labour transformations.

the functions they perform for 'their' government (Musacchio, Lazzarini, and Aguilera 2015). Similarly, sovereign funds are diverse in terms of the institutional, organizational, and legal arrangements that underpin them, including different missions, mandates, and investment objectives. Economic nationalism encompasses a wide diversity of doctrines, practices, and policies, from neo-mercantilism and neo-developmentalism to trade wars. We also witness considerable variety in industrial and planning policies. On the other hand, these landscapes of state intervention and state capitalist impulses are also diverse in the sense that they have unfolded across highly varied political economic contexts, with their own national, regional, or local specificities, and which are underpinned by diverse material bases and articulation of class forces.

This heterogeneity seems to have led students of state capitalism to eschew systemic explanations of the global character of state capitalism. However, barring such explanation, we are left with the idea that these joint and concurrent trajectories in the landscapes of state intervention are largely coincidental. Besides, state capitalist impulses in particular territories are seen as the product of the political economic dynamics specific to this place, not as processes associated with the wider restructuring and geographical remaking of global capitalism. Following the U&CD principles outlined earlier, we propose a different approach, which consists in seeing the new state capitalism as not merely heterogenous or polymorphous, but as 'variegated' (Brenner, Peck, and Theodore 2010). This means that geo-institutional differentiation is not simply derivative. It is systemically produced and constitutive of the new state capitalism. Our argument here is that acknowledging the plurality of the political economic projects, modalities of intervention, and institutional forms which compose present-day state capitalism must be complemented with an account of the development and entanglement of their trajectories together and in relation to each other in a co-constitutive movement, which, far from leading to any sort of institutional or policy convergence, (re)produces institutional heterogeneity over time. As we demonstrate throughout the book, the polymorphism of contemporary landscapes of state capitalism is not merely contingent, it is relational and dialectical.

This leads us to our third point, which is that our *problématique* of uneven and combined state capitalism redefines the nature of comparison away from an exercise in identifying the institutional contours of neatly demarcated territories categorized as state capitalist, and towards relational-comparative work consisting in tracing difference in connection, interdependencies, and co-evolution between different instantiations and repertoires of state action, and in particular, between state-capital hybrids and muscular forms of statism (Hart 2018; Sparke 2020). It becomes less a question of accounting for national varieties of state capitalism as one of grasping the inner relational nature of contemporary state capitalism as a variegated, world-historical totality. This calls for a relational social ontology, where the various repertoires of state action that make state capitalist impulses are not seen as relatively autonomous 'building blocs' of state capitalism, but as part and parcel of a relational whole. The relations between the parts, and between the parts and the whole, are seen as intrinsic to the various repertoires of state intervention, with the whole greater than the sum of its parts. Relationality is therefore key to understanding the structure and modality of each repertoire of state intervention. To paraphrase Massey (1995, 3), what constructs these repertoires as relational are the spatialized and 'power-filled' social relations that underpin them and 'which link them together (or not) in their mutual constitution'. Accordingly, by better understanding the interweaving of spatialized social relations underpinning and connecting the various repertoires of state action, we will aim to reveal in this book something qualitatively new about state capitalism as a world-historical totality.

Hence our fourth point: as we examine this interweaving of spatialized social relations, we will emphasize dynamics pertaining to the uneven geographical development of global capitalism (as previously argued), as well as the causal significance of *direct political relations* between states in shaping contemporary state capitalism. This relates to the notion of political multiplicity briefly mentioned earlier in this section. Consider the following examples. As noted in the introductory chapter, contemporary calls for renewed state activism in the West are often explicitly articulated in explicit reference to the extended state prerogatives elsewhere, notably in East Asia. Witness, for instance, Margrethe Vestager, executive vice president of the European Commission: 'One thing we could learn [from China] is to make a strategy and stick to it.'[5] The ongoing European project to relax rules limiting state aid in a bid to spur the creation of digital champions is a direct response to successes of China and the United States in nurturing the activities of their own brand of platform capitalism. Similarly, efforts to strengthen the EU-wide capacity to regulate inward foreign investments, such as Regulation EU 2019/425, have been justified by the need to monitor foreign state-sponsored entities operating in the European Union.[6] Another telling example is that of the United States, and the current re-articulation of state

[5] https://www.wsj.com/articles/western-economies-embrace-state-intervention-emulating-asia-11604574001.

[6] https://trade.ec.europa.eu/doclib/press/index.cfm?id=2124.

power which is happening in the context of the 'New' or 'Second' Cold War happening with China (Baltz 2022; van Apeldoorn and de Graaff 2022). The design and deployment of stronger industrial policies in the United States, in the form of the Bipartisan Infrastructure Investment and Jobs Act, the US Science and Chips Act and the Inflation Reduction Act, has been a response to initiatives such as the Made in China 2025 and other modalities of industrial policy in China. The EU is itself responding with its Green Deal Industrial Plan, European Chips Act, and other industrial policy initiatives. What these brief examples suggest is that the landscapes of contemporary state capitalism develop through various forms of conflict and confrontation, cooperation and collaboration, hierarchical subordination, and other modalities of unequal articulation.

In order to theorize these various forms of causal interaction between states in shaping the overall trajectory of present-day state capitalism, we foreground in this book the notion of 'combination' (the C in U&CD). Combination, Jamie Peck argues, 'indexes the fundamentally dialectical and relational character' of U&CD. Peck writes (2019a, 50):

> 'Combination', in this sense, denotes hybrid complexity, structural asymmetry, and contradictory coexistence, rather than systemic singularity, equilibrium, or purity, invoking an ontology of mutually entangled social formations fashioned from elements old and new, near and far. This is, moreover, a *landscape* ontology, the inconstant outcome of a moving and unequal matrix of articulations, (inter)relations, and unbalanced interdependencies.

The question that combination rises in the context of state capitalism is the following: what are the mechanisms through which state capitalist impulses develop in dynamic, inter-referential, combinatorial forms, resulting in cumulative effects and producing further expansion in state prerogatives across scale and territory? Indeed, as Peck (2019a, 54) notes, combination 'presents as a potentially boundless source of "multiplier" effects in both socioeconomic and explanatory terms'. Hence, this invites us to problematize the constitutive and catalytic role of combination in the current expansion of states' roles as promoter, supervisor, and owner of capital, and the cascading impacts of state capitalist impulses from one place to another, as well as between policy domains (geopolitical, techno-industrial, energy, finance, infrastructure, development, and so on), both at home and abroad. Thus, the argument that we develop in the book is that this combinatory, 'multiplier' effect is a particularly potent source of dynamism in contemporary state capitalism, and its tendency to develop in a spiral that both shapes and is shaped by world capitalist development. We fully flesh out this argument on the causal power of combination in Chapter 5.

Conclusion

The work of theoretical reconstruction we conducted in this chapter aimed at bolstering the analytical purchase and rigor of state capitalism as a representational category and a lens for analysis. It consisted in three conceptual moves. The first one consisted in recasting state capitalism as a set of critical interrogations concerning the role and place of ongoing state transformations (particularly, the combined expansion of state-capital hybrids and muscular forms of statism) in the (geo)political re-organization of global capitalism. We argued that wrestling with these interrogations while destabilizing the problematic familiar dichotomies which have entrapped the field of state capitalism studies is precisely what makes the *problématique* of state capitalism both challenging and generative.

Our second conceptual move consisted in defining state capitalism in relation to the capitalist state and capital accumulation. Drawing upon materialist state theory, we argued that state capitalism is an immanent potentiality, an impulse which is contained in the form of the capitalist state and built into its genetic code. This invites reflection as to what factors lead to the actualization of this potentiality at the current historical juncture, and the conflictual processes of politicization that accompany them. This double theoretical move allows understanding the current advent of state capitalism as a process of self-transformation of the state as it politically mediates the historical-geographical mutations in the material forms of production of (relative) surplus-value on a world scale. Simply put, rather than the negation of an abstract model of free-market capitalism, or the rise of a nationally scaled and relatively coherent variant of capitalism, we posit contemporary state capitalism as a global process of restructuring of the capitalist state, including in its liberal form.

Finally, our third conceptual move consisted in bringing the methodological predispositions and principles of uneven and combined development (U&CD) front and centre to the study of contemporary state capitalism, as a means to probe into its multiple spatialities and temporalities. This opens up space for theorizing the synchronicity of present-day state capitalist impulses, by locating them within a set of determinate processes pertaining to the historical development and geographical remaking of global capitalism (notably those which relate to labour), and by shedding light on the

Table 3.1 An alternative conceptual framework and research agenda for the study of contemporary state capitalism

	Ontology	Framework of spatial assumptions	Temporalities	Causal explanation for contemporary advent	Institutional diversity	Implications
Existing approaches to state capitalism	Entire nation-states (or blocs of nation-states) and/or specific organizational forms and institutional arrangements	State capitalism as the outcome of domestic structures and conflicts and primarily contained within national territories (but can be exported). Methodological nationalism	Incomplete privatization, catch-up development, and Polanyian countermovement	Rise and consolidation of a nationally scaled and relatively coherent national variant of capitalism	National varieties of state capitalism, characterized by distinct institutional contours, and distinguishable from more conventional varieties of capitalism	Growing competition of state capitalism with other varieties of (neo)liberal capitalism, both for access to global markets and as a model for other countries to emulate
The *problématique* of uneven and combined state capitalism	Historic arc in the global trajectories of state intervention, characterized by the co-development of muscular forms of statism and the expansion of state-capital hybrids	U&CD as a methodological predisposition. State transformations can unfold at a multiplicity of scales and across territorial borders. Their geographical horizon is global	Locating state capitalism in the historical developmental trajectory and geographical remaking of global capitalism	State capitalist impulses rooted in the state's political mediation of capital accumulation, social antagonism, and crisis tendencies	State capitalism as a variegated, world-historical totality Uneven and hybrid articulations of state capitalist impulses	The (geo)political re-organization of global capitalism. Changing role of state power in the territorial organization of the planetary circuits of capital

	This aggregate expansion of state's role as owner, supervisor and promoter of capital is understood as a process of restructuring of the capitalist state, including in its liberal form	Social and spatial relationality as key to understanding the structure, modality of each repertoire of state capitalism across the spaces of the world economy	State capitalism defined in relation to inherited landscapes of state intervention	Expansion of the state's role as means to overcome blockages to capital accumulation Synchronicity as causal factor in state capitalist impulses	Geo-institutional heterogeneity is constitutive of state capitalism. It is relational and dialectical	Cascading impacts of state capitalist impulses Towards secular transformations in the form and nature of the capitalist state in the latest phase of capitalist development?

causal significance of political multiplicity (how various forms of conflict, cooperation and emulation between states shape the various trajectories in the repertoires of state intervention). Moreover, we made the case for a relational social ontology of contemporary state capitalism, one that sees geo-institutional differentiation as systematically (re)produced and constitutive of state capitalism as a variegated, world-historical totality. The key features of our conceptual framework are summarized and presented in Table 3.1.

4
Rooting State Capitalism in the Churn of Uneven Development

Let us now put to work the conceptual framework developed in the previous chapter. Specifically, we will aim to answer the following questions: What are the processes and relations pertaining to the historical development and geographical remaking of global capitalism which underpin the recent aggregate expansion of the state's role as promoter, supervisor, and owner of capital? What are the political economic transformations undergirding this historic arc in the trajectories of state intervention on a global scale, and especially the co-expansion of state-capital hybrids and of muscular forms of statism? In other words, we now move to a lower (i.e., more concrete) level of abstraction in our analysis, in order to explain the uneven and combined development of state capitalism at the current temporal juncture.

Our main claim is that the fundamental sources of present-day state capitalism are to be found in two world-historical economic mutations, both of which stem from determinate material transformations in the capitalist labour process and changing forms of labour exploitation: on the one hand, the emergence of a more complex constellation of 'old' and 'new' international divisions of labour; and on the other, deep-seated tendencies towards economic stagnation and industrial overcapacity. We show in the first section that these phenomena have had multifaceted ramifications in terms of the temporal and geographical dynamics of value production, circulation, and distribution, and in terms of corporate strategies.

Far from being passive observers of these processes, states have been directly implicated in these transformations. They have aided, accompanied, and occasionally expedited them by deploying a range of instruments, policies, regulations, and other modes of economic practice, in the context of their role as promoters of capital accumulation. As they have done so, states have themselves experienced a process of restructuring, involving profound transformations in pre-existing landscapes of state intervention, a rearticulation of the relations between states and the circuits of capital, shifting boundaries between the state and civil society,

The Spectre of State Capitalism. Ilias Alami and Adam D. Dixon, Oxford University Press.
 DOI: 10.1093/9780198925224.003.0004

and a dramatic expansion of their role as promoter of capital accumulation, direct owner of capital, and investor-shareholder. We argue that this is precisely the phenomenon that is now increasingly being referred to as the 'new' state capitalism. In short, present-day state capitalism must be understood as a process of self-transformation of capitalist states as they have politically mediated these global (but regionally uneven) secular mutations.

In the next section, we offer a panorama of this polymorphous process of state restructuring since the turn of the millennium, and particularly in the post-2008 global financial crisis environment. We identify four tendencies, which we call the 'productivist', 'absorptive', 'stabilizing', and 'disciplinary' state capitalist impulses. Combinations of these four state capitalist impulses have been observable to various degrees across the world economy, and have profoundly shaped global trajectories of state intervention. Needless to say, conceptualizing such a broad-range and multi-scaled set of state transformations is at risk of reductionism and tendencies towards overly stylized facts. We however think that this is a risk worth taking in order to provide a comprehensive picture of state capitalism as a variegated, world-historical totality, and a better understanding of its drivers, logics, and effects.

From Labour Transformations to the Geographical Remaking of Capitalism

Recall that we argued in the previous chapter that the determinants of the expansion of present-day state capitalism must be sought in global transformations in the material forms of surplus value production, and more precisely, in changing forms of labour exploitation by capital through the transformation of capitalist production. Accordingly, we must start our analysis from the proverbial 'hidden abode of production'.

Transformations of the Labour Process under Large-Scale Industry

Global capitalist production, and particularly large-scale industry, experienced several rounds of transformation in the twentieth century. Each round was associated with emerging spatial patterns of production, new divisions of labour, the reorganization of the circuits of capital, and changing forms of labour exploitation. The 1960s marked a key moment in the development of the international division of labour (Fröbel, Heinrichs, and Kreye 1978). The fragmentation of the labour process, the deskilling of factory work, and the standardization of tasks and products in sectors such as clothing and textiles, footwear, and simple consumer electronics facilitated a geographic shift in the global organization of production. A range of production processes and component assembly operations were relocated from the core of the world economy to low-cost and labour-intensive peripheral regions. This 'new' international division of labour led to significant degrees of industrialization in East Asia (the Four Asian Tigers famously benefited from this process and experienced rapid industrialization and socio-economic transformation from the 1960s to the 1990s), and to a lesser extent, in some other parts of the Third World (including in countries such as Brazil, Mexico, Argentina, South Africa, Turkey, and others). Nevertheless, this did not signal the demise of the 'classic' or 'old' international division of labour which had prevailed since colonial times. Many resource-rich countries remained integrated into the world market as exporters of primary commodities (minerals, energy, and agricultural products) notably in Latin America, Africa, South East Asia, and the Arab states of the Persian Gulf.

At the turn of the twenty-first century, the international division of labour developed into more complex forms, as a result of the capitalist compulsion to increase labour productivity via technological change and revolutions in communication and transportation methods. The development of advanced semiconductors based on integrated circuits (following the microelectronics revolution) and their subsequent application to the labour process enabled a rapid process of automation, robotization, computerization, and digitalization of large-scale industry (Charnock and Starosta 2016; Arboleda 2020). This in turn facilitated profound transformations in the world of work, changing forms of labour exploitation, and an increasing fragmentation of the global working class. This process involved three main dimensions (in what follows, we draw significantly on Charnock and Starosta 2016, chapter 4).

First, there was a valorization of intellectual labour implicated in the deployment of science and technology to the production process. Think about, for instance, applied research and development, engineering, programming, industrial design, and other forms of white-collar work involved in the planning of manufacturing and the organization of supply and production chains. Second, we observed an increasing codification of tacit knowledge (which used to be developed by blue-collar workers through experience) and the 'objectification of formerly manual tasks as automated functions of machines' (Charnock and Starosta 2016, 7). This transformative process had a double implication for a large stratum of the working class. On the one hand, it accelerated the de-skilling and degradation of simpler manual and non-mechanized labour, which pushed more workers to toil in assembly lines and contemporary sweatshops as an 'appendage of machinery'. On the other, the computer-aided codification of tacit knowledge also facilitated a process of re-skilling. Indeed, soft skills such as digital literacy, problem-solving, and other flexible and transferable skills have become essential and generalized across a range of occupations involving the handling and distribution of information. Examples include the various types of labour conducted by office clerks, low-level programmers, accountants, legal aids, customer service workers, and the armies of labourers processing data for tech companies.

Third, there was a multiplication of 'relative surplus populations', that is, surplus relative to the needs of capital for formal waged labour (Davis 2006; Bernards and Soederberg 2021). Automation and labour-saving technologies combined with the worsening economic stagnation of the last couple of decades (more on this below) have depressed the global demand for labour (Benanav 2020). Manifestations of this phenomenon include the pace of job creation lagging behind that of job destruction, jobless recoveries after recessions, high structural unemployment, persistent underemployment, and falling labour shares of income. In the Global South, the worsening impacts of ecological degradation, expulsions from non-capitalist livelihoods, and other forms of dispossession have led to the increasing integration of impoverished populations into capitalist social relations as consumers and debtors, swelling the ranks of surplus populations and amplifying forms of displacement (Bernards and Soederberg 2021). Unable to access a full wage—although their life is now structured by it—growing masses must look to survive in low labour-productivity activities, the 'gig' economy, informal sectors, and other highly contingent, irregular, and often immiserating pursuits, from street hawking to app-mediated services delivery (Jones 2021; Smith 2021).

Overall, these transformations associated with the technical revolution and computer-assisted automation of the labour process greatly intensified the real subsumption of labour to capital (see previous chapter), subjecting an ever more global proletariat to the coercive laws of world market competition. This led to an increasing fragmentation of the global working class in terms of the costs and productive attributes of labour power (or, in mainstream economics and policymaking jargon, unit labour cost and productivity) providing the basis for enhanced global labour arbitrage (which firms can leverage to organize production across territorial borders) and for the expansion and complexification of the international division of labour.[1]

Contemporary Constellations of International Division of Labour

The late 1990s–2000s saw a drastic acceleration and deepening of the 'new' international division of labour. It penetrated into more sophisticated economic sectors, including high-tech and other sectors characterized by technological dynamism and a high intensity of intellectual labour (Charnock and Starosta 2016). East Asian late-industrializers (South Korea, Taiwan, Singapore) moved up the value chain into sectors closer to the technological and productivity frontier (semiconductors, biotech, 5G technology, telecoms, artificial intelligence, advanced robotics, and green tech). This was accompanied by a reorganization and deepening of global and regional production networks, with the relocation of less complex, low-skilled, labour-intensive manufacturing activities to China and Southeast Asia (Vietnam, Thailand, Indonesia, and the Philippines) and to new manufacturing frontiers in Cambodia, Myanmar, Bangladesh, Sri Lanka, Laos and pockets of industrialization in some parts of Central America (Costa Rica, Honduras, the Dominican Republic), northern Mexico, Central and Eastern Europe, and North Africa. Importantly, this migration of factory work to poorer regions (notably those with easy access to large developed markets) was facilitated by trade and economic liberalization, the establishment of special economic zones (low or no-tax zones paying low wages to process commodities for exports, with little or no labour and environmental regulations). However, as we will see below, states have also increasingly facilitated this reorganization of global production via more interventionist policy instruments.

The fast-paced processes of industrialization—and concomitant mega-urbanization and mass proletarianization—experienced in the above world-regions went hand in hand with dynamics of (de)industrialization unfolding elsewhere. Exporters of primary commodities in large swaths of Latin America, Africa, Central Asia, and the Persian Gulf benefitted from East and Southeast Asia's huge appetite for raw materials, food staples, mining commodities, and energy products. This created a boom in their prices, the so-called 'commodity super-cycle', which lasted from early 2000s to the

[1] Arbitrage operations tend to also leverage other oppressive social relations, such as race, gender, and nationality.

mid-2010s. Nevertheless, the downside was 'premature deindustrialization' in these resource-rich economies (Rodrik 2016), partly as a direct result of the macroeconomic impacts of the commodity super-cycle (a strong appreciation of the exchange rate contributing to the deterioration of the external competitiveness of manufactured goods), and partly due to the increased competition of manufactured goods from China and Southeast Asia. These two factors contributed to decimating local industries. Many of these countries thus experienced economic 're-primarization', meaning that the weight of the primary sector in the economy grew in comparison to that of the manufacturing and service sectors, with important implications for structural change (or lack thereof), income distribution, employment levels, the informal economy, and pressures on the environment. The deepening of the 'new' international division of labour therefore drastically heightened certain detrimental aspects of the 'classic' or 'old' international division of labour.

In advanced capitalist economies, the further unfolding of the 'new' international division of labour manifested itself as accelerated deindustrialization and the growth of service-oriented economies, reinforcing patterns of spatial polarization between, on the one hand, 'rust belts' and other 'left-behind' regions which concentrate declining industries, and on the other, dynamic regions where the leading edge of higher value–producing activities clustered, such as knowledge-intensive business services (financial, legal, accountancy, management consultancy, and marketing services) as well as sectors at the technological and productivity frontier (advanced manufacturing and electrical equipment, aerospace, nano-technologies, digital services, software development, 5G, big data, the internet of things, intelligent robotics, materials science, green energy). As we will see in Chapter 6, this is important insofar as these geographies and sectors are now primary transnational investment targets of contemporary state-capital hybrids (notably state enterprises and sovereign funds), which have also become increasingly integrated with established financial centres and global financial networks.

All in all, then, transformations in the material forms of production of relative surplus value over the past twenty to thirty years resulted in an increasingly complex constellation of old and new international divisions of labour (Charnock and Starosta 2018), with far-reaching implications for the temporal rhythms and geographical patterns of global capital accumulation. One such implication is that we have seen the emergence and consolidation of new geographies of extraction, production, and consumption characterized by differential rates of accumulation between and within countries, with extremely dynamic growth poles and laggard regions. While not displacing the centrality of the 'Triad' (North America, Western Europe, and Japan)—notably as spaces of consumption, finance, and high-tech development—there has however been an extraordinary eastward geoeconomic pivot from the North Atlantic, and a reorganization of spaces of extraction and production around the Pacific Rim. This is best illustrated by the massive flows of agricultural, energy, and mining commodities extracted from Latin America and shipped to the East Asian 'global factory'. Enabling this extraordinary expansion of metabolic flows has required the establishment of a transpacific logistical corridor, connecting mines and agricultural hinterlands in Latin America to port and manufacturing cities in East Asia (Arboleda 2020).

More broadly speaking, as the emergent pattern of geographical uneven development consolidates, there is a growing need for new spatial and territorial arrangements linking up distant frontiers of resource extraction, sites of agro-industrial production, industrial agglomerations and spaces of consumption. This explains why the last two decades have seen a renewed interest in large-scale connective infrastructure, notably transnational multimodal logistical systems spanning oceans and continents to integrate distant spaces and facilitate the flow of capital, commodities, money, people, information, standards, and technical know-how along production networks (Danyluk 2018; Arboleda 2020; Schindler and Kanai 2021; Schindler, Alami, and Jepson 2022). We will further comment on the extensive state involvement in these dynamics of territorialization later in this chapter.

Tendencies towards Economic Stagnation

Now, if changing forms of labour exploitation and the consolidation of new planetary geographies of extraction, production, and consumption have led to an unprecedented accumulation of profits—especially for the transnational capitalist firms able to coordinate the various stages of production along criss-crossing value chains—they have nevertheless accelerated tendencies towards economic malaise. Mainstream economists and policymakers call this phenomenon 'secular stagnation' (cf. Baldwin and Teulings 2014). This notion gained popularity in the 2010s and refers to the idea that advanced capitalist economies appear to have entered a period of long-term economic slump whose roots predate the 2008 global financial crisis by decades, with no prospect of a return to 'normal'. This manifests as slow growth, low investment, and a savings glut. Mainstream economists attribute (incorrectly in our view) secular stagnation to manufacturing decline in advanced capitalist economies, which is counterpoised to economic vitality in emerging capitalist economies.

We see this phenomenon as affecting the accumulation of capital as a whole. It is therefore global (albeit uneven, as evidenced by differential rates of accumulation between spaces across the world capitalist economy). Following economic historians and theorists Robert Brenner, Giovanni Arrighi, Simon Clarke, and others, we locate the sources of economic stagnation in the 'long downturn'—the generalized capitalist crisis of overproduction which started in the 1970s (Arrighi 1994; Clarke 1994;Brenner 2006).[2] The argument here is that, although the 'neoliberal offensive' (Harvey 2006), the deepening of the new international division of labour described earlier, and the integration of vast pools of labourers into global capitalism provided powerful counter-tendencies to capital overaccumulation in the short term, they nevertheless ended up radically worsening global overproduction and industrial overcapacity across a wide range of sectors.

Indeed, while it is rational from the perspective of individual capitalist firms to invest in technology and fixed capital as a means to raise labour productivity and capture relative surplus value under the form of above-average profit rates, in the aggregate, this competitive drive raises the productivity standards prevailing in a particular sector, and reduces socially necessary labour time. Living labour being the source of capitalist value, this therefore results in a growing gap between the volumes of commodities produced, and the amount of value embedded in these commodities (see Moraitis 2022 for a brilliant exposition of the argument). Firms can compensate ensuing falling profitability rates by producing more commodities, yet this only exacerbates tendencies towards overproduction, industrial overcapacity, and intensified competition between industrial capitals as global product markets become saturated. This results in a slowing pace of investment, low manufacturing-output growth, and low labour-productivity gains.

Thus, as a result of the revolution in the technological basis of the forces of production and the immense increase in manufacturing capacities which took place over the past couple of decades globally, deep-seated overaccumulation tendencies have returned with a vengeance, becoming particularly visible since the mid-2010s in a wide range of sectors, from agro-chemicals to shipbuilding, aluminium, steel, coal power, solar panels, and others (cf. inter alia, IMF 2020; Copley 2022). Furthermore, policy responses to the 2008 global financial crisis in the form of economic stimulus packages in large

[2] These authors' interpretations of the causes of over-accumulation are inspired by different understandings of Marxian crisis theory, but this has no bearing on the essence of our argument here.

economies (notably China) may well have played a crucial role in preventing a catastrophic economic collapse globally, but have also compounded underlying global overaccumulation (Hung 2016).

Corporate Strategies of Adaptation: Rentiership, Logistics, Centralization, Finance

Before we turn to a sustained examination of the role of the state in politically mediating the above processes, let us briefly review the corporate strategies deployed by capitalist firms to secure profit rates in the face of tendencies towards economic stagnation, industrial overcapacity, intensifying competition, and the globalization of production. This quick detour is necessary, insofar as these corporate strategies have profoundly shaped institutional developments and state policymaking. Four trends are noteworthy.

The first is well known and has been discussed at length in the booming literature on financialization over the past couple of decades. It refers to firms' increasing resort to financial markets as a means to shore up corporate profits (Krippner 2011; Mader, Mertens, and van der Zwan 2021). Here we do not simply mean that firms have turned to short-term speculative financial activities instead of investing long term in the sphere of production. Rather, we draw on works which emphasize that privileged access to deep and liquid financial markets allows large capitalist firms (often from the Global North) to establish dominance in global value chains and squeeze out competitors and sub-contracting firms (Milberg 2008; Durand 2017; Bonizzi, Kaltenbrunner, and Powell 2020; Newman 2022). Financial markets and instruments are therefore not simply a means to generate revenue streams in anticipation of future surplus value production, they are also a tool leveraged by dominant firms focused on so-called 'core competencies' to enhance market power, pass on shocks and cost-disciplines to sub-contracting firms (at the expense of their labourers and a deterioration in work conditions), and therefore maximize their capacity to syphon profits out of global production networks, before channelling them to tax heavens jurisdictions (Bair et al. 2023).

Second, firms have sought to grow, acquire market share, secure monopolistic positions, enhance market power, and increase profitability through the transfer of ownership in the sphere of circulation instead of investing in new production facilities (Alami and Dixon 2022). This redistribution of ownership and control of existing capital in fewer hands has taken place across a wide range of industrial sectors, and has been facilitated by mergers and acquisitions, takeovers, joint ventures, and other modalities of alliance. It has fuelled an unprecedented round of transnational centralization of capital mediated by the financial system and actively supported by states and state-owned capital, which we explain and document at length in Chapter 6.

Third, firms have sought to leverage advances in logistics to shore up corporate profits and gain competitive advantages. Simply put, logistics itself has become a corporate strategy and site of value creation, leading to a blurring of the boundary between production and circulation (Bernes 2013; Cowen 2014; Arboleda 2020; Brennan 2021). The incorporation of logistics calculations into production flows, the management of entire supply chains as an integrated, total-cost system, the development of just-in-time production methods, and other innovations in infrastructural planning, circulatory systems, and logistical flows have allowed firms to compress turnover times, cheapen the circulation of commodities, and exponentially expand the volume of commodities in transit in a relatively secure and reliable way (Bernes 2013; Cowen 2014; Clover 2016; Chua et al. 2018). This has enhanced the mobility of both commodity capital and the production process itself (Danyluk 2018). Although the 'logistics revolution' started in the 1970s, there was a qualitative leap forward at the turn of the millennium, catalysed by developments in computer-assisted automation, AI, and data processing. These equipped lead firms with new tools for 'manipulating space' to match supply with demand, thus neutralizing risks of devaluations (Danyluk 2018, 632). They also afforded firms with the ability to manage the dense circulation of information (about labour processes, workflows, inventory fluctuations, consumer behaviour, etc.) within production networks (Chua et al. 2018; Durand and Milberg 2020) and exert control over the wider division of labour, both of which facilitate value capture (and thus extra profits) along the circuits of capital (Baglioni, Campling, and Hanlon 2023). Furthermore, algorithmic surveillance of labour processes and the tight monitoring of bodies allowed firms to intensify the exploitation of transportation and distribution workers, often employed in precarious and heavily policed labour regimes (Danyluk 2018; Strauss 2020).

Fourth, firms have aimed to secure high profits by developing new forms of rentiership (Christophers 2020; Birch, Ward, and Tretter 2022; Schwartz 2022). Of particular importance here are a host of corporate profit strategies, often called 'intellectual monopoly capitalism' (Durand and Milberg 2020; Rikap 2021) consisting of locking in monopoly control of intangible assets, from trademarks and patents to other forms of intellectual property rights, as a source of market power and/or revenue generation (Monk 2009). Securing monopoly control of intangible assets for extended periods of time affords firms the ability to create and exploit artificial scarcity. It also allows them to erect barriers to entry and prevent competitors from entering clusters of innovation with great commercial potential (Smith 2017). Finally, it allows lead firms to exert control over subordinate firms and the wider division of labour along value chains, thereby empowering them to capture value produced elsewhere within the circuit of capital (Baglioni, Campling, and Hanlon 2023).

***

In sum, the transformations in the capitalist labour process analysed in this section have had fundamental implications in terms of the temporal and geographical dynamics of value production, circulation, and distribution, and in terms of corporate strategies. Our argument so far is presented visually in Figure 4.1.

So where does contemporary state capitalism fit in this narrative? To use the conceptual language developed in the previous chapter, contemporary state capitalist *impulses* have been rooted in these global (but regionally uneven) capitalist mutations. Our key argument is that, far from being passive observers, states have been directly implicated in these mutations, which they have politically mediated. They have (more or less willingly) aided, accompanied, and occasionally expedited them by deploying a range of instruments, policies, regulations, and other modalities of intervention, in the context of their role as promoters of capital accumulation within their territory (ensuring favourable conditions and disciplining social relations in line with accumulation imperatives) and abroad (opening markets and defending the interests of the capitals they represent). States have also assisted firms in the design and implementation of the four corporate profit strategies mentioned earlier. As they have done so, they have themselves experienced a polymorphous process of self-transformation, involving significant mutations in pre-existing landscapes of state intervention, a rearticulation of the relations between states and the circuits of capital, shifting boundaries between the state and civil society, and a dramatic aggregate expansion of their role as supervisor, regulator, guarantor, and direct owner of capital. Crucially, this is because the capitalist transformations discussed in this section have reconfigured the challenges and constraints that capitalist states face, but they have also simultaneously provided them with new opportunities and capacities to perform such role. We show in the next section that

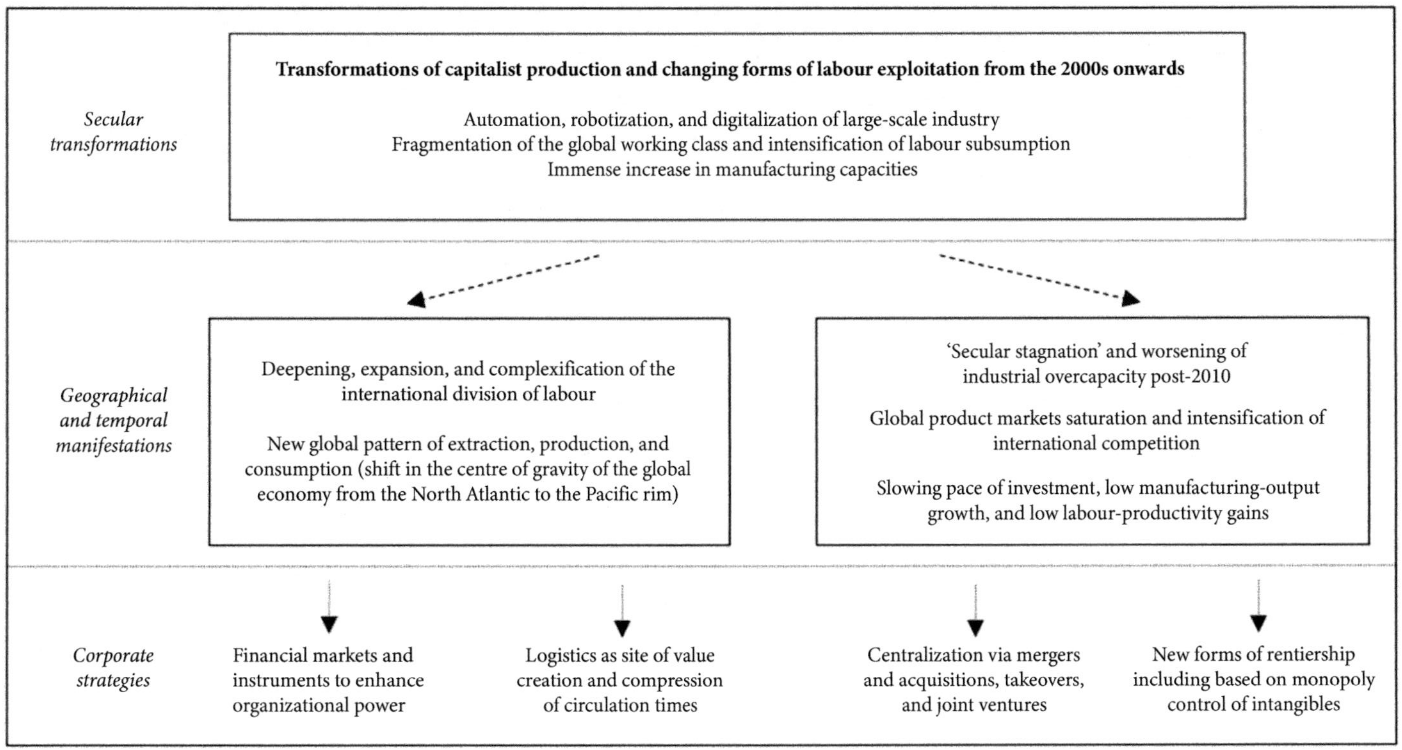

Figure 4.1 Material determinations of contemporary state capitalism

the remarkable expansion of state-capital hybrids and of muscular forms of statism observed since the early 2000s and particularly after the 2008 crisis must be understood in this light.

Four Tendencies towards State Capitalist Impulses

In order to structure our account of how states have politically mediated the above processes of capitalist restructuring and associated mutations in the spheres of production, circulation, distribution of value, we offer a typology of contemporary state capitalist impulses. We identify four types, which we call the 'productivist', 'absorptive', 'stabilizing', and 'disciplinary' state capitalist impulses. While there is much overlap and reciprocal interaction between them, the four state capitalist impulses follow distinct logics.

'Productivist' State Capitalist Impulses

The first set of transformations that we single out is what we call the 'productivist' state capitalist impulse, insofar as it designates processes of state restructuring geared towards increased direct state intervention in production arrangements and the competitive dynamics of productive and extractive capital. Several trends can be observed.

The moving frontier of technological innovation and the establishment of global and regional production networks have prompted states to develop new forms of intervention (notably in the domain of techno-industrial policymaking) and modalities of government-business cooperation. This is because global and regional production networks have presented states with emergent political economic challenges, such as favouring the dynamic articulation of domestic firms with said networks (Yeung 2016). In addition to attracting high-value added foreign direct investment and coordinating the emergence of new technological frontiers for firms to reach competitive positions in cutting-edge industries (Thurbon and Weiss 2021; Maggor 2021), the challenge is to help domestic companies position themselves as 'anchor' or 'lead' firms of production networks, both at home and abroad. Indeed, by coordinating various stages of production in those networks, firms can secure market power and maximize value capture. In this respect, and in line with the tendency towards rentiership and the growing importance of logistics mentioned earlier, states have aimed to boost their national innovation systems (encompassing large public and private funding for

R&D and scientific-technical training, government procurement policies, credit subsidies, tax breaks, and other policies encouraging innovation) to help firms acquire and monopolize strategic technological and organizational capabilities over extended periods of time. In short, these new challenges have elicited a reconfiguration of techno-industrial and innovation policy.

Thus, we saw a proliferation of 'entrepreneurial' states and various forms of state support to industry and innovation, often under the leadership of public innovation agencies, such as Israel's Office of the Chief Scientist, Singapore's A*Star, Enterprise Ireland, Finland's Sitra, the US Defense Advanced Research Projects Agency, and BPI France Creation (Mazzucato 2011; Maggor 2021). These offer 'targeted government funding in R&D and training, support for marketing and exporting, networking and brokerage services, and building of facilities and science parks' in order to foster innovation technologies and products (Maggor 2021, 452). Some countries have designed national industrial strategies as an overall framework for techno-industrial policymaking. For instance, Germany's *National Industrial Strategy 2030* aims to develop so-called 'Industrie 4.0' (cf. Germann 2022). France launched *France 2030* to develop strategic sectors (automotive, aerospace, digital, green industry, biotechnology) and national champions. Britain successively launched two national plans, *Industrial Strategy* and *Build Back Better* (see Berry et al. 2021). A range of smaller European economies such as Finland, Denmark, and Ireland have experimented with various forms of active innovation policies (Ornston 2012). Industrial policy also made a remarkable comeback at the European Union level, and re-industrialization has been identified as a top priority (Wigger 2023). The *2020 Industrial Strategy* aims to support the green and digital transitions of EU industry, while protecting and expanding Europe's industrial base and technological lead. Flagship initiatives such as *Smart Specialization* blend cohesion policy with industrial policy goals. More recently, the EU has passed a series of ambitious plans—*REPowerEU*, *EU Green Deal* and the *EU Chips act*—designed to reduce the EU's energy and technological dependency, foster reindustrialization, and accelerate the green transition.

Made in China 2025 was launched to help Chinese state- and privately owned firms break into high tech manufacturing (Zhang and Lan 2023). *Singapore Economy 2030* and *Smart Nation* aim to boost the roboticization, digitalization, and greening of Singapore. The South Korean state launched a range of national initiatives to accelerate the development of intelligent robotics and other 'growth engines' and 'frontier technologies' (Thurbon and

Weiss 2021). Other East Asian initiatives have been set up at the regional and municipal levels (see for instance Doucette and Park 2018, on 'East Asian developmental urbanism'). After years if not decades during which the US had reframed from formulating national industrial plans, relying instead on government procurement and mission-oriented developmental projects to boost innovation and technological development (Block and Keller 2011; Weiss 2014; Baltz 2022), national industrial policy has made a resounding comeback in the US, focusing in particular on chipmakers and EV manufacturers.

As the few above examples show, this trend mainly concerns those advanced capitalist economies in the west and East Asia at the cutting edge of the technology and productivity frontier, yet low- and middle-income countries also face the challenge of positioning themselves favourably in global production networks, in order to attract foreign investment, achieve economic diversification, industrial upgrading, and enhance firm competitiveness and labour productivity. Vast differences in terms of institutional capacity notwithstanding, the important point here is that there has been an increasing awareness in countries across the income spectrum that these policy goals cannot be achieved by relying solely on the 'open-market' and 'horizontal' forms of industrial policy that predominated in the 1990s (industrial clusters, tax breaks, public-private partnerships, and loose labour market regulations) (Bulfone 2023). States have therefore increasingly experimented with new combinations of both horizontal and vertical forms of industrial policy designed to nurture strategic sectors and firms, from national champion policies to targeted state aid packages and subsidized credit lines via state investment funds, policy banks and other state-owned instruments. These have been deployed both in a defensive way (protecting sectors and restructuring declining industries at home in the face of competition) and in a more offensive manner (favouring transitions to new areas of sectoral competitiveness and supporting capitals abroad).

Across the Global South, this renewed interest in industrial policy has often taken an explicitly territorial dimension, and has manifested itself as a profusion of spatial planning and national development strategies (Schindler and Kanai 2021). We mentioned earlier that the current pattern of uneven geographical development requires the production of new territories and spatial arrangements, including a dense network of connective infrastructure to integrate distant places and to facilitate the ever-growing flow of capital, commodities, money, people, data, and technical standards along value chains. Producing flexible territorial regimes has thus become essential for countries to participate in global production networks (Schindler and Kanai 2021; McGregor and Coe 2023; Su and Lim 2023). Hence, we witnessed a re-emergence of spatial planning strategies in order to 'constitute functional territories that can be "plugged in" to global value chains' (Schindler and Kanai 2021, 44). In addition to large-scale state-supported investment in energy grids, digital networks, public works, and air, maritime and terrestrial transports, we saw the creation and empowerment of economic and spatial planning agencies in charge of developing spatialized industrial policies and rolling out zoning technologies, from special economic zones and economic corridors to new towns and integrated systems of logistical connectivity (Lee, Wainwright, and Glassman 2018; Arboleda 2020; Schindler, Alami, and Jepson 2022). Such policies are currently being deployed in dozens of countries across Central and Eastern Europe, Latin America, Asia, and Africa, from Ecuador's *Plan Nacional de Desarrollo* to *Plan Sénégal Emergent*, Kenya's *Vision 2030*, Indonesia's *Vision 2045*, *Thailand 4.0*, Pakistan's *Vision 2025*, Poland's *National Development Concept 2050*, and Morocco's *New Development Model*. They aim to comprehensively redesign national territory in ways that will enhance economic diversification, industrial upgrading, and balanced regional growth. They place inter- and intra-regional connectivity and transnational integration as key to enhancing firm/sector competitiveness and national comparative advantages.

Relatedly, we witnessed a turn to more aggressive forms of competitive economic nationalism in the policy fields of development finance and infrastructure. Here, too, the tendencies discussed earlier of capital overaccumulation and the growing importance of logistics and connectivity matter significantly. States in advanced and large emerging economies have used their international development agencies, export-import banks, and other modalities of strategic support to develop the operations of 'their' own capitalist firms (state-owned or not) in countries across the Global South. According to a 2022 OECD report, in 2019 and 2020, donor countries like the US, Australia, Finland, Canada, Japan, Japan, the UK, Denmark, France, the Netherlands, Korea, Switzerland, Czech Republic, and others awarded between 50 and 100 per cent of their official development assistance contracts to their own supplier firms. This is to achieve a double objective: opening up market opportunities for their over-accumulated capital (Mawdsley, Murray, Overton, et al. 2018) and competing to finance, build, and control infrastructure-led connectivity in ways that facilitate the integration of their firms in regional production networks and accelerate the circulation of capital. Schindler and Kanai (2021) refer to this as an 'infrastructure race' (see also Di Carlo and Schindler 2022). Examples include China's *Belt and Road Initiative*, a range of programmes launched by advanced capitalist states (EU's *Global Gateway*, the G7's *Build Back Better World*, UK's *Global Britain*), as well as numerous initiatives on the part of mid-size powers and regional actors, such as South Korea, Turkey, India, the United Arab Emirates, Brazil, Morocco, Saudi Arabia, Vietnam, and others.

Other trends towards productivist state capitalist impulses were directly rooted in the commodity super-cycle. As discussed earlier, large rents generated from the export of foodstuff, agricultural, mining, and energy commodities flowed into resource-rich economies. This provided the material basis for the reincorporation of state enterprises into developmentalist-redistributive strategies. States increased their direct participation and ownership in primary sectors in order to leverage the commodity boom (albeit at the cost of reinforcing extractivist development models heavily dependent on primary resources and extremely destructive for the environment). Thus, we saw 'the renationalisation of privatized assets in the mining sector and the reorganization of the oil and gas industry in favour of direct state participation' (Nem Singh and Chen 2018, 1087). This was to make sure that states would capture significant portions of these rents. In mining, oil, gas and agro-chemicals, direct state participation, and ownership aimed at facilitating the strategic coupling of firms and territories within global production networks (Lim 2018; Horner and Alford 2019; Werner 2021).

State enterprises have also been used, in the context of the turn to more muscular forms of statism, to deliver energy, raw materials, and industrial inputs priced below prices of production, thereby transferring surplus-value (produced from their own process of labour exploitation) to productive capitals in other industrial sectors (such as petrochemicals, manufacturing, and construction) to catalyse structural change (Kim and Sumner 2019). Moreover, some of these sectors have been particularly affected by structural dynamics of overcapacity and intensified competition, which states and 'their' state enterprises have sought to address by extending transnational control over resources and markets, thereby fuelling dynamics of capital centralization (Lim 2018; Werner 2021). For instance, many Brazilian, Indonesian, Malaysian, and Chinese state enterprises operating in the food, agro-chemicals, energy, hydrocarbons, and mining sectors have expanded their global operations to acquire competitors. These dynamics of centralization, however, did not only concern state enterprises in resource-rich developing and emerging economies. States in advanced capitalist economies have also increasingly provided support to their state enterprises to help them become globalized champions (Babic, Garcia-Bernardo, and Heemskerk 2020; Bulfone 2023), especially in large-scale infrastructure construction, transports, logistics, telecoms (sectors which have received a boost as part of the global geographical reorganization of the circuits of capital discussed earlier) as well as sectors closer to the technology and productivity frontier (renewables, advanced manufacturing, aerospace, and defence). We offer an in-depth analysis of these trends in Chapter 6.

Moreover, in the context of their increasing direct participation in the circuits of productive/extractive capital, states in both advanced capitalist economies and in the global South have expanded their role as owner and provider of finance and credit, often at a low cost and with long time-horizons, to support specific segments of capital or sectors (Marois 2021; Mertens, Thiemann, and Volberding 2021). This includes the provision of subsidized credit, but also so-called patient capital, equity participation, capital transfers, and financial products such as insurance and state guarantees, via organizational forms as diverse as development and policy banks, state-owned commercial banks, and other development finance institutions. These have been redeployed, and often repurposed, to serve the needs of industrial policy, infrastructure development, and the internationalization of national champions (Kim and Sumner 2019). Examples include the creation of the Polish Development Fund to finance infrastructure, high tech projects, start-ups, and to channel long-term liquidity from pension funds to listed companies (Naczyk 2022). The UK launched in 2021 its own state-owned bank focused on infrastructure development, the UK Infrastructure Bank. In France, a range of state-owned financial institutions were merged and repurposed in 2014 to form a public investment bank, Bpifrance, to offer guarantees, equity financing, and export credit to small-and-medium enterprises. At the EU level, the European Investment Bank vastly increased its operations and institutional ties with existing national development banks, testifying to the existence of a nascent 'hidden' European investment state (Mertens and Thiemann 2019). The National Integrated Circuit Industry Investment Fund, aka the 'Big Fund', was created in 2014 to develop China's integrated circuit industry and reduce reliance on imported technology. In South Korea, the revival of state-led credit activism and investment via five large specialized state-owned banks (including the Korean Development Bank) since the Asian financial crisis has served the needs of industrial policy and supported export-led development by funding small-and-medium enterprises in strategic manufacturing sectors such as semiconductors and green energy (Thurbon 2016; Klingler-Vidra 2018; Henow 2022).

'Absorptive' State Capitalist Impulses

The second type of state capitalist impulse that we identify we call 'absorptive' for two reasons. On the one hand, it refers to a set of state transformations oriented towards absorbing and recycling economic surpluses by putting them into motion as financial capital, and facilitating their investment across sectors and geographies. On the other, it designates state transformations targeted at absorbing over-accumulated capital, 'toxic' assets, and socializing 'bad' debt and risks.

The consolidation of complex constellations of old and new international divisions of labour, and the associated emergence of new geographies of extraction, production, and consumption, have resulted in a highly uneven planetary distribution of large and persistent current account deficits and surpluses over the past twenty to thirty years, or what mainstream economists and policymakers call 'global imbalances'. According to a recent IMF (2021, 15) report, 'overall current account deficits and surpluses amounted to 3.2 percent of world GDP in 2020'. In the same year, the IMF estimated that 'global excessive' imbalances, that is, the global sum of 'absolute current account gaps compared with their desirable medium-term levels' represented about 1.2 per cent of world GDP (2021, 15.). These have been rooted in diverging rates and patterns of accumulation between world-regions, with continued concentration of deficits in debtor countries and sustained surpluses in creditor countries. A key manifestation of global imbalances is that countries such as China, Japan, Switzerland, Russia, India, Taiwan, Saudi Arabia, South Korea, and Singapore have generated vast current account surpluses and accumulated massive amounts of foreign exchange reserves over the past couple of decades, while countries such as the United States, France, the United Kingdom, and Canada have sustained deficits.

These imbalances have had a range of global repercussions, notably in terms of patterns of global capital flows, asset formation, financial instability, currency fluctuations, rising inequality, and trade tensions (Klein and Pettis 2020). Their role in the build-up on the 2008 global financial crisis is notorious. Importantly for our purpose, the accentuation of global imbalances has provided the material basis for a historically unprecedented expansion of state ownership (the role of states as owners of capital and as investor-shareholder) and state property (the mass of capital and assets controlled by states) since the turn of the century (Alami and Dixon 2022). Several trends can be observed.

The accumulation of vast amounts of surpluses (stemming from commodity export revenues to balance-of-payments surpluses and the build-up of foreign exchange reserves) due to the consolidation of export-oriented models in East and South East Asian economies and the 're-primarization' of many developing economies in Latin America and Africa, have fuelled the multiplication of sovereign wealth funds and a spectacular expansion of the assets they control globally (see figures cited in Chapter 1). Indeed, states across Asia, the Middle East and Africa have created new sovereign wealth funds (or repurposed and extended the prerogatives of existing ones) in order to absorb and recycle these vast surpluses. Sovereign funds have expanded their operations at home and abroad since the early 2000s, occasionally in partnership with state enterprises.

Some of these funds invest their resources following a conventional portfolio diversification strategy, generating long-term risk-adjusted returns from global financial markets. Funds which resources come from foreign exchange reserves, for instance, often seek to diversify foreign exchange assets and earn a higher return by investing in a broader range of asset classes, from real estate and property to finance and insurance, trade and retail, media, healthcare, and manufacturing (Babic 2021). For instance, South Korea and China created (respectively) the Korea Investment Corporation in 2005 and the China Investment Corporation in 2007 as vehicles to diversify their gigantic foreign exchange reserves. These funds invest across a wide range of geographies and sectors in public equity, bonds, private equity, hedge funds, infrastructure, energy, Treasury bills, and more.

Other sovereign funds, often referred to as development funds or strategic investment funds, have been more directly implicated in state activism and techno-industrial strategy. These funds are actively managed in a similar fashion to a private equity or venture capital fund, and their mandate is to invest in sectors, firms, assets, and projects that are deemed strategic to fomenting economic growth and the diversification of the economy, pointing to overlap between productivist and absorptive state capitalist impulses (Dixon and Monk 2012).

Examples of strategic investment funds include Samruk-Kazyna, established in 2008 in Kazakhstan through the merger of Samruk, a state holding company, with Kazyna, a state development fund, with a dual mandate to improve national welfare and to support the modernization of the economy. Singapore's Temasek and Malaysia's Khazanah began as passive holding companies for the state's shares in national enterprises and have since transformed into strategic investment funds with domestic and global remits

(Dixon 2022). Morocco's strategic investment fund Ithmar Capital, created in 2011, aims at stimulating productive sectors, national projects and innovation in accordance with the sectoral strategies identified by the Moroccan state. Senegal's Fonds Souverain d'Investissements Stratégiques (FONSIS) was launched in 2012 with a similar mission to boost productive economic activity by investing in the strategic sectors identified by the national development strategy (*Plan Sénégal Emergent*), from infrastructure to energy, logistics, agriculture, and mining. While its resources have so far come from state-owned assets, FONSIS will also be in charge of managing and investing revenues from recent oil and gas discoveries.

Both FONSIS and Ithmar Capital explicitly aim to co-invest through partnerships with international investors, which speaks to another objective that many of the newly created strategic investment funds strive to achieve, notably (but not only) in low- and middle-income countries. The objective is indeed to use the relatively limited investment fire power of these funds to attract investment from a range of international partners, including global asset managers, index funds, pension and sovereign funds, multilateral development banks, and international development agencies. This is particularly the case for infrastructure projects, which are considered too risky for many Northern-based institutional investors. In conjunction with development and policy banks, recently created strategic investment funds thus increasingly aim to 'de-risk' and crowd-in private investment into large-scale infrastructure and industrial projects, via a range of practices and vehicles, from public-private partnerships to 'blended finance' (Gabor 2021; Mawdsley and Taggart 2022; Schindler, Alami, and Jepson 2022). In short, these instruments are meant to recalibrate the risk-return profile of infrastructure projects by institutionalizing a new distribution of risk, reward and responsibility between the borrowing state and investors, with the hope of attracting the large pools of liquidity circulating in the world market. This policy—effectively consisting of borrowing states socializing financial risks—is actively promoted by multilateral and regional development institutions, notably to finance the Sustainable Development Goals (for a critique, see Gabor 2021).

The multiplication of strategic investment funds does not concern only developing countries. Several richer economies created or repurposed their own strategic investment funds, both as de-risking tools to mobilize private finance and as vehicles to channel investment from East Asian and Middle Eastern sovereign wealth funds into particular sectors or projects. For instance, France's Fonds Stratégique d'Investissement (then brought under the aegis of Bpifrance), Italy's Fondo Strategico Italiano (then renamed Cassa

Depositi e Prestiti Equity) and Ireland Strategic Investment Fund all serve these purposes.[3]

Moreover, many states across the income spectrum created state asset management companies to pool resources and centralize within the same corporate structure their equity stakes in other firms and state-owned assets. These corporate structures afford states the ability to exercise (more or less distant) forms of control over industries and sectors. Thus, Bpifrance and Cassa Depositi e Prestiti (which also perform state asset management functions) have built hundreds of billions of euros' worth of stakes in both listed and unlisted companies in strategic sectors such as telecoms and high tech, and actively support the internationalization of national champions.

State asset management companies and sovereign funds have also been used by states to influence the corporate restructuring of state-owned enterprises and the private sector, by intervening in their business decisions, introducing a shareholder value orientation, changing their management team, injecting liquidity, or by absorbing over-accumulated capital and 'bad' debt. For instance, Indonesia's recently created Indonesia Investment Authority will help state-owned enterprises in utilities, transportation, and construction deleverage by purchasing their assets so they can continue to expand and finance large-scale infrastructure projects (Kim 2021). In China, four large state asset management companies—Cinda, Huarong, Great Wall, and Orient—have been set up to takeover and handle the state-owned commercial banks' non-performing loans in 1999, allowing them to survive. The state asset management companies thus performed a function of absorbing and centralizing geographically diverse financial risks gone bad, thereby displacing them in both spatial and temporal terms (Ho and Marois 2019). They then expanded their functions and undertook debt-to-equity swaps with heavily indebted state-owned enterprises and offered restructuring support, so the latter could consolidate and expand. In the following decade, they transformed into fully fledged, commercially oriented financial institutions, operating in all areas of banking, futures, securities, trust, and real estate, and simultaneously playing a strategic role in supporting Chinese state authorities' project of world market integration while retaining control of key nodes in the economy (Wang 2015; Ho and Marois 2019).

Finally, central banking in advanced capitalist economies, although rarely discussed in state capitalism debates (Hillier 2022; Sokol 2023), has performed an increasingly important role in absorbing bad debt and managing

[3] While 'de-risking' logics are at play in both the global South and in advanced capitalist economies, it is reasonable to think that states in the latter are generally able to strike better deals with investors (in terms of the allocation of risks, rewards, and responsibility) than poorer states.

toxic assets (via large-scale asset purchase programmes which expose their balance sheets to various credit, interest rate, and market risks). Indeed, practices such as 'quantitative easing' and the backstopping of securities market liquidity (Braun and Gabor 2020; Musthaq 2023), as well as the fiscal role that central banks have increasingly come to play in the post-COVID-19 context, respond to similar logics of absorption of risks and over-accumulated capital. This is closely related to a third type of state capitalist impulse.

'Stabilizing' State Capitalist Impulses

Taking inspiration from Shih (2009) and Carney (2018, 2015), we call this third logic the 'stabilizing' state capitalist impulse. Carney's work focuses on the rise of dominant-party authoritarian regimes in the first decade of the twenty-first century (Carney 2018). These regimes, Carney argues, increasingly rely on ownership of large corporate entities to maintain their rule. Partially state-owned enterprises and sovereign wealth funds have provided them the capacity to deal with an increasingly important source of instability—financial globalization. More precisely, these instruments have allowed regimes to reap the benefits of economic and financial globalization by 'aggressively pursu[ing] higher investment returns in foreign markets to maintain the support of voter-investors' (Carney 2018, 19). State enterprises and sovereign funds have also been used to aggressively intervene in the domestic corporate sector to strengthen the state's control of vital resources and information. As such, they have significantly contributed to the efforts of ruling factions to reduce risks to regime survival (see also Shih 2009).

In developing our notion of 'stabilizing' state capitalist impulse, we take our cue from Shih's and Carney's identification of a logic of regime survival in the increasing reliance on state ownership, yet we conceive of stabilization in broader terms. First, as we explain below, we see such logics at play in a much broader range of political economic configurations than simply dominant-party authoritarian regime, including in so-called liberal-democratic heartlands. Second, our notion encompasses a wider set of state transformations which specifically aim at mitigating crisis and economic volatility, propping up the value of financial assets, preventing the disorderly unfolding of crises, maintaining economic sovereignty, and preserving domestic political orders.

We argue that stabilizing state capitalist impulses must be understood as a response to the turbulent disarticulations catalysed by the processes of capitalist restructuring discussed in the first part of this chapter. Deepening market interdependence and the planetary integration of the circuits of capital have intensified the coercive laws of world market competition and heightened the tension between the global character of capital accumulation and the national form of the state, resulting in what Mezzadra and Neilson (2019, 130) call a partial 'explosion' of the national scale. This has been experienced by governments and ruling parties as the relative erosion of a range of national economic policy tools, repeated economic crises, ensuing political turmoil, and difficulties maintaining social stability. Macroeconomic management, in particular, has proved decidedly difficult in the face of the unprecedently high mobility of money-capital and speculative finance and volatile primary commodity prices. Stabilizing state capitalist impulses, then, consist of attempts to produce a modicum of economic and political stability in this context.

The 1997–1998 Asian financial crisis, the early 2000s emerging markets crises (in Brazil, Argentina, Russia, South Africa, Turkey, and many others), and the 2008 global financial crisis have been watersheds in spurring remarkable processes of institutional innovation and policy experimentation, notably in the realm of cross-border finance management and financial stabilization. Many states in developing and emerging economies deliberately accumulated massive amounts of foreign exchange reserves throughout the 2000s as a war chest to 'self-insure' against sudden capital account reversals. State-financial apparatuses (central banks, national treasuries, and financial regulatory authorities) were empowered and adopted strict macroprudential regulations and tightly regulated, monitored, and supervised domestic banking systems (with the regulation of the latter often tighter that international norms and best practices) (Marois 2012). The aftermaths of the 2008 global financial crisis, however, proved that these policy and institutional developments failed to provide sufficient financial and macroeconomic stability. Indeed, between 2009 and 2014, developing and emerging economies faced extraordinary volatile patterns of cross-border finance, the procyclicality of which was enhanced by the expansionary monetary policies conducted by central banks and governments in advanced capitalist economies (Alami 2019).

We therefore witnessed another round of policy experimentation. Countries as diverse as Brazil, South Korea, Indonesia, China, Costa Rica, Uruguay, the Philippines, Peru, Taiwan, Colombia, Argentina, Thailand, Turkey, and India implemented different forms of capital controls (on both portfolio flows and bank loans), stricter macroprudential regulations, foreign exchange derivatives regulations, unconventional monetary policy tools, and 'aggressive' foreign exchange market interventions in a context of acute financial instability (Gallagher 2015; Prates and Fritz 2016; da Silva 2022). Importantly, these policies neither challenged long-term commitments to capital account liberalization, nor did they signal a break with norms of free capital mobility and other pillars of orthodox macroeconomic policymaking (such as central bank independence, inflation targeting, and relatively tight fiscal discipline). Insofar as they were designed to allow for the continuation of growth strategies and development models relying on external finance, while mitigating some of their worst short-term consequences, they answered to a logic of stabilization (Alami 2019).

Many governments had similar objectives in mind when they deployed so-called stabilization sovereign funds in order to buffer the economy from external macro-financial shocks or economic downturns. By investing in domestic equities, these funds helped mitigate externally induced financial markets volatility. In resource-rich economies, stabilization funds aimed to address the 'Dutch disease' (also known as 'resource curse') by holding highly liquid low-risk assets offshore (Alsweilem and Rietveld 2018). Thus, they not only diversified natural resource revenue savings, they also played a role in fiscal policy, by smoothing resource revenue spending over time, and in monetary policy, by limiting the appreciation of the exchange rate. During crises, they helped sustain government spending or bail out certain industries. Governments could thus avoid the need for international assistance from the Bretton Woods institutions and the accompanying conditionalities, which often mean severe cuts to public spending and other politically contentious economic reforms (Dixon and Monk 2012). Examples of stabilization funds created over the past two decades include the Fondo Mexicano del Petroleo, the Fundo Soberano de Angola, the Petroleum Fund of Timor-Leste, and the Ghana Stabilization Fund, all designed to manage revenues from oil; Chile's Economic and Social Stabilization Fund, to handle revenues from copper; the Pula Fund managing Botswana's revenues from diamond exports; the Stabilization fund of the Russian Federation to manage volatile oil and gas prices.

Crucially, these funds are often firmly integrated within their country's core political and authority structure, and therefore perform the above tasks in ways that serve extant power configurations and ruling parties' policy agendas. Their ability to distribute investment according to particular policy objectives has proved crucial in this regard. For instance, the restructuring and extended purview of Saudi Arabia's Public Investment Fund since 2017 has helped Crown Prince and de facto ruler Mohamed Bin Salman concentrate political and economic power. The fund not only played an essential role as emergency liquidity provider when oil prices collapsed in 2014–2015 and after the COVID-19 crisis, it is also the cornerstone of the Saudi regime's strategy of preparing for a world after oil (Montambault Trudelle 2022). A similar dynamic has been at play in Turkey, where the newly created Turkey Wealth Fund has facilitated a transition to hyper-presidentialism and resource centralization under Recep Tayyip Erdoğan and the AK Parti (İpek 2019; Öniş and Kutlay 2021; Altınörs and Akçay 2022; Güven 2022).

Stabilizing state capitalist impulses have also involved the mobilization of state-owned banking. National and regional development banks played an essential role as counter-cyclical tools to offset private credit crunches, particularly following the 2008 global financial crisis (Griffith-Jones and Ocampo 2018; Marois 2021; Mertens, Thiemann, and Volberding 2021). Their vastly expanded loan portfolios and financial capacities allowed states to channel finance and credit to serve particular political objectives and spatial strategies, while presenting the additional benefit of allowing states to avoid fiscal constraints. For example, in Bolivia, the *Movimiento al Socialismo*, empowered by popular pressure from below, re-established state-owned banks and implemented a financial reform in a bid to reduce external vulnerabilities and ensure political stability (Naqvi 2021). In Indonesia, the state has responded to the instabilities generated by shrinking external development finance and underdeveloped domestic capital markets by enhancing its role as patient capitalist and development financier since the early 2000s (Kim 2021). By financing the expansion of state enterprises and large-scale infrastructure projects, state banks such as Bank Rakyat Indonesia, Bank Mandiri, and Bank Negara Indonesia have been at the heart of the Indonesian state-led development model, and have helped Jokowi's administration secure some degree of political legitimacy (Kim 2019a, 2019b, 2020). In Brazil, under the *Partido dos Trabalhadores* (PT), the Banco Nacional de Desenvolvimento Econômico e Social not only played a vital counter-cyclical role which helped the country withstand the global financial crisis, it was also instrumental in temporarily securing the relative support of some sections of the 'internal bourgeoisie' (Boito and Saad-Filho 2016). The PT also relied on federal banks Caixa Econômica and Banco do Brasil to promote a particular conception of citizenship and social inclusion of the poor and lower middle classes based on credit-fuelled consumption (Lavinas 2017).

This points to a related trend: a wide range of regimes have relied upon state-owned banking to engineer particular social contracts with various segments of the population, notably by facilitating the expansion of consumer debt and real estate markets. In Hungary, the nationalization of a large share of foreign-owned commercial banks, and the re-politicization of the central bank in 2014–2015 enhanced the ability of the state to contain the destabilizing effects of foreign capital inflows but also facilitated a centralization of political control over credit provision. The Hungarian state used this power to engineer a boom in construction and housing markets, to further financialize social policy, and to earmark lending to small-and-medium enterprises, in order to strike rentier bargains between state and society (Scheiring 2020; Karas 2022; Piroska 2022). Relatively similar processes took place in Turkey (Öniş and Kutlay 2021; Altınörs and Akçay 2022), as well as in Russia, where resurgent state activism has been a direct response to the fragilities of the 2000s, namely speculative patterns of cross-border finance and volatile hydrocarbon prices. A wave of renationalization and banking sector concentration facilitated the emergence of several state-controlled national champions, which allowed the state to exert considerable political control over the financial system, consolidate authoritarian tendencies, and catalyse forms of financialization that served its interests (Viktorov and Abramov 2020; Mishura and Ageeva 2022).

In advanced capitalist economies, in addition to sizable state rescue packages, bank recapitalizations, and selective industry bailouts in the aftermath of crises (which allowed politically controlling the devalorization of capital and the distribution of the costs), stabilizing state capitalist impulses manifested in particularly interesting ways in the realms of central banking. The US Federal Reserve, the European Central Bank, the Bank of England, the Bank of Japan, and others set up low or negative interest rates and implemented extraordinary monetary stimuluses to prop up the value of financial assets, preventing the collapse of financial markets, and maintaining a host of 'zombie firms' on life-support. These are firms unable to cover debt servicing costs from current profits over an extended period, and their prevalence has ratcheted-up since the 2008 crisis (Banerjee and Hofman 2018). Moreover, the stabilizing role of central banks has not been limited to crisis management and temporary dysfunction. As the critical macro-finance literature has shown, central banks have developed new and permanent instruments to maintain the plumbing of finance and guarantee cheap liquidity in noncrisis times, to accompany the institutional development and deepening of market-based financial systems. In the process they have concentrated extraordinary discretionary authority to govern in and through financial markets (Braun and Gabor 2020; Musthaq 2021; Wullweber 2021). The complex hybrid entanglements of public monetary governance and private financial market practices resulting from these transformations have become increasingly important for the reproduction of global capitalism. In short, central banks have become fundamental 'marshals of statist modalities', concentrating great powers to shape trajectories of capitalist development (Hillier 2022, 127).

'Disciplinary' State Capitalist Impulses

We call the fourth and final set of state transformations the 'disciplinary' state capitalist impulse. It encompasses a double logic. On the one hand, it refers to the disciplining of a state's own domestic social relations in line with the competitive imperatives of global capitalism. On the other, it designates muscular attempts on the part of governments to shift the burden of economic adjustment to other states, and/or to engage in aggressive forms of geopolitics which actively mobilize economic power. These two aspects of the disciplinary state capitalist impulse, the domestic and the geo-economic one, are intimately connected, both on a material and ideological level. Let us start with the second one.

Commentators have noted an increasing 'securitisation of economic policy and economisation of strategic policy' (Roberts, Choer Moraes, and Ferguson 2019), a key manifestation of which has been the 'weaponization' of economic interdependence and networks (Farrell and Newman 2019). The use of the US dollar or the SWIFT interbank messaging system to impose sanctions, and the confiscation of the foreign exchange reserves of the Afghan central bank by the US state are cases in point. More recently, the all-out financial war launched by western capitalist economies against the Russian state in retaliation for its war of aggression in Ukraine has involved freezing foreign exchange reserve assets, a ban on transactions with the Russian central bank, and exclusion from the global dollar-based clearing and settlement system. These examples are indicative of a broader trend observable over the past couple of decades in a wide range of political regimes, namely a general turn towards assertive forms of economic nationalism which collapse the distinction between economic interest and national security (Gertz and Evers 2020).

This is clearly discernible in the field of technology, where the emergence of dynamic new poles of accumulation over the past twenty years has contributed to the 'proliferation of reasonably effective national innovation systems' (Smith 2017, 286). This has intensified inter-capitalist competition in sectors close to the technological frontier, with advanced capitalist states deploying a host of offensive and defensive measures. Offensive measures have included support for the internationalization of national champions and state enterprises (facilitating foreign investment and the acquisition of foreign competitors), government procurement policies guaranteeing markets, economic diplomacy (states negotiating contracts for high tech firms and opening markets abroad), and the weaponization of cybersecurity and intellectual property law to exclude competitors. Defensive measures have encompassed the use of tariffs and government purchase bans on foreign technologies (cf. the ban on Huawei's and ZTE's technologies in Britain and the US), export controls on strategic technologies (from microchips to AI software), the reshoring of critical value chains (from critical minerals and clean energy tech to pharmaceuticals), and the deployment of foreign investment screening and merger control mechanisms giving states the power to block inward foreign investment in critical firms, technologies, and assets (on the latter, see Alami 2023, 2024).

We will discuss this escalation of both offensive and defensive measures in further detail in the next chapter, insofar as they exemplify the catalytic role of combination in the cumulative expansion of contemporary state capitalism. For now, our point is that this is not simply about inter-imperial rivalry and strategic competition between leading capitalist powers for technological supremacy and leadership in science, engineering, and high-tech manufacturing. Rather, this trend must be understood against the backdrop of the transformations in the capitalist labour process and the development of more complex constellations of international division of labour discussed earlier. These have contributed to (1) a new multipolarity of power and economic activity in the world market, underpinning a certain reshuffling of geoeconomic force fields; and (2) intensified competition in the realms of trade, investment, and technology. This has led to a profusion of neo-mercantilist policies, trade and investment restrictions, beggar-thy-neighbour measures in the realms of exchange rates and monetary policy (so-called currency wars), and other explicit attempts by states to leverage their economic positions to favour themselves over others.

Recent UNCTAD reports document many of these trends. Forty-two per cent of national investment policies adopted in 2021 introduced restrictive measures on foreign investment, which is the highest proportion ever recorded (UNCTAD 2022b, 56). This brought the total of countries conducting investment screening for 'national security' purposes to thirty-seven, including the US, Canada, France, Japan, Germany, Sweden, Spain, South Africa, Mexico, Australia, Russia, Czechia, Denmark, Slovakia, and Saudi Arabia (UNCTAD 2022b, 58). Trade restrictions also increased since 2015. While these measures have been largely at the initiative of large advanced and emerging economies, they have been implemented in every world-regions except Africa (UNCTAD 2022a). UNCTAD (2020, x-xi, xiii) expects these trends towards 'growing economic nationalism' and 'towards more interventionism, rising protectionism' amidst 'geopolitical and financial risks and continuing trade tensions' to continue in the next decade.

Far from a backlash against (neo)liberal globalization, these trends are best seen as what Kanishka Jayasuriya (2022) calls 'new modes of geo-capitalist engagement', where state power is increasingly mobilized in the political management of economic competition and geo-economic relations. These new modes of geo-capitalist engagement have been adopted in a wide range of both illiberal and nominally liberal political regimes across all continents, where they serve highly variegated social blocs and sections of capital. This diversity notwithstanding, they are often accompanied and justified by appeals to national identity and a rhetoric which portray economic competitors as threats to the sovereignty, autonomy, and integrity of the nation. Economic warfare against competitors is thus framed as an existential matter. This is particularly obvious in radical right-wing and conservative-populist regimes, which directly mobilize various forms of ethno-nationalism in economic policy narratives (think about the likes of Trump, Bolsonaro, Duterte, and Modi). This is also visible in beacons of 'progressive neoliberalism', such as 'extreme centre' governments (à la Macron) or the European Union, which mobilize notions of civilizational differences in geoeconomic competition, albeit in subtler forms than the authoritarian populist earlier mentioned.[4] Consider, for instance, the EU's 'strategic autonomy' framework, which is meant to guide as a long-term policy orientation in response to external and domestic threats. 'Strategic autonomy' effectively affirms a form of techno-nationalism allegedly grounded in 'European values' and designed to secure sovereignty, industrial leadership, and geopolitical independence in the face of internal tensions, Russian expansionism, high dependency on energy and critical raw materials, and unfair trade practices from global competitors (Lavery, McDaniel, and Schmid 2022). It plays a key role in the EU's move towards 'competitive globalism', which is an attempt to 'craft a globalization more tightly attuned to its own concerns' (Youngs and Ülgen 2022, 52).

These new modes of geo-capitalist engagement are intimately related, both materially and ideologically, to the management of social relations at home, or what we referred to earlier as the domestic dimension of the disciplinary state capitalist impulse. For example, in Germany, political struggles between various domestic segments of capital differentially exposed to world market value-disciplines (and in particular, to Chinese firms catching up and US companies forging ahead) have shaped the modalities of 'defensive-mercantilism' adopted by the German state (Germann 2022). The

[4] We borrow the expressions 'progressive neoliberalism' and 'extreme centre' from Nancy Fraser and Tariq Ali (respectively).

disciplinary impulse is not simply about reconciling divergent capitalist interests or favouring internationally connected domestic capital, it is also linked to the development of coercive and repressive forms of rule. In both the Global North and the Global South, we witnessed a move towards the more explicit use of naked state violence to suppress dissent and impose social control, as ostensibly technocratic and depoliticized modes of managing class relations have become largely ineffective, as a result of rising inequalities, political polarization, waning economic dynamism, a partial collapse of social contracts, and a general disconnection between governments and citizens (Jayasuriya 2022).

In this context, racialized calls to restore the powers of the sovereign have justified deep restructurings of the welfare state (where it still exists) and enduring austerity. Increasingly exclusionary notions of national identity and citizenship have been used to cultivate support from insiders and divide populations. Disciplinary state capitalist impulses, then, are inseparable from the recent resurfacing of national and racial hierarchy in the context of a mutating neoliberalism (Davies and Gane 2021). That said, state violence is not only directed at specific subaltern subjects (such as refugees, undocumented migrants, and racialized populations) or confined to edge spaces (the violent policing of borders, *banlieues*, ghettos, slums, *favelas*, ...), it is also ramped up across vast sections of societies. Indeed, disciplining and governing populations rendered surplus (see above) has involved transformations in state power, from aggressive border militarization, the development of AI-powered systems of mass surveillance, incarceration and social control, the criminalization and brutal repression of social movements and various forms of protest and dissent (from the *Gilets Jaunes* insurrection to the climate movement), to the suspension of the rule of law and civil liberties. These increasing difficulties for the capitalist state to sustain its liberal form, and the development of increasingly coercive and repressive forms of rule, have been captured by, among others, notions of 'global police state' (Robinson 2020), 'planetary illiberalism' (Sparke 2020), 'authoritarian neoliberalism' (Bruff and Tansel 2019), and 'neo-illiberalism' (Hendrikse 2018, 2021).[5] Although neglected by the near entire literature on state capitalism, we see these transformations in the technologies of labour containment, and particularly of surplus populations, as fundamental to contemporary state capitalism. Table 4.1 recaps our mapping of contemporary state capitalist impulses.

[5] There are reasons to believe that the intersecting crises of climate catastrophe, economic stagnation, and surplus humanity will compound the tensions at the heart of the capitalist state, resulting in an increasing inability to perform its role while sustaining its liberal form (cf. Alami, Copley, and Moraitis 2023).

Table 4.1 Mapping state capitalist impulses

	Logic	Key trends and manifestations	Main instruments and institutional forms
Productivist state capitalist impulse	Processes of state restructuring geared towards increased direct state intervention in production arrangements and the competitive dynamics of productive and extractive capital	Helping firms reach competitive positions in cutting-edge industries; assisting firms in developing and monopolizing technological capabilities; restructuring declining industries at home Fostering and supporting the internationalization of national champions; facilitating the 'strategic coupling' of firms with global value chains; opening markets abroad; building large-scale connective infrastructure to facilitate transnational integration Provision of long-term finance to support specific segments of capital; redistribution of rents from primary to secondary sector to foster industrialization	New forms of technology and innovation policies implemented by public innovation agencies; novel combinations of horizontal and vertical industrial policies; Executive planning agencies; international development agencies; national industrial strategies; national development plans; state enterprises; government procurement; credit subsidies; development and policy banks
Absorptive state capitalist impulse	State transformations oriented towards absorbing surpluses, by putting them into motion as financial capital, and facilitating their investment across sectors, assets, and geographies	Channelling surpluses to strategic sectors in order to catalyse development, economic diversification, growth, and structural change Absorption of over-accumulated capital and redirection to more economically dynamic sectors Crowding-in private capital by co-investing with international investors (including using public resources to 'de-risk'); Using public authorities to socialize 'bad' debt and economic risks	Sovereign wealth funds; strategic investment funds; state asset management companies State enterprises; policy banks; central banks

Table 4.1 *Continued*

	Logic	Key trends and manifestations	Main instruments and institutional forms
Stabilizing state capitalist impulse	State transformations aiming at propping up the value of financial assets, preventing the disorderly unfolding of crises, maintaining economic sovereignty, and preserving domestic political orders	Strengthening state control over key economic sectors and resources; distributing rents to engineer social contracts and secure political support to elite projects Mitigating externally induced financial volatility and the resource curse; smoothing fiscal revenues; counter-cyclical macroeconomic management; avoiding Bretton Woods conditionalities; bailing out financial systems and select industries; backstopping financial market liquidity	Stabilization funds; state enterprises; capital controls; 'aggressive' foreign exchange market interventions; nationalization of large chunks of banking sectors; policy and development banks; central banks
Disciplinary state capitalist impulse	State restructuring geared towards: (1) muscular forms of geopolitics, which actively mobilize economic power and attempt to shift the burden of economic adjustment to other states; (2) enhanced disciplining of a state's own working classes and surplus populations	Asserting forms of economic nationalism which collapse the distinction between economic interest and national security; trade and currency wars; defensive and offensive mercantilism Violent modes of managing class relations mobilizing naked state power; development of coercive technologies of labour containment; increasing difficulties for the capitalist state to sustain its liberal form	Trade restrictions; export controls; foreign investment screening mechanisms; weaponization of cybersecurity and intellectual property law Border militarization; AI-powered systems of mass surveillance and social control; criminalization and brutal repression of social movements; suspension of the rule of law and civil liberties

Conclusion

This chapter offered our 'first cut' at theorizing the relational properties of contemporary state capitalism, and more precisely, the interweaving of spatialized social relations underpinning and connecting the various transformations constituting state capitalism. We located the uneven and combined development of contemporary state capitalism in the historical development and geographical remaking of global capitalism. Importantly, we showed that this process of state restructuring is not merely a historically contingent form of reconstruction of the capitalist state. It is determined by secular transformations in the materiality of surplus-value production and changing forms of labour exploitation. We thus substantiated claims that the new state capitalism is *qualitatively* different from previous modalities of state capitalism. Moving beyond existing forms of periodization which emphasize cyclical temporalities (e.g., the ebb-and-flow of state intervention in response to market deepening and crises; catch-up development), our analysis traced the expanded role of the state to historically specific transformations. This is fundamental to considering present-day state capitalism in its historical fullness, that is, as a product of *determinate historical* processes rather than a merely episodic phenomenon. This also opens up space for a theoretical reflection concerning the potential mutation of the general place and role of the state in contemporary capitalism. We return to these important questions in the conclusion of this book. Moreover, we developed an account of how geo-institutional differentiation is constitutive of state capitalism as a variegated and dynamic world-historical totality. The roots of geo-institutional differentiation are to be found in the globally uneven manifestations of labour transformations, rather than in the divergence between competing national variants of capitalism.

Let us close the chapter with a few words of caution. First, although we aimed for our list of examples to be as diverse and wide-ranging as possible to illustrate the remarkably varied nature of present-day state capitalism, it is by no means exhaustive. Second, the bird's-eye view we adopted to offer a comprehensive overview of recent state transformations did not allow us to do justice to the politics of said transformations. This would have required a careful examination of their embedding in political projects and shifting class landscapes (some of which we have briefly mentioned), the support or opposition of select capital fractions and political elites, and the implications for state-business and intra-corporate dynamics. Nor could we offer an analysis of the winners and losers of these transformations, including their distributive consequences for the lives of everyday people. In short, although we focused here on historical determinations, processual analyses of the contingent, open-ended, and messy socio-political struggles shaping state capitalist trajectories are no less important. Finally, it is important not to overemphasize the durability, coherence, stability, and functionality of the four state capitalist impulses we identified in this chapter. The picture we want to give here is not one of all-powerful capitalist states unproblematically mediating capitalist transformations. On the contrary, we underline the precarious and experimental character of these state transformations, which are often riddled with policy failure and characterized by widely divergent developmental outcomes.

5 State Capitalism Begets State Capitalism

On Combination and Political Multiplicity

In this chapter, we add a second layer to our theorization of the uneven and combined development of contemporary state capitalism. Our 'first cut' theorization, developed in the previous chapter, emphasized the *uneven* in uneven and combined state capitalism. It traced the current advent of state capitalism to a deep process of state restructuring rooted in the historical development and geographical remaking of global capitalism: as they have politically mediated world-historical, but regionally uneven, capitalist mutations in value production, circulation, and distribution, states have transformed themselves and drastically expanded their role as promoter of capital accumulation, direct owner of capital, and investor-shareholder. In short, our first cut theorization firmly situated contemporary state capitalist impulses within the churn of uneven development. Our 'second cut' theorization, developed in the present chapter, will now enrich and complement this first cut, this time by focusing on the notion of combination (the *combined* in uneven and combined development), and the role it plays in the advent of contemporary state capitalism, its evolution, and its socio-spatial power geometries.

Recall that in Chapter 3, drawing on the work of contemporary theorists of uneven and combined development, we argued that the notion of combination is important insofar as it invites us to scrutinize the constitutive and catalytic role of combination and political multiplicity in the current expansion of state capitalism. Simply put, *multiple states interact with each other* as they politically mediate the churn of uneven development, and these relations and connections have causal significance. Our 'second cut' theorization therefore explores the role of combination and political multiplicity, in the context of a highly unevenly structured world market, as *constituent properties* of state capitalism. More precisely, we emphasize here the 'multiplier effect' (a term we borrow from Peck 2019a) of combination and political multiplicity as a particularly potent source of dynamism in contemporary state capitalism.

The Spectre of State Capitalism. Ilias Alami and Adam D. Dixon, Oxford University Press.
 DOI: 10.1093/9780198925224.003.0005

Our overall contention is that relational co-constitution shapes the form and outcome of emerging state capitalist landscapes. This is because the various repertoires of state intervention that make up contemporary state capitalism develop in dynamic, inter-referential, and combinatorial forms, resulting in cumulative effects, which themselves produce further extensions of state prerogatives. Indeed, a particular form of state activism in a specific location may have cascading impacts and ricocheting effects across geographic space, including in non-adjacent locations and faraway places, insofar as they spark a policy response on the part of states which are directly affected. Effects may be less direct (but no less significant) when a particular modality of state intervention in one place transforms economic conditions and sociopolitical relations elsewhere, in turn prompting other states to react to this new context by developing novel prerogatives, capacities, institutional forms, and modes of economic practice. The picture that emerges, then, is less one of a mosaic of neatly demarcated varieties of capitalism, than one of moving landscapes of state intervention that are created, constituted, and transformed over time through interconnected socio-spatial processes and interactions. We substantiate this argument by tracing three types of multiplier effect which have powerfully contributed to the cumulative unfolding of the landscapes of state capitalism: (1) competitive emulation in the context of geoeconomic and geopolitical rivalry; (2) peer group learning and mimetic behaviour; (3) enabling and mutual reinforcement. Note that they are not mutually exclusive, and in any given situation or case, they can operate simultaneously.

Geopolitically Driven Competitive Emulation in the Making of State Capitalism

Let us begin by examining mechanisms of competitive emulation and their role as an impetus in the current expansion of state capitalism. We define emulation as a process through which states monitor and scrutinize each other's policies and modes of intervention, and strategically adapt their own. This process can, in some cases, lead to the adoption of relatively similar policy designs, institutional forms, policy programmes, or modes of economic practice across states, but, more often than not, emulation reproduces considerable policy and institutional diversity over time. Thus, more than strict policy or institutional convergence, we conceive of emulation as reactive, strategic, or pre-emptive adaptation (Baybeck, Berry, and Siegel 2011). We are particularly interested in how states strategically adapt by experimenting with new modalities of state intervention, notably those identified earlier in this book: state-capital hybrids (sovereign wealth funds, state enterprises, policy and development banks, central banks) and muscular forms of statism (techno-industrial policy, spatial development strategies, economic nationalism, trade and investment restrictions).

Now, while emulation across states may be driven by a wide range of factors or motives, such as coercive donor–recipient aid relationships or collaborative policy diffusion among peers (cf. Shipan and Volden 2012; Baldwin, Carley, and Nicholson-Crotty 2019), our concern in this section is with patterns of emulation which are specifically driven by geopolitical and geoeconomic competition, or in other words, strategic policy adaptation and experimentation with new modalities of intervention in order to protect or improve existing competitive positions, or secure new competitive advantages. We are therefore interested in the specific form of policy emulation driven by what theorists of uneven and combined development, following Trotsky, call the 'whip of external necessity'. This refers to the existential imperative to grow and survive in a world capitalist economy characterized by asymmetrical geopolitical economic and military relations. The 'whip' compounds and intensifies competitive pressures and rivalry, thereby compelling states to take developmental initiatives, including in reaction to what others do (Rosenberg 2013, 196; Rolf 2021). Competitive emulation, spurred by the 'whip of external necessity', has been a powerful factor of cumulative causation in contemporary state capitalism (Alami 2023). In what follows, we explore various examples, each of them offering insights into how competitive emulation manifests in practice, and with what implications.

We have seen a multiplication of cases where states lock themselves into a pattern of escalation in offensive and defensive commercial measures, whereby the deployment of a particular policy is followed by retaliation and countermeasures in a tit-for-tat manner. The proliferation of trade and investment restrictions between the United States and China is a case in point. Starting in 2018–2019, under the Trump administration, the US slammed tariffs on more than $350 billion worth of imports from China (notably on steel, aluminium, solar panels), to which China responded by imposing tariffs on an additional $100 billion worth of US imports (Fajgelbaum et al. 2023). An agreement in January 2020 has halted further tariff hikes, but trade and investment restrictions have since then focused on the high-tech sector, in the context of ramped up competition on the future of global tech. The US banned Chinese telecommunication giants Huawei and ZTE from its 5G networks and is pressuring allies to follow suit. From October 2022, it started implementing an increasingly comprehensive set of stringent investment restrictions and export controls on advanced semiconductors and AI tech. The two most advanced Chinese semiconductor players (Yangtze Memory and Shanghai Micro) were added to the US 'entity list' (meaning that they are now subject to licence requirements for the export or transfer of specified technological items). The US also banned American citizens from working in the Chinese semiconductor sector and put in place a ban on some US tech investment in China. At the time of writing, China has retaliated by blocking corporate mergers and acquisitions involving a US semiconductor company that operates in China; it banned the purchase of microchips developed by Micron (the leading US chipmaker) in China's critical infrastructure sector; finally, it is now subjecting gallium and germanium (two rare earth metals critical for computer chips and other electronic components) to export controls, and is threatening to exercise its control over the broader mineral supply chains (Allen 2023). China is also responding by massively investing and subsidizing firms to expand the production of so-called 'legacy' chips (which are less sophisticated than advanced semiconductor technology, but remain strategically significant and central to the production of automobiles, aircraft, home appliances, broadband, consumer electronics, factory automation systems, military systems, medical devices, and green technologies), in an attempt to maintain influence on the global semiconductor sector by controlling the mature chips market (Shilov 2023; Shivakumar, Wessner, and Howell 2023). Selling these chips at a discount price could simultaneously undercut western chipmakers, and create new dependencies on components produced in China (Miller 2023).

Competitive escalation in this case has therefore led to a broadening of the repertoire of trade and investment restrictions (combining broad tariffs on a wide range of goods and surgical measures targeting chokepoints in critical value chains, including restrictions on the movement of highly skilled labour) but also to a reconfiguration of the role of the state as investor and promoter of critical science, key technologies, and strategic sectors. In addition, this competitive escalation has cascading impacts beyond the two main protagonists (the US and China): for example, Sweden has also excluded Huawei's and ZTE's technologies from its 5G networks (to which China has retaliated by imposing trade sanctions on Nokia); Japan and the Netherlands have agreed to join the US in controlling the export of advanced chipmaking machinery and equipment to China (Lewis 2023). Besides, there is evidence that the US is pressuring allies to adopt tighter foreign investment screening mechanisms to block investment from China (Chan and Meunier 2022).

Competitive emulation also manifests as state attempts to outbid each other in the support they offer to firms and industries. Here, too, we have recently seen this dynamic accelerating and reaching new highs. As briefly mentioned in a previous chapter, many western and East Asian capitalist economies are currently designing large-scale state plans to boost investment in the design and manufacturing of next-generation semiconductors within their own territory. Plans such as the European Chips Act and the UK's National Semiconductor Strategy have either been explicitly drafted, or have been significantly ramped up, in order to keep up with the 2022 US CHIPS and Science Act and with the various industrial policies deployed in China. The cases of South Korea and Japan are particularly interesting. South Korea's President Yoon Suk Yeol referred to semiconductor competition as a 'national, all-out war', and vowed in June 2023 to provide additional support to the semiconductor industry in addition to the extensive tax cuts already offered in the context of the K-Chips Act passed in March earlier this year (Lee 2023). Japan has announced a vast programme of subsidies to incentivize world industry leaders (TSMC, Micron, Samsung Electronics, Rapidus, and others) to invest in new production facilities in its territory. Moreover, the Japan Investment Corporation, a state-backed investment fund overseen by the Ministry of Economy, Trade and Industry, is now directly acquiring controlling interests in strategic firms, such as the Tokyo-based company JSR (Lewis 2023). This takeover deal is not only unprecedented because of its value ($6.4 billion), but also because it is the first time the Japan Investment Corporation is mobilized to effectively nationalize (although in a market-friendly way) a firm which controls a critical link in the global semiconductor supply chain. Compelled by the 'whip of external necessity', the Japanese state is reinventing its role as investor-shareholder and experimenting with its state-capital hybrids in new ways.

Dynamics of competitive emulation are also evident in the so-called global green subsidies race. This encompasses generous tax breaks, tax credits, loans and guarantees, technical assistance grants, local content requirements, government procurement policies, and other forms of government aid and incentives to expand the production of wind, solar, and other renewable energies, but also, increasingly, state-led investment to strengthen entire supply chains, from the extraction and processing of critical minerals to the design and manufacturing of electric vehicles, lithium-ion batteries, power storage, and other low-carbon tech (Allan, Lewis, and Oatley 2021; Thurbon, Kim, Tan, and Mathews 2023). The landmark green policy packages recently launched in the US, the 2022 Inflation Reduction Act (IRA), has been explicitly framed as an attempt to enhance competition with Chinese state-led green developmentalism. The IRA plans to spend at least $369 billion (and potentially much more, insofar as many tax credits are uncapped) on green energy and green tech investment. In conjunction with the US CHIPS and Science Act mentioned earlier (worth $52bn), and with the bipartisan Infrastructure Investment and Jobs Act ($550bn), this piece of legislation evidences a policy stance reorientation towards much more explicit and muscular forms of industrial policy, one that few had anticipated or even thought possible in the US today.

This has in turn prompted the European Union to design its own response in order to offset the IRA's potentially negative impacts on the EU economy, such as EU firms relocating to the US and further contributing to a deterioration of its techno-industrial base. The IRA poses a risk for the 'competitiveness of the European industry', declared European Commission Executive Vice President Margrethe Vestager (Allenbach-Ammann 2023). In response to the IRA, and in addition to the €503 billion that the EU already plans to spend in the context of the European Green Deal Investment Plan and NextGenerationEU programme (designed in the aftermath of the COVID-19 pandemic and Russia's invasion of Ukraine), the EU Green Deal Industrial Plan for the Net-Zero Age proposes to relax EU State Aid rules (a cornerstone of its competition policy) in order to allow EU member states more leeway in directly supporting firms and national champions, including through tax benefits and subsidies (Scheinert 2023). Overall, the EU is projected to spend €800bn on renewable energy subsidies and €35bn on clean tech manufacturing subsidies between 2022 and 2031 (Chazan, Fleming, and Inagaki 2023). The European Commission is also preparing to launch the European Sovereignty Fund, to 'preserve a European edge on critical and emerging technologies relevant to the green and digital transitions' (Bourgery-Gonse 2023). The objective of this new strategic investment fund will be to finance companies in key sectors, crowd in private investment in green tech, and help buy specific firms which, in the words of Internal Market Commissioner Thierry Breton, hold 'strategic, if not systemic, roles' in value chains (Bourgery-Gonse 2023). South Korea, too, designed a specific response to the IRA: a newly formed alliance between the state and industry leaders such as LG Energy Solutions and Samsung has pledged to invest $35 billion over the next eight years in the domestic renewable battery ecosystem; and two of its state-capital hybrids, the Export-Import Bank of Korea and the Korea Trade Insurance Corp., will offer $2.3 in loans and guarantees to battery makers (Kim, Lee, and Kim 2022). At the time of writing, Japan is currently drafting its own response under the form of a debt-financed $150-billion green subsidy package, the Green Transformation Act, with the aim of catalysing $1 trillion worth of green investment over the next ten years (Komachi, Neilson, and Voss 2023).

The digital economy is another area where patterns of competitive emulation have been particularly visible and have led to the combined expansion of state prerogatives and shifts in state-firm relations over time. The rise of the digital economy has been driven by the development of frontier technologies and by the emergence of a novel corporate form at its centre, the platform. Digital platforms, particularly the few US and Chinese giants that dominate the digital economy (Alibaba, Alphabet, Amazon, Apple, Facebook, Microsoft, Tencent and others) have been able to concentrate more and more business power (Kenney and Zysman 2016). As Rolf and Schindler argue (2023), the US and Chinese states are increasingly seeking to instrumentalize and mobilize this power in pursuit of state objectives. On the one hand, this is resulting in the growing reliance of states on platform tech and operations as a means of establishing and exercising extraterritorial economic and political power. On the other, this is deepening the dependence of tech giants on their home state institutions. Rolf and Schindler (2023) call this structural integration and interdependency between hyper-scaling platforms and geopolitical superpowers 'state-platform capitalism'.[1] The global development of state-platform capitalism is not only profoundly shaped by competitive emulation between the US and China and their state-led efforts to leap ahead in areas such as cloud computing, big data, 5G, artificial intelligence, quantum computing, and smart cities, it is also deeply structuring the trajectory of the digital economy as a whole (Rikap and Lundavll 2021).

Again, this is prompting other state actors to adapt. For instance, the European Union found itself caught between US and Chinese digital giants. Indeed, only eight out of the world's top 200 digital firms are European. Even more pointedly, none of the top fifteen digital firms are European (all of them are from the US or China) (Negreiro and Madiega 2019). The European Union increasingly sees this as a problem for industrial competitiveness and technological sovereignty and has therefore recently deployed a variety of policy measures under the umbrella of the programme A Europe fit for the Digital Age. It is using the changes to EU competition law and changes in EU state aid rules to both further regulate the tech giant and to foster the development of its own digital champions. It is also aiming at positioning itself as a leader in digital standard setting, data privacy protection, and digital governance. Furthermore, the EU has significantly scaled up its role as tech investor and innovation catalyst by expanding the prerogatives of the European Investment Fund and other state-capital hybrids in the various

[1] This, however, does not mean that the priorities and interests of states and 'their' platforms are always aligned.

segments of European venture capital markets, with the hope of favouring the growth of European frontier tech start-ups and their maturing into 'unicorns' (Mocanu and Thiemann 2023).

Finance for infrastructure development is another area where competitive emulation has led to a combined expansion of the state's role over the past few years, notably in the form of state-capital hybrids. This policy area has recently become an increasingly significant terrain and object of geopolitical and geoeconomic competition (Di Carlo and Schindler 2022). Advanced capitalist states and mid-range powers are competing to finance, build, and control connective infrastructure and, increasingly, green industrialization projects (e.g., solar, green hydrogen), in the global South (Anguelov 2021; Schindler and Kanai 2021; Hoffmann and Ergenc 2023; Reboredo and Gambino 2023; Gabor and Sylla 2023). In this context, they have launched overarching programmes and strategies, starting with China's Belt and Road Initiative (BRI). The European Union and the US are pushing for co-operation on international infrastructure projects to counter the BRI, including by spearheading the G7's Build Back Better World. Many G7 powers have also designed their own initiatives, including the UK's Global Britain, the EU's Global Gateway, and Japan's 2025 Policy Program for Promotion of Overseas Infrastructure Systems.

Perhaps more significantly, states competing in this infrastructure race have also created new dedicated state-capital hybrids and have expanded the firepower of existing ones. Under the umbrella of the BRI, China famously coordinates a range of government agencies (e.g., National Development and Reform Commission), development and policy banks (e.g., China Import–Export Bank and China Development Bank), state enterprises (e.g., China Railway International and China Machinery Engineering Company), and sovereign funds (e.g., Silk Road Fund and China Africa Development Fund), which blend development-oriented aid, grants and below-market interest loans, commercially oriented export credits, and market-based funding mechanisms (Chen 2021; Liu and Dixon 2022). Japan's strategy to finance and construct infrastructure in developing countries combines the operations of multiple state-capital hybrids, including the Japan International Cooperation Agency (in charge of official development assistance), the Japan Bank for International Cooperation (in charge of offering export credits), the Nippon Export and Investment Insurance (providing trade insurance), as well as two recently created specialized state-owned infrastructure investment funds: the Japan Overseas Infrastructure Investment Corporation for Transport and Urban Development created in 2014; and the Fund Corporation for the Overseas Development of Japan's Information and

Communication Technology, created in 2015. The EU has also reconfigured its development finance architecture to adapt to intensifying geoeconomic competition. The relation between the European Investment Bank, the European Bank for Reconstruction and Development, national development banks, and the EU Member States was repurposed to better align them with the geostrategic objectives of the EU in developing countries (Bougrea, Orbie, and Vermeiren 2022; Piroska and Schlett 2024).

Even the US, often considered to be relatively reluctant to engage in state-owned development banking, has extended the prerogatives and budget of the recently created US International Development Finance Corporation (IDFC) to compete more effectively in the infrastructure race. In January 2021, the *Financial Times* reported that the IDFC struck a deal with Ecuador that will help the country repay billions of dollars in loans to China, in exchange for excluding Chinese telecoms services and equipment providers as they build out their high-speed 5G mobile networks. The chief executive of the IDFC and the American administration have been reported to say that this could be a 'novel model', or 'template that will encourage other nations to wean themselves off Chinese debt and remove Chinese telecoms companies from their networks' (Sevastopoulo and Long 2021).

Much of this competition is indeed framed by the competing actors themselves as a clash of rival, antithetical models of infrastructure finance: a Western-led liberal model of market-based development finance allegedly promoting the rule of law, human rights, and international norms and standards, opposed to a more politicized model focusing on state-to-state loans, supposedly practised by China and non-traditional development actors. However, as we have just seen, a common trend is the increasing mobilization by all competitors of various forms of state-capital hybrids, such as strategic investment funds and state-owned banks, which are driven by both market and geopolitical logics. Furthermore, the operations of competing state-capital hybrids from both traditional and emerging actors shape each other to a considerable extent (Alami, Dixon, and Mawdsley 2021; Liu and Dixon 2022; Mawdsley and Taggart 2022; Skalamera Groce and Köstem 2023). This is particularly visible in lending and investment practices, such as the securitization of infrastructure assets, the promotion of public–private partnerships, 'de-risking' initiatives to produce 'bankable' projects and enlist private capital, the adoption of environmental targets, and so on. This is neither to downplay the very real differences in worldviews between the various actors involved, nor deep institutional diversity. Rather, competitive emulation results in the adoption of lending and investment practices and of institutional forms that are relational and mutually constituted, rather than representative of diametrically opposed models of finance for infrastructure development.

To conclude this section, let us draw a few analytical lessons from the various examples of geopolitically and geoeconomically driven competitive emulation explored so far. The 'whip of external necessity' shapes with forcefulness the evolving landscapes of state capitalism, insofar as it pushes governments to develop new forms of intervention. This is to either leap ahead, or simply keep up with what competitors are doing. By reshuffling the cards of domestic politics and by destabilizing existing institutional configurations, the 'whip' can compel intervention on the part of governments that would otherwise be disinclined or reluctant to act. This can in turn lead to the gradual normalization of some form of policy intervention previously considered illegitimate and can open space for further policy experimentation (we will come back to this important topic in Chapter 8). In addition, more often than not, state interventions rip through complex value chains, and can redirect investment and trade flows in unexpected ways, potentially compelling other states to intervene as well in order to adapt. All in all, combinatorial dynamics of emulation and escalation (whether in the form of tit-for-tat retaliation, competitive outbidding, attempts to undercut rivals, and other forms of reactive and strategic adaptation) have no doubt played a major role in countries edging towards more aggressive forms of industrial and economic nationalist policies, and in experimenting with new modalities of state-capital hybrids. Thus, these examples underline the causal significance of geopolitical and geoeconomic competition in the 'productivist' and 'disciplinary' state capitalist impulses analysed in the previous chapter, as much as they exemplify the co-evolution of repertoires of state intervention.

Peer-Group Learning and Mimetic Behaviour

Relations between the various repertoires of state intervention which make up contemporary state capitalism can also be based on less confrontational and more collaborative rationalities. In this section, we examine the diffusion and circulation of policy designs, institutional forms, policy programmes, or modes of economic practice based on patterns of peer-to-peer learning and mimetic behaviour. More precisely, this refers to states drawing inspiration from each other's actions and experiences, either informally or by establishing formal mechanisms of cooperation to produce and exchange policy knowledge, ideas, experiences, and best practices. We follow the literature on policy diffusion in establishing a distinction between policy learning and mimetic behaviour: while learning involves the adoption of a particular policy or institutional form after a thorough assessment of peers' policy decisions, objectives, and outcomes, mimetic behaviour does not imply such process of strategic diagnosis and evaluation (Shipan and Volden 2008, 2012). Mimetic behaviour can, for instance, be driven by the prevalence of policy 'fashions', 'fads', and policy paradigms (Brooks 2005). As Chwieroth (2014, 755) puts it, 'when a particular practice becomes fashionable or a fad among a relevant peer group, uncertain and rationally-bounded actors within that peer group may be more likely to adopt it'. A peer group refers to countries which currently face similar political economic challenges (Brooks and Kurtz 2012), notably due to their position in the international division of labour, and therefore can leverage this common experience. This, however, does not mean that relations between peers are necessarily horizontal or exempt from unequal power differential.

Several examples will serve to substantiate the argument that patterns of peer-to-peer learning are a potent driver of state capitalist transformations. Let us first look at cross-border finance management in developing and emerging economies. In the previous chapter, we saw that many developing and emerging economies have recently experimented with a wide range of policy tools, from various types of capital controls, stricter macroprudential regulations, foreign exchange derivatives regulations, to unconventional monetary policy tools, and aggressive foreign exchange market interventions. We interpreted this process of policy innovation and institutional development as a manifestation of a 'stabilizing' state capitalist impulse, an attempt at maintaining a modicum of stability in a context of acute macro-financial volatility. We add here that this process of policy innovation and experimentation has been shaped by peer-based learning. Such learning has happened via the formation of 'translocal networks of policy transfer, knowledge and expertise' (Peck and Theodore 2015), involving financial regulators, central bankers, and other state actors from a variety of developing and emerging economies, with the additional participation of staff from International Monetary Fund and the Bank for International Settlements, central bankers from advanced capitalist economies, private financial actors, and high-profile international economists and financial experts.

The objective of these networks is to collectively reflect on the common challenges faced by emerging markets in terms of cross-border finance management and monetary stability; to share and consolidate knowledge and expertise; to monitor, compare, and contrast policy experiences and the effectiveness of policy tools; and to promote best practices between emerging markets. These sophisticated policy-making circuits manifest as international conferences regularly organized by central banks, open channels of communication between central bankers and financial regulators, bilateral country visits, and invitations of experts from peer countries to share experiences, consult on a variety of topics, or testify before policy commissions and participate in working groups. Our own research on the management of cross-border finance in Brazil and South Africa in the post-2008 global financial crisis environment provides ample evidence for this (cf. Alami 2019). For instance, the implementation of diverse capital controls in Brazil between 2009 and late 2012 was informed by the policies deployed at the time in China, South Korea, and Taiwan. This emboldened Brazilian state managers to design ambitious policy measures (including a tax on foreign exchange derivatives to limit carry trade operations) which they themselves saw as much more interventionist than what they would normally be inclined to do. Central bankers from Chile, South Korea, India, and Brazil were invited to share their experience in South Africa in 2013, as South African policymakers were designing their own policy response to mitigate cross-border financial volatility. The South African Reserve Bank also organized an international conference in 2016 (attended by one of the authors of this book) with the specific aim to learn from other emerging markets. Central bankers from Colombia, Turkey, and India delivered presentations on the policy challenges experienced in their respective countries, and the forms of intervention deployed to address them. In sum, the increasingly institutionalized character of translocal networks of cross-border finance management has collectively enhanced state capacity for peer-based learning and policy experimentation and has favoured the diffusion of statist modalities of intervention.

Similarly dense translocal networks of policy transfer have formed over the past twenty years on the theme of sovereign wealth funds, how to integrate them into development strategies, and how to govern them. The networks involve practitioners (fund managers, investors, and policymakers) and academics (one of us, Adam Dixon, has been a long-time participant in them as an expert and associated researcher). They organize conferences, public and private discussions, working groups, the publication of briefings, and public representation and advocacy activities. For instance, the International Forum of Sovereign Wealth Funds, created in 2008, represents a group of more than thirty sovereign wealth funds. The Forum aims to encourage the adoption of good governance and accountability structures and practices (the so-called Santiago Principles); it produces research on the political economic issues sovereign funds face; it 'facilitates peer assistance and holds workshops and seminars to help members enhance their existing investment capabilities';

and it represents its members to the global financial and policy communities (we will return to the Santiago Principles in Chapters 6 and 8).[2] Just like in the case of cross-border finance management, what we see here with the International Forum of Sovereign Wealth Funds is an example of an institutionalized site of peer-to-peer learning, where the collective production of policy knowledge and practices shapes the behaviour of members. Moreover, the experience and operational knowledge developed by sovereign wealth funds can also offer models for the creation of new ones.

Consider the example of Kazakhstan's state-owned investment fund, Samruk-Kazyna. Samruk-Kazyna is a major or sole shareholder of many of the country's largest enterprises including KazMunayGas, the state-owned oil and gas company, Kazpost, the national postal operator, and Kazatomprom, one of the world's largest suppliers of uranium products for the atomic energy sector. According to data from the Sovereign Wealth Fund Institute, the value of Samruk-Kazyna's assets at the time of writing (August 2023) was $77 billion. When first established in 2008, one of its main objectives was to support the partial privatization of state-owned enterprises, but it then took on a much greater role in national economic development after the global financial crisis, and it is now embedded in *Kazakhstan 2050 Strategy*, which is Kazhakstan's national development plan. For this, Samruk-Kazyna undertook a comprehensive transformation (Samruk-Kazyna 2014). First, Samruk-Kazyna aimed to improve the performance and global competitiveness of portfolio companies by becoming a 'private-equity like owner', implementing business process re-engineering, establishing strategic key performance indicators for companies and aligning the companies' strategies with these indicators. Second, Samruk-Kazyna would become an 'active investor', restructuring its portfolio by simplifying the legal structure of portfolio companies, attracting outside investors through IPOs to provide market discipline, removing non-core business assets and social assets from the portfolio, and redefining the fund's investment strategy to turn it into a catalytic investor able to mobilize capital for new sectors and economic opportunities in support of national economic development. Third, Samruk-Kazyna would become a 'commercial strategic holding' by reforming the corporate governance of the fund and of portfolio companies, to reduce and formalize government involvement in operations and investment decision-making. Importantly for our purpose, these policy aims, governance arrangements, and investment practices were directly inspired by the aims and evolution of two East Asian strategic investment funds, Singapore's Temasek and

[2] https://www.ifswf.org/about-us

Malaysia's Khazanah (established in 1974 and 1993 respectively). These are considered mature, sophisticated, and world-renowned strategic investment funds. Both have been cornerstones of Singapore's and Malaysia's national economic development models (see Dixon 2022). This example is instructive insofar as it shows how peer-learning can contribute not only to the diffusion of a particular organizational form of state-capital hybrid (sovereign wealth funds), but also a specific way of integrating them into national development strategies and associating them with a 'developmental mindset' (Thurbon 2016).

There is evidence that similar patterns of peer learning or mimetic behaviour have played a role in the diffusion of funds elsewhere (Chwieroth 2014). For instance, witnessing the expansion of East Asian and Middle Eastern sovereign wealth funds, many states across the African continent have created their own state-sponsored funds. Africa now counts twenty-two sovereign funds, including in Senegal, Morocco, Egypt, Rwanda, Angola, Zimbabwe, Ghana, Nigeria, Namibia, Kenya, and seven are in project. In Senegal and Kenya, where we conducted research on the creation of sovereign wealth funds, planning agencies, and their embedding in national industrial strategies, our interviewees emphasized the crucial role of what they called 'benchmarks', that is, studying, comparing, and drawing lessons from policies and institutional forms deployed elsewhere, before making policy choices at home. This knowledge was developed by producing desk studies, visiting other countries, or inviting foreign experts. For instance, the *Plan Senegal Emergent*, the national development strategy currently deployed in Senegal to achieve 'emerging market' status by 2035 through a series of successive five-year plans, draws inspiration from a wide range of country experiences: for policies to manage mining and agricultural commodities, Senegalese policymakers learned from Latin American resource-rich economies; the policies concerning infrastructure development, tax and administrative reform, spatial planning, special economic zones, public-private partnerships, and sovereign funds were designed by drawing inspiration from African neighbours (Mauritius, Morocco, Ethiopia), but also Malaysia and Singapore. Similarly, Kenyan planners and policy elites consciously emulated Malaysian and Singaporean policy designs in the formulation and execution of Kenya Vision 2030, a long-term development plan to turn Kenya into a newly industrializing, middle-income country (Fourie 2014).

Other examples abound: Kazakhstan has articulated a model of development closely aligned with the East Asian experience, aiming to be the first 'Asian Snow Leopard'—a reference to the so-called 'Asian Tigers'. Over the past two decades, Rwanda has developed what Pritish Behuria (2018) calls a 'learning-oriented developmental state strategy', which has (inconsistently) emulated various institutional forms and policy designs associated with Singapore's development experience: the Rwanda Development Board was modelled on Singapore's Economic Development Board; the Rwandan financial sector was reformed to give a central role to state-capital hybrids (the Rwandan Development Bank, the Rwanda Social Security Board, and military banks), in a way that emulates the strong presence of state actors in the Singaporean financial system. More broadly, successful industrial policy intervention in East and Southeast Asia has 'inspired low-and middle-income economies to build on their experience and push industrial development through greater participation in global value chains' (UNCTAD 2018, 129). According to UNCTAD, this learning and emulation process has significantly contributed to the proliferation of industrial policies national development strategies across the Global South.

This omnipresence of East Asian late industrializers as a model and source of learning for developing countries can be explained by what theorists of uneven and combined development call the 'privilege of historic backwardness' (Rosenberg 2013, 196; Rolf 2021, 27–28). This notion refers to the fact that asynchronous national and regional development trajectories present developmental laggards (regions or states where labour productivity lags behind prevailing world-market standards) with the opportunity to adopt technologies, productive techniques, and more importantly for our purpose, policy designs and institutional forms, from more advanced poles of capitalist production. This points to the possibility of 'leapfrogging' by learning from the policy experiences of early adopters and first movers, particularly from countries who used to be peers, in the sense that they faced similar political economic challenges in the past. Clearly, by widening the gap between development trajectories, the deepening and complexification of the 'new' international division of labour described in the previous chapter has presented development laggards with additional opportunities to learn from and emulate policy designs and institutional forms designed elsewhere, notably muscular forms of statism and empowered state-capital hybrids, thereby contributing to their combined expansion.

The final case of peer-based learning and mimetic behaviour we explore in this section is in a somewhat different register but is no less significant: the global diffusion of AI-based and digital surveillance technologies, and their deployment by states for repressive purposes. This relates to what we have referred to in the previous chapter as the 'disciplinary' state capitalist impulse in its domestic dimensions, that is, the use of a range of techniques to curtail freedom, quell dissent and impose social control domestically, particularly in the context of expanding and increasingly restive relative surplus populations. This includes the deployment of digital tools and technologies enabling state-ordered censorship and information control or manipulation (e.g., content-shaping algorithms), automated espionage and surveillance systems allowing digital repression (geospatial tracking systems, CCTV equipment and face recognition capabilities, biometric identification systems, malware and spyware); laws requiring private sector tech actors to provide for hardware or software backdoor tools to access citizens' data; and institutional arrangements and policy programmes bringing these bundles of practices, technologies, and legal tools together.

Contrary to liberal narratives, the diffusion of these techniques and practices has not been limited to illiberal and autocratic regimes such as China, Russia, Iran, India, or Saudi Arabia. Rather, we have seen the increasing adoption of digital authoritarian practices across a wide range of states, including nominally liberal-democratic political systems (Luger 2020). This trend towards 'global digital authoritarianism' (see Glasius 2018; Bhorat and Rauchbauer 2023) proliferates via a range of channels, including illiberal states promoting their own brands of digital authoritarianism, and private firms from advanced capitalist economies (especially the UK, France, Germany, Italy, Sweden, and Israel) exporting their surveillance technologies around the world. More pointedly for our purpose, peer-to-peer emulation and mimetic behaviour also participate in the diffusion of the trend: as states scrutinize each other's digital authoritarian practices, what is considered necessary, permissible, and acceptable in the matter evolves, contributing to both amplifying global demand for digital tech and the growing adoption of digital authoritarian practices (Glasius 2018).

In addition, digital authoritarian practices and technologies travel via dense transnational elite networks, who are not necessarily geopolitically or ideologically likeminded (Gurol et al. 2023). These networks involve complex ecosystems of state and private actors, including national security agencies, state-owned and private firms developing military intelligence and cybersecurity tech, digital platforms, state-funded public and private research institutions, and the like. Despite the intensifying tech and 'state-platform capitalism' competition between rivals discussed earlier, these state-private elite networks feature a remarkable degree of transnational collaboration and cooperation, through the establishment of joint ventures for technological development, formal partnerships for policy design and implementation, economic agreements, the circulation of key individuals, and informal if not entirely opaque channels. As they travel through these networks, digital authoritarian practices, technologies, and their accompanying discourses and political imaginaries (fighting the 'war on terror', restoring digital sovereignty, maintaining cybersecurity, curbing crime and foreign interference, controlling 'fake news', and other legitimating tropes) are reshaped. They build upon and integrate multiple regional experiences of digitally enabled state control and repression. They make their way into even more policy areas and social spheres, from healthcare to policing, finance, welfare administration, extractive activities, airports, ports, logistical hubs, cities, and border control (Arboleda 2020; Jenss and Schuetze 2021; Bernards 2023; Bhagat and Phillips 2023; Gurol, Zumbrägel, and Demmelhuber 2023). They tend to be used to repress ever larger populations, such as when technologies developed to police borders are then used to monitor and discipline protests (Tyler 2022).

A few concrete examples will suffice to illustrate the above points. Luger (2020) offers a fascinating study of the 'worlding' of the Singaporean digital authoritarian practices aiming at curbing freedom of expression and policing cyberspaces, and especially preventing the critique of government officials. These practices are the product of a multidirectional flow of 'global bits and pieces', including local projects to govern state-society relations, legal devices inherited from British colonial rule, American-Trumpian rhetoric on 'fake news' as a method of stifling critical press, assemblages of content-shaping algorithms and profit-maximizing strategies developed US tech platforms, memes and other digital content globally produced and circulated, and authoritarian practices to protest and dissent developed in other countries, including Western liberal democracies (Luger 2020).

Likewise, the 'preventative policing system' and 'coercive internment camp system' deployed by the Chinese state to target Uyghurs and Turkic Muslims in Xinjiang is a product of geographically diverse practices and technologies. While it is often considered to be representative of both a putative Chinese model of digital authoritarianism and of a dystopian future, it is in fact built on century-old models of European settler colonialism, and counterinsurgency techniques that emerged from the United States, Israel, and Europe, but adapted to 'Chinese characteristics' (中国特色) that came from China's Maoist past' (Byler 2019, 89). Its brand of Islamophobia and counterinsurgent militarism is indeed similar to and inspired from those of post-9/11 United States and other states involved in the 'war on terror' (Brophy 2019). Furthermore, Byler (2020) shows that the comprehensive, AI-assisted biometric and digital surveillance technologies that supports the system are developed and deployed by a range of state and private actors, some of which operate well beyond China. These include foreign AI companies and universities involved in the scientific partnerships developing audio and DNA tracking capabilities, facial recognition, and heat-sensing systems, and other surveillance and data analysis applications (Franceschini and Loubere 2022). Some of these repressive techniques and technologies are then re-circulated globally: they are purchased by transnational firms such as Amazon, IBM, and Chrysler to monitor their workers, and diffused within transnational law enforcement networks, thereby influencing policing and incarceration practices worldwide (Byler 2020). The Chinese experience with tech-powered repressive practices also feeds into integrated tech solutions which are marketed globally as commodities and sold to governments. For instance, Huawei's Safe City and ZTE's Smart City tech solutions travel globally on the back of megaprojects or economic agreements between China and countries across the Global South, such as those developed under the umbrella of the Digital Silk Road. These tech solutions are present in at least twenty African countries. Importantly, they are not simply deployed and translated locally, but are shaped by African state elites and other stakeholders' specific demand for repressive and disciplinary technologies, which then feeds back into the urban surveillance techniques and solutions offered by the companies (Gagliardone 2019; Jili 2023).

All in all, the various examples explored in this section show that unpacking interrelated patterns of diffusion based on mimetic behaviour and peer-based learning is central to understanding both individual policy interventions as well as how complex global landscapes of state capitalism move and evolve over time. Diverse modalities of state-capital hybrids and statism are not simply copied and replicated by peers and emulators, they are relationally constituted as they travel across space-time, often resulting in the further extension of state intervention.

Mutually Reinforcing Trajectories

Finally, trajectories of state intervention can also mutually enable or reinforce each other. This happens when they develop in relations of complementarity or relatively stable and functional integration. These relations therefore act as a combinatory, multiplier effect in state capitalism, insofar as they facilitate the consolidation, deepening, or further extension of state prerogatives over time. As the various cases explored below show, the urban—understood not only as cities but also as extended territories of planetary urbanization and global infrastructure (Wiig and Silver 2019; Brenner 2014)—is oftentimes where state capitalist modalities touch ground and articulate to each other, where state capitalist actors meet and interact, where state spatial projects intertwine, and where various forms of state and private ownership fuse together.

Let us start with the case of the inflow of Chinese state-owned capital into diverse European economies. As geoeconomic competition has intensified, these investments have triggered increasingly defensive reactions on the part of western European states over the past few years, such as the deployment of foreign investment screening mechanisms to protect key firms, critical supply chains, and strategic technologies. Here, we see that the expansion of a particular state capitalist modality (transnational investment by Chinese state-owned enterprises and investment funds) acts as a catalyst for the development of another one (foreign investment screening mechanisms implemented on the receiving end of investment flows). The tightening of foreign investment screening mechanisms then impacts the transnational operations of Chinese state-owned capital, either because Chinese firms are forced to adapt the channels and vehicles they use to invest, or because flows are redirected towards other investment destinations. This is therefore a case where two repertoires of state intervention develop through mutual, if antagonistic, interaction.

There are also plenty of cases where the inflow of foreign state-owned capital has not triggered a backlash or negative response, but has actually been welcome and encouraged, insofar as it has served and enabled state strategies in Europe. For instance, Ward et al. (2023) demonstrate that sovereign wealth fund investment into London real estate markets must be understood as the 'strategic coupling' of intersecting state spatial projects. More precisely, they show that Qatari Investment Authority's involvement in London's Olympic Village is the relational outcome of three projects: Qatar's attempt to project power transnationally (which is itself inseparable from domestic policy objectives and regional politics, notably fraught relations with its neighbour Saudi Arabia); the British state's post-imperial global ambition of retaining its centrality in global finance; and London government authorities seeking to address the city's housing crisis by creating investment vehicles to attract foreign 'patient' state capitalist investment.

Similar strategic coupling dynamics are at play in the case of Manchester Life, a real estate development joint venture between Manchester City Council (the city's local government authority) and the Abu Dhabi United Group for Development and Investment (a private equity firm owned by Sheikh Mansour bin Zayed Al Nahyan, member of the Abu Dhabi Royal Family and Minister of Presidential Affairs for the United Arab Emirates)

(Goulding, Leaver, and Silver 2023).[3] Manchester City Life aims to finance urban development under conditions of austerity and property-led financial accumulation. The project brings together and articulates the state spatial strategies of the two leading actors involved in mutually reinforcing ways: while the Manchester City Council seeks to integrate the city into global production networks (notably by engaging in state-led gentrification policies) and engages in urban diplomacy to attract global investment, by investing in Manchester's real estate the private equity fund promotes Abu Dhabi's 'soft' power, and contributes to positioning the United Arab Emirates as a world leading exporter of real estate capital. As Goulding, Leaver, and Silver (2023) astutely put it, the city thus plays a constitutive role 'as a subject and object of new state capitalist strategy' and a site of mutually reinforcing state capitalist trajectories.[4]

The work of Sarah Hall (2021) on the presence and operations of Chinese banks in the City of London offers another case of mutually beneficial imbrication of state spatial projects, this time at the scale of the financial district. The presence of these banks is inseparable from the Chinese state's strategy of currency internationalization, and its broader attempt to improve China's position in global financial and monetary relations. The depth and liquidity of the City of London's financial markets provided Chinese state managers with an attractive opportunity for renminbi internationalization. Indeed, using London as a 'western partner of choice' served as a means to leverage its strategic position in the global financial system and to 'legitimize RMB internationalization as a policy project' (Hall 2021, 157). Moreover, positioning London as a hub for renminbi internationalization also served (geo)political ambitions on the part of the British state. It provided the City with an opportunity to develop new financial products, markets, and expertise, which helped cement its position as a leading global financial centre. It also proved crucial in the larger British state project to pivot towards China as a means to catalyse economic growth in the UK after the 2008 global financial crisis. Thus, the making of London's financial district as an offshore hub for renminbi internationalization was shaped by an interpenetration and co-development of various forms of state power, driven by their own geopolitical and geoeconomic ambitions (Hall 2021; see also Green and Gruin 2020). The

[3] Thus, strictly speaking, the fund is not state-owned, but the boundaries between state, capital, and ruling families are porous in Gulf Monarchies (Hanieh 2018). As such, Hanieh recommends avoiding overly sharp conceptual divisions between them, and proposes to conceive of 'private' Gulf capital as inclusive of state elites and ruling families (2018, 66).

[4] Koelemaij (2022) presents a wealth of examples where sovereign fund investing in real estate markets bring together strategies of 'geo-entrepreneurialism' on the part of municipal governments across the world, and the geopolitical strategies of Gulf states.

rapid deterioration of UK-Chinese relations over the past few years shows that the alignment of interests necessary to maintain this strategic coupling was highly precarious and temporary.

This, however, need not be the case, and relations of complementarity can be more stable, as evidenced in Jensen's work (2023) on the dynamic interactions between Chinese state-owned shipping enterprises and Spanish port authorities. Focusing on the relationships between the port of Valencia in Spain and the Chinese state-owned COSCO shipping group, Jensen demonstrate that while Chinese state-owned shipping enterprises and Spanish port authorities have varied political-economic strategies, these have not been mutually exclusive or incompatible. On the contrary, synergetic relations have developed between the two types of actors. Establishing new relationships with Chinese firms allows Spanish port authorities to access new capital and maximize profits. The very same relationships enhance the capacity of Chinese state-owned firms to increase market share in European shipping markets and boost their ability to integrate vertically. Both dynamics also benefit the Chinese and Spanish national states and their respective attempts at positioning themselves globally as leading logistical and industrial powers (Jensen 2023). This case is all the more interesting that it highlights the role of infrastructure as a key site and medium of strategic coupling and imbrication of state capitalist modalities.

Indeed, in post-Soviet spaces and across the Global South, the inflow of foreign state-supported or state-owned capital into large-scale infrastructure projects has enabled various forms of state agency and spatial projects. For example, the Great Stone Industrial Park, a mega-infrastructure project jointly developed by Belarus and China, permits the coupling of Chinese and Belarusian state strategies in ways through which each side expects to benefit (Liu, Dunford, and Liu 2021). The project aims to establish a high-tech industrial and export zone in Belarus, and position a new 'green' satellite city of Minsk as a hub on the Eurasian Land Bridge connecting China to the Eurasian Economic Union and the European Union. The project would allow Belarus to reduce its dependence on Russian gas and oil, develop a state-led economic diversification plan, and strengthen its integration with Eurasia and find new partners. The mega-infrastructure project thus enables the formation and alignment of interests and strategies in a complimentary manner (Liu, Dunford, and Liu 2021).

Likewise, energy and connectivity infrastructure projects in Central and Eastern Europe have been instrumental in enabling an expansion of state power, while simultaneously facilitating the accumulation of Chinese state-owned capital and China's geopolitical and geoeconomic expansion. For instance, the strategic partnership between Serbia and China, in the context of the BRI, fostered a series of legislative reforms and policy transformations that have strengthened the capacity of the Serbian state to establish BRI projects and mobilize Chinese finance for state-led industrial development (Liu 2024). Starting with the 2009 Agreement on Economic and Technical Cooperation in the Area signed between the two countries, a series of bills empowered the state to expedite state-coordinated infrastructure projects, from the selection of contractors to land expropriation, at the cost of democratic due process (Liu 2024). Relatedly, Rogers (2022) argues that inward state-owned capital investment in infrastructure has contributed to the concentration of political power and the consolidation of illiberalism in Serbia. Szabó and Jelinek (2023) show that the Belgrade–Budapest Railway (a flagship Belt and Road project in the Central and Eastern European region) is bolstering a process of state restructuring that offers the ruling Serbian and Hungarian political elites an opportunity to pursue economic nationalist policies that cater primarily to the Hungarian firms and segments of capital most tightly connected to state power.

The inflow of foreign state-owned capital can also enable increasingly assertive geopolitical stances. For the members of the '16+1' mechanism (that is, the institutional arrangement facilitating the relations between China and sixteen Central and European states), partnering with China to fund and develop state-led infrastructure projects is a means to project power regionally and globally, and increase their leverage vis-à-vis other partners, such as the European Union (Kavalski 2018). This suggests that smaller actors may be able to benefit from intensifying competition between hegemonic contenders by exercising various forms of state power and agency, but also, that the very act of 'hedging' (Kuik 2016) may be conducive to state transformations. Laos and Nepal, for example, have been able to hedge between the US, China, and powerful regional actors such as India and Vietnam who compete to finance and control infrastructure-led connectivity and integrate regional value chains on the region (Schindler, DiCarlo, and Paudel 2022). Indeed, these two low-income, landlocked countries have gained strategic importance due to their geographic location in relation to BRI corridors and other projects of territorial integration. Hedging has been predicated upon, and has fostered, a process of state restructuring, through which both states have developed enhanced capacities to mobilize foreign capital in support of ambitious state-led spatial planning strategies (Schindler, DiCarlo, and Paudel 2022; see also the diverse cases in Di Carlo and Schindler 2022).

Reciprocal dynamics between geostrategic hedging and state transformations have been at play in other countries across the developing world.

China's ambition to connect to western Europe via Central Asia has unintentionally amplified Kazakhstan's ability to hedge between great powers, notably between Russia and China, allowing it to punch above its weight in the regional economy, and bolstering its capacity to engage in state-led economic development and export diversification (Tjia 2022). Interestingly, the Kazakh state has increasingly mobilized and expanded the capacity of its various sovereign funds (including Samruk-Kazyna discussed earlier) in order to link together its geostrategic hedging and national development strategies.

The case of Senegal exemplifies how the availability of state-supported development finance from a broader range of sources has opened up space for spatialized industrial strategies centred on the state-coordinated expansion of infrastructure in smaller low-income countries. The Senegalese state has deliberately tapped into geographically diverse sources of funding, and stimulated competition between various foreign actors on the ground, to finance the Plan Senegal Emergent and dozens of large-scale infrastructure projects. It has, for instance, taken concessional loans from traditional partners such as the World Bank and the French Treasury, raised money on Eurobond markets, and taped into state-supported infrastructure finance from new partners such as China, Turkey, the UAE, South Korea, India, and Morocco. Multinational construction companies and contractors from France (Eiffage, RATP, SNCF, Bolloré Africa Logistics and others), Turkey (Summa, Limak, and Yapı Merkezi Group) and China (China Road and Bridge Corporation, China Geo-engineering Construction Overseas Corporation) have all been major actors in the execution of the Plan Senegal Emergent, building infrastructure with the support of multiple state-owned financial institutions (respectively, Proparco, BPIfrance and Agence Française de Développement; Türk EximBank; The Export-Import Bank of China).

At the same time as it has strategically mobilized foreign finance and negotiated messy relations of competition and collaboration between these foreign state and private actors, the Senegalese state has expanded its spatial planning and investment capacities, notably by creatively deploying a host of policy instruments such as specialized para-statal agencies (including the Agence pour la Promotion des Investissements et des Grands Travaux), state enterprises, policy and development banks, and sovereign funds (including the Fonds Souverain d'Investissements Stratégiques). Importantly, it has done so while maintaining a firm and unambiguous commitment to orthodox notions of competitiveness, fiscal discipline, public–private and 'de-risking' partnerships, and public sector reform in order to ameliorate the business environment and attract foreign investment. Thus, in this case as in others across the Global South, the strategic coupling of foreign state-supported development finance and spatialized industrial strategies centred on infrastructure development has not been associated with a clean break from neoliberalization logics in development. Rather, this configuration has contributed to the establishment of a field of experimentation in marketized statecraft blending public and private power, where various types of private and state-owned capital fuse in messy configurations (see, e.g., O'Sullivan and Rethel 2023). Furthermore, while these mutually reinforcing state capitalist trajectories have undoubtedly enabled various forms of state agency and more assertive state interventionism in developing and emerging economies (Jepson 2020; Kaplan 2021; Carmody and Murphy 2022; Chiyemura, Gambino, and Zajontz 2023), they have at times (unintentionally) deepened relations of hierarchical subordination and dependency. This has been the case, for instance, where the patterns of indebtedness and capital accumulation fostered by infrastructure-led development have deepened the 'malintegration' of places into the world economy (enclave-oriented development, extractivism, etc.) and reinforced internal socio-economic inequalities and uneven development (Gonzalez-Vicente 2017; Carmody, Kragelund, and Reboredo 2020; Carmody 2020; Taylor and Zajontz 2020; Zajontz 2022).

Combinatory dynamics of (foreign) state-backed capital and (local) state-led industrialization projects are increasingly at play in the area of competition for electric vehicles, transition minerals, and green energy. These are likely to profoundly shape developmental outcomes in a broad range of developing and emerging economies, particularly those strategically positioned in this competition due to factors such as natural resource endowment, favourable climatic conditions, geographic location, and existing transport infrastructure. On the African continent, countries such as South Africa, Kenya, Mauritania, Egypt, Djibouti, Tunisia, Morocco, and Namibia have become strategic players in the global race to scale up green hydrogen, and have all designed state-led plans to leverage this opportunity. In May 2022, six of them (Egypt, Kenya, Mauritania, Morocco, Namibia and South Africa) have announced the Africa Green Hydrogen Alliance, a platform bringing together African governments, the private sector, civil society, and development partners for capacity building and 'to intensify collaboration and supercharge development of green hydrogen projects on the African continent'.[5] France, Germany, Spain, the Netherlands, Italy, and

[5] Africa Green Hydrogen Alliance. (2022). Realizing Africa's green hydrogen potential through government leadership. Available at: https://gh2.org/africa-green-hydrogen-alliance-agha (last accessed 14 August 2023).

the European Union, eager to reduce dependence on Russia's oil and gas and accelerate the energy transition, have launched initiatives to support the development of green hydrogen production capacities in the region as a source of cheap and sustainable energy. This coupling of strategic initiatives from both African and European state actors is leading to mutually reinforcing, and highly diverse, configurations of state-capital hybrids and statist modalities.

Consider, for instance, the EU–Egypt Renewable Hydrogen Partnership, which brings together the climate ambitions of Egypt's Vision 2030 (Egypt's long-term national development strategy) and the green hydrogen objectives of the REPowerEU plan. In the context of this partnership, the European Bank for Reconstruction and Development is providing an $80 million equity bridge loan to Egypt Green, a company established for the purpose of developing and operating the first green hydrogen production facility in the Suez Canal Economic Zone. Hydrogen Egypt is a joint venture between: Scatec ASA (the leading Norwegian renewable power company, whose main shareholder is the Norwegian state-owned multinational energy company Equinor); Fertiglobe (one of the largest nitrogen fertilizer and ammonia producers in the Middle East and North Africa, itself a joint venture between the Abu Dhabi National Oil Company and petrochemical giant OCI); Orascom (a leading engineering and construction group in the region); and the Sovereign Fund of Egypt.[6] In Mauritania, it is via the European Investment Bank that the EU is partnering with local state and private actors to develop renewable hydrogen capacities.[7]

Namibia adopted a Green Hydrogen and Derivatives Strategy in 2022 to establish itself as a major global hydrogen producer.[8] The plan involves the construction of transport and logistics infrastructures, the development of economic corridors, and industrial capacities to produce not only green hydrogen but also to manufacture locally some of the industrial components and equipment required for its production. At the core of this strategy, the state has set up an infrastructure fund, SDG Namibia One, whose purpose is to coordinate public investment and crowd in global and local private capital in green hydrogen. SDG Namibia One has attracted both concessional and commercial funding (including from the European

[6] https://www.ebrd.com/work-with-us/projects/psd/53558.html.

[7] https://www.eib.org/en/press/all/2022-290-mauritania-and-the-eib-strengthen-renewable-energy-and-green-hydrogen-cooperation.

[8] Ministry of Mines and Energy Namibia. 2022. Namibia: Green Hydrogen and Derivatives Strategy. Available at: https://www.ensafrica.com/uploads/newsarticles/0_namibia-gh2-strategy-rev2.pdf (last accessed 14 August 2023).

Investment Bank), and it is jointly managed by the Environmental Investment Fund of Namibia (a Namibian state-owned strategic investment fund), Invest International (a Dutch state-owned impact investment and infrastructure fund, which also put €40 million in SDG Namibia One as grant funding) and Climate Fund Managers (a Dutch private asset management firm specialized in blended finance and impact investing). Institutional and private investors have already made commitments to invest in SDG Namibia One, not least Bank Windhoek, the largest Namibian bank which is owned by Capricorn Group, itself co-owned by Capricorn Investment (a Silicon Valley impact investment firm), the Government Institutions Pension Fund (the largest Namibian public pension fund), and NAM-MIC (the investment vehicle of the Mineworkers Union of Namibia), alongside smaller shareholders (Gabor and Sylla 2023). Another key actor in the national hydrogen strategy is Hyphen Hydrogen Energy, a corporate entity created to develop green energy projects and jointly managed by the German renewable company ENERTRAG and the international private equity firm Nicholas Holding, with a 24 per cent equity stake from the Namibian government (via Welwitschia Fund, the Sovereign Wealth Fund of Namibia).[9] Hyphen has signed a Memorandum of Understanding to deliver green hydrogen and ammonia to RWE (a German energy firm), Gasunie (a Dutch energy network operator), and the Port of Rotterdam Authority (Gabor and Sylla 2023).[10] Overall, then, the remarkably diverse landscape of state interventionism and state-capital hybrids that we see in this case is an outcome of the strategic coupling of Namibian, German, Dutch, and EU state-led green hydrogen strategies. To be sure, there are many reasons (astutely analysed by Gabor and Sylla) to doubt that such projects of 'de-risking developmentalism' will achieve its industrialization and developmental objectives. But it offers a clear example of state strategies and modes of intervention that are designed to be synergetic, and to further enable each other.

In sum, the various cases discussed in this section show that the complementarity between repertoires of state intervention, or their (relatively) functional integration, can themselves become a powerful factor of cumulative causation in state transformations. Trajectories of state capitalism can indeed mutually reinforce each other, therefore facilitating their consolidation and deepening over time, or enabling additional restructuring of state power.

[9] https://hyphenafrica.com/shareholders/

[10] Environmental Investment Fund of Namibia. 2023. SDG Namibia One Press Release 20 June 2023. Available at: https://www.eif.org.na/post/sdg-namibia-one-press-release-20-june-2023.

Conclusion

If our 'first cut' theorization of uneven and combined state capitalism (developed in Chapter 4) emphasized the systemic drivers and historical determinations underpinning the 'productivist', 'absorptive', 'stabilizing', and 'disciplinary' state capitalist impulses, the 'second cut' theorization developed in the present chapter introduced a richer sense of state capitalist politics, actors, interests, and strategies, notably by embracing a more explicit focus on the individual and collective agency of states and firms in the realms of geopolitics and geoeconomics. This also allowed introducing a sense of open-endedness, contingency, and a more processual understanding of the multiple trajectories that make up contemporary state capitalism. By tracing various forms of interrelations, co-evolution, and interaction between repertoires of state intervention, we showed that combination and political multiplicity forcefully shape trajectories of state transformation. An analytical focus on these relations is hence particularly useful for understanding the current rise of state capitalism as well as its *variegated*, *multilinear*, and *interactive* character.

We examined in particular three types of combinatorial mechanisms: competitive emulation in the context of geoeconomic and geopolitical rivalry; (2) peer group learning and mimetic behaviour; (3) enabling and mutual reinforcement; and we unpacked some of their catalysing effects, by looking at a wide array of examples from various places and world-regions. Of course, there are no doubt many more combinatorial mechanisms at play between different repertoires of state intervention, which perhaps have an equally potent and catalytic role in contemporary state capitalism, but our intention with this selection was to cover a wide range of relations, from confrontational, restrictive, and punitive rationalities, to self-conscious emulation, collaboration, and occasionally mutually beneficial configurations.

These relations, we argued, must be seen as constituent properties of contemporary state capitalism, insofar as they play a constitutive role in the aggregate expansion of the state's role as promoter, supervisor, and owner of capital. This compounding and multiplier effect, we have sought to capture with the aphorism (and title of this chapter) 'state capitalism begets state capitalism', as well as with the metaphor of the *spiral* (cf. Alami 2023; Alami and Dixon 2023). At the heart of contemporary state capitalism, there is a tendential dynamic which resemble the movement of a spiral.

With this metaphor, we aim to grasp how self-reinforcing state capitalist transformations unfold geographically and temporally. The movement of the spiral widens, inasmuch as state restructuring intensifies, and state-capital hybrids and muscular forms of statism proliferate across geographic space. Their dynamic interaction and combination produce further state capitalist modalities, which in turn can have cascading impacts from one place to another, as well as between policy domains (geopolitical, techno-industrial, energy, money and finance, infrastructure, development, labour, and so on), both at home and abroad. Importantly, as we hope to have shown in this chapter and the previous one, there is no single central point or axis in this spiralling movement. State capitalist impulses do not emanate and spread geographically from a unique centre. Rather, the landscapes of contemporary state capitalism are 'polycentric' (Peck 2019) and comprise multiple, spiralling trajectories which develop in parallel and at various speeds.

The metaphor of the spiral also helps us understand the temporal dimensions of state capitalist trajectories. On the one hand, these trajectories are gradual. They follow the protracted character of state restructuring, and the slow build-up and intensification of state power (after all, expanding state capacities, reconfiguring institutions, passing new laws and regulations, learning from peers, building translocal networks of policy transfer and expertise, and fine-tuning new modalities of intervention takes time). On the other hand, the gradual pace of state capitalist transformations is at times punctuated by temporal ruptures, which can be induced by violent crises, the 'whip of external necessity' (geoeconomic and geopolitical rivalry), or cumulative changes leading to tipping points. These temporal ruptures are characterized by a sudden acceleration, intensification, or a leap forward in state transformations, in a spiralling movement, such as the one we recently witnessed in areas such as techno-industrial policy and trade and investment restrictions.

Finally, the metaphor of the spiral can help us rethink the (geo)political repercussions of state capitalism for the future of the global political economy and the world order. Political economists and theorists of capitalist diversity tend to study recent and ongoing state transformations through the lenses of convergence and divergence (e.g., Milanović 2019; Boyer 2020). Their central concern is this: will national and regional political economies converge towards one or several 'models' of capitalist organization? According to the analysis and arguments developed in this book, we would argue that there is no reason to expect any pattern of institutional and political convergence (or divergence) towards one particular model of capitalism. The spiral of state capitalism leads not to the consolidation of distinct national models, but to recombinant pathways and hybrid trajectories of state transformations, which both shape and are shaped by world capitalist development. State capitalism may well continue to beget more state capitalism in the near future (we will offer a series of speculative thoughts in this in the concluding chapter of the book), but this evolutionary dynamic will continue to reproduce institutional heterogeneity in a relational and dialectical way.

6
Expropriation of Capitalist by *State* Capitalist

Centralizing Capital as State Property

This chapter goes a step further in our analysis of the morphology of contemporary state capitalism. Here we will zoom in on some of the paradigmatic organizational forms of the new state capitalism: state enterprises, sovereign funds, and other modalities of state-owed, state-sponsored, or state-controlled corporate entities. In Chapters 4 and 5, we have articulated a series of arguments about how and why states have increasingly mobilized them over the past two decades, as part of their expanded role as promoter of capital accumulation, owner of capital, and as investor-shareholder. In other words, we have so far discussed contemporary state-capital hybrids as *creatures of the state*. This chapter adopts a different yet complementary perspective. It looks at state-capital hybrids as *competitive organizations in their own right*, that is, as corporate entities facing strategic opportunities and operational dilemmas, which they address by consciously devising business strategies, sometimes in relative independence and autonomy from their state sponsors. Simply put, our account in this chapter emphasizes the *agency of state-capital hybrids as business organizations*, in order to enrich the theorization of uneven and combined state capitalism developed so far. Before we dive any further, allow us to remind the reader some of the data points mentioned earlier in this book to document the proliferation of these state-capital hybrids and the magnitude of their expansion across the world economy.

State-owned enterprises (SOEs) certainly did not wither away, as predicted by theorists of the firm and neoliberals in the 1980s–90s (cf. Peng, Bruton, Stan, and Huang 2016). On the contrary, they experienced a remarkable revival. Their share among the world's 2000 largest firms doubled to 20 per cent over the last two decades. Over the same period, the assets controlled by SOEs grew from about \$13 trillion in 2000 to \$45 trillion (equivalent to half of global GDP) (IMF 2020, 5–6). Many SOEs are in top rankings such as the Fortune Global 500. According to the OECD, half of the top ten

The Spectre of State Capitalism. Ilias Alami and Adam D. Dixon, Oxford University Press.
 DOI: 10.1093/9780198925224.003.0006

non-financial firms as measured by revenue are SOEs. In 2021, they made up 132 of the world's 500 largest companies—up from thirty-two just two decades ago.[1] UNCTAD (2019b) estimates that there are at least 1,500 state-owned *multinational* enterprises, which are SOEs that control assets or other entities in countries other than its home country. In other words, many SOEs now compete on the world market, and perform as efficiently as private capitalist firms in some sectors. These new SOEs are a highly diversified group in terms of size, complexity, structures of ownership and control, sectors of operation (including energy, mining, utilities, transportation, construction, defence, semiconductors) and the functions they perform for 'their' government. Importantly, there are new ways of governing them, which hardly resemble the 'old' model of SOE—wholly owned by the state and acting as an extension of public bureaucracy (Musacchio and Lazzarini 2014). Contemporary SOEs are often characterized by sophisticated hybrid structures of ownership, control, and management, where states own majority or minority equity positions in firms, or use golden shares that give veto rights (Cuervo-Cazurra 2018). Among the largest state enterprises, nearly 60 per cent have a mix of public and private owners (IMF 2020, 49).

Simultaneously, sovereign wealth funds (SWFs) have grown in size and number. Between 2005 and 2023, their number increased from fifty to 176. Assets under management over the same period grew to over $11.8 trillion, which is more than hedge funds and private equity firms combined.[2] Like SOEs, SWFs are a heterogeneous group, not least in terms of size. Some, like Norway Government Pension Fund Global and China Investment Corporation, control assets upwards of $1 trillion, whereas others, such as Ghana Heritage Fund or Bolivia's Fund for Productive Industrial Revolution, manage less than $1 billion. SWFs are diverse in terms of their institutional and organizational arrangements, including different missions, mandates, and investment objectives. Some are diversified portfolio investors, while others serve national industrial objectives by making investments in strategic enterprises and infrastructure projects (Dixon 2017). As intimated in previous chapters, they have become at once important components of national development plans and global financial markets, investing in some of the world's largest companies and partnering with other institutional investors.

This heterogeneity notwithstanding, these relatively new state-capital organizational forms share significant commonalities. Due to the presence of

[1] https://oecdonthelevel.com/2022/02/01/state-owned-enterprises-are-on-the-rise-should-we-worry/.

[2] https://www.swfinstitute.org/fund-rankings/sovereign-wealth-fund.

state actors, they are perceived to be vulnerable to political influence, whether such influence is effectively exercised at all. They simultaneously display an invariably profit-seeking orientation, and follow other aims and logics, such as strategic, (geo)political, and developmental objectives, or a combination thereof. As such, they manifest multiple bottom lines (Musacchio, Lazzarini, and Aguilera 2015; Haberly 2017). These new state-capital entities not only participate in what is supposedly private market activity but do so in a commercial manner. Many of these new SWFs and SOEs have purposefully adopted principles of market transparency, embraced the tools of modern financial management and shareholder value logics in the administration of state assets (Wang 2015). Managerial 'best practices' from the private sector, ranging from public listings to establishing independent expert boards, developing in-house financial skills and capabilities, and hiring professional staff from the private sector are becoming the norm (Bachher, Dixon, and Monk 2016; Clark and Monk 2017).

Given this explicitly 'commercial' conduct, we refer to these various forms of state-owned, state-sponsored, state-controlled, and state-directed capital as *marketized* and *corporatized* state-capital *hybrids*. They are *marketized* insofar as they operate in a businesslike manner and efficiently compete with private capital on the world market. They are also *corporatized* inasmuch as they constitute corporate entities with their own legal personality separate from the government, and they significantly emulate the practices and organizational goals of comparable private-sector entities. We observe, for instance, a distinctive 'organizational isomorphism' of SWFs (DiMaggio and Powell 1983) with conventional investment funds and of SOEs with investor-owned transnational corporations. We use the notion of *hybridity* to refer to the diversity in their structure of ownership (often mixing public and private ownership) (Bruton et al. 2015), in their governance and legal arrangements, but also, as we will see below, to refer to what Labban (2008) calls the growing fusion of domestic/transnational capital, financial/productive capital, and private/state capital which these corporate entities increasingly embody.

Together, these state-capital hybrids constitute a major engine of global capitalism (Haberly and Wójcik 2017; Babic, Garcia-Bernardo, and Heemskerk 2020). They are increasingly integrated with global circuits of capital, including global networks of production, trade, finance, infrastructure, and corporate ownership. Their business operations stretch across sectors and geographies, notably via practices such as foreign listing, international portfolio investment, and mergers and acquisitions. Furthermore, they come from and are present in countries across the income spectrum and from nearly all types of political regimes (IMF 2020).[3] Their growing significance as leading vehicles of economic activity across political, geographical, and ideological contexts demands reflection. How can we explain the global rise of these modern state-capital hybrids and their *organizational transformation* into more marketized, corporatized, and increasingly sophisticated and globally competitive forms? Why do they increasingly emulate the practices and organizational goals of comparable private-sector entities, adopt the techniques of modern finance, resort to mixed ownership, and extend their operations across geographic space?

The burgeoning literature on new SOEs and SWFs, which spans bodies of scholarship as diverse as international business, strategic management, international political economy, development studies, and economic geography, provides a partial answer to these questions by emphasizing factors such as the role of firm strategies, developmentalist logics, state-capitalist elites, the adoption of global norms such as shareholder value orientation, and Polanyian double movements. These explanations are valuable but incomplete. As a result of their methodological focus on individual corporate entities and/or individual nation-states, they fail to locate the rise of marketized state-capital hybrids within broader dynamics of geographically uneven capitalist development on a planetary scale (see Chapter 4). This is problematic insofar as, without an account of the capitalist imperatives and structural properties in which the above factors are embedded, the literature is unable to fully grasp their role in the transformations of state-capital hybrids into competitive marketized and globally spread organizations. Furthermore, it is unable to explain why such organizational structures have become so prevalent in aggregate, macro-terms. Without a theory of their emergence as a macro-historical process, we are left with the impression that the global rise of state-capital hybrids is largely coincidental.

In this chapter, we take a different methodological approach. Combining a historical-geographical materialist perspective on organizational change (Smith 1984/2008; Harvey 2006[1982]; Adler 2009) and economic geography theories of the firm (Schoenberger 2000, 1999; Taylor and Asheim 2001; Yeung 2017), we develop an account of the mutations in the organizational structures, capacities, and operations of state-capital hybrids grounded in material processes of capital accumulation. We conceive of the modern, marketized, globally spread state-capital hybrid as an 'organizational fix' which provides a temporary resolution to a specific set of geographical

[3] More than a third of state-owned multinationals are European (many originate from countries like France, Germany, and Italy), and about 45 per cent from developing Asian economies (UNCTAD 2019b).

contradictions, imperatives, and crisis-tendencies in the current phase of capitalist development. In Chapter 4, we showed how transformations in the planetary circuits of accumulation, and in particular, the emergence of a new constellation of divisions of labour, created the conditions for a massive round of centralization of capital as state property since the early 2000s. Building from this discussion, we argue in this chapter that the historical specificity of this process of capital centralization is that it has been *geographically dispersed.* Due to its vast financing requirements, it has also been intensely mediated by the global financial system. Our main argument is that, by participating in this process, state-capital hybrids have faced strategic and operational dilemmas, to which they have reacted with purposive organizational adaptation: in order to be able to invest across geographies and sectors, acquire target firms across borders, develop portfolio diversification strategies, and manage global operations, they developed new skills and competencies, reconfigured their internal structures and relations with other firms and financial actors, and developed more flexible and liquid forms of property in order to expand control across the planetary circuits of capital without full ownership.

The remainder of this chapter is divided in three parts. The next section critically engages with the extant literature on SOEs and SWFs, unpacking the strengths and weaknesses of the various explanations for the rise of state-capital hybrids. The section thereafter develops a theoretical framework for the study of organizational change considering the historical development and geographical remaking of global capitalism. The following section puts the framework to work and provides a geographic reconstruction of the rise of the globally spread, marketized and corporatized state-capital hybrid as an organizational fix. The final section concludes and discusses our contribution to conceptualizations and empirical investigations of the 'firm–state nexus', the burgeoning literature on the role of the state in global production and financial networks, and debates about the nature of contemporary state capitalism.

Explaining the Rise of State-Capital Hybrids

States and corporations have often acted in concert throughout the history of global capitalism. Not only are state power and capital fundamentally integrated, as has been discussed at length in debates concerning the nature of the capitalist state (Clarke 1991), states and corporations have also historically shared sovereign and commercial prerogatives (Barkan 2013). Hybrid entities blending public and private power—such as 'company-states' (e.g., the Dutch East India Company, the Royal African Company, the Hudson's Bay Company) and corporatized forms of government—have played a fundamental role in the making of global capitalism (Stern 2011). What we now recognize as a relatively strict boundary between public and private has been historically characterized by remarkable fluidity (Phillips and Sharman 2020). This is not merely to say that contemporary state-capital hybrids have many historical antecedents. This suggests that past mutations in state-capital organizational forms have gone hand in hand with processes of state transformation. Consequently, explaining the rise of contemporary state-capital hybrids, and their mutation into more marketized, corporatized, and increasingly sophisticated and globally competitive forms, requires studying how they relate to ongoing processes of state transformation.

There is a vast body of scholarship of interest here, spanning international business, strategic management, international political economy, development studies, and economic geography. The key claims as to the rise of the marketized state-capital hybrids can be grouped into four categories: explanations that underline, (1) strategic decisions at the firm-level, (2) a revival of developmentalist or state-capitalist institutional logics, (3) the role of state-capital hybrids in the preservation of political authority, or (4) a Polanyian double movement. This is a schematic categorization, and we acknowledge that there is overlap between the categories and some of the literatures therein. In what follows, we briefly review the strengths and weaknesses of these four explanations, before synthetizing them and developing our own.

Strategic Decisions at the Firm-Level

In the first category, formulated mostly within management scholarship, the rise of marketized state-capital hybrids is interpreted as a modernization process of SOEs. Organizational change is seen mainly as the result of strategic decisions at the firm-level. SOEs have gained experience from their past operations and initiated a process of corporate governance reform to address previous problems of inefficiency, poor management and performance, rent-seeking, and general principal-agent dilemmas (Musacchio and Lazzarini 2014; Cuervo-Cazurra 2018). They have adopted the practices, organizational goals, and mechanisms of monitoring and performance control of comparable private-sector entities (especially investor-owned transnational corporations) in order to motivate managers and employees with material incentives and prevent, 'the slack, waste, and, in the worst case, abuse' (Peng, Bruton, Stan, and Huang 2016, 306), which characterized (or was assumed to characterize) many of the old-style state enterprises. Modernization does not mean, however, complete separation from the state or that full privatization is an ultimate objective. Access to state power can be a source (alongside more market-based resources and capabilities) of competitive advantage, which other corporate competitors may not have. State enterprises leverage state support as a political resource and a source of strategic competencies. This is useful with respect to internationalization activities, such as FDI and mergers and acquisitions (Li, Cui, and Lu 2017).

Nonetheless, state support for international operations can be a disadvantage where it is perceived as politically motivated. Hence, the modernization process embraces professionalization and internalization of global norms, such as shareholder value. This secures legitimacy and trust of both state and market actors, while contributing, in principle, to better financial performance. This behaviour is also seen in SWFs. This is rationalized in terms of efficiency and expertise in the management and employment of state resources, but also to mitigate perceptions, domestic and foreign, that investment decision-making is driven by political considerations (see also, Aguilera, Capapé, and Santiso 2016).

In summary, the organizational isomorphism of SWFs with conventional investment funds and of SOEs with conventional transnational corporations is explained as the outcome of a strategic decision to implement corporate governance reform at the firm-level. This literature makes a valuable contribution inasmuch as it emphasizes the agency of state-capital hybrids, the variegated strategies that they deploy in a competitive market context, and the micro-level distribution of power between civil servants and managers in the firm, drawing important connections between corporate governance reform and internationalization strategies. Yet, there are three limitations to these arguments.

First, the literature does not adequately problematize the presence of the state in state-capital hybrids. The state, as such, is seen through the lens of state personnel, such as civil servants, politicians, and other state representatives acting as managers or sitting on the board of directors of SOEs and SWFs. This can be descriptively valid, yet this conceptualization fails to sufficiently problematize the relations between the new state-capital hybrids and wider transformations in state configurations, which, as we will see below, are key to understanding their contemporary rise.

Second, as Coe and Yeung (2015, 159) underline, the strategic management literature 'tends to focus more narrowly on the strategy–structure–performance of firms in global competition' and less on the capitalist imperatives and structural properties in which these are embedded. This results in an inability to account for aggregate, macro developments. Third, this is compounded by a propensity to privilege agential explanations at the expense of more systemic processes and by inattention to spatial-territorial processes beyond descriptions of firm internationalization practices. These limitations are particularly problematic from an economic geography perspective. As Maskell (2001, 338) notes, 'elements highlighted in the theory [of the firm; in this case, the state-capital hybrid] should not only be valuable when addressing issues on the level of the firm, but should be applicable and useful when studying the economic dynamics of localities, regions, nations, or continents'. Such theory should be able to 'lend itself to theoretical and empirical work on different levels of spatial aggregation' (2001, 338).

The Developmentalist and State-Capitalist Revival

The limitations of agential explanations are, to be fair, acknowledged by several contributions, which emphasize that firm strategies are embedded in broader institutional settings (Butzbach, Fuller, Schnyder, and Svystunova, 2021). Here, strategic choices are the outcome of dynamic interactions with institutions, where organizational transformation within the firm is seen as a response to institutional change at the level of the national economy (Peng, Bruton, Stan, and Huang 2016). These institutionalist approaches also explain the increasing marketization and internationalization of SOEs as a response to a series of institutional reforms, particularly in post-socialist and emerging economies, ranging from market liberalization, partial privatization, industrial restructuring, and administrative decentralization.

Mostly from international political economy, development studies, and economic geography, a complementary historical-institutionalist literature focuses on intermediate-level variables, corporatist arrangements, policy networks, and the relationships among political elites and economic groups to explain the emergence (or retention) of state-capital hybrids (see, e.g., Nölke 2014). This work is framed typically in the context of a post-Washington Consensus scepticism of neoliberal privatization and the revival of industrial policy that sees a significant role for state-capital hybrids. By reforming and strengthening the capabilities of state-capital hybrids, governments can simultaneously achieve commercial and non-commercial (developmental) objectives.

Thus, this literature sees the reinvention of state-capital hybrids as a path-dependent evolution of existing 'developmentalist' or 'state capitalist' elements in the political economy (Kim 2019a). As Nem Singh and Chen (2018, p. 1091) argue in an analysis of Chinese SOEs and resource-based SOEs from other emerging markets, 'there are many factors that influence the decision to retain SOEs and support their developmental roles—a country's model of development based on state capitalism, the strategic relevance of a sector to government policy, and the particular features of an industry'. The state fosters SOEs and national champions in the name of national development, with an aim of integrating them and/or upgrading their position in global production networks and the global technology frontier. This speaks to the 'productivist state capitalist impulse' analysed in Chapter 4. Furthermore, some governments are increasingly utilizing SWFs, specifically the development-focused variety, to improve the operational and financial performance of SOEs (Carney 2018; Braunstein 2019; Dixon 2022).

The analytical advantage of this institutionalist lens is its ability to position state-capital hybrids within broader domestic institutional constellations and developmentalist objectives. Although the appreciation of path-dependent historical process provides some explanatory purchase to the renewal of state-capital hybrids, this is incomplete. There is an element of circular reasoning in much of this literature: a decision to establish or retain SOEs or SWFs is attributed to a country's model of development based on state capitalism, while state capitalism is itself defined by the presence of state-capital hybrids. What needs explaining is assumed away.

Reinforcing Political Authority

In a related vein of research, the role of new state-capital hybrids has been seen as a preservation strategy for existing structures of political authority. At a basic level, state-capital hybrids are policy tools to manage integration in the global economy. For example, in addition to facilitating the achievement of some macroeconomic management objectives, such as providing a means of managing natural resource revenues or investing foreign exchange reserves, an SWF can also afford its sponsoring political authority political benefits. Indeed, having an accumulated global investment portfolio in a SWF and/or control over parts of the domestic economy through a strategic investment fund, the sponsoring political authority has a means of deploying economic resources to ensure support and loyalty, with the objective of securing stability of the political regime (Shih 2009; Carney 2018). This relates to the 'stabilizing state capitalist impulse' discussed in Chapter 4.

To be sure, deploying resources is a regular part of what all governments do through existing parliamentary and executive channels. But a marketized state-capital hybrid provides an additional channel with different capabilities. The SWF brings the tools and opportunities of modern finance to the state's capabilities and decision-making schema. If we take financial globalization as a constraint to policy space and policy manoeuvrability, but also an opportunity whereby states can link up with the leading edge of the global economy, the SWF (like the SOE in the productive sphere) is an access point that bridges the public–private divide. It provides access without necessitating change of the extant structure of political authority. If anything, it may enhance that political authority.

A key limitation of this literature is that it treats state-capital hybrids as mere political instruments in this power balance, with little agency of their own. Their emergence and actions are subordinated to the logics of developmentalism, state capitalism, and/or elite power reproduction. As we will see below, this is problematic insofar as state-capital hybrids are competitive entities capable of devising their own strategies and adapting to the dilemmas they face, which bears on the organizational forms they assume. Moreover, the argument for their emergence rests primarily at the level of a national social formation, resulting in difficulties explaining the *global* rise of marketized state-capital hybrids.

Polanyian Double Movements

The closest we arrive at a macro-explanation of the global rise of marketized, corporatized state-capital hybrids is literature that invokes a Polanyian double-movement logic in debates on contemporary state capitalism. Here, state-capital hybrids are policy tools to engage with the global political economy, and to tame or resist the potential negative consequences of an otherwise self-regulated market (see, e.g., Dixon and Monk 2012; Haberly 2017; Haberly and Wójcik 2017; Dolfsma and Grosman 2019). The value of this argument is the effort at theorizing state-capital hybrids beyond the national institutional setting. It also draws useful connections between the rise of state-capital hybrids and crisis-prone transformations in the world capitalist economy such as financialization and neoliberalization.

However, the explanatory power of the mechanical metaphor of the double movement, where the state intervenes to deal with the adverse consequences of a self-regulated market system, is limited. For example, Dolfsma and Grosman (2019, p. 579) note that 'state involvement is perhaps the most prominent way in which society is seen to be protected from the vagaries of market forces. The perceived inability of market systems to ensure stability and equality has led to suggestions that the movement (back) to statism is predictable, and even overdue.' There is thus a tendency to reproduce binaries (e.g., state vs market, political vs commercial), which seem ill-adapted to grasp the current rise of state-capital hybrids and their simultaneous embodiment of political and market logics. This is even more problematic that contemporary state-capital hybrids, as indicated earlier, have become key players in global market expansion. As such, the basis for the Polanyian argument, according to which state-capital hybrids manifest as a reaction to excessive market forces, seems tenuous at best.

To recap, while the extant literature put forward valuable arguments, it also falls short in several respects, as summarized in Table 6.1. Furthermore, we note that it does not address what is arguably the elephant in the room: in

Table 6.1 Explaining the contemporary rise of state-capital hybrids

Categories of argument	Key claims	Strengths	Weaknesses
Strategic decisions at firm level	Corporate governance reform and marketization as a process of modernization	Keen attention to organizational change, governance and legal arrangements, and the agency of firms	Difficulties dealing with aggregate developments
	Adoption of private sector best practices and mixed ownership to address previous problems of inefficiency, poor management and performance, rent-seeking and clientelism, principal-agency dilemmas	Link between corporate governance reform and internationalization strategies	Grounded in mainstream theories of the firm which consider state enterprises as an anomaly
	Connection to state actors as a source of strategic competencies and of competitive advantage over private firms	Micro-level distribution of power in the firm	Weak theorization of the state and tendency to aspatial forms of reasoning
The role of institutional change	Changes in state enterprises' organizational dynamics and internationalization strategies as a result of market liberalization, partial privatization, and decentralization	Focus on institutional path-dependency and on the link between firm capabilities, national institutions and developmentalist objectives	State-capital hybrids as mere instruments of states (little or no agency of their own)

Continued

Table 6.1 *Continued*

Categories of argument	Key claims	Strengths	Weaknesses
	Increasing use of SOEs and SWFs as the result of the reconfiguration of the developmental state	Link to broader reconfiguration of the forms of state action under conditions of globalization and financialization	Rise of state-capital hybrids subsumed under a broader developmentalist or state-capitalist logic
	State-capital hybrids as instruments of industrial policy and tools of engagement with the global economy	Focus on the role of SOEs and SWFs in global production and financial networks	Methodological nationalism: state-capital hybrids as primarily national creatures
The reproduction of political authority	Role of SOEs and SWFs in preserving existing structures of political order and authority	The benefits particular political and economic elites draw from state-capital hybrids	Their emergence and actions are subordinated to the logic of developmentalism, state capitalism, and/or to the logic of elite power reproduction
	State-capital hybrids as a power resource for ruling elites, and tools for domestic political survival and to enhance and project power abroad	Articulation of domestic politics and geopolitics	Difficulties explaining organizational change and aggregate developments
Polanyian double movements	State-capital hybrids as tools to tame and resist the negative consequences of the market	Effort at explaining macro-developments beyond the national institutional setting	Tendency towards mechanistic type of explanation
	The role of state-capital hybrids in the reconfiguration of economic sovereignty	Connections between the rise of state-capital hybrids and crisis-prone transformations in the world capitalist economy such as financialization and neoliberalization	Tendency to reproduce problematic binaries (e.g., state vs market, political vs commercial)

aggregate, macro-terms, the growing size and multiplication of state-capital hybrids have contributed to an historically unprecedented *centralization of capital as state property* on a global scale. As the figures mentioned in the introduction demonstrate, the sheer size of the new state-capital hybrids and the mass of capital they control is nothing short of remarkable. This significant transformation in the morphology of present-day capitalism has of course not gone unnoticed in both the academic and policy-oriented literature (see, e.g., IMF 2020), yet it has not informed theorizations of the recent rise of marketized state-capital hybrids as a new organizational form. In the remainder of this chapter, we integrate the various strands of arguments and factors identified in the literature into a coherent explanation, while addressing this significant blind spot by linking dynamics of organizational change to the self-transformation of global capitalism. For this, we need a different set of conceptual tools.

Theorizing Firms and Organizational Change in Capitalism

Theories have sought to explain organizational change in the firm by focusing on a diversity of factors, including rules and routines, transaction costs, bundles of resources, skills, and competencies, capabilities to learn, networks, discourses, sunk costs and power inequalities (see Taylor and Asheim 2001). By contrast, a historical-geographical materialist theory of organizational change posits transformations in organizational structures, capacities, and operations as being grounded in material processes of capital accumulation.

Towards a Historical-Geographical Perspective on Organizational Change

Building on Marx's insights, Harvey (2006[1982], 137) writes that both government and business have experienced 'massive organizational changes' since the birth of capitalism, and that their 'sheer scale and complexity of organization ... have changed out of all recognition in the last two hundred years'. Capitalism not only propels technological innovation (via processes of inter-capitalist competition and the compulsive logic of accumulation) but also catalyses profound transformations in the modes of organizing and governing production. Put differently, capital periodically revolutionizes the forces of production, and organizational change is a key component of this remarkable dynamism (see also Adler 2009).

Before we proceed, a caveat is in order. The notion of organizational change can cover a very wide range of processes, including transformations in ownership structures, product and market specialization, the social and technical division of labour within the firm, the geographical boundaries of the firm, power relations with partners such as suppliers, and so on. We are primarily concerned here with state-capital hybrids' organizational isomorphism with comparable private-sector entities, their transformation into more marketized, corporatized, and globally competitive forms, their adoption of the techniques of modern finance, their resort to mixed ownership, and the geographical dispersion of their economic activities.

The approach we develop is explicitly geographical insofar as we foreground the dynamic role of space in shaping firms' operations (Schoenberger 2000, 1999; Taylor and Oinas 2006; Yeung 2017; Zhang 2017). Moreover, we heed corporate geographers' advice to conceptualize firms (in our case, state-capital hybrids) as organizations with agency. Although the dynamic process of capital valorization sets limits on their behaviour, state-capital hybrids, just like any firm (and despite the presence of the state in their structure of ownership), are competitive organizations in their own right. They are not only caught up in the process of capital valorization but also act upon it. Put simply, they are not mere sites where the contradictions, imperatives, and crisis-tendencies of accumulation play out; nor are they simply tools deployed by states; they face strategic and operational dilemmas, and act accordingly, notably by devising strategies in order to seize what they perceive to be opportunities (Schoenberger 2000). As Coe and Yeung put it (2015, 125), 'strategy matters: ... in identifying the causal properties of strategy, we argue for the analytical importance of intentionality and agency in accounting for empirical outcomes ... actor-specific strategic choices lead to diverse modes of organizing global production networks ... strategy matters because it represents the purposeful response of actors to the challenges of competitive dynamics in the face of the real-world uncertainty'.

Importantly, and with some notable exceptions (see, Clark and Dear 1984), neither historical-geographical materialist perspectives on organizational change and economic geography theories of the firm are known for their sophisticated analysis of the state, which if it is recognized at all is typically seen as external to economic activity. Nor have they paid significant attention to state-capital hybrids. The explanatory model we develop below therefore aims to remedy these blind spots. We contribute to theorizing state-capital hybrids in their relation to the capitalist state and to other (privately owned) capitals. The originality of our approach resides in that we conceive of organizational change as resulting from state-capital hybrids' strategies to address operational dilemmas, thereby emphasizing their agency, which we firmly situate within broader capitalist transformations, notably concerning the state's role as owner of capital and as investor-shareholder.

The strategies pursued by state-capital hybrids are not necessarily aligned with those of 'their' state. Indeed, the relation between state-capital hybrids and their sponsors, albeit fundamentally structured by the broader role of the state in capital accumulation, is necessarily contingent and context dependent. State-capital hybrids may be more or less regulated by state apparatuses, and they are likely regulated differently at home than abroad. They may have more or less power and autonomy to pursue profit-making activities, which state actors may attempt to control where their interests are at stake (Jones and Zou 2017). We therefore cannot assume a priori that the agency of state-capital hybrids in terms of business decisions is *necessarily* different than that of comparable private-sector firms.

To theorize the ways in which organizational change results from the above process, we mobilize what Bok (2019) calls 'fix thinking' in geographical political economy. More precisely, we aim to leverage the role that the metaphor of the 'fix' can play as 'a vehicle for theory-making' (Bok 2019, 1100). Conceived as such, the 'fix' encourages us to think about organizational transformations as the search for a temporary resolution to a specific set of geographical contradictions, compulsions, and crisis-tendencies, which manifest as practical requirements and operational dilemmas for state-capital hybrids. The contradictions and imperatives, while never resolved, become expressed in organizational structures. As such, we define an *organizational fix* as purposive organizational adaptation leading to the reconfiguration of existing (and/or the production of new) juridical, institutional, governance, and territorial arrangements. 'Fix' is conceived here in the metaphorical sense, in that the organizational fix is always precarious, partial, and unstable. It is also conceived in a more literal sense, in that capitalist contradictions and imperatives are temporarily displaced in space and time by means of restructuring organizational structures, capacities, and operations. We also draw attention to the role of cultural and political discourses, meanings, values, and semiosis in the development of a fix, which we call 'the politics of representation' of the contemporary state-capital hybrid, following previous theoretical elaborations (MacLeod 2001; Sum and Jessop 2013). Our explanatory model is represented visually in Figure 6.1.

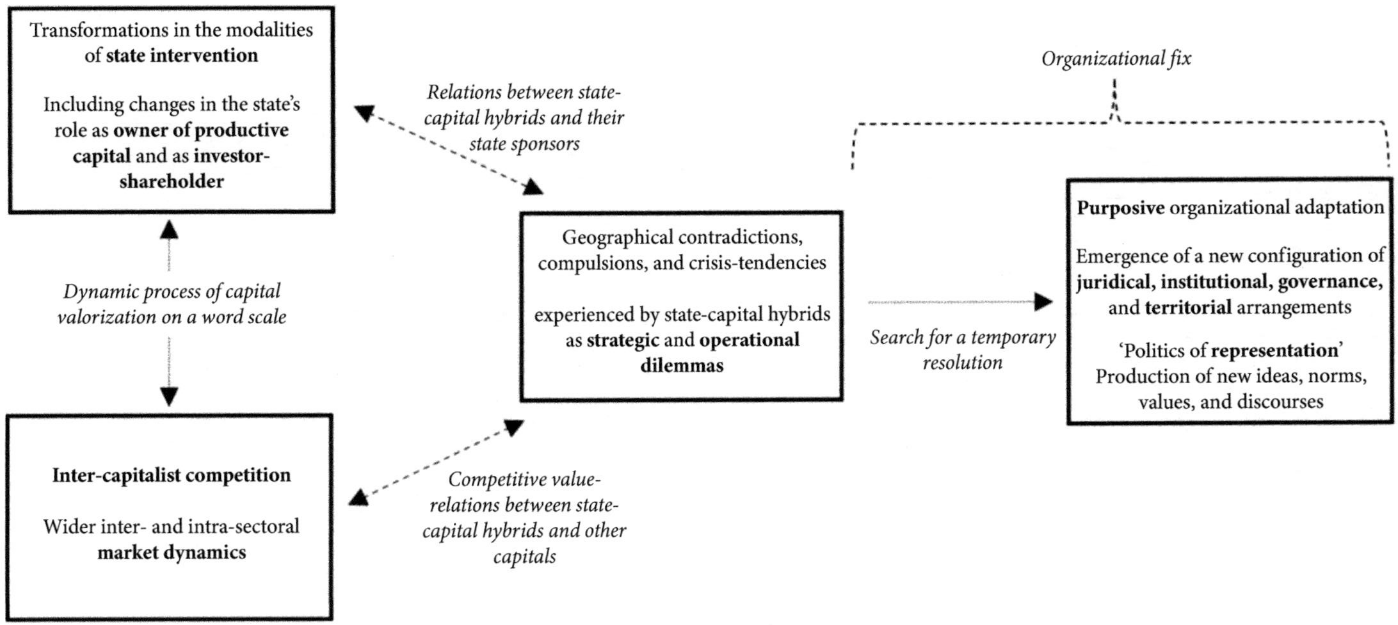

Figure 6.1 Explanatory model of organizational change

Thus, we conceive of the recent transformation of state-capital hybrids into more marketized, corporatized, and increasingly geographically spread entities as the ongoing search for an organizational fix. What, then, are the capitalist contradictions, imperatives, and crisis-tendencies that this fix seeks to negotiate? What does this tell us about the nature of the fix and the conditions of its emergence?

Centralization of Capital and Organizational Change

As aforementioned, modern state-capital hybrids have been implicated in an historically unprecedented round of centralization of capital. This is a good place to start answering the above questions because the contradictory tendencies of centralization/decentralization and concentration/fragmentation are major drivers of organizational change (Marx 1867/1991; Smith 1984/2008; Harvey 2006[1982]). Let us briefly explain why.

First, we must establish a distinction between centralization and concentration of capital. Concentration (or what Marx calls 'accumulation proper') refers to individual capitals growing by accumulating more capital, that is, by reinvesting and putting into motion increasing quantities of surplus value as capital (Marx 1867/1991; Smith 1984/2008, 161). This results in an increase in total social capital, which is the magnitude of capital in circulation (the contradictory unity of all individual capitals, including state-owned capitals). By contrast, centralization is a process of redistribution of ownership and control of existing capital in fewer hands, rather than investment in new capital outlays. Insofar as it consists in the combination of previously independent capitals into a single one, centralization does not contribute to an increase of total social capital. As Marx puts it, 'Capital grows to a huge mass in a single hand in one place, because it has been lost by many in another place. This is centralization proper, as distinct from accumulation and concentration' (Marx 1867/1991, 777). Marx also refers to this as 'expropriation of capitalist by capitalist' (Marx 1867/1991, 777). Centralization, often directly through a merger or takeover, or indirectly through the credit system, is 'thus simultaneously the destruction of one capital and the surge in valorization of another' (Smith 1984/2008, 162, 163). Note that centralization does not necessarily imply physical location. Centralization is above all a *social* process 'according to which individual units of capital come to control larger and larger quantities of capital' (Smith 1984/2008, 160). As such, it can take a range of spatial forms, as we discuss below.

Both tendencies (concentration and centralization) and their counter-tendencies (fragmentation and decentralization) are directly given in the form of capital (Harvey 2006[1982]). Concentration and centralization are centripetal forces catalysed by the immanent drive to expand control over production, achieve economies of scale and scope (to increase labour productivity and lower production costs), raise the mass of capital in circulation, and concentrate market power. Fragmentation and decentralization are centrifugal forces driven by, among other things, the need to reduce the costs of coordinating production, which tend to increase as capitals grow in scope and scale of operations. These tendencies form a contradictory unity which is mediated by inter-capitalist competition but also by the state. The latter may sanction, supervise, or indeed encourage the centralization of capital, or on the contrary, it may force decentralization via laws and regulations such as antitrust and anti-monopoly legislations (Christophers 2016). The dialectical movement of this contradictory unity stimulates organizational change, and the organizational fixes that emerge constitute variegated ways to negotiate its contradictions in space.

Equipped with this conceptual apparatus, we can now turn to an examination of the rise of the marketized state-capital hybrid.

The Emergence of the Marketized State-Capital Hybrid as an Organizational Fix

Recall that, in Chapter 4, we located the dramatic *expansion of state ownership* (the role of states as owners of capital and as investor-shareholders) in the historical development and geographical remaking of global capitalism. More precisely, we emphasized two world-historical economic mutations, both of which stem from determinate material transformations in the capitalist labour process and changing forms of labour exploitation: one the one hand, the emergence of a more complex constellation of 'old' and 'new' international divisions of labour; and on the other, deep-seated tendencies towards economic stagnation and industrial overcapacity. We showed that these two tendencies have had multifaceted ramifications in terms of the temporal and geographical dynamics of value production, circulation, and distribution, which created the conditions for a massive *expansion of capital as state property* (the mass of capital and assets owned or controlled by states) since the early 2000s. We now turn our attention to the concrete dynamics of capital centralization which have developed out of this expansion of state property, to explain the concrete organizational forms that this process has taken.

Social and Spatial Patterns of Centralization of Capital as State Property

As argued earlier, state-capital hybrids are competitive economic entities. They engage in competitive value-relations with other capitals in the context of wider inter- and intra-sectoral market dynamics and the valorization of capital as a whole. As such, they face strategic and operational dilemmas and devise strategies to address them, including those that stem from centralization/decentralization tendencies. Consequently, to gain a better understanding of the historically specific social and spatial forms taken by the recent massive centralization of capital as state property (and, ultimately, explain organizational change), we must examine state-capital hybrids' strategic motives and the modalities of their participation in this process. In what follows, we therefore complement the state-oriented perspective adopted in Chapters 4 and 5, with one that focuses on the agency of state-capital hybrids as competitive entities in themselves, as capitals which valorize.

Let us note from the outset that the economic sectors most concerned by centralization were, unsurprisingly, those most fundamentally affected by the unfolding of the constellation of old and new international divisions of labour discussed in Chapter 4, notably: food and agro-chemicals (Belesky and Lawrence 2019), energy, hydrocarbons, and mining (Bridge and Bradshaw 2017; Lim 2018; Nem Singh, and Chen 2018), infrastructure construction and telecom (Florio, Ferraris, and Vandone 2018); aluminium, steel, semiconductors, and high tech (IMF 2020), and financial services (to which we reprise below). Resultingly, these sectors have all become extremely concentrated (i.e., dominated by a few powerful actors), and this even more so that they are highly capital intensive and therefore inherently prone to oligopoly. While the precise strategic motives for centralization have differed across sectors and geographies, it is possible to identify commonalities in their drivers, with important implications for understanding the macro-aggregate dynamic of centralization and its spatial and organizational forms.

One of the common strategic drivers of participation of state-capital hybrids in the centralization of capital has been the *geographical expansion of control over resources and markets*. SOEs, notably in food, agro-chemicals, energy, hydrocarbons, and mining sought to acquire other firms in order to secure independent and geographically diverse supplies of raw materials, or to allow for a more rapid expansion in the scale and scope of production. Examples include the merger of two massive Chinese state-run chemical groups Sinochem and ChemChina (with a combined asset value of $245 billion) and their high-profile acquisition of Syngenta, the Switzerland-based global chemical crop, fertilizers, and pesticides producer.[4] Japan Tobacco (a public company where the Japanese government owns one-third of the shares) facing market saturation and aggressive competition at home started a strategy of global expansion in the early 2000s. The takeover of transnational tobacco corporations, such as US-based RJ Reynolds and UK-based Gallaher, and the acquisition of flagship international brands and distributors, allowed access to large markets in North America, western Europe, and former Soviet Union countries, particularly Russia, as well as penetration in fast-growing markets in the Middle East, North Africa, Asia, and Africa. It also seeks to secure tobacco leaf at lower price by investing in leaf growers in African countries (MacKenzie, Eckhardt, and Widyati Prastyani 2017).

Examples abound in the oil and gas sector. In a bid to remain globally competitive, Petrobras expanded its geographical operations (notably in the Southern Cone and advanced capitalist economies) seeking to enter new markets and acquire strategic assets to become a vertically integrated energy company. Russia's Gazprom and Lukoil, Thailand's PTT, Malaysia's Petronas, and Indonesia's Petramina similarly all expanded their global operations to acquire key assets and secure long-term energy supplies. China's CNOOC acquired Canada-based Nexen, allowing it to secure oil from geographical sources across four continents and to diversify its international portfolio into oil sands and shale gas (Lim 2018).

Other SOEs, in sectors such as power generation and manufacturing, sought to gain access to productive capacity abroad unavailable in their domestic economy, by acquiring strategic firms for their technologies, intellectual property, technical skills, or operational know-how. Here, we can cite the hotly debated case of Chinese state-capital hybrids seeking to acquire small-and-medium enterprises in advanced manufacturing and high-tech sectors in western Europe, such as German producers of industrial robots, or chipmakers in the UK and elsewhere. Another less conspicuous but equally significant example is that of Leonardo (partially owned by the Italian state) which grew to become one of the world's largest arms and defence manufacturers by acquiring smaller firms in aerospace and electrical equipment, taking participations in other large European consortiums such as Avions de Transport Régional and Eurofighter, and engaging in joint ventures with other partially owned state-capital hybrids such as Thalès.

Both logics of geographical expansion of control over resources were driven by the need to address a rapidly growing demand (at least until the

[4] https://www.spglobal.com/platts/en/market-insights/latest-news/oil/041321-analysis-sinochem-chemchina-merger-to-bring-flexibility-to-oil-business-expand-in-chemicals [accessed 17 August 2023].

commodity super-cycle came to an end circa 2014), but also to cope with more structural concerns of industrial overcapacity and market saturation (notably in sectors such as aluminium, steel, and semiconductors) which became even more visible at the end of the commodity boom (IMF 2020). As we saw in Chapter 4, overcapacity and market saturation result in intensifying global competition (Brenner 2006), and it becomes easier to grow and sustain profitability rates by acquiring other capitals than by *accumulation proper*.

This leads us to logics of geographical expansion geared towards market access and control. SOEs have acquired competitors to expand their geographical reach (and gain access to new markets, notably in sectors such as large-scale infrastructure construction, transports, logistics, telecoms, and other network industries where questions of geographic range are key) and to strengthen competitive market positions. Prominent examples include the expansion of French and German SOEs in the British railway sector (respectively, SNCF and Deutsche Bahn) and in the electricity sector, where EDF and E.On acquired British Energy and Powergen respectively. Telefónica (where the Spanish state holds a golden share) expanded across Europe and the Americas. Vattenfall (fully state-owned by the Swedish state) has become the major foreign player on the German electricity market and is active across Northern Europe.

Finally, capital centralization has also been driven by three other strategies on the part of state-capital hybrids. First, the *redeployment of capital into more profitable sectors or with better growth potential*. An example is Norwegian oil producer Equinor, formerly Statoil, which recently acquired solar energy producer Scatec Solar, Danish power and gas trading firm Danske Commodities, and Polish onshore renewable energy developer Wento, as part of its strategy to grow exposure to fast-growing alternative energy sectors. Equinor is also investing in hydrogen power in the Netherlands and northern England and created a venture capital fund to invest in low carbon energy technologies. ENI, where the Italian government owns a golden share, follows a similar strategy (Asmelash and Gorini 2021).

Second, state-capital hybrids have developed *cross-ownership to expand control in a network-like manner* and reinforce relationship with key firms (such as strategic suppliers) or related sectors. For instance, the Chinese State-owned Assets Supervision and Administration Commission (SASAC), credited to be the largest economic entity in the world, is the sole shareholder of ninety-six parent holding companies, each of them owning multiple shares of downstream subsidiaries, and serving as an intermediary between SASAC and other group member firms. 'A single SOE business group under SASAC's supervision may have a labyrinthine network of hundreds of subsidiaries, several of which may be linked through equity ownership to firms in other SOE business group', many of which are listed on a stock exchange in mainland China and often cross-listed in Hong Kong or a foreign stock exchange (Milhaupt 2020, 366).

Third, state-capital hybrids have deployed strategies of *risk management by means of geographic and sectoral diversification*. The case of Japanese Tobacco mentioned above is illustrative insofar as it diversified in food, pharmaceuticals, and vaping technologies by acquiring European firms. SWFs are investing in sectors as diverse as real estate and property (notably in world financial centres such as London and New York), finance and insurance, trade and retail, sports (football clubs), media, advanced manufacturing, and high tech in North America and western Europe (Babic 2021). A telling example is the Saudi SWF Public Investment Fund, which invests internationally in various sectors and asset classes in pursuit of higher returns and key technologies and knowledge. It partners with diverse global investors such as SoftBank Vision Fund (notably to invest in high tech), with American asset manager Blackstone (to invest in US infrastructure), with French private equity managers, as well as with other state-capital hybrids (such as the Russian Direct Investment Fund). The 2008 global financial crisis, the COVID-19 pandemic, and associated market turmoil presented opportunities for state-capital hybrids to scale up these strategies by taking stakes in distressed firms and assets. SWFs, for instance, bailed out automobile sectors in Germany and France, and overexposed financial institutions such as Citigroup or Merrill Lynch in the United States (Haberly 2014; Thatcher and Vlandas 2022). In the aftermath of Russia's invasion of Ukraine, SWFs from oil exporting Middle Eastern countries, particularly the UAE and Saudi Arabia have taken advantage of massive capital injections derived from soaring oil and gas revenues, and have massively invested in infrastructure, software, and generative AI globally. They are also purchasing large quantities of high-performance semiconductors from Nvidia and other top chipmakers and offering generous pay packages to attract AI engineers and software developers from around the world (particularly from China) to support their AI development efforts and ambitions.

These various strategies of geographical expansion have unfolded across territorial borders, with state-capital hybrids either acquiring firms (via total acquisition, majority acquisition, or acquisition by majority share) or buying shares in firms based in other countries (Florio, Ferraris, and Vandone 2018). Moreover, the target firms have been disproportionately privately owned. While this is self-evident in the case of portfolio diversification strategies (which are about the holding of assets with different risk/reward ratios across geographies), this has also been the case for mergers and acquisitions (M&As). For instance, between 2002 and 2012, in 75 per cent of the M&A deals where the acquirer was an SOE, the target firm was privately owned (Florio, Ferraris, and Vandone 2018, 144, 147). Put differently, the recent centralization of capital as state property is not simply a process whereby state-capital hybrids have absorbed each other, thereby redistributing ownership and control of existing state-owned capital in fewer (state) hands. Rather, there has been a net increase in the magnitude of total social capital owned or controlled by states. To paraphrase Marx's expression introduced earlier, this is 'expropriation of capitalist by *state* capitalist'. The result is a growing fusion of domestic/transnational capital, financial/productive capital, and private/state capital (under the aegis of the latter) (Labban 2008).

Examining these various strategic motives for geographical expansion has allowed us to specify the key spatial contours of the centralization of capital as state property which has unfolded since the early 2000s. We can now explain some of the organizational transformations which state-capital hybrids have undergone as a result of this process. Our key contention is that a particular set of juridical, institutional, corporate governance, and territorial arrangements, or what we have referred to earlier as an organizational fix, has emerged to address the structural imperatives of what is effectively *a highly geographically dispersed form of centralization of capital as state property*. From the perspective of state-capital hybrids, these structural imperatives have manifested as practical requirements and operational dilemmas, to which state-capital hybrids have reacted with purposive organizational adaptation.

This explains why, among the various modalities of transnationalization that could facilitate the global dispersion of the economic activities of state-capital hybrids (e.g., strategic alliances, joint ventures, and so on), the preferred techniques have been cross-border M&As and international portfolio investment, despite adverse market reactions (Florio, Ferraris, and Vandone 2018). This is because they enable a transnational redistribution of ownership and control, which in turn allows state-capital hybrids to control larger and larger quantities of capital across geographic space. This also explains why they have become more globally competitive. At the scale of individual state-capital hybrids, the transnational absorption of competitors allows consolidating globally competitive market positions. At the aggregate level, a larger magnitude of total social capital is now owned or controlled by state-capital hybrids.

These dynamics have also required certain transformations in the internal organizational structures, capacities, and operations of state-capital hybrids, such as the hiring of professional staff from financial firms or transnational corporations, the development of in-house financial skills and managerial capabilities. These were fundamentally driven by the need for state-capital hybrids to strategically address specific operational dilemmas faced by virtue of their participation in the highly geographically dispersed form of capital centralization, including: investing across geographies and sectors, identifying target firms and closing cross-border M&A deals, developing international portfolio diversification strategies, and managing global operations. These require developing new competencies (such as risk management and business valuation) and relationships with a broader range of service providers (such as financial services firms), gaining access to infrastructures such as stock exchanges, reorganizing internal operations, governance structures, and the like. As such, *pace* the extant literature, these transformations are not merely the result of the adoption of shareholder value orientation and other financial(ized) norms and practices. Nor are they simply motivated by the belief that embracing private sector practices would deliver better performance. The role of these ideas and norms is undoubtedly important—notably in their cultural, ideological, and discursive dimensions, as we discuss below. However, we argue that what explains their recent adoption is that they found resonance with the set of practical requirements and operational dilemmas rooted in the highly geographically dispersed form of capital centralization. Succinctly put, the convergence of the practices and organizational goals of state-capital hybrids with comparable private-sector entities must be understood in terms of purposive organizational adaptation to this material process.

To further unpack these dynamics of organizational change, notably the increasing resort to mixed public-private ownership, we must now turn to the financial system, which has fundamentally shaped the process of capital centralization.

The Role of the Financial System as a 'Lever' of Centralization

The financial system is a major lever of capital centralization and organizational change. Marx calls it a 'terrible weapon in the battle of competition and … an enormous social mechanism for the centralization of capitals' (Marx 1867/1991, 778). He writes that the financial system allows 'absolute control within certain limits over the capital and property of others.... Success and failure both lead here to a centralization of capital, and thus to expropriation on the most enormous scale' (Marx 1894/1991, 570). Marx (1894/1991, 512–514, 570–573) connects this process to the emergence of the joint-stock company as a new form of organizing production, hence drawing an explicit link between the financial system as a lever of centralization and organizational change. The financial system is crucial insofar as 'the centralization of capital depends on its availability in money form' (Labban 2008, 62) and because it enables the separation of ownership and control of capital. Our argument is that the forms taken by both aspects during the recent round of capital centralization have had implications for the organizational transformations of contemporary state-capital hybrids.

Implicit from our account so far is how the massive centralization of capital as state property has been intensely mediated by the global financial system. We mentioned that many contemporary state-capital hybrids now either directly participate in the global financial system by investing in other firms and/or by issuing and publicly listing shares, and how this has contributed to both the centralization of money capital and assets, and the centralization of productive capital though financial means. We also indicated that low-cost borrowing from global financial markets was instrumental in the expansion of state-capital hybrids, notably during the commodity boom. We may add that the post-2008 financial crisis and post pandemic policies aiming at preventing the destruction of fictitious value (including Quantitative Easing and other forms of unconventional monetary policy) provided vast amounts of cheap liquidity that state-capital hybrids could tap into.

The highly geographically dispersed process of capital centralization discussed earlier has required extremely vast financing needs, which state-capital hybrids often could not meet with the mass of capital they possessed. Consequently, they resorted to global finance in order to acquire (or take stakes in) other firms. This took the form of loans (from domestic and transnational banks) and public offerings (listing a portion of shares on stock exchanges). The latter is particularly interesting for our purpose, insofar as it has involved a turn to mixed forms of public–private ownership. This type of private capital injection is often explained in the literature as a strategic means to improve corporate performance (Milhaupt and Pargendler 2017). There is also little doubt that beliefs in the superiority of the private sector have penetrated the corporate culture of many state-capital hybrids, thereby contributing to the spread of mixed public–private ownership.

Our approach, however, suggests a different explanation: the growing resort to partial state ownership (states owning majority or minority equity positions, or using golden shares to retain veto rights) constitutes an organizational fix to address the contradiction between direct full state ownership and the need to establish 'control over greater geographical space and masses of capital', as Mazen Labban (2008, 60) astutely puts it. Public offerings enable state-capital hybrids to deploy more capital than they possess, while retaining a degree of control (2008, 60). Cross-listing (listing on more than one stock exchange, with the second listing often in another country than the one of incorporation) allows accessing an even larger investor base and facilitates foreign acquisitions. As such, it enables a networked form of expansion across the world capitalist economy. In short, the growing resort to mixed public–private ownership emerged as means to overcome the limitations of full state ownership, insofar as the latter constitutes an obstacle to the highly dispersed centralization of capital that has taken place. It is *a juridical form of ownership more adequate to the development of flexible and liquid forms of state property* increasingly integrated into the global circuits of capital.

We now turn to the impact of ideas and norms in organizational change, or what we have referred to earlier as the 'politics of representation' of the marketized state-capital hybrids. These politics involve the production of ideas, norms, values, and discourses concerning the perception of state-capital hybrids (especially when they originate from a foreign country), the definition of 'best practices' for governing them, the establishment of norms and criteria of 'good conduct' for investing state resources, and the distinction between what are considered market-oriented activities (versus politically driven ones). Our main argument here is that these politics of representation of the fix have been fundamentally shaped by the ways in which state-capital hybrids have been rendered amenable to the institutional, cultural, and social norms of neoliberalized global finance, and vice versa.

As indicated earlier, the literature provides a partial treatment of these issues, emphasizing that state-capital hybrids and their sponsoring states have developed strategies to be perceived as legitimate and responsible market actors. For instance, to address anxiety on the part of state and market participants, notably in the West, SWFs have adopted the Santiago Principles, the shorthand name for the Generally Accepted Principles and Practices for Sovereign Wealth Funds. We mentioned the Santiago Principles in the previous chapter when we discussed emulation between SWFs. These principles, inspired from the conventional Western model practised by cognate institutional investors such as supplementary occupational pension funds, are designed to demonstrate good governance, transparency, and disclosure (Clark and Dixon 2017). This illustrates that the international financial community plays a crucial role in the politics of representation of the fix, and that state-capital hybrids must engage with such politics as a *condition of participation in global financial markets.*

We complement this argument in two significant ways. First, we stress that state-capital hybrids are not passive norm-takers. For example, if adopting some of the institutional, cultural, and social norms of neoliberalized global finance may indeed result in deep corporate restructuring, we can also envisage scenarios where state-capital hybrids strategically use the jargon of shareholder value and other financial(ized) discourses in order to discursively reframe their existing operations and mandates, without necessarily restructuring them. (In fact, there is evidence that the Santiago Principles may be something of an in-between of these two scenarios).

Second, global finance does not constitute a monolithic force in the politics of representation of contemporary state-capital hybrids. Various interests are at stake. Global financial professionals such as investment bankers and corporate lawyers, looking to profit from the lucrative market of rapidly expanding transnational state-capital hybrids, have a vested interest in normalizing their status as legitimate financial market actors through technocratic, expert-driven practice (Liu and Dixon 2021). By contrast, multilateral financial institutions such as the International Monetary Fund and the World Bank have primarily been concerned with controlling the proliferation of state-capital hybrids (especially those from southern countries), ensuring that they assume liberal forms and that their increasing cross-border activities create the fewest frictions possible in the global circuits of trade, production, and finance (we will discuss this at length in chapter 8). As such, they have sought to present themselves as centres of knowledge, technical expertise, and self-endorsed authority to assist in the reform and marketization of state-capital hybrids. Other coalitions of Western and business state actors have sought to cast doubt on the legitimacy of non-Western state-capital hybrids, in the context of geopolitical competition with China and other emerging capitalist economies (see Chapter 7). As Ruben Gonzalez-Vicente perceptively notes (in Alami, Dixon, Gonzalez-Vicente, et al. 2022, 1000), the growth of state-capital hybrids from these economies 'creates new poles of competitiveness and accumulation' and introduces emerging capitalist classes and fractions of capital into the competitive world market, challenging pre-established market hierarchies and the hegemony of traditional actors.

These examples tell us that the politics of representation of the fix are determined by a much wider field of struggles and relations than is commonly acknowledged in the literature. These struggles are neither contained within the boundaries of the state-capital hybrid (as the focus of the management literature on principal-agent problems suggests), nor within national social formations (as the literature on the reproduction of political authority argues). These politics also cannot be reduced to the financialization of state ownership. Rather, we submit that the flexible and strategic adoption of the institutional, cultural, and social norms of neoliberalized global finance is a means by which state-capital hybrids attempt to negotiate a wide range of conflictual relations, including antagonisms between and within various segments of capital, intra-capitalist class struggles, North/South geopolitical relations, and great power competition between hegemonic contenders. These relations therefore shape the cultural, normative, and ideological dimensions of the marketized state-capital hybrid as an organizational fix.

Conclusion

SOEs, SWFs, and other forms of state-capital hybrids have become major engines of global capitalism, which makes them a compelling area of empirical and theoretical study. They are also often considered to be the paradigmatic organizational forms of the new state capitalism. In this chapter, we set out to answer the following questions: How can we explain their global advent and their organizational transformation into more marketized, corporatized, and increasingly sophisticated and globally competitive forms? Why do they increasingly emulate the practices and organizational goals of comparable private-sector entities, adopt the techniques of modern finance, resort to mixed ownership, and extend their operations across geographic space?

To answer these questions, we developed an explanatory model of organizational change grounded in historical-geographical materialism and economic geographies of the firm. Our explanatory model built on the argument presented in Chapter 4, which is that the expansion of state ownership (the role of states as owners and investor-shareholders) is a phenomenon rooted in the historical development and geographical remaking of global capitalism, and in particular, the emergence of a new constellation of old and new divisions of labor, and tendencies towards economic stagnation and industrial overcapacity. This created the conditions for a massive round of centralization of capital as state property (the mass of capital and assets owned of controlled by states) since the early 2000s. We showed in this chapter that the modern, marketized, globally spread state-capital hybrid emerged as an 'organizational fix' to mediate the geographical contradictions, capitalist imperatives, and material requirements associated with this process. Purposive organizational adaptation consisted in developing new skills, operational capabilities, and mixed ownership structures in order to leverage the financial system, allow for the development of flexible and liquid forms of state property, and facilitate the expansion of the latter into the global circuits of capital.

Our analysis has implications for three sets of scholarly debates. First, it contributes to conceptualizations and empirical investigations of the dialectical relationships between nation-states and (trans)national corporations, that is, the 'firm-state nexus', which has emerged as a leading frontier in economic geography (Yeung 2017). While studies of SWFs and SOEs typically tend to be compartmentalized, we sought to study contemporary state-capital hybrids as a particular form of embodiment of the firm–state nexus. This allowed scrutinizing the context in which they are (re)produced as well as the structural imperatives in which their corporate strategies are embedded. Theoretically, we showed that understanding their operations and organizational transformations requires studying them not only as creatures of nation-states but also as complex spatial and territorial entities in their own right (Dicken and Malmberg 2001; Zhang 2017). We have demonstrated that contemporary state-capital hybrids constitute a particularly productive entry point to study firm–state nexus reconfigurations and their place in dynamics of uneven development.

Second, our analysis contributes to debates on the modalities of state intervention in global production networks. Noting that states often do much more in global production networks than simply enabling markets, recent scholarship identified the need to scrutinize their role as producers (Lim 2018; Horner and Alford 2019; Werner 2021; McGregor and Coe 2023). In this chapter, we scrutinized the multiplication and growing significance of state-capital hybrids, and the organizational transformations they experience in order to become increasingly active, and sometimes acquire leading positions, in global production and financial arrangements. Future geographical research may further investigate the role of state-capital hybrids in shaping wider development outcomes in the case of specific value chains, notably with respect to territorial embeddedness and their relations with other public and private actors.

Finally, our analysis in this chapter uncovered a phenomenon that, albeit not completely ignored by the existing literature, has not been methodically investigated and has not informed theorizations of state-capital hybrids and debates on state capitalism: the role of the massive and geographically dispersed centralization of capital as state property. We showed that this process has fundamentally undergirded the global rise of SOEs and SWFs. More generally, the question of state ownership has featured little in state-theoretical debates. Our analysis suggested that contemporary mutations in modalities of state ownership must be studied in relation to shifting patterns of uneven development and state transformations, as well as in relation to changing corporate strategies. Both state-oriented and firm-oriented perspectives are required. Both must be grounded in material processes of capital accumulation.

7
The Rhetorical Weaponization of the New State Capitalism

Now that we have theorized and explained the rise of contemporary state capitalism as a distinct set of material transformations, characterized by an aggregate expansion of the state's role as promoter, supervisor, and owner of capital across the spaces of the world capitalist economy, we turn our attention to the *discursive* and *ideological* dimensions of this phenomenon. As we will see in this chapter and the next, power struggles in the realms of discourses, narratives, geographical representations, ideas, and ideology are *integral* to the uneven and combined state transformations currently unfolding. Let us start by focusing on how Western state and private actors are strategically mobilizing discourses of state capitalism.

Narratives of state capitalism conjure up a variety of powerful geographical imaginaries and representations. None of them are innocent. Consider the front-cover of a 2012 special report of *The Economist* entitled 'The rise of state capitalism: the emerging world's new model', figuring a picture of Lenin smoking a cigar. In another issue of *The Economist*, published two years earlier and dedicated to state-backed Chinese takeovers, the front cover featured a picture of Mao handing over a wad of one-hundred-dollar bills.[1]

In short, these geographical imaginaries comprise a myriad of value-laden symbols and scripts. They are saturated with sedimented meanings, which mobilize familiar histories and narratives. The red background colour as well as the pictures of the two charismatic leaders elicit the histories of 'really existing socialism' in the ex-Soviet Union, China, and elsewhere, but also that of the Cold War. Those representations link the contemporary polymorphism of state intervention to the past by reactivating vivid memories of the Cold War and communism, while depicting imaginaries that manifest suspicion and duplicity. The covers suggest that in state capitalism, what lies behind the veil of capitalist money and markets—symbolized by the US dollar, both on Lenin's cigar and Mao's banknotes—is the concentration of political power in

[1] The reader can see the covers at the following link: https://cdn2.opendemocracy.net/media/images/Economist_covers.width-800.jpg.

The Spectre of State Capitalism. Ilias Alami and Adam D. Dixon, Oxford University Press.
 DOI: 10.1093/9780198925224.003.0007

the hands of strong, illiberal states. The covers imply that the recent commercial success of the practitioners of the new state capitalism is being harnessed to achieve (geo)political gains. There is something inauspicious, if not threatening, about the fact that money is not allocated by the invisible hand of the market, but by the very visible hand of Mao. State capitalist models are not governed by the impersonal rule of law, money, and private property, but by power politics.

These imaginaries are live as well in policy thinktanks and geopolitical consultancies. For Ian Bremmer (2009), political pundit and president of Eurasia Group, the rise of state capitalism in the developing world is antithetical to Western liberal capitalism and seriously risks impairing the functioning of the free market. For Council on Foreign Relations fellow Joshua Kurlantzick (2016, 23), the return of state capitalism 'presents a real potential alternative to the free-market model, and as an alternative it presents serious threats to political and economic stability around the world'. For Harvard economist and Cato Institute research fellow Jeffrey Miron (2015), '[China] has state capitalism, not true capitalism'. Not only do those imaginaries overwhelmingly locate state capitalism in spaces outside of the Western core of the world economy, but they also construct the *abnormality* and *alterity* of state capitalism in reference to a presumed universal template of capitalist organization which dominates in the West. This is evident in Bremmer's account, which explicitly pits state capitalism against (Western-dominated) democratic liberal free-market capitalism, and in Miron's characterization of Chinese state capitalism as some kind of impure form of capitalism.

These imaginaries are likewise present in much of the Comparative Capitalism literature. For instance, Vasileva-Dienes and Schmidt (2019, 255) recently underlined that the variety of capitalism that predominates in the BRICs is characterized by the state 'as a central force organizing the market', but also by 'patrimonialism, meaning a political-economic configuration marked by clientelism, informal politics and corruption'. By contrast with the varieties of capitalism that prevail in the West and Japan, patrimonialism in the BRICs is 'a distinct *structural* principle of economic and social organization that systematically affects the relationship between the state, business and labor' (2019, 257; emphasis added).

Our key contention in this chapter is that this discursive and representational construction of the new state capitalism as deviating from a Western norm of capitalist political organization functions as an extremely potent *geopolitical category*. As we argued in the introduction, in the current context of turbulent geographical changes in the global dynamics of capital accumulation and in the planetary configuration of hegemonic power, the recent resurgence and redefinition of state capitalism in academic, policy-making, and popular analyses is no coincidence. Conversely, we posit that it plays a powerful role in categorizing, disciplining, and hierarchizing the spaces of world politics. In this chapter, we demonstrate this claim by offering a critical interrogation of the representations and narratives of state capitalism, as well as the power-geometries and geographical imaginaries that underpin them, to uncover how it operates as a geopolitical category.

Accordingly, we take inspiration from critical geopolitics, a body of literature concerned with the 'politics of writing and envisioning global space' (Ó Tuathail 2005, 14), and scrutinizing how geopolitical imaginaries, scripts, narratives, and other forms of representational practices have 'a contextuality, and [how they are] implicated in the ongoing social reproduction of power and political economy' (Ó Tuathail and Dalby 1998/2002, 2). It posits that there is power in representing the world economy in particular ways and in imposing order and meaning upon space. The social construction of geographical significance and the attribution of meaning and identity across global political space play a crucial role in spatializing (geo)politics (Dodds 2005). Critical geopolitics encourages us to scrutinize the taken-for-granted assumptions, temporalities, and framings of Western geographical narratives, revealing how such narratives, often taken as universal truths, are deeply enmeshed in the world they analyse (Sidaway 2000). Thus, we ask: how does the narrative of the return of state capitalism work as a form of geopolitical knowledge and practice? To answer this question, we proceed in four steps. In the next section we reprise the context of wider geopolitical and geo-economic shifts as discussed in previous chapters to situate the social construction of 'state capitalism' as a geo-category. We contend that the emerging new spatiality of the global economy, as outlined in Chapter 4, has prompted the need for new discursive frames and geopolitical lines of reasoning. We then scrutinize thereafter how the category operates in this geographical contextuality, that is, how it projects meaning and identity across space, and how it relates to other geopolitical meta-narratives. In the penultimate section, we develop the argument that what we call the 'strange geographies' of the new state capitalism (borrowing an expression from Sidaway and Pryke 2000) operate as a form of geopolitical knowledge which enables Western business and state actors to justify tougher policy stances. In particular, we focus on two areas: (1) diplomacy and foreign policy, and (2) trade, technology, competition regulation, and investment screening. The final section concludes.

The Geographical Contextuality of the New State Capitalism

As Mamadouh and Dijkink (2006, 357, our emphasis) note, 'Geopolitical representations become more explicit but also *more divisive* when important decisions have to be taken or a *crisis* occurs. *Major changes in the geopolitical context* generally bring the reformulation of geopolitical visions, a re-articulation of geographical representations that is necessary to acknowledge and justify foreign policy changes.' We argue that the re-emergence and reconfiguration of imaginaries of state capitalism must be considered against the backdrop of a series of interrelated geopolitical and geo-economic shifts in the global political economy, or what we call, following Ó Tuathail and Dalby (1998/2002), the geographical contextuality of the new state capitalism.

As noted in previous chapters, one of the most profound changes in the global dynamics of capital accumulation and the geographies of power that underpin them has been the shift in the centre of gravity of the global economy from the North Atlantic to the Pacific Rim, leading to the emergence and consolidation of new geographies of extraction, production, and consumption characterized by differential rates of accumulation between and within countries, with extremely dynamic growth poles and laggard regions. The rise of so-called 'emerging markets' (the BRICS but also other acronyms) appeared as the new engines of the global economy in the second half of the 2000s and in the immediate aftermath of the 2008 global financial crisis, as advanced capitalist economies were struggling to recover from the crisis. The fad about the BRICS is largely over now, with many emerging economies embroiled in deep financial and political crises. But the geographical reconfiguration of the global economy nonetheless led to a significant phase of geopolitical power dispersal away from the traditional Western centres of power. There has been a limited but noticeable move towards a new multipolarity of power and economic activity in the world market, underpinning a certain reshuffling of geoeconomic force fields, with for instance, some adjustments in global governance arrangements (e.g., the formation of the G20; the emergence of new multilateral development banks such as the Asian Infrastructure Investment Bank).

A concomitant geopolitical development has been the growing assertiveness in world politics of several states outside the traditional core (West/Global North) of the global economy. Most notably is the rise of China as a relative counterweight to the United States as the dominant hegemonic power, expressed through growing tensions, territorial disputes, and risks of military confrontation in the Pacific Ocean and South China Sea. This new mixture of confidence and assertiveness has also manifested as acts of intimidation towards Taiwan, and retaliations using trade restrictions and commercial coercion. For instance, the Philippines, Japan, and South Korea have been targeted because of territorial disputes, or because of military and defense cooperation with the US. Imports of soybeans meat and other products from Canada were blocked in 2018, after authorities there detained Huawei's chief financial officer at the request of the US. Beef, barley, and wine imports from Australia were subjected to restrictions after Canberra called for an independent investigation into the causes of the COVID-19 pandemic. In November 2021, bilateral trade with Lithuania was blocked after a Taiwan Representative Office was opened in Vilnius (Anderlini 2020; Reynolds and Goodman 2022). More broadly, Chinese diplomats have increasingly engaged in so-called 'Wolf warrior diplomacy', a new assertive brand of Chinese diplomatic tactics and coercive commercial statecraft on the global stage.

Furthermore, Putin's Russia has reasserted its imperialistic ambitions in global power politics through its annexation of Crimea, the invasions of Ukraine and Georgia, its support for the Assad regime in Syria, increased military presence in Africa, and the alleged intervention in the 2016 US presidential election. The rise of both China and Russia is increasingly interpreted as a global threat, some even arguing that this signals the advent of a 'new' or 'Second' Cold War (Ciută and Klinke 2010; Ó Tuathail 2018; Medby 2020; Schindler, Alami, DiCarlo, et al. 2023), with an additional fear of the two coming together and becoming geopolitical allies. We come back in the next section to how the re-emergence of the Cold War narrative in geopolitical discourse is intimately related to the redefinition of the state capitalism category. Beyond China and Russia, the vast majority of developing countries in Asia, Africa, and Latin America have refused to immediately align themselves behind the Western-led NATO alliance in its proxy war against Russia, and have refused to condemn Russia's invasion of Ukraine. Many of these countries also explicitly refuse to fall in line behind the US in its economic war against China, which they see as against their own foreign policy and economic interest. For former Chilean ambassador to China Jorge Heine and colleagues (Fortin, Heine, and Ominami 2023), this form of 'active non-alignment' reflects a deep and widespread disenchantment in the Global South with the Western-led liberal international order. This active non-alignment, and more generally, the perception of a real and growing divide between the Global North has been met with a mix of surprise and confusion in the west. However, it remains to be seen if active nonalignment will translate into a coherent form of collective geopolitical agency, one able of delivering real and tangible gains for the developing world, given the diversity of interests across the Global South and the uneven positioning of developing countries with respect to great power rivalry.

These geopolitical developments have been accompanied with, and facilitated by, profound transformations in the global distribution of surplus (as discussed in Chapter 4). Recall that the consolidating pattern of planetary uneven geographical development has led to a massive expansion of capital as state property (the mass of capital and assets owned or controlled by states) since the early 2000s, and associated changes in global patterns of finance and investment (as we saw in Chapter 6). Much of this capital has been funnelled into new sovereign funds, multinational state enterprises, and other state-capital hybrids to access a broader range of asset classes, markets, and geographies for investment in both the Global North and the Global South, in a broad range of sectors (real estate, health, tech, education, financial services, etc.). Some of it has also been channelled into sovereign and infrastructure lending, via state-owned development finance institutions. Chinese state-supported sovereign lending, for instance, has become a major source of funding for large infrastructure projects in Latin America, Africa, and Asia (Schindler 2018). In short, we are witnessing a reconfiguration of the global political economy, an uptick in state ownership of assets, a geographical expansion of state-capital hybrids' control over resources and markets, increasingly murky boundaries between state-owned and private firms, and a partial breakdown of the North/South axis which has structured much of the thinking and practice in world politics over the past eighty years (Mawdsley and Taggart 2022). Non-Western contenders (especially China) are more assertive and increasingly appear as capable competitors to the hegemony of the United States. Many are dissatisfied with the liberal international order. As we argue below, those turbulent changes have prompted a loss of credibility of existing geo-categories to make sense of the variegated spaces of this brave new world order.

The third fundamental contextual element, which we have discussed at length in previous chapters, is an historic arc in the trajectories of state intervention across the world economy. New global landscapes of state intervention have gradually emerged at the turn of the millennium and consolidated in the aftermaths of the 2008 global financial crisis and the COVID-19 pandemic, including in economies not typically considered as featuring large state sectors (cf. Wright, Wood, Musacchio, et al. 2021; Nölke 2022). Governments across the world have increased their role as promoter, supervisor, and owner of capital by expanding and experimenting with several political, organizational, and institutional forms. In addition to the multiplication of state-capital hybrids just mentioned, we saw the concomitant development of more assertive and muscular forms of statism (encompassing techno-industrial policy, spatial development strategies, economic nationalism, and trade and investment restrictions). In addition, we have seen a quantitative increase in the fiscal size of the state to historically unprecedented levels,[2] and central banks have become increasingly powerful actors in supporting economies worldwide. Broadly speaking, combinations of 'productivist', 'absorptive', 'stabilizing', and 'disciplinary' state capitalist impulses have been observable to various degrees across the world economy and have profoundly shaped global trajectories of state intervention (see Chapter 4). Their development in dynamic, inter-referential, and combinatorial forms has triggered cascading impacts and ricocheting effects, resulting in a proliferation of state-capital hybrids and muscular forms of statism across geographic space (Chapter 5).

After the 2008 financial crisis, as financial analysts MacDonald and Lemco (2015, viii) insist in their book on state capitalism, 'state capitalism appeared to be the core of a "new normal" of geo-economics that was like a juggernaut on the world stage'. This is particularly relevant for our argument because this 'new normal' is currently posing a double issue for both Western state and private actors, in a context of intensified competition in the realms of trade, investment, and technology. On the one hand, there are concerns among policymakers and legislators that key firms and assets can fall prey to what is euphemistically termed in the policy jargon 'opportunistic investment behaviour'. This refers to foreign state capitalist investors (state enterprises, sovereign funds, or other state-capital hybrids) seizing crises as opportunities to acquire (or take controlling stakes in) distressed firms and underpriced assets, particularly in sectors considered strategic (see Chapter 6). Furthermore, there are concerns that opportunistic investments can be controlled or influenced by foreign governments aiming to achieve geostrategic goals, such as taking control of key firms, assets, core technologies, or critical infrastructure. This in turn poses risks in terms of the loss of intellectual property and economic sovereignty (sectors or supply chains becoming overly dependent on foreign firms), and increased vulnerability to foreign geopolitical influence. In short, there are increasing concerns amongst state actors that inward investment on the part of foreign state-capital hybrids can pose risks for 'national security' and 'public order'. For instance, by portraying the figures

[2] The global averages as measured by the IMF are freely accessible at: https://www.imf.org/external/datamapper/exp@FPP/USA/FRA/JPN/GBR/SWE/ESP/ITA/ZAF/IND.

of Mao and Lenin in the shadow of the new state capitalism, *The Economist*, as discussed earlier, strongly suggests that such ulterior political motives exist and are dangerous, even where the investment practices of state-capital hybrids have been broadly speaking market-conforming. These concerns are of course inseparable from Western anxieties about the loss of geopolitical status and global market shares across a range of industrial sectors, where foreign state-capital hybrids are suspected to be distorting markets and generating unfair competitive advantages over private firms.

On the other hand, the contemporary polymorphism of state intervention is igniting struggles over the political legitimacy of emergent and reconstituted landscapes of state intervention, and over the definition of the relations between the state qua public and the private. Indeed, at times where state capitalist impulses have ostensible implications for the circuits of capital, the balance of power between and within classes and segments of capital, and in terms of geoeconomic force fields (as it is the case at the current historical juncture), the prevailing norms establishing a clear separation between the state qua public and the private may appear to be suddenly crumbling, notably from the standpoint of state and business actors who either stand to lose from such reconfigurations, or who anxiously perceive that they are. Importantly, these struggles are happening in the context of a partial crisis of legitimacy of neoliberalism due to its role in the aftermath of the 2008 crisis (Peck 2010), coupled with the failure of neoliberal prescriptions to deliver developmental gains across the world (and the comparatively better performance of non-Western states that have followed development strategies that diverge in significant ways from neoliberal prescriptions). This ideational struggle around the legitimacy, form, modalities, content, and purposes of state intervention, and about what is considered appropriate and 'tolerable' state–economy relations, is ridden with class tensions, but also with geopolitical power relations (Peck, 2021; Meulbroek, 2023; Whiteside, Alami, Dixon, and Peck 2023). It is unfolding against the backdrop of the deep geographical and power reconfigurations previously unpacked. We return to this crucial point in the penultimate section.

In sum, in the face of profound material transformations in the global dynamics of accumulation, the geographical redistribution of power in world politics, the multiplication of new forms of state-capital entanglements, and renewed legitimacy struggles around the role of the state in capitalist society, a sense of epochal transformations has captured the imaginations of Western corporate and policy-making elites. Simultaneously, and partly as result of those transformations, some of the older signifiers used to make sense of the spaces of world politics, such as the geopolitical division of the world into 'Third', 'Second', and 'First', or between Global North and Global South, between developed and developing countries, but also some of the post-Cold War narratives framed in the context of 'globalization' and the 'end of history', have lost (at least some) traction and credibility (Sidaway and Pryke 2000, 189; Slater 2004, 5; Sidaway 2012, 53). This has created a need for new discursive frames and geopolitical lines of reasoning, both to render intelligible those messy material and ideational epochal transformations, and to justify specific policy stances with regards to those transformations, as we successively discuss in the next sections. For now, our claim is that this geographical 'contextuality' of state capitalism is key to understanding both the process of social construction of the geo-category new state capitalism and how it functions as a form of geopolitical knowledge and practice. We now turn to an examination of how the category operates in this contextuality and how it projects meaning and identity across space.

Searching for a 'New Global Drama' ...

> Cold War geopolitics, in short, was a powerful and pervasive political ideology that lasted for over forty years.... Strategic analysts have been searching ever since for a new global drama to replace it, launching 'the end of history,' 'the clash of civilizations' and 'the coming anarchy' among others as new blockbuster visions of global space, only to see them fade before the heterogeneity of international affairs and proliferating signs of geographical difference. Political leaders have struggled to articulate visions of the new world (dis)order amidst the overwhelming flux of contemporary international affairs.
>
> **(Ó Tuathail and Dalby 1998/2002, 1–2)**

Our overall contention in this section is that geopolitical discourses announcing the return of state capitalism participate in the search for 'a new global drama'. Strategic analysts, political leaders, foreign policy professionals, opinion leaders, but also corporate and academic circles have been looking for a 'new blockbuster vision of global space' in order to render intelligible the global transformations analysed in the previous section, and the re-mobilization of the geo-category state capitalism plays a key role in this. While acknowledging, following Sidaway (2012, 50), that geo-categories such as 'emerging markets', 'rogue states', the 'end of history' narrative, and so on, are not stable and fixed but 'dynamic and frequently contested' objects, and that the new state capitalism is no different in that regard, we argue that it is nonetheless possible to identify a distinctive set of meanings, signifiers, and power-geometries that lie at the core of how the geo-category operates. We unpack in this section how the new state capitalism acts as a 'an operating system formatting large sections of global space' (Ó Tuathail 1997, 313). We look not only at how the new state capitalism attributes specific geographical and historical significance and identities to regions, places, and territories, but also at its embedding in meta-narratives of capitalist modernity, democracy, development, and world order. We make four main arguments.

First, imaginaries of state capitalism establish a sense of simplicity and straightforwardness in the face of the messy political-economic transformations scrutinized in the previous section, reducing their complexity, heterogeneity and dynamic character to a grand geopolitical narrative characterized by a clear-cut binary opposition between *free-market capitalism* and *state capitalism*. Much like the category 'new Cold War', which is currently emerging as another central frame of analysis of world politics (as we further discuss below), state capitalism frames a 'recognizable narrative that reduces complex events to a digestible storyline of good and bad' (Medby 2020, 152). The state capitalism narrative is a familiar story of heroes and villains which, through discourses of competition, (more or less open) hostility, and expanding influence, constructs a sense of 'ideological directness', to borrow another term of Ó Tuathail and Dalby (1998, 1–2). The two main protagonists are easily identifiable, two radically different and incompatible models of capitalism. Their material and ideological competition is what structures contemporary world politics, and what is at stake is the future of the rule of law, democracy, free trade, and international security (or in short, the liberal world order). The expansion of the new state capitalism threatens what capitalism brings best. As a leader from *The Economist* (2012) magazine speculates, this 'spread of a new sort of business in the emerging world will cause increasing problems'. The geographical imaginary which underpins this narrative, too, is unequivocal: it depicts an unambiguous geography of rival geopolitical blocs. According to a senior analyst at a prominent Washington-based think tank, 'One of the most pressing challenges the Biden administration will face is how to compete with, and push back against, China's increasingly powerful and disruptive state capitalist system, which not only threatens U.S. economic and strategic interests, but also undermines the regulatory and legal architecture that underpins the global economy' (Blanchette 2021, np). For Blanchette, the solution to this challenge is not only to expand state intervention and capacity at home (as we will see below), it is also to consolidate a geopolitical bloc to face the threat of state capitalism: 'it is imperative the United States find overlap and synergies with like-minded countries that share apprehensions about the statist elements of China's economic rise'.

Second, the geo-category establishes this sense of simplicity, directness, and familiarity by reactivating and redefining older grand geopolitical narratives. Indeed, as Mamadouh and Dijkink 2006, 357–358) emphasize, the production of new geopolitical knowledges often involves the 'renegotiation of past experiences, geopolitical visions, and national identities', and existing and past geopolitical visions often act 'as potential resources for the formulation of new geopolitical lines of reasoning'. This is precisely how the new state capitalism narrative operates as a form of geopolitical knowledge. In particular, it revisits the narratives and imaginaries of the *old* state capitalism, that is, imaginaries of a bureaucratic and ossified system of social organization and central planning, characterized by large, inefficient, and poorly run state-owned companies, which misallocate resources and undermine the smooth functioning of private markets, and which are controlled by politicians in their own interests (clientelism, corruption, etc.). If this form of state capitalism might have been useful in its time, it is now undoubtedly a thing of the past: capitalist globalization has rendered it obsolete. This old capitalism also conjures up the historical experiences and associated imaginaries of post-Second World War Europe, the Third World developmental state, Nazi Germany and fascist Italy before the war, but also, and perhaps especially, the histories of really existing socialism in the ex-Soviet Union, China, and elsewhere.

Furthermore, and as is evident from the two covers of *The Economist* discussed in the introduction, it mobilizes and re-actualizes several scripts and idioms that were central to the repertoire of Cold War geopolitics. Interestingly, the 'new Cold War' is also a category that is currently emerging as a central frame of geopolitical discourses.

As Ciută and Klinke (2010, 325–326) put it, the narrative of the new Cold War 'reproduces the symbolic order and hybrid vernacular—part description, part prescription—embedded in Cold War geopolitics, working with the same binaries that portray the identities of the protagonists and the bonds of interaction, conflict and in/security that structure their relationship: East/West, aggression/defence, authoritarianism/democracy, irrationality/rationality, and politics/economics'. We submit that the new state capitalism must be understood in tandem with the discourses of new Cold War. Discourses of the new state capitalism, just like of the new Cold War, are 'characterized by the associative: linking current events to the past, painting vivid linguistic imageries .... By calling it the new version of something supposedly already "known", it translates the present moment into a version of the past—albeit a *new* version [...]' (Medby 2020, 151, original emphasis). The new state capitalism both relies upon and contributes to reproducing the well-known identities and grand narratives of the old state capitalism and the old Cold War (and their associated bipolar structure and cultural/moral hierarchy), and its sense of familiarity is derived from it. Nonetheless, as Medby (2020, 153) notes, the recycling of narrative frames such as the new Cold War 'cannot be understood simply as a repetition of the past. On the contrary, it prompts the question of what is "new", and how we can understand today in light of both continuity and change.' This perceptive remark equally applies to the new state capitalism.

What is new, of course, is that according to the Cold War narrative, the West had won: the victory of democratic free-market capitalism established a new world order, characterized by the spread of liberal values and the expansion of capitalist globalization, beneficial to everyone, and signalling the 'end of history' (Fukuyama 1992). But with the rise of the new state capitalism, the non-West re-enters world history and threatens the liberal world order. Importantly, this new threat is different from the old one in two ways. On the one hand, by contrast with the ossified, sclerotic, and inefficient old state capitalism, the new state capitalism is depicted as decidedly modern and remarkably *dynamic* and *creative*. This bears some similarity with the emerging markets narrative, which for the first time represented 'selected parts of what was the Third World ... as more dynamic and modern than the West' (Sidaway 2012, 54). However, unlike in the case of emerging markets, the dynamism of the new state capitalism is not only presented as a business/investment opportunity, but also the source of a threat. The danger does not reside in the new state capitalism refusing capitalist globalization, but on the contrary, being particularly good at it. The new state capitalism narrative, then, is a wake-up call for the West to adapt and face this remarkable dynamism and inventiveness. On the other hand, the threat to the liberal world order and capitalist democracy this time does not come from communism, but from an impure version of capitalism. Put differently, the radical alterity of the contestant is constructed differently. As postcolonial scholars would put it, the new dominant image of capitalism's 'Other' is not a competing mode of production, it is a deviant, perverted version of the very selfsame one. We can speculate that in the current context of enduring crisis, widespread social unrest, extreme high levels of inequality, rising illiberal polities, etc., the new state capitalism narrative embodies a partial recognition that capitalism *can* yield harmful outcomes. But it pictures those harmful outcomes as the product of capitalist deviances, which are located elsewhere, in other (largely non-Western) spaces of the world economy. It renders them external to capitalist modernity in its purest version.

This leads us to our third argument. The new state capitalism narrative is enfolded within two entangled discourses that have a much longer historical sweep. By locating the threat to the world order and the West in the East, the new state capitalism is firmly embedded in the dominant imaginative geographies of Anglo-American geopolitics since the early twentieth century. As Dodds (2005, 33–34) underlines:

> many writers from Mackinder [considered a founding father of geopolitics] onwards have argued that the countries and regions of the 'East' have threatened the Western world. Mackinder's earliest geopolitical paper (1904) on 'The geographical pivot of history' identified a 'Heartland' within the Soviet Union and claimed that Western powers would be threatened by Eastern powers: 'Were the Chinese, for instance, organized by the Japanese, to overthrow the Russian empire and conquer its territory, they might constitute the yellow peril to the world's freedom' (1904, 430). In a similar vein, American geopolitical writers in the 1940s and 1950s argued that the menace from the East in the form of the Soviet Union threatened to imperil the free world.

In many ways, the production of the geographical imaginaries of the new state capitalism constitutes a new round in the longer histories of dominant representations of Anglo-American geopolitics. For instance, in 2019, Secretary of State Mike Pompeo under Trump declared that 'when capitalism competes with state-owned enterprises, I am confident capitalism will prevail.'[3] In 2020, he stated that 'we need a strategy that protects the American economy, and indeed our way of life. The free world must triumph over this new tyranny.... We, the freedom-loving nations of the world, must induce China to change, just as President Nixon wanted. We must induce China to change in more creative and assertive ways, because Beijing's actions threaten our people and our prosperity.... We can't treat this incarnation of China as a normal country, just like any other' (Pompeo 2020, np). In an address at the George Washington University in 2022, Current US Secretary of State Anthony Blinken declared that Chinese 'aggressive and expansive authoritarian one-party state capitalism' is the 'most serious long-term' threat to world order.[4]

Finally, representations of state capitalism also have a firm grounding in discourses that have an even longer history: the rhetoric of empire. Indeed, by

[3] Mike Pompeo on US–China trade talks. https://www.foxbusiness.com/video/6005173408001 [last accessed 22 August 2023].

[4] Secretary Blinken on the Administration's Policy towards China. Video available at: https://www.youtube.com/watch?v=VA3NS9BZong [last accessed 22 August 2023].

constructing the non-West (China, Russia, the newly emerging economies, the Arab countries, or the Global South more generally) as 'spaces of exception' (Power 2010), and places with peculiar characteristics of impurity and deviance (clientelism, corruption, dysfunctional political interference, economic inefficiencies...), the new state capitalism narrative both mobilizes and reproduces racialized colonial and imperial discourses. Those discourses, by characterizing the non-West as embodied 'otherness', simultaneously construct a picture of (Western) 'selfhood' and establish cultural/moral hierarchy. As studied at length by postcolonial scholars, the orientalist gaze (Said 1978) is an eminently political process. Indeed, as Slater (2004, 11) argues, 'Not only is there a process of self-affirmation, but also a denial of a potentially beneficial association with the non-Western other.' Furthermore, there is a 'politics of power' at play in this process, which 'strives to deny that what is thereby continuously reinstated as other is, rather, a facet (at the very least) of self and a powerful ongoing *relation of mutual formation*' (Lee 2011, 74, our emphasis). By depicting state capitalism in non-Western spaces as deviant, corrupt, politically driven, undemocratic, and irrational, imaginaries of the new state capitalism deny that those traits and attributes are potential facets of Western capitalism too, which is simultaneously represented as a fundamentally democratic, rational, efficient, meritocratic, virtuous, and pure version of capitalism. Hence, this Western capitalism is constituted not only as morally superior, but also as the ideal norm. This is evident in much of the work of foreign policy analysts, political pundits, think tanks, and business commentary that we have discussed at length so far, but also in many academic writings on the new state capitalism in developing and emerging economies.

Some of the Comparative Capitalism literature on the topic is a case in point. Becker (2014, 35–36, emphasis added), an influential scholar in the field, states that emerging economies are characterized by 'patrimonial capitalism', defined as 'an *allegedly* capitalist economy in which success in business depends on close relationships between businessmen and government officials' and by 'a structural relation between the state and the economy'. But, as Wehr notes (2015, 139), by depicting a patrimonial, *quasi*-capitalism prone to clientelism and corruption in 'emerging' countries, Uwe Becker constructs an image of a competitive, meritocratic, rational, and functional capitalism in the West, regulated by the rule of law, where the economy is *structurally separated* from the state, and where success in business *does not* depend on tight and informal relationships between private and state actors. 'In no meaningful way', as Tilley (2015, 210) adds, 'is a comparative lens turned back on Western countries to examine forms of corruption', and pejorative labels such as patrimonialism, cronyism, and so on are reserved for non-Western capitalist formations.

Another telling example is the recent work of national business systems theorists Fainshmidt, Judge, Aguilera, and Smith (2018, 316), who characterize state-led capitalist configurations in non-West spaces as systems where 'the state takes an active and direct role in the economic ordering of society. In these systems, political networks often serve as the mechanism thorough which economic activity is coordinated. These networks tend to monopolize and sustain power, introducing predatory elements to the state.' What is implied here is that in Western capitalisms, 'political networks' do not serve as mechanisms of economic coordination, and the Western capitalist state is devoid of 'predatory elements'. This rhetoric is employed in policy as well. Consider, for example, the 2018 US National Defense Strategy, which refers to China as a 'a strategic competitor using predatory economics to intimidate its neighbors while militarizing features in the South China Sea'.[5] Therefore, in this characterization too, state capitalism is imagined as deviant, and its apparent *abnormality* and *alterity* is constructed in reference to a presumed universal template of capitalist organization that dominates in the West. As Sidaway (2003, 166) puts it, 'the western state is identical with itself a replica of nothing other than its own model statehood', and non-West state capitalist configurations are mere supplements to it.

To be clear, our point here is not to level a critique of those commentators individually, but rather to point at profound difficulties in how (state) capitalist configurations outside of the West are imagined in the field of Comparative Capitalism in general, as has been discussed at length by Wehr (2015) and Tilley (2015). Even the more critical and reflexive work of Nölke, ten Brink, Claar, and May (2015), whose project is to demonstrate the viability of alternatives to the varieties of capitalism that predominate in spaces of the West, tends to inadvertently reproduce some of this Western-centric bias. For example, their model of 'state-permeated market economy' is constructed with reference to the Western varieties of coordinated-market economies and liberal-market economies. The model of state-permeated capitalism is characterized by the extent to which it differs from Western ideal-type varieties of capitalism. Here too, the West is the standard against which the rest of the world is seen to deviate, which tends to 'unconsciously universalize the western parochial' (Pollard, McEwan, Laurie, and Stenning 2009, 139). All in all, in the words of Pollard, McEwan, Laurie, and Stenning (2009, 138),

[5] Available at: https://dod.defense.gov/Portals/1/Documents/pubs/2018-National-Defense-Strategy-Summary.pdf [last accessed 20 August 2023].

much theorization of state capitalist configurations in the non-West happens 'through conceptual lenses that almost always have antecedents in western theorizations'. The spatial-historical contexts, and the institutions and forms of state power of countries across the Global South are established, not necessarily in explicit terms, as different from Western ideal-types. They are not considered in their own right, but rather the extent to which they resemble Western contexts and theoretical frames. Hence, they can only be deviant cases, or at best, another, or alternative, model of capitalism. An implication of this process of othering is that we may miss that although modalities of state intervention look different, they may actually perform, as Pollard and Samers (2007, 324) note, 'very familiar acts of economic coordination'. Much influential academic writing, then, inadvertently contributes to the construction and dissemination of value-laden and Western-centric geographical imaginaries of the new state capitalism.

The geo-category state capitalism produces a powerful 'regime of truth'—to use a Foucauldian term—which scripts the West (spearheaded by the United States) as the guarantor of a liberal, rational, efficient, virtuous, and pure version of capitalism. This is a seductive story in times of enduring capitalist crisis and political malaise, worsening levels of inequality, deep tensions between capitalist dynamics and democratic politics, and the rise of illiberal political forces in many spaces across the global political economy. Yet, as we show in the next section, the new state capitalism is more than an appealing narrative that the West tells itself: it also serves as a condition of possibility and plays a powerful role of justification of specific policy adjustments.

Material Interests and Strategic Policy Adjustments

We mentioned in the introduction that a key premise of critical geopolitics is that the production of geopolitical visions and associated political identities and rationalities is 'implicated in the ongoing social reproduction of power and political economy' (Ó Tuathail and Dalby 1998/2002, 2). Indeed, as Dodds (2005, 33–34) explains, 'the strategies employed by Great Powers to maximize specific interests are frequently "scripted" through particular representations about the world economy and international politics'. In this section we further unpack the specific material interests that are scripted through the construction of geographical imaginaries of state capitalism. We offer an analysis of the policy re-adjustments that the geo-category discursively enables and politically justifies, in the face of the geopolitical and geo-economic changes discussed earlier. Our key contention is that it is possible to identify some significant trends in how state and business actors in the United States and western European countries have mobilized imaginaries of state capitalism to allow for and provide legitimacy to specific policy stances in two interrelated and overlapping policy areas: (1) diplomacy and foreign policy; and (2) trade, technology, competition regulation and investment screening. In the next chapter we also discuss comparable dynamics occurring in the field of international development. These categories and our analysis are by no means exhaustive.

Diplomacy and Foreign Policy

Here we are concerned with the mobilization of the geo-category new state capitalism by several state actors and foreign policy analysts close to policy-making circles, mostly in the United States but not exclusively, who are specifically concerned with the expansion of Chinese influence abroad, especially in Asia and the Pacific (where the risk of military confrontation has ostensibly increased). For many of those commentators, a multi-faceted competitive struggle between the United States and China is already happening, as evidenced by intense cyber military conflicts, technological and industrial catch-up, but also the risk of 'export' of Chinese state capitalism as a development model, which is perceived as a key facet of this competitive struggle.

Our argument is that the geo-category state capitalism, in tandem with narratives of a new Cold War, is key to the construction of the geopolitical tensions between the United States and China as a 'philosophical divide', and not simply as the competition between a 'declining hegemon with erratic politics and a track record of aggression'—as Tooze (2018, 21) puts it—and a rising power. For instance, Kaplan (2019), a prominent American international relations commentator wrote in the pages of the prestigious US-based journal *Foreign Policy* that 'the philosophical divide between the American and Chinese systems is becoming as great as the gap between American democracy and Soviet communism'. According to Edel and Brands (2019), two other prominent US political pundits writing in the same journal, 'addressing the Chinese challenge will be central to preserving the relatively stable, open, and democratic world that has taken hold over the past seven decades'. What is at stake in 'the next superpower showdown', then, is not simply a power struggle between two competitors. Conversely, for Edel and Brands, the current competition between the United States and China is in direct continuity with past struggles (presumably the Second World War, the Cold War, the War on Terror) to defend the liberal world order and global peace.

Such discourse is not exclusive to punditry but is now used in official US government discourse. In reference to the National Defense Strategy's claim that China and Russia want to reshape the world in an authoritarian mould, Christopher Ford, US Assistant Secretary for International Security and Nonproliferation at the US Department of State during the Trump administration, in official remarks stated that 'China, in particular, has become notably interested in exporting its state-capitalist, high-technology police state model of government to other countries [...] even while ensnaring ever-greater portions of the developing world in manipulated debt dependencies and "neo-neocolonial" economic relationships. The global competition, in other words, is becoming ideological. Increasingly, it seems to be not just about *who* will dominate the 21st century world, but also about what the *operating system* of that world will be, and the predominant mode of governance within it. Clearly, this is serious stuff.' The operating system Ford arguably implies here is that of 'state capitalism'.[6] Moreover, as this quote suggests, narratives of hostile Chinese state capitalism are also often tangled with tropes of 'debt trap diplomacy', that is, the idea that China lures poor countries into agreeing unsustainable loans to pursue infrastructure projects so that, when they experience financial difficulty, Beijing can seize the asset, thereby extending its strategic or military reach (for a debunking of such myths, see Brautigam 2020; Jones and Hameiri 2021).

Whereas Great Power competition of the Cold War could be framed easily as competing economic systems, China's embrace of capitalism and its integration within the capitalist global economy renders this comparison obsolete. The geo-category of state capitalism reprises this binary tension, providing a frame for the US government's competitive foreign and economic policy posturing vis-à-vis Russia and China outlined in key policy documents such as the National Defense Strategy and the National Security Strategy, since at least 2017 under the Obama Administration. The construction, mobilization, and dissemination of imaginaries of the new state capitalism serve strategic thinking in terms of US diplomacy and foreign policy, primarily regarding the rise of China as

[6] 'Re-learning a competitive mindset in great-power competition', official remarks given at Los Alamos National Laboratory by Christopher Ford, Assistant Secretary, United States Department of State, 14 March 2019. Available at: https://2017-2021.state.gov/re-learning-a-competitive-mindset-in-great-power-competition/index.html [last accessed 20 September 2022].

a global power. This allows portraying this struggle as a new Cold War (not as an attempt from a declining hegemon to contain the rise of an increasingly capable competitor), providing ideological justification for the current toughening in US diplomacy and foreign policy, as a well-intended and rational reaction to the objective threat of Chinese state capitalism.

For instance, the trilateral security partnership 'AUKUS' (a strategic alliance between the US, the UK and Australia announced in 2021) has been justified by US policymakers, such as US Congressman and Chairman of the House Foreign Affairs Committee Michael T. McCaul, by the 'clear and present dangers' of 'the malign actions of the Chinese Communist Party', and its 'increasingly aggressive posture in the waters surrounding Taiwan' and in the Indo-Pacific. These actions demand that AUKUS establish 'critical deterrence measures', boost industrial-military capabilities, facilitate military technology transfers between allies and transfer, in order to deter potential Chinese military action and maintain shared security in the Indo Pacific. This is presented as an existential matter.[7] Likewise, the 'Quad alliance' (formally the Quadrilateral Security Dialogue between the US, Japan, Australia, and India) created in 2004 but largely dormant for the years that followed, has been revived from 2017 onwards as 'as a bulwark against Chinese state capitalism' in the Indo-Pacific (in the words of a former Senior Advisor for Strategic Engagement at USAID (Arha 2022).

Key figures of the Biden administration such as national security advisor Jake Sullivan, Secretary of State Antony Blinken and Treasury Secretary Janet Yellen, have adopted a less aggressive tone in their public statements in order to steady increasingly tense and volatile US–China relations. Yet they continue to denounce distorting and unfair Chinese state capitalist practices as obstacles to any improvement in US–China relations (insofar as they are portrayed as incompatible with US national security interests), and continue to mobilize such narratives in order to legitimize the tougher diplomatic and foreign policy stances of the Biden administration. According to Sullivan's landmark speech of April 2023, US domestic and foreign policy must be comprehensively integrated in order to protect US workers and companies in the face of the 'abuses' conducted by competitors such as China and Russia. In his words:

[7] See 'Transcript: Assistant Secretary of Defense for Strategy, Plans, and Capabilities Dr. Mara Karlin Testimony to the House Foreign Affairs Committee Hearing on Modernizing U.S. Army Exports and a Stronger AUKUS'. Available at: https://www.defense.gov/News/Transcripts/Transcript/Article/3408956/assistant-secretary-of-defense-for-strategy-plans-and-capabilities-dr-mara-karl/ [last accessed 22 August 2023].

> The People's Republic of China continued to subsidize at a massive scale both traditional industrial sectors, like steel, as well as key industries of the future, like clean energy, digital infrastructure, and advanced biotechnologies. America didn't just lose manufacturing—we eroded our competitiveness in critical technologies that would define the future. Economic integration didn't stop China from expanding its military ambitions in the region, or stop Russia from invading its democratic neighbors. Neither country had become more responsible or cooperative.
>
> **(Sullivan 2023, np)**

Similar foreign policy adjustments in the European Union have also explicitly been framed as attempts to adapt to the challenges of state capitalism. A good example is the EU's *Open Strategic Autonomy*, a new foreign policy orientation designed to better defend the EU's interests, security, and standing in the world. *Open Strategic Autonomy* has come to embody a general ambition to secure greater European independence, and has been heralded as ending Europe's naivety with respect to the global distribution of the benefits of globalization, and adopting a more realist policy stance, while staying open to global trade and rules-based cooperation. The concept originates in defence but has gradually emerged as a hegemonic and geoeconomics-permeated foreign policy discourse covering an ever-greater array of issues (Lavery, McDaniel, and Schmid 2022; Veselinovič 2022). In the *2021 Strategic Foresight Report* which articulates the essence of this new foreign policy orientation, the European Commission argues that the EU must strengthen its open strategic autonomy and global leadership to adapt to a series of key global trends, including the rise of 'Chinese state capitalism [which] is not always compatible with open global regulation, human-centred standards and sustainable values' (European Commission 2021a, 12). European Commission President von der Leyen's recent remarks (March 2023) on what she calls the 'de-risking through diplomacy' of EU's relations with China are worth quoting at length:

> Our [EU's] relationship is *unbalanced* and increasingly *affected by distortions created by China's state capitalist system*. So we need to rebalance this relationship on the basis of transparency, predictability and reciprocity. We have to ensure that our trade and investment relations promote prosperity in China and in the European Union. The Comprehensive Agreement on Investment, the so-called CAI—for which negotiations concluded in 2020—aimed at such rebalancing. But we have to recognize that the world and China have changed significantly in the last three years—and we need to reassess the CAI in light of our wider China strategy. And we know there are some areas where *trade and investment poses risks to our*

> *economic and national security*, particularly in the context of *China's explicit fusion of its military and commercial sectors*. This is true for certain sensitive technologies, dual-use goods or even investment which comes with forced technology or knowledge transfers. This is why—after *de-risking through diplomacy*—the second strand of our future China strategy must be *economic de-risking.*
>
> **(von der Leyen 2023, np)**

Again, the discursive/ideological justification for the set of policies and strategic reorientation von der Leyen refers to as 'de-risking' EU–China relations hinges upon the rhetorical mobilization of the geo-category state capitalism.

Trade, Technology, Competition and Investment Screening

Narratives and geographical imaginaries of new state capitalism also enable significant domestic policy adjustments in the United States and other advanced capitalist economies, especially in the areas of trade, technology, competition, and investment policy. In previous chapters, we have characterized this trend as increasingly muscular and assertive, if not aggressive, techno-industrial policy, neo-mercantilism, economic nationalism, and trade and investment restrictions. Much-discussed examples are the trade war initiated by the Trump administration, and the Biden's administration turn to techno-industrial policy, export controls on tech, inbound and outbound investment screening, and the like, all of which have been politically justified by the need to counter the specific commercial challenges and security threats presumed to be associated with Chinese state capitalism. In the words of US Senator John Cornyn, one of the cosponsors of a 2018 bipartisan bill significantly tightening the US foreign investment screening mechanism (Foreign Investment Risk Review Modernization Act), 'There is no real difference between a Chinese state-owned enterprise and a "private" Chinese firm in terms of the national security risks that exist when a U.S. company partners with one' (cited in Pearson, Rithmire, and Tsai, 2022, 158). US policies towards Chinese tech firms have been justified by, in the words of the Executive Director of the Paul Tsai China Center at Yale Law School, 'resurgent state capitalism', 'the pervasive nature of CCP [Chinese Communist Party] power in China's domestic economic and legal system', and its tightening 'grip on companies and citizens alike' (Williams 2020, 17, 18). Or, as former US Secretary of State Mike Pompeo put it,

> We know too that doing business with a CCP-backed company is not the same as doing business with, say, a Canadian company. They don't answer to independent boards, and many of them are state-sponsored and so have no need to pursue profits. A good example is Huawei. We stopped pretending Huawei is an innocent telecommunications company that's just showing up to make sure you can talk to your friends. We've called it what it is—a true national security threat—and we've taken action accordingly.
>
> **(Pompeo 2020, np)**

More generally, according to a senior analyst at a prominent Washington-based think tank, 'There is no long-term strategy for successfully competing against Chinese state capitalism that does not include significant investments in the United States' own domestic infrastructure, educational system, health care, and governance capacity ... the United States should begin a conversation on creating its own market-friendly industrial policy' (Blanchette 2021, np). Current Secretary of State Anthony Blinken made a similar point in 2019 when he declared that 'We should insist on competing in a rules-based system that *protects our people from the aggressive state capitalism of modern autocracies*. We should use our market power to set the highest standards for protecting workers, the environment, intellectual property and middle-class wages, while insisting on transparency and basic commercial reciprocity. In other words, we'll treat you the way you treat us' (Blinken and Kagan 2019, np; our emphasis).

The European Union has also toughened its trade policy stance after a series of controversial trade disputes with China between the mid-2000s and 2016 (De Ville 2019). At the core of those disputes lies a concern over Chinese state capitalism's alleged misappropriation of foreign technology (Branstetter 2018). There is also the concern of unfair competitive practices: US and European companies allegedly struggle to compete with Chinese companies which are state-owned, state-controlled, or receive intensive state support, resulting in the loss of market share, both at home and abroad. Moreover, there is the suspicion that foreign state-led investment in Europe and North America (conducted by state-capital hybrids such as SWFs and SOEs), especially in sectors considered strategic (national security, high tech), is motivated by geopolitical objectives, and concerns about technological dependence on foreign firms susceptible to political interference (Zettelmeyer 2019). In addition, growing anxieties and fears developed in Europe circa 2018 concerning the impacts of China's state-led industrial plan *Made in China 2025*. For instance, in 2018, Max Zenglein, the Chief Economist of The *Mercator Institute for China Studies* (one of the most influential European think tanks with a focus on China) called for Europe 'to stand up to China's state capitalist model'. Zenglein (2018, np) claimed that

> As Chinese state-owned and private companies align their global ambitions with those of the government, the strategy [Made In China 2025] represents an export of China's state-led economic system. This presents a challenge to the affected industries as well as to the economies of industrialized countries, in which innovation is driven by profit expectations rather than by strategic national targets. In more drastic terms: it represents a threat to the core of liberal democratic economic systems.

To be clear, our argument is not that those concerns are completely unjustified (some are), but that the dissemination of the geo-category state capitalism plays a key role in framing those concerns within particular geographical imaginations, thereby calling for and justifying a particular policy response: we have mentioned the toughening of trade and technology policy already (and the increasing use or threat of sanctions, for example against Huawei, amidst concerns over its ties to the Chinese state and suspicion that this could be used for spying), but also a shift in competition law (encouraged at the EU level), a hardening in investment screening policy (in France, Italy, the UK, Germany, Spain, the United States, Australia, Canada, Japan, and at the EU level, with the EU framework on foreign investment screening, as further discussed below), and a renewal of industrial policy and support to domestic capitalist firms.

The National Industrial Strategy 2030 announced by German economy minister Peter Altmaier in February 2019 is a case in point.[8] Some of the key measures include: strategic support to domestic companies, closing key EU value chains to imports from outside the European Union, designating specific German firms as 'national champions', allowing the German state to buy shares of companies in order to prevent foreign takeovers, modifying EU competition law to facilitate the creation of EU champions, even when this hurts competition in the European Union, extensive state support of industrial sectors of 'great economic significance'. As Zettelmyer (2019, 2), a fellow

[8] Although the National Industrial Strategy 2030 does not directly mention state capitalism, the term was used by commentators in the German press at the time. For example, economic columnist Olaf Gersemann of *Die Welt* in a 5 February 2019 piece entitled 'Danke, Peter Altmaier', stated [our translation], 'Germany and the rest of the world face systemic competition with Chinese state capitalism that is not interested in participation, but rather its own hegemonic ambitions.' https://www.welt.de/debatte/kommentare/article188255653/Industrie-Strategie-2030-Danke-Peter-Altmaier.html [last accessed 22 August 2023].

at the Peterson Institute for International Economics (a liberal US-based think tank), underlines, one of the assumptions on which the policy proposal relies is that 'Germany's automobile industry, the core of its manufacturing sector, will be threatened unless Germany performs better in areas such as robotics, artificial intelligence, and battery cell production, where it faces massive competition from the United States, Japan, and particularly China, whose success is attributed to industrial policy'; hence, the 'document calls for a new industrial policy based mainly on three instruments: subsidies, direct state participation in companies, and a reform of competition policy at the EU level'.

More recently, Monopolkommission, an independent expert committee which advises the German government and legislature in the areas of competition policy-making, competition law, and regulation, issued a report entitled *Chinese state capitalism: A challenge for the European market economy* (2020). The report states that

> China pursues a hybrid economic model that contains both state-economy and market-economy elements. More strongly than in European market economies, the Chinese state intervenes in economic affairs in many different ways to achieve its industrial policy goals. Of particular importance in this context are economic benefits (subsidies) which state or private undertakings enjoy. In the international context, such state intervention can lead to competitive advantages for Chinese undertakings over non-subsidized undertakings. Due to China's growing economic importance, such state intervention is increasingly affecting the EU economy and putting European undertakings at a competitive disadvantage vis-à-vis their Chinese competitors.
>
> **(Monopolkommission, 2020, 1)**

The report then goes on to list a number of policy recommendations to reform EU competition and foreign trade law, and develop policy instruments in order to protect the EU internal market and the competitiveness of European firms against Chinese state capitalism and the distorting effects of third-country subsidies. In its own working documents on how to address foreign subsidies distorting the internal market, the European Commission reprises the same jargon, and explicitly mentions the economic risks posed by Chinese industrial policy and state enterprises (European Commission 2021b). Expanding the EU policy toolbox is presented as a necessity to protect the EU internal market from 'unfair and abusive practices' of Chinese state capitalism and other 'developmental' states (European Commission 2021b, 4, 11). Relatedly, the brand new *Open, Sustainable and Assertive*

Trade Strategy developed by the European Commission aims to repurpose European trade policy to address urgent geoeconomic challenges, notably

> the rapid rise of China, demonstrating global ambitions and pursuing *a distinct state-capitalist model*, has fundamentally changed the global economic and political order. This poses increasing challenges for the established global economic governance system and affects a level playing field for European companies competing globally and at home. [footnote 3: This challenge is particularly visible in the area of energy intensive industries and notably the steel sector, where global solutions are needed to address the immense imbalances on the world market negatively affecting European companies and undermining the successful green transition of this ecosystem.]
>
> **(European Commission 2021c, np; our emphasis)**

We can clearly see how narratives of rogue Chinese state capitalism discursively enable and legitimize competitive policy emulation and strategic policy adaptation at home, notably the adoption of trade defence instruments (see Chapter 5). Another telling example, in the area of investment screening, is that of Regulation EU 2019/425, the purpose of which is to ensure coordination, exchange of information, but also greater freedom at both EU and national level to regulate inward investments. The regulation, in effect since October 2020, aims at protecting strategic technologies and infrastructure. This is in reaction to growing volumes of Chinese state-led investment in Europe. As Franck Proust, one of the leading EU lawmakers on the regulation, declared: 'We're not looking to bar foreign investment. It is essential for EU countries, we need it. It's to pay attention to the investments that are strange, that do not make economic sense but are political' (quoted in Reuters 2019).[9] Elsewhere, he asserted that the regulation will 'mark the end of European naivety' (quoted in Reuters 2018).[10]

In the case of France, President Macron's call *For European Renewal* (April 2019) advocated for a reform of EU trade and competition policy and the adoption of European preference in strategic industries. When Macron declared 'Our [EU] borders also need to guarantee fair competition. What power in the world would accept continued trade with those who respect none of their rules? We cannot suffer in silence', he made explicit reference to

[9] See https://www.reuters.com/article/us-eu-china-investment-idUSKCN1Q31JU [last accessed 22 August 2023].

[10] See https://www.reuters.com/article/us-eu-china-investment-idUSKCN1NP1IJ [last accessed 22 August 2023].

Chinese but also American state-supported competitors.[11] In a recent public speech outlining the logics and objective of his strategy to 'accelerate re-industrialization', Macron argued that France now faces a strategic context for industrial policymaking which is shaped by intensifying geopolitical tensions between the US and China, each with their 'own, and diametrically opposed, models of production' [in French: 'avec deux modèles de production, deux choix très polaires']. He then added:

> The Americans are our allies, we share the same values ... but we have no desire to be dependent [on them]... China is investing massively with a very state-centric model [un modèle très stato-centré] and a relationship to civil liberties that is not ours. And we have an American choice which is a break with the last 20 years, which is ... to over-subsidize the parts of [US] industry that [they] want to keep because, basically, [they] want to defend [their] national economic security and produce at home what [they] consider to be critical in digital technology or cleantech, and therefore industries that are strategic (our translation from French).[12]

In the United Kingdom, British Prime Minister Rishi Sunak called China the 'biggest state threat to our economic interests and this is a systemic challenge to the world order. That's why it's important we stake steps to protect ourselves again .... This regime is not aligned with the values that we share between the US, the UK, Australia and other allies.'[13] Similar tirades have been used to justify bills such as the 2021 UK's *National Security & Investment Act* 2021 (which establishes a foreign investment screening mechanism) and techno-industrial policies to position the UK as a leader in artificial intelligence.[14]

All in all, imaginaries of the new state capitalism are useful to provide justification for policy adjustments in the realms of trade, technology, competition, investment, and industrial policy in at least two important regards. On the one hand, and while those policies could be interpreted as aggressive moves which infringe upon the rules of the liberal order in order to contain the rise of an increasingly capable competitor which has managed to significantly improve the position of its firms in global value chains and global production networks, narratives of the new state capitalism instead allow portraying those policies as relatively benign and perfectly legitimate

[11] See https://www.elysee.fr/emmanuel-macron/2019/03/04/for-european-renewal.en [last accessed 22 August 2023].

[12] See https://www.elysee.fr/emmanuel-macron/2023/05/11/accelerer-notre-reindustrialisation-le-president-presente-sa-strategie [last accessed 22 August 2023].

[13] See 'British PM Rishi Sunak says China is the "biggest state threat" to economic interests'. https://www.youtube.com/watch?v=Sx9Kf26DVWc [last accessed 22 August 2023].

[14] See https://www.telegraph.co.uk/business/2023/08/20/sunak-spend-100m-taxpayer-cash-ai-chips-global-race/ [last accessed 22 August 2023].

measures, which do not violate liberal principles overall, but simply provide means to protect oneself against politically motivated, potentially dangerous state capitalism which is providing extensive support to its firms and which is 'cheating its way to the top by stealing technology' (Economist 2019). This tension is perfectly captured by Jeromin Zettelmeyer, the fellow at the Peterson Institute for International Economics mentioned earlier, when he argues that 'The rise of China requires a comprehensive response—not because the West should seek to suppress an increasingly capable competitor but because it needs to protect its firms from unfair practices and its citizens from the possibility that an authoritarian system may abuse its economic power' (Zettelmeyer 2019, 14). According to this narrative, those policy measures are all the more justified and necessary because the WTO—the international organization in charge of governing trade and trade-related issues (technology, property rights, investment) along liberal lines—does not provide the appropriate tools to adequately address the atypical practices of Chinese state capitalism (De Ville 2019; Leonard, Pisani-Ferry, Ribakova, et al. 2019).

On the other hand, imaginaries of state capitalism play a central role in the context of the renewed ideological conflicts around the legitimate role and place of the state which we discussed earlier. They simultaneously allow casting doubt on the legitimacy of Chinese state intervention in the circuits of capital at home and abroad, and legitimating renewed state action by advanced capitalist states. The alleged threat, duplicity, and exceptionality of state capitalism allow justifying strong state intervention in the realms of trade, technology, competition, investment, and industrial development as a *pragmatic* and *necessary* response, while not fundamentally proposing a political and ideological reordering of what constitutes the appropriate scope for state intervention in capitalist society.

To be sure, we do not argue that all those policy re-adjustments are *always* being made in explicit reference to state capitalism, or by directly mobilizing the geo-category in public policy discourse (though many certainly are). Rather, our contention is that the framing of political concerns in the areas of trade, competition, investment, and tech consistently draws upon the geographical imaginaries of state capitalism dissected throughout the chapter.

Conclusions

The category state capitalism is rapidly becoming a central geopolitical marker. Drawing upon critical geopolitics, we argued in this chapter that this process must be understood in light of a rapidly shifting geo-economic and geopolitical terrain of the global political economy, which has prompted the need for new discursive frames and geopolitical lines of reasoning. While acknowledging that the geo-category state capitalism is fluid and multidimensional, we have unearthed how it operates, and scrutinized the role that it plays in the contested reproduction of geopolitical power. The geo-category is increasingly used to order and classify the spaces of world politics, and in particular, the emerging landscapes of state intervention in the context of a planetary reconfiguration of hegemonic power.

Geographical imaginaries of the new state capitalism, we have shown, are saturated with notions of hostility, danger, competition, but also deviance and abnormality, which portray non-Western political geographies of capital as a threat to Western and global security and the liberal world order, largely due to its reactivation of older grand geopolitical tropes, such as the Cold War. By characterizing those geographies as essentially and ostensibly deviant, corrupt, and authoritarian, the political identity of Western capitalism is simultaneously represented as fundamentally democratic, meritocratic, rational, and as a universal template of capitalist organization, a model of social progress, and given a leading civilizational role in world politics. As such, the geo-category is embedded in long-lasting discourses of Anglo-American geopolitics and racialized discourses of a deviant and threatening non-West (and associated notions of Western moral superiority), reproducing an imperial gaze.

Not only is this a seductive story in times of enduring capitalist crisis and political malaise, deep tensions between capitalist dynamics and democratic politics, and the rise of illiberal political forces in many spaces across the global political economy, geographical imaginaries of the new state capitalism also serve the material interests of a number of state and business actors in advanced capitalist economies. We have underlined the salience of the new state capitalism geo-category in enabling and justifying specific policy adjustments in the realms of foreign policy, trade, technology, competition, and investment. The next chapter also considers international development. We have showed how the new state capitalism as a form of geopolitical knowledge plays a key role in—in the same movement—casting doubt on the legitimacy of Chinese state intervention in support of accumulation at home and abroad, and legitimating extensive state action in the circuits of capital valorization on the part of advanced capitalist states. Concisely put, the rhetorical weaponization of state capitalism is integral to the uneven and combined movement of state transformations.

8
Liberal Anxieties and Ideological Adjustment in Global Development

In this chapter, we continue our exploration of the ideological and discursive changes accompanying the tumultuous state transformations discussed earlier in the book. We focus on the official discourses, practices, and agendas of global Development, defined as a project of transformation in the majority world.[1] Empirically, our analysis relies upon a close reading of research and policy documents recently released by multilateral and supranational development actors such as the International Monetary Fund (IMF), the World Bank, the Organization for Economic Co-operation and Development (OECD), the United Nations Conference on Trade and Development (UNCTAD), and the G-20. Since the early 2010s, these institutions have produced a remarkable wealth of material explicitly concerned with old and new forms of state ownership and intervention. We searched the publication databases and research repositories of these multilaterals for keywords including 'state ownership', 'state-owned banks', 'state enterprises', 'sovereign wealth funds', 'state interventionism', 'industrial policy', and selected documents which were either entirely dedicated to (or featured at least an entire chapter about) the changing role of the state as owner, supervisor, and promoter of capital. We used this material as a source of data to scrutinize the discursive construction of the new vision of the state in Development. We focus here on multilaterals, which we conceive as regulative agencies committed to the global imposition of the social relations and disciplines central to capitalist reproduction, with the reordering of states at the core of their task (Cammack 2010).

Our analysis is interested in how discourses, practices, and agendas of global Development are articulated in relation with material political economic dynamics and framed within specific geographical imaginations

[1] In this chapter, we draw on Gillian Hart's distinction between 'big D' Development and 'little d' development (Hart 2010). 'Big D' Development refers to projects of political and economic transformation in the global South. By contrast, 'small d' development refers to the crisis-ridden expansion of capitalism as an economic system. We further elaborate on this distinction and on how the two phenomena relate to each other below.

The Spectre of State Capitalism. Ilias Alami and Adam D. Dixon, Oxford University Press.
 DOI: 10.1093/9780198925224.003.0008

(Slater 2004; Hart 2010; Power 2010). The distinction made by Gillian Hart between 'big D' Development and 'little d' capitalist development is particularly useful. She defines 'big D' Development

> as the multiply-scaled projects of intervention in the 'Third World' that emerged in the context of decolonization struggles and the Cold War; and then following paradigmatic shifts in the 1970s, into the era of the Washington and post-Washington Consensuses. 'Little d' development refers to the development of capitalism as geographically uneven but spatially interconnected processes of creation and destruction, dialectically interconnected with discourses and practices of Development.
>
> **(Hart 2010, 119)**

Hart argues that the official discourses and practices of Development have undergone significant rounds of reconfiguration since the 1950s in relation to global capital accumulation, geopolitical forcefields and the contradictions, struggles, and crises that accompany them. Our main contention is simple: if the key historical events and trends shaping the post-war Development project were decolonization and the Cold War, and more recently the 'interregnum' followed by the 'war on terror' and other non-state security threats, the defining world-historical transformations shaping the emerging vision of Development in the current period are (1) the *expansion of the new state capitalism*, as defined in this book as a polymorphous process of global state restructuring; and (2) the *rise of China* and the intensification of the Second Cold War (Schindler, Alami, DiCarlo, et al. 2024). These two distinct yet intimately related developments are pushing traditional Development actors to adapt.

We show that the IMF, World Bank, and other multilaterals are increasingly taking stock of the presence and significance of state capitalism in the global Development landscape and have (often reluctantly) acknowledged some of its developmental successes. This is prompting them to react and adapt to this new 'state capitalist normal'. So far this has taken the form of a *strategic discursive and ideological adjustment* involving a certain re-legitimation of the place of the state in Development, and a limited embrace of its role as promoter, supervisor, and owner of capital.

We see the articulation of this new vision of the state in Development, not only as an attempt from these actors to remain relevant in a rapidly changing world, but as playing a fundamentally political role: it is an attempt at minimizing the multiple risks and dangers that are perceived to be associated with the current rise of state capitalism. This includes minimizing the potential for the political 'use' of state-capital hybrids, which would risk creating a further (geo)politicization of economic relations and a spiral of protectionism, or what the IMF now refers to as 'geoeconomic fragmentation' (Aiyar, Chen, Ebeke, et al. 2023), particularly in the tense geopolitical context. This also includes controlling the proliferation of state-capital hybrids and making sure that they assume liberal forms, especially in developing countries. Finally, this involves ensuring that their increasing cross-border activities create the least frictions possible in the global circuits of trade, production, and finance, and do not disrupt the competitive operations of the law of value. Put differently, we see the discursive re-legitimation of the state in Development, and its limited embrace of state-capital hybrids, as a way of addressing liberal anxieties regarding the direction in which the political form of global capital accumulation may be heading (the unchecked proliferation of state-capital hybrids possibly blunting competition, politicizing economic relations, and intensifying geoeconomic tensions), in order to preserve and further enshrine the centrality of market regulation in Development in an age of rising state capitalism and turbulent geopolitical reordering.

State Capitalism in the Global Development Landscape

In Chapters 4, 5, and 6, we documented and provided an explanation for the world-historical process of state transformation that has happened over the past two decades. This process has been characterized by, on the one hand, a multiplication of state-capital hybrids (including sovereign wealth funds, state enterprises, policy and development banks, central banks) and a geographical expansion of their control over resources and markets, and on the other, the concomitant development of more assertive and muscular forms of statism (encompassing techno-industrial policy, spatial development strategies, economic nationalism, and trade and investment restrictions). In this section, we look at these developments from the perspective of multilaterals and global Development actors. We examine *how* these institutions are accounting for the contemporary advent of state capitalism and its impacts across the global Development landscape. We do this by drawing upon the multiple research reports, case studies, guidelines, and other policy documents issued by multilaterals on old and new forms of state ownership and intervention.

Sovereign Wealth Funds

The rise of sovereign wealth funds has been widely commented upon by multilaterals. Virtually all reports on Development finance now mention sovereign funds as a new class of institutional investor which is durably changing the landscapes of Development finance. There are several reasons for that. First, multilaterals note that sovereign funds offer a rational response to a set of policy challenges associated with global imbalances and a volatile macro-financial environment. In this context, in the words of John Lipsky, First Deputy Managing Director of the IMF, 'effective wealth management has become an important public sector responsibility' (Lipsky 2008). Sovereign funds are useful tools in that regard, insofar as they can help smooth government expenditures across the business cycle. The IMF's own research has recently shown that 'stabilization sovereign wealth funds do indeed help smooth government consumption by reducing fiscal policy volatility associated with commodity price fluctuations' (Al-Sadiq and Gutiérrez 2023, 1). Insofar as neither global imbalances and liquidity cycles nor the need for macroeconomic stabilization will go away, multilaterals posit that sovereign funds will continue to be important domestic financial actors in the future. This is all the more so given sovereign funds' ability to act as long-term providers of capital (Gelb, Tordo, Halland, et al. 2014; OECD 2020).

Second, multilaterals increasingly recognize that, in addition to their commercial mandates, sovereign funds will increasingly be called to invest for developmental purposes (although, as we will see below, they are also worried of the risks that may come with such investment practices). The reason for this is that there are vast 'financing gaps', in sectors such as infrastructure and development projects, as well as the low-carbon transition (Gelb, Tordo, Halland, et al. 2014; OECD 2020; Al-Sadiq and Gutiérrez 2023). Accordingly, sovereign funds can contribute to plugging these gaps by mobilizing public funds to complement and 'crowd in' private investment. For instance, a 2020 OECD report argues that sovereign funds 'can contribute to the low-carbon transition by providing equity and other forms of investment capital to sectors and stages of the investment process where the private sector does not invest by itself' (OECD 2020, np). This points to the role of sovereign funds not only as macroeconomic stabilizers, but also as domestic strategic development institutions. The latter role is increasingly embraced by multilaterals, and even encouraged, although under specific conditions. The multilaterals also recognize that sovereign fund holdings are highly unevenly distributed globally, but that even funds with modest resources can be useful tools in smaller countries: '[f]unds holdings are highly concentrated, with almost 90 per cent of total developing-country funds being held by just 7 countries [China, Kuwait, Qatar, Korea, Saudi Arabia, Singapore, and the United Arab Emirates], but even in the remaining countries, where asset values are relatively small, the amounts are still sufficiently large to make a development impact' (UNCTAD 2015, xvii).

Third, multilaterals indeed emphasize in their reports that sovereign funds have not only grown in size and significance within their own countries, they have also acquired increasing relevance for the global financial system. For instance, in the key document outlining the *Maximizing Finance for Development* agenda, the World Bank, and the IMF state that 'the global development landscape has changed', which is at least partly due to 'growing sources of official financing, in particular from the BRICS', resulting in the emergence of 'a new development finance architecture' (IMF/WorldBank 2015, 5–6). Attracting large pools of liquidity from these new actors and channelling them towards development objectives is therefore presented as a top priority: their massive financial resources, largely untapped inasmuch as only a small portion of their assets are in developing economies, could help fund the Sustainable Development Goals, infrastructure development, and climate change adaptation. This is also a recurring theme of recent UNCTAD *Trade and Development Reports* and *World Investment Reports*. The 2020 iteration of the *World Investment Report* argues that a key objective of investment promotion policy in developing countries should be to attract '[t]he large amounts of institutional capital [sovereign funds but also public pension and insurance funds] looking for investment opportunities in global markets' (UNCTAD 2020, iv).

Therefore, in addition to acknowledging the increasing place and significance of sovereign wealth funds as macroeconomic stabilizers and strategic investors, the World Bank and UNCTAD have adapted their policy prescriptions concerning Development finance, and now afford a central and multifaceted role to sovereign wealth funds in what Daniela Gabor calls the 'de-risking state' (2021). More precisely, sovereign funds are presented as key to both sides of the 'de-risking' equation: on the one hand, domestically focused sovereign funds can help create 'bankable' opportunities in infrastructure, water, climate adaptation, health and education, notably by socializing the risks of private capital and partnering with global financial investors (for instance, by offering guarantees and blended finance arrangements); on the other hand, these very 'de-risking' practices are also supposed to crowd in and leverage the vast resources of deep-pocketed sovereign wealth funds from other countries.

Furthermore, the IMF and the OECD have reacted to the rise of sovereign wealth funds by taking an active role since 2008 in the definition of global standards and best practices to manage them. This includes participation in the Santiago Principles, a governance framework encouraging the adoption of good governance and accountability structures and practices inspired from the private financial sector (we touched upon the Santiago Principles in Chapters 5 when we discussed the International Forum of Sovereign Wealth Funds, and in Chapter 6 when we examined the organizational isomorphism of sovereign funds with conventional investment funds). In other words, more than simply producing policy-oriented research, reviewing case study evidence, offering policy guidance and formulating prescriptions, the IMF and OECD have aimed to directly shape how sovereign funds operate globally. We will see later that this is intimately connected to their broader attempts to regulate and control the global proliferation of state-capital hybrids and render it compatible with the deepening of market-based finance in Development.

National Development and Policy Banks

Our analysis of recent research and policy material from multilateral Development institutions shows that they now acknowledge, albeit not unambiguously and often reluctantly, that national development and policy banks have become major Development actors and are here to stay. A 2015 OECD report notes that '[i]nternational investment by [state-owned banks] increased dramatically during the global financial crisis, and it seems likely that [they] will remain an important source of investment' (OECD 2015, 12). The World Bank has noted this trend too. The inaugural *Global Financial Development Report*, released by the World Bank in 2013, is called *Rethinking the role of the state in finance*. The report covers not just the state as a supervisor and regulator of financial systems, but also the 'the state as owner'. It dedicates a whole chapter to state-owned banks, and reviews some of their developmental success. The report nonetheless argues that, as crises recede, governments should privilege less direct forms of intervention (WorldBank 2013). The World Bank also published two comprehensive surveys of national development banks in 2012 and 2017. The latter notes that state-owned banks 'are relevant, and governments use them to provide financial services in sectors or regions that private financial intermediaries do not serve sufficiently. New [development banks] continue to be established in developing and developed countries alike to expand infrastructure finance, provide financing for new types of environmentally-friendly projects, and mobilize additional financing to meet a wide range of developmental objectives' (OECD 2017, 6). The report also importantly demonstrates the World Bank's growing interest in the ownership structures, business operations, and management practices of contemporary state-owned, development, and policy banks, with the explicit objective of governing their operations and lending practices.

A recent IMF report acknowledges that state-owned banks, although 'they have struggled to achieve their socioeconomic mandates ... can also play a positive role' (2020, 25). The report adds that state-owned banks can assist firms and support households during economic downturns as countercyclical lenders, while providing credit to marginalized groups or sectors underserved by private financial institutions (IMF 2020). More generally speaking, the OECD, World Bank, and IMF now regularly acknowledge in their policy documents and public statements that development and policy banks will have an essential role in addressing climate change or responding to global shocks such as the recent COVID-19 pandemic. Importantly, the OECD, World Bank, and IMF now encourage national development and policy banks to 'move beyond their traditional role of financing projects and companies to attracting commercial investors to public and private projects, through approaches such as blended finance to support the creation of new markets' (OECD/UN Environment/World Bank 2018, 1). We therefore see similar 'de-risking' policy prescriptions than that given to domestically oriented sovereign funds: state-owned banks are encouraged to act as intermediaries in blending finance from donor governments, host countries, and investors to scale up commercial investment in infrastructure projects.

UNCTAD, characteristically, sees a role for development banks beyond that of simply de-risking. It argues not only that '[s]uch banks have been a major feature of the development finance architecture for many years', but also that they should be counted as key partners in development finance by traditional international financial institutions (UNCTAD 2016, 5). In another report, it notes that 'the landscape of development banking is changing considerably, both in response to new investment needs and as a reflection of the wider trend of South–South cooperation and global engagement' (UNCTAD 2015, xvii). This refers to the growing role in the global financial architecture of alternative institutions for liquidity provision and development finance, many of which are Southern-led. These include bilateral and regional mechanisms of financial cooperation (such as the Chiang Mai Initiative in East Asia and the Latin America Reserve Fund) and the multiplication of development finance initiatives, such as the Eurasian Development Bank, the Asian Infrastructure Investment Bank, and the New Development Bank. Emerging and developing countries now account for 63 per cent of liquidity finance and 80 per cent of development bank finance (Kring and Gallagher 2019, 4). These national, bilateral, and regional initiatives have been attractive to countries across the Global South because they provide an opportunity to escape (to some extent) the orbit of the 'old multilateralism' of Bretton Woods institutions and its intrusive conditionality, but also due to the failure of the (post)Washington Consensus to deliver financial stability. As a result of this, a 2017 UNCTAD report argues (UNCTAD 2017, 6) that:

> The time is ripe to promote development bank. At the national level, the global financial crisis in 2008 has opened space for national policymakers to selectively break with the Washington Consensus policy package and an opportunity to support pro-development finance initiatives. At the regional and South-South levels, there is a new momentum of initiatives for the creation of Southern banks, which could tap into global savings, especially those that originate in the South. Taking advantage of such opportunities is fundamental to supporting future development in the South.

The same report discusses a variety of case studies, including Brazil's Banco Nacional de Desenvolvimento Econômico e Social, the Korea Development Bank, the Industrial Development Bank of India, and China Development Bank, and conclude that state-owned banks have 'considerable firepower to ignite the creation of new industries and provide support to a more inclusive development strategy' (UNCTAD 2017, 45). More recently, an UNCTAD policy brief argues that 'since the 2007–2009 North Atlantic financial crisis, and even more since the COVID-19 crisis, there has been a real renaissance of development banks, and a growing appreciation of their important roles, including in providing counter-cyclical finance in "bad" times, and in providing, at all times, long-term funding to help finance the major structural transformation and catch-up growth urgently needed to achieve more dynamic, inclusive and low-carbon economies' (Griffith-Jones 2022, 3).

State Enterprises

Both the global prevalence of state-owned enterprises (SOEs) and their developmental role have been increasingly acknowledged by multilaterals.

As an International Finance Corporation (the private arm of the World Bank) policy brief puts it: 'Despite extensive privatization, governments continue to own and operate national commercial enterprises in key industries. State-owned industries in high-income countries, in major emerging market economies, and in many low-and middle-income countries have *endured* and *expanded*' (Wong 2018). Witnessing the rise of state enterprises and their growing role in the global economy, UNCTAD has constructed a database on state-owned multinational corporations (that is SOEs that control assets, subsidiaries, or other entities in countries other than its home country) in 2017. It regularly comments on their evolution in its World Investment Report (see for instance the 2017 and 2019 editions). The database includes 1,500 state-owned firms, owing more than 86,000 foreign affiliates, or close to 10 per cent of all foreign affiliates (UNCTAD 2019b). The IMF dedicated a whole chapter to state ownership in its high-profile Fiscal Monitor 2020 report, entitled *State-owned enterprises: the other government*. It takes stock of their increasingly widespread prevalence in 'virtually every country', with 'many governments rely[ing] on them to serve their citizens and to foster economic and social development', and notes that 'SOE cross-border activity has diversified and increased in this century' (IMF 2020, x, 47). The IMF report raises the question: 'How can countries get the most out of them? At their best, they can help countries achieve economic and social goals. At their worst, they need large bailouts from taxpayers and hinder economic growth' (IMF, 2020, 61). To avoid this, the IMF is developing new tools, including a recently published *How to Note* on how to assess the fiscal risks of SOEs (Baum, Medas, Soler, and Sy 2021). This *How to Note* 'describes a newly developed SOE risk assessment tool to help country authorities and IMF country teams' (2021, 1).

The OECD released a landmark policy document in 2015 titled *State-Owned Enterprises in the Development Process*. It frames this endeavour as follows: 'This publication is a first response of the OECD to the issue of what role is, or can be, assigned to SOEs as part of national development strategies' (OECD 2015, 3). While it makes sure to insist that '[t]he OECD's long-standing position is that policy works better when it is aligned with market principles and supports necessary structural reform' (2015, 4), it is forced to recognize that 'in an interesting twist, there is growing evidence that foreign greenfield investment by SOEs located in emerging economies has a positive developmental impact in the recipient countries' (2015, 36). The OECD has also increasingly focused on state enterprises over the past ten years, producing influential documents like the 2015 OECD *Guidelines on Corporate Governance of State-Owned Enterprises*, the 2021 *Ownership and Governance of State-Owned Enterprises: A Compendium of National Practices*, the 2022 *Monitoring the Performance of State-Owned Enterprises: Good Practice Guide for Annual Aggregate Reporting*, and numerous case studies and comprehensive surveys.

Similarly, the World Bank issued several reports on the governance of SOEs over the past few years, in addition to multiple country case studies. In 2014, the World Bank released a key document *Corporate Governance of State-Owned Enterprises: A Toolkit* to help policymakers design and implement corporate governance reforms for state-owned enterprises (WorldBank 2014). At the time of writing (August 2023), the World Bank is also about to release its *Integrated State-Owned Enterprises Framework* (iSOEF), which outlines a comprehensive methodology to assess the importance of SOEs in a particular economy, evaluate their place in market dynamics, their relation with other firms, and their potential adverse market effects, in order to guide reform efforts. The World Bank sees the iSOEF as its own response to the recent expansion of state enterprises. A document introducing the iSOEF argues that

> The COVID-19 crisis has also tested the state's ownership role and the effectiveness of SOE management teams by exposing the underlying weaknesses in countries' and SOEs' corporate governance frameworks and capacity. The call to 'rebuild better' post-pandemic will increasingly obligate SOEs to demonstrate sustainable approaches that take into consideration the management of environmental and social risks as well as the impact of their economic activity on climate change and communities. Silver linings of this crisis include increased recognition of improved corporate governance standards, and practices and *a sense of urgency to strengthen the performance of SOEs*, to ensure their sustainability and mitigate mounting fiscal risks. The World Bank Group's new Integrated SOE Framework (iSOEF) *responds to these developments and provides a holistic approach to SOE reform.*
>
> **(International Finance Corporation and World Bank 2021, vii; our emphasis)**

The World Bank has also produced dozens of case study analyses on state-owned enterprises in particular countries over the past few years, some of which already apply the iSOEF (cf. technical notes released in 2021–2022 on Croatia, Bulgaria, Kyrgyzstan, Niger, and Gambia). The 2020 annual report of the European Bank of Reconstruction and Development report also devotes an entire chapter to state ownership.

Importantly, multilaterals have been very attentive to the uneven geography of SOE expansion. The OECD (2015, 36) insists that 'China plays an important role in this story ... [which] is partly the result of a deliberate policy, known in Chinese as the "going out strategy"'. UNCTAD underlines that 'their [multinational SOEs] headquarters are widely dispersed, with more than half in developing economies and almost a third in the European Union. China is the largest home economy' (UNCTAD 2017, xi). Similarly, the IMF notes that '[t]he recent growth of SOEs on the world stage primarily reflects the rise of China's economy—where SOEs still play a large role—along with other emerging market economies' (IMF 2020, 1).

One area where state-capital hybrids have been particularly successful is infrastructure investment and project implementation, including in sectors such as rail and road transport, ports, airports, water, mining, and energy. A report co-authored by the World Bank and the Public-Private Infrastructure Advisory Facility (PPIAF) notes that 83 per cent of investments in infrastructure projects in 2017 were sponsored by government-sponsored entities and SOEs in developing countries.[2] It also notes that 73 per cent of SOE investment commitments were financed by public banks and public equity. According to a 2016 report written by the consultancy firm KPMG for the Global Infrastructure Hub (created by the G-20 in 2014 to coordinate infrastructure investment initiatives): 'Essentially, governments are starting to recognize that it is the public sector that needs to energize projects and that, to date, they have relied far too much on the private sector to achieve their economic, social and environmental objectives' (KPMG 2016, np). The report goes on to add: 'Ever since the rise of privatization and public-private partnership models in the 1980s, most governments have operated under the assumption that the private sector outperforms the public sector when it comes to procuring and delivering infrastructure. But *this can no longer be taken for granted*' (KPMG 2016, np; our emphasis). The discursive shift concerning the role of the state is absolutely clear here, as well as its geoeconomic dimension, with the World Bank-PPIAF report underlining that 'East Asia Pacific accounts for up to half of global public and private investments, with China alone accounting for a quarter' (World Bank-PPIAF 2017, 43), and the KPMG report insisting that 'the center of gravity in the global infrastructure market is fundamentally shifting towards the East' (KPMG 2016, np).

[2] The PPIAF is an organization funded by western donors and dedicated to 'strengthening the foundation of governments in emerging markets and developing countries so they can generate a pipeline of bankable projects' (see https://ppiaf.org). The report is available at: https://ppi.worldbank.org/content/dam/PPI/documents/SPIReport_2017_small_interactive.pdf.

Techno-Industrial Policies and National Development Plans

Multilateral development institutions have also been increasingly concerned with the profusion of muscular forms of statism, including techno-industrial policies, spatial development strategies, economic nationalism, and trade and investment restrictions. A (pre-pandemic) UNCTAD *World Investment Report* dedicated to the topic notes that 'industrial policies have become ubiquitous. UNCTAD's global survey of industrial policies shows that, over the past 10 years, at least 101 economies across the developed and developing world (accounting for more than 90 percent of global GDP) have adopted formal industrial development strategies. The last five years have seen an acceleration in the formulation of new strategies' (UNCTAD 2018, xiv). The report adds that 'the rate of adoption of both formal industrial policies and individual policy measures targeted at industrial sectors appears to be at an all-time high' (UNCTAD 2018, 128–129). Furthermore, the report argues that if the 1980s–1990s period was characterized by 'low political legitimacy for interventionist development strategies', the period from 2000s onwards has seen 'regained legitimacy for national development strategies' (UNCTAD 2018, 130).

UNCTAD also interestingly mentions that 'the success of fast-growing economies in East and South-East Asia has put pressure on developed countries to respond to intensified competition in trade, investment and technology. It has also inspired low-and middle-income economies to build on their experience and push industrial development through greater participation in GVCs [global value chains]' (UNCTAD 2018, 129). This speaks to the mechanisms of competitive emulation we unpacked in Chapter 5. UNCTAD has seized the renewed interest in industrial policy and Development strategies to consistently make the case for stronger developmental interventionism in the Global South, notably to address the climate crisis. For instance, in its 2021 *Trade and Development Report*, UNCTAD makes the case for a 'retrofitted' and 'climate conscious' developmental state, one that would implement green development plans and a public investment-led strategy of diversification (UNCTAD 2021).

Other multilateral Development institutions have also started to adapt their discourse in the face of the renewal of industrial policy. A telling example is that of a recent IMF research paper called *The Return of the Policy that Shall Not Be Named*, which not only takes stocks of the return of industrial policy but also revisits the evidence for its effectiveness (or lack thereof). It argues that '[i]ndustrial policy is tainted with bad reputation among policymakers and academics and is often viewed as the road to perdition for developing economies. Yet the success of the Asian Miracles with industrial policy stands as an uncomfortable story that many ignore or claim it cannot be replicated' (Cherif and Hasanov 2019, 2). The paper concludes that 'their high sustained growth was the outcome of the implementation of an ambitious technology and innovation policy over decades that kept adapting to changing conditions and moving to the next level of sophistication' (Cherif and Hasanov 2019, 63). More recently, the IMF has released a paper entitled *Industrial Policy for Growth and Diversification: A Conceptual Framework* (Cherif, Hasanov, Spatafora, et al. 2022). The paper not only takes for granted that industrial policy is widespread and exists in many forms, it also outlines 'a stylized decision-making framework' to guide industrial policy efforts (Cherif, Hasanov, Spatafora, et al. 2022). This is a far cry from the type of knee-jerk reaction to industrial policy that the IMF has often expressed in the past.

This significant evolution reflects a broader trend amongst mainstream economists and policymakers, who are now developing, in the words of Rodrik, Juhász, and Lane (2023, np), a 'more nuanced and contextual understanding of such policies [which] yields a generally more positive assessment' (see Juhász, Lane, and Rodrik 2023). This is the case too at the OECD, where a research project has recently been launched in order to 'gather and harmonize publicly available data' on industrial policies, develop a new methodology to 'quantify them', 'analyze their structure' and 'evaluate their effectiveness' (Criscuolo, Díaz, Lalanne, et al. 2023, 3, 9). This, again, is justified by the fact that 'Industrial policy has resurfaced prominently in academic and policy discussions in the wake of major shocks and long-term trends' (Criscuolo, Díaz, Lalanne, et al. 2023, 3).

While the World Bank overall expressed a clear scepticism of industrial policy throughout the 1990s, its position gradually shifted throughout the 2000s, with a selective embrace of industrial policy not as a last resort policy tool to fix market failures, but as a wholly legitimate set of policy interventions to foster competitiveness and alter a country's industrial structure. This is reflected, for instance, in the 'new structural economics' articulated by Justin Yifu Lin, who was World Bank Chief Economist between 2008 and 2012 (Lin 2011; see, Andreoni and Chang 2019 for a critique). A World Bank policy paper co-authored by Justin Lin and Joseph Stiglitz in 2013 states that 'Today, the relevance and pertinence of industrial policies are acknowledged by mainstream economists and political leaders from all sides of the ideological spectrum' (Stiglitz, Lin, and Monga 2013, 2). It adds that 'the blind faith in the magic virtues of market forces in which rational agents would naturally create an optimal environment for growth and economic development has been disproved by the enormity of the Great Recession—and the swift policy responses that governments around the world adopted to weather the crisis' (Stiglitz, Lin, and Monga 2013, 18). According to the paper, the debate must no longer be about industrial policy 'yes' or 'no', but rather, 'how can it be designed to avoid the pitfalls of some of the seeming past failures and to emulate some of the past successes?' (Stiglitz, Lin, and Monga 2013, 4).

In addition, the Bank's own evaluation of its industry specific interventions between 2008 and 2014 concludes that the World Bank 'has not had a distinct, overarching approach to supporting industry competitiveness in the past decade', that it should clarify and 'strengthen its industry level support (including through knowledge, policy advice, and financing) to inclusive and sustainable industrialization, taking into account specific country circumstances and, in particular, the challenges faced by low-income countries' in terms of deindustrialization and job creation (Independent Evaluation Group 2016, xvii–xix). The Bank's Management response to this independent evaluation is instructive and worth quoting at length:

> discussions around industrial policy are complex and disagreement persists on the merits of targeting policies to specific industries. Management agrees with IEG [Independent Evaluation Group] that the effectiveness of industry specific measures can be enhanced in ways to promote productivity gains, job growth, and rising incomes. Management further believes that the efficacy of industry specific efforts requires not only bundling complementary elements of an industry's ecosystem, but more often than not, they require the deepening of economy-wide frameworks that support well-functioning factor and product markets. Indeed, in a number of countries, economy-wide incentives in and of themselves contribute to industry competitiveness and jobs. Sector-specific policies do not necessarily imply 'picking winners,' but rather policies (resolving credit, infrastructure etc.) that might apply to any sector ex ante but wind up affecting particular sectors. These types of policies are probably still where the World Bank should have its primary focus, although perhaps *more aggressively than in the past.*
>
> **(Independent Evaluation Group 2016, xxi–xxii)**

Two additional papers are worth mentioning here insofar as they exemplify this discursive shift at the Word Bank. The first one, published in 2018, is framed in conventional economics (standard welfare theory) but aims at identifying guiding principles for industrial policy rather than negating its legitimacy and usefulness (Maloney and Nayyar 2018). The second one is a 2020 World Bank policy note which argues that contrary to the 'conventional wisdom that industrial policies can be at odds with competitive markets ... competition policy and certain types of industrial policy can be crafted as complements' (Pop and Connon 2020, 3). Both papers signal a concern with shaping industrial policymaking rather than arguing against it.

Economic Nationalism and Trade and Investment Restrictions

The turn to economic nationalism and the multiplication of investment restrictions over the past few years, in the context of intensifying geoeconomic tensions discussed in Chapter 4 and 5, has captured the imagination of multilateral Development institutions. UNCTAD (2020, x–xi, xiii) expects trends towards 'growing economic nationalism' and 'towards more interventionism, rising protectionism' amidst 'geopolitical and financial risks and continuing trade tensions' to continue in the next decade. In particular, UNCTAD carefully monitors the adoption of restrictive investment policies, and regularly updates its Investment Policy Monitor database.[3] According to the 2022 *World Investment Report* 'together, countries that conduct FDI screening account for 63 per cent of global FDI inflows and 70 per cent of stock (up from 52 and 67 per cent, respectively, in 2020)' (UNCTAD 2022b, 13). Thus, 'the trend towards tighter regulation of investment continued, and the ratio of measures less favourable to investment over those more favourable was the highest on record (42 per cent, a point higher than in 2020) (UNCTAD 2022b, 56). UNCTAD has reacted by developing a new position on the matter: 'In the context of the expanding use and scope of investment screening mechanisms, it is ever more relevant to take a balanced approach to policymaking, so as to enhance the State's ability to address essential security concerns without weakening its FDI promotion efforts in the interest of sustainable development' (UNCTAD 2023, 1). It has released several policy notes to help enhance the predictability and transparency and efficiency of foreign investment screening regimes (UNCTAD 2023, 2019a).

Regarding trade restrictions, UNCTAD's 2022 *Trade and Development* report identifies 'geopolitical trade disruptions' as a major risk which could lead to a 'pessimistic' scenario 'centred on deepening geo-political tensions and military escalation' (UNCTAD 2022a, iv). This scenario is seen as particularly harmful for developing countries, who could be vulnerable to the 'policies adopted by the geopolitical blocs of major economies on trade, finance and climate' (UNCTAD 2022a, 91; the IMF makes a similar point in

[3] The database is available at https://investmentpolicy.unctad.org/investment-policy-monitor (last accessed 28 August 2023).

IMF [2023, 94]). Besides, 'the increasing attention to geopolitics in the design of trade policy reflects growing tensions at the global level that are challenging the rationale for multilateralism' (UNCTAD 2022a, 149). In the face of this new reality, UNCTAD makes the case for what it calls 'open developmental regionalism as a bulwark against an increasingly challenging world order' (UNCTAD 2022a, 150). This consists in offering more policy space for heterodox state policy experimentation, but also making the multilateral trading regime more inclusive and more developmentally oriented, by 'rolling back of elements of the multilateral trade agenda that have encroached too far into the responsibilities of the state' (2022a, 150).

'Geoeconomic fragmentation' in both trade and investment relations has become a major theme of IMF reports and public statements as of late. The term was coined by IMF researchers (Aiyar, Chen, Ebeke, et al. 2023) and refers to a 'policy-driven reversal of global economic integration' (IMF 2023, 91). The processes is attributed to 'rising geopolitical tensions and the uneven distribution of the gains from globalization have contributed to increasing skepticism toward multilateralism and to the growing appeal of inward-looking policies' (IMF 2023, 91; also Aiyar, Chen, Ebeke, et al. 2023, 12). The report asserts that 'if geopolitical tensions were to increase and countries were to move farther apart along geopolitical fault lines, FDI is likely to become more concentrated within blocs of aligned countries' (IMF 2023, 94). While the IMF dedicates much efforts to warn against the risks and quantify the economic costs of such scenario (more on this below), it also makes policy recommendations to reduce exposure to geoeconomic fragmentation, notably for emerging and developing economies that are 'nonaligned' with either geopolitical bloc. On the one hand, as we may expect, it argues that 'the large and widespread economic costs from strategic decoupling provide a rationale for a robust defense of global integration, at a time when several actors are advocating more barriers and inward-looking policies' (IMF 2023, 105). It therefore makes the case for policies promoting private sector development as a means to reduce uncertainty. However, on the other hand, it argues that some inward-looking policies may be driven by 'legitimate security concerns', and that countries should implement policies to ensure that gains from trade must be shared more broadly (Aiyar, Chen, Ebeke, et al. 2023, 13, 23; IMF 2023). In addition, 'the rules-based multilateral system must adapt to the changing world economy' (IMF 2023, 105). The new system would be 'fairer' and 'would preserve legitimate policy space while maintaining the stability and effectiveness of the trade system and helping sustain a minimum level of critical cross-border flows of goods, services, and finance' (Aiyar Chen, Ebeke, et al. 2023, 25).

In several publications, the World Bank has argued that the multiplication of trade and investment restrictions and the turn to various forms of economic nationalism can be explained by a reversal in attitudes towards globalization. A landmark World Bank report entitled *The Distributional Impacts of Trade* published in 2021 argues that 'At the heart of the tensions between trade's supporters and detractors is the fact that the gains from trade accrue unequally among countries and among different groups, sectors, and regions within countries' (Engel, Kokas, Lopez-Acevedo, and Maliszewska 2021, xiii). 'These impacts increasingly serve as an argument for protectionism and greater economic nationalism. The case against trade has increased in countries that have been unable to attract better export-oriented jobs or that offer little help for workers who experience trade-related dislocation' (2021, 1). However, the report is quick to add that 'we must be clear from the start: the relationship between trade and growth is unequivocal.... But while the aggregate gains from trade are clearly established, a burgeoning literature within economics has shown that the losses from trade may be deeper, more concentrated, and longer-lasting than previously understood ... the report also shows where previous analysis may have fallen short and provides new resources and actionable guidance for policy makers to ensure greater gains from trade while minimizing the losses' (Engel, Kokas, Lopez-Acevedo, and Maliszewska 2021, xiii–xiv). Another flagship World Bank publication emphasizes the role of subsidies and attempts to delink from global financial and trade networks ('re-shoring', 'onshoring', 'friend-shoring', etc.) in fuelling trade tensions and contributing to trade fragmentation and heightened global trade policy uncertainty (World Bank 2023, 32). For Pinelopi Goldberg, Chief Economist of the World Bank between 2018 and 2020, the new global context demands a more nuanced assessment of trade liberalization, which takes into account the distributional impacts of trade, information asymmetries, market failures, market concentration in critical product markets, market externalities along global value chains, and national security concerns, all of which '*could* provide a justification' for place-based policies, strategic trade policy, targeted subsidies, to complement trade liberalization. These, she argues, have not sufficiently been acknowledged by trade practitioners and free trade proponents (Goldberg 2023; Goldberg and Reed 2023).

Before concluding this section, let us mention a paper jointly authored by staff at the IMF, World Bank, OECD, and World Trade Organization entitled *Subsidies, Trade, and International Cooperation* (2022). The report argues that 'There are good reasons why this issue [subsidies in global commerce], which has challenged policymakers for decades, should be addressed now. The renewed drive toward industrial policies to promote "strategic" sectors may distort international competition, especially against smaller, fiscally constrained developing countries. With the frequency and complexity of distortive subsidies increasing, even as the need grows for active policies to address climate, health, food, and other emergencies, subsidies and the subsidies debate have brought significant discord to the trading system. The issue demands global attention and cooperation' (IMF/World Bank/OECD/WTO 2022, 3). Interestingly, the report acknowledges that 'Many subsidies are explicitly aimed at the important task of correcting market failures and *may do this well*. Many others, however, are designed in ways that do little to advance their stated objective, or do so at high domestic cost or with harmful effects on the global commons and on other countries, notably the poorest and most vulnerable countries. International cooperation can reduce the overall use of subsidies and improve their design' (IMF/World Bank/OECD/WTO 2022, 3; our emphasis). The report then adds that while international rules on subsidies regulations exist,

> both longstanding and recently-exposed gaps remain in these international rules .... The recognition of gaps is shaped by such developments as the emergence of global value chains; digital markets and related network concentration effects; *the global importance of economies in which the state plays a central role, and of international SOEs*; the urgent challenge of climate change; and the *recognition that well-crafted subsidies can be an important part of the public response* to economic and health emergencies. These developments make the issue of subsidies in the trading system both more complex and more urgent.
>
> **(IMF/World Bank/OECD/WTO 2022, 3; our emphasis)**

***

To sum up, our exploratory analysis of some of the recent intellectual output of multilaterals suggests that they have taken stock of the rise of contemporary state capitalism, and in particular, the growing presence and significance of state-capital hybrids and statist interventionism in global Development landscapes since the early 2000s. Multilaterals have accepted that these transformations are here to stay in the foreseeable future. They are keenly aware of the geographies of these transformations, and particularly, of the concentration of wealth and massive financial resources outside of the capitalist core, with important geoeconomic implications. They have reluctantly acknowledged some of the developmental successes of state capitalism, while expressing the need to adapt to this new 'state capitalist normal'. This is remarkable inasmuch as state enterprises and state-owned financial entities were considered relics of the past, a legacy of centrally planned economies destined to be privatized as countries develop and transition to modern capitalist economies and had long been neglected by conventional Development theory and practice. Similarly, spatial development plans and industrial strategies had largely lost legitimacy in mainstream Development policy-making circles. The discursive and ideological reorientation is therefore noticeable and significant. Questions of state ownership, state subsidies and other forms of intervention are now much higher on the reform agenda of these institutions. Multilaterals are also developing new tools to monitor these developments, new theoretical frameworks to analyse them, and adapting their policy prescriptions, guidelines, and best practices, on how to govern them. This is because, as we show in the next section, this accommodation of greater state ownership and intervention is also accompanied by considerable anxieties.

Liberal Anxieties: The Risks and Dangers of State Capitalism

The rise of state capitalism in global Development is presented as problematic by multilaterals. Research and policy reports emphasize several challenges and risks allegedly associated with it, which we examine in this section. This is a task worth our attention for the following reasons. On the one hand, we see this discursive construction of risks as having a double political objective: nuancing the success and developmental effectiveness of state capitalist instruments, by emphasizing that significant risks and dangers come with them, is a means of attempting to limit their appeal (see again Chapter 7). On the other, it will help us understand how multilaterals are positioning themselves with respect to the rise of state capitalism, and how they are gradually developing a policy line on the matter. Notwithstanding a degree of diversity of views among the actors considered, we identify a certain level of commonality in the discursive construction of challenges, risks, and dangers of state capitalism.[4] Unsurprisingly, many of the risks mentioned concern an alleged proneness to rent-seeking, fiscal proclivity, inefficient management, resource misallocation, lower productivity, corruption, and economic underperformance at the local level (see, inter alia, Gelb, Tordo, Halland, et al. 2014;

[4] UNCTAD, for instance, is characteristically more open to direct state intervention than, say, the World Bank. There is also heterogeneity within institutions. For example, the research output of the IMF tends to be less orthodox than its more policy-oriented material or its 'institutional views'.

OECD 2015; World Bank 2017; IMF 2020; IMF/World Bank/OECD/WTO 2022). These are familiar concerns that multilaterals have expressed at length since the early days of the Washington Consensus. The reports and policy documents that multilaterals have released on sovereign funds, state-owned enterprises, policy banks, industrial policy, trade, and investment restrictions, are replete with them. In this sense, a strong emphasis on these risks denotes an element of continuity in the intellectual production of the multilaterals. However, we also single out three additional types of risk: (1) uncontrolled policy emulation, (2) distorted economic competition, and (3) protectionist backlash.

The Risks of Uncontrolled Policy Emulation

Competitive emulation and peer-based learning (see Chapter 5 for an in-depth analysis of these mechanisms of policy diffusion) are widely identified as a mechanism which may contribute to the proliferation of state capitalist instruments. For instance, the 2015 OECD report on the role of SOEs in Development asserts: 'we are not blind to the fact that a number of countries have been looking for the apparent success of, for example, some Asian governments that have relied on more state-interventionist practices to obtain growth and development' (OECD 2015, 4). The report then argues:

> Whether the Washington Consensus has succeeded or failed goes beyond the scope of this report. In any case, it has fallen out of fashion in a number of developing countries, which are keenly aware of the developmental success of Asian economies (currently China, but previously Japan, Korea, Singapore and Chinese Taipei) that did not subscribe to market fundamentalism in the early stages of their development process. All of these countries depended heavily on state intervention to further economic development, in some cases (especially in China and Singapore) including widespread state ownership of enterprises.
>
> **(OECD 2015, 19)**

However, the report is quick to emphasize that 'the policy implications of this approach may in practice run into major obstacles', and goes on to list 'a malfunctioning or corrupt public sector', and the 'hijacking' of policies by 'interest groups and entrenched businesses' (OECD 2015, 21). In sum, '[e]ven if one accepts as a fact (and for the reasons suggested above, this is not obvious) that the state can and should play a role in developing industries, it is far from obvious that this needs to extend to corporate ownership' (OECD

2015, 26). Policy emulation and learning in circumstances beyond a narrow set of parameters (which we discuss below) is considered risky.

UNCTAD also identifies emulation as a mechanism of proliferation of state capitalist instruments (although it does not necessarily see risks in this), not just in developing countries, but across the North/South divide: 'The success of fast-growing economies in East and South-East Asia has ... inspired low-and middle-income economies to build on their experience and push industrial development through greater participation in GVCs' and it has also 'put pressure on developed countries to respond to intensified competition in trade, investment and technology' (UNCTAD 2018, 129).

The IMF, World Bank, and OECD see competitive emulation in the context of tit-for tat-retaliation as a particularly risky dynamic. They write: 'subsidies in one country can trigger subsidies in others. For example, in using tax incentives to attract foreign direct investment (FDI), countries may engage in a race to the bottom that hurts all of the subsidizing countries while blunting the intended effect of the subsidy for each one. Subsidies can also lead to competition between sub-central jurisdictions within a country, causing over- and under-investment and raising questions on opportunity costs for public resources' (IMF/World Bank/OECD/WTO 2022, 9).

The 2013 *Global Financial Development Report* issued by the World Bank (2013, 4) argues '[t]he state can try to run parts of the financial system directly, but evidence shows that approach to be very costly'. The report is at pains to portray emulation as risky, especially in poorer countries that do not have 'appropriate' institutional frameworks: 'In less developed economies, there may seem to be more scope for the government's involvement in spearheading financial development. However, less development is often accompanied by a less effective institutional framework, which in turn increases the risk of inappropriate interventions' (2013, 4). In other words, there is a specific geography to the risks of state capitalism: if its unchecked proliferation is a general source of concern, it is perceived as a particularly dangerous risk in non-Western, poorer countries, where the separation of the economic and the political is seen as more fragile than in (Western) liberal heartlands. Presumably, expanding the scope of direct state intervention and ownership in developing countries is dangerous because it may trigger a move away from liberal modes of governance and development, or encroach on sacrosanct private property rights, when the stability of liberal institutions and strong property rights in Western countries would prevent such drift. As we discuss in the next section, the injunction to 'reform' and 'modernize' state-capital hybrids in developing countries (following OECD guidelines,

World Bank professional training, and IMF expertise) is not only aimed at improving their governance and transparency, but also at governing their conduct, and keeping processes of policy emulation and peer-based learning in check.

Multilaterals also warn that industrial policies, large-scale state subsidies, and trade restrictions, although now increasingly practiced by large, advanced capitalist economies, would be too costly and risky for developing economies. For instance, in the pages of the IMF's flagship magazine *Finance and Development*, Peterson Institute for International Economics fellow Douglas Irwin argues that developing economies should not follow the new 'Washington-Beijing-Brussels Consensus of building up certain national industries through government subsidies and trade restrictions' (Irwin 2023, 14). This is because 'Large-scale industrial subsidies seem to be a luxury that rich countries can indulge. Just because the US, China, and the EU can afford subsidies does not mean that others should follow. As Ricardo Hausmann has warned, 'Copying other countries' solutions to problems you do not have, or focusing on trendy issues that are not really important, is a recipe for inefficiency, if not disaster.' Fiscally strapped developing economies cannot afford lavish subsidies for domestic producers when fiscal balances are precarious and the payoffs uncertain' (Irwin 2023, 14).

The Risks of Market Distortion and 'Unfair' Competition

One of the main risks which multilaterals associate with the rise of state capitalism is that of market distortion and flawed or 'unfair' competition. Here the concern is threefold. First, that state-capital hybrids themselves may not be subject to strict market disciplines, insofar as they can benefit from the direct support of their sponsors, leading to an 'uneven playing field'. The policy recommendations of the IMF in its 2020 *Fiscal Monitor* report regarding SOEs are precisely about making sure that they are subject to market disciplines. It makes the case for designing 'effective governance frameworks' to ensure 'transparency of economic performance and of relationships with governments', to provide the 'right incentives' so that 'SOEs set prices that reflect costs' and that SOEs are under rigorous financial oversight and monitoring (IMF 2020, xi). The objective is that SOEs are themselves disciplined by market or market-like mechanisms, following principles of so-called 'competitive neutrality' between firms, which means 'avoiding offering undue advantages that distort competition and selectively benefit some firms over others' (IMF/World Bank/OECD/WTO 2022, 25).

Indeed, state-capital hybrids must compete 'fairly' (as the same IMF report puts it) with privately owned capitals. Importantly, multilaterals emphasize that this concern is compounded by the fact that state-capital hybrids are now very large actors which operate internationally: 'This concern has long been present in domestic markets, but, more recently—with the internationalization of SOEs and their large size—it has spilled across national borders' (IMF 2020, xi). A 2015 OECD report echoes this: 'SOEs in emerging economies are increasingly making their presence felt in the international marketplace though foreign trade and investment. As a corollary, they are more likely to find themselves competing with foreign private enterprises.... If those SOEs still enjoy government subsidies or other material advantages at the time of internationalization, this may be a cause for concern' (OECD 2015, 12). The report adds: 'China plays an important role in this story.... Chinese investments in the African resource sector have grown rapidly in recent years. This development has given rise to some concern about unwanted side-effects' (OECD 2015, 36). Relatedly, the profusion of state subsidies is seen as particularly problematic insofar as production and trade are organized along global value chains. Thus, 'Regardless of any domestic benefits, subsidies may distort trade and investment and disrupt other economies. . . . Subsidies can accumulate along supply chains.... This not only complicates the attribution of benefit to a firm or sector, but it also underscores that subsidies matter not just for a particular sector but for the global trading system. Further, the increased role of multinational enterprises in global value chains raises the possibility that certain government subsidies may be provided transnationally' (IMF/World Bank/OECD/WTO 2022, 9).

This relates to the third concern, which is that state-capital hybrids may not invest their vast resources in market-conforming ways, whether in the form of sovereign lending, or investment in private firms and infrastructure projects. What is seen as a risk here is that the 'patient' capital provided by state-capital hybrids, can lead to a shift away from liberal (and Western-dominated) market-centric finance, and/or to a distortion in market forces. A firm receiving investment from a sovereign fund, a subsidy from a government, or lending from a policy bank may appear in a better financial position than its economic performance would warrant. According to a KPMG report written for the G20's Global Infrastructure Hub, state-controlled investments in infrastructure 'often prioritize objectives other than pure return on investment and therefore tend to distort capital market flows and returns', which is seen as an obstacle to 'predictable and stable investment environment' (KPMG 2016, np). Multilaterals indeed underline that such objectives can be, or can be perceived to be, 'noncommercial'. For instance, the IMF notes that 'SOE expansion abroad is not always based on commercial objectives but may reflect other home country goals, such as control of natural resources, acquisition of technology, or political or diplomatic objectives' (IMF 2020, 21). This, to some extent, mirrors growing angst among Western business and policy circles that the huge resources and market power of non-Western state-capital hybrids can be used for achieving geostrategic objectives or for expanding statecraft, as discussed in the previous chapter. Furthermore, this is further complicated by the fact that state-capital hybrids have evolved novel structures of ownership, control, and management which 'blur the distinction between *state owned* and *privately owned*—making it more difficult to ascertain when governments are influencing a firm's business decisions' (IMF 2020, 50, original emphasis). This ambiguity may lead trade partners and states on the receiving end of investment flows to implement protectionist measures (IMF 2020, 65). Similarly, in practice there is 'no bright line between prudential [read: legitimate, potentially beneficial] and protectionist [read: detrimental, costly] policies (IMF/World Bank/OECD/WTO 2022, 5).

Risks of (Geo)politicization, Protectionist Backlash, and Runaway Geoeconomic Fragmentation

The pursuit of noncommercial objectives via state-capital hybrids, or perception thereof by both market and state actors (particularly in the West), is the source of another risk category clearly identified by multilaterals, namely that the rise of state capitalism may lead to a politicization of economic relations and to protectionist reactions, especially in the current geopolitical context of mounting tensions between the United States and China. According to the OECD: 'Partly in consequence [to the increase in outward state-controlled investment from emerging economies], governments around the world have become more active in their effort to formulate policies for dealing with international investment from SOEs.... [And there are risks that] such practices will spark a protectionist backlash abroad' (OECD 2015, 12, 21). This is also noted by the IMF, who argues that '[a]s SOEs have grown in scope and size, their drawbacks have spilled over to other countries, leading to calls for protectionist measures' (IMF 2020, 21). The IMF underlines that these risks are compounded by the absence of a global governance framework in the matter: 'Domestically, some countries have frameworks that seek to promote fair competition between SOEs and private firms (for example, in Australia and the European Union). At the global level, however, there is no common framework' (IMF 2020, 1).

Overall, multilaterals are increasingly concerned that globally active state-capital hybrids may fuel a protectionist backlash followed by tit-for-tat, counter-acting, and punitive retaliatory measures. This could contribute to anti-globalization sentiment and distrust in multilateralism, destabilize the rules-based liberal order and market liberalization, and introduce a considerable degree of arbitrariness, unpredictability, and incoherence in global trade and investment relations (Aiyar, Chen, Ebeke, et al. 2023; IMF 2023; World Bank 2023).

While multilaterals are careful not to single out any particular state actor, some reports occasionally display a more hawkish inclination. For example, a KPMG report for the G20's Global Infrastructure Hub is explicit in its identification of a new Cold War as a key contextual element and potential factor of politicization of economic relations. It argues that one of the key trends that will influence the world of infrastructure in the next years is geopolitical reordering in a context of global uncertainty: 'Interestingly, it's largely the emerging and developing markets that are using this uncertainty to make big plays', and goes on to note in particular the rise of China as well as 'Gulf States' continued investment into western assets' (2016, np). Here too, the geographies of these risks are uneven: while the danger of protectionist backlash is clearly portrayed as global, it is nonetheless largely attributed to the threat of state-capital hybrids coming from the east. Western states may also be to blame for the global protectionist backlash, but theirs (according to the report) is a relatively rational and understandable reaction in the face of the threat of Eastern state-capital hybrids.

In sum, the three categories of risks identified in multilaterals' discourse largely exceed the general scepticism with state intervention that one may typically expect from (neo)liberal-minded institutions (market distortions, proneness to corruption, public mismanagement, economic inefficiency, waste of resources, etc.). These categories betray a profound apprehension about the direction in which the political form of global capital accumulation may be rapidly heading, namely, one in which the unchecked proliferation of statism and non-market conforming state-capital hybrids may blunt competitive value-disciplines, trigger a certain move away from liberal (Western-dominated) market-centric governance, politicize economic relations and intensify geopolitical and geoeconomic tensions between nation-states. This may in turn erect drastic barriers to the circulation of capital as a whole, effectively putting an end, if not reversing, the project of global economic integration. In short, the contemporary advent of state capitalism poses mounting risks of geo-economic fragmentation, all the more so that the international legal and institutional economic architecture is struggling to accommodate its rise (Alami and Taggart 2024). In this fast changing geopolitical and Development landscape, as IMF Managing Director Kristalina Georgieva and WTO Director-General Ngozi Okonjo-Iweala recently put it, 'we cannot afford to stand still' (2023, 11). It is this deep liberal anxiety which underwrites the current re-articulation of 'big D' Development, and the multilaterals' conditional embrace of more direct forms of state ownership and state intervention.

Articulating a New Vision of the State in Development

As the evidence provides, there have been noticeable shifts in the discourse of multilaterals (and, not covered in this chapter, bilateral development agencies) concerning the role of the state in Development. Evidence supports the argument that a gradual 'normalization' of the role and place of state-capital hybrids in the global economy is under way (Kim 2020; Alami and Taggart 2024). We argue, though, that this normalization is currently happening under specific parameters. To emphasize the *political* nature of this process, we prefer to speak of an articulation of a new vision of the state, of the like that Hart, following the distinction introduced earlier, calls 'big D' Development. In this section we outline its emerging contours. Certainly, the emergence of such a vision can only be a protracted, ambiguous, if not contradictory process. Fully characterizing it would also require examining a multiplicity of actors beyond multilaterals. Notwithstanding these caveats, we contend that it is possible to clearly identify some of the key features of this new vision of Development, which sheds light on some of the political objectives this vision hopes to achieve. We make three arguments.

First, we note that the emerging vision is characterized by an embrace of a fuller role of the state in Development (than the post-Washington Consensus), including *as promoter, supervisor*, and *owner of capital*. Importantly, such a view of the state does not provide unconditional support to all forms of statism and state-capital hybrids. On the contrary, it is highly selective and circumscribed. This much is clear from the multiple statements where multilaterals define their project of carving out a new view for the state in Development. For instance, the 2013 *Global Financial Development Report* is explicit in its attempt to navigate the following tensions while articulating a new role for the state: 'Two building blocks underlie the report's view of the role of the state in finance. First, there are sound economic reasons for the state to play an active role in financial systems. Second, there are practical reasons to be wary of the state playing too active a role in financial systems' (2013, 1). A 2017 World Bank report on state-owned banks aims to strike a sort of balance between 'laissez faire' and 'interventionism'. Similarly, the vision articulated by multilaterals in the context of debates about participation in GVC is one where state interventions are 'directed towards various constellations of firm and non-firm actors as a "third way" between state-minimalist and state-coordinated approaches' (Werner, Bair, and Fernández 2014, 1219). This makes clear that the new view of the state involves a certain re-adjustment of what is considered the appropriate scope and extent of state intervention, one which nonetheless remains resolutely within the liberal ambit. However, its exact parameters remain elusive.

To further characterize this adjustment, consider a concrete example: the partial (and for some still reluctant) recognition that state-capital hybrids *can be* legitimate developmental tools, which is a fundamental feature of this adjustment. The new agenda walks a tightrope, acknowledging the existence and relative success of a wide range of complex hybrids of public and private actors in development, while simultaneously remaining rooted in a firm commitment to liberal forms of governance, which are by definition predicated on a neat separation of the economic and the political (more on this below). The way in which it reconciles these two seemingly opposite propositions is by conducting a rather subtle operation, epitomized by the following statement from a World Bank official: 'The goal is to professionalize and depoliticize state ownership' (see forward by Alexander Berg in, Wong 2018, 1). This is the stated objective of the World Bank's *Integrated State-Owned Enterprises Framework* (iSOEF) and the Santiago Principles mentioned earlier, as well as training programmes such as the World Bank's *Leadership Training Toolkit for State-Owned Enterprises* (International Finance Corporation and World Bank 2021), which aim to promote entrepreneurial, depoliticized, and commercially efficient versions of state-capital hybrids, fully integrated into (and non-disruptive of) private markets. Put differently, the emerging view of the state developed by Development multilaterals strives to *extract some forms of state ownership* (the modern, professionally managed, well-governed, market-oriented state-capital hybrid—possibly indicating one in which management consultants and large-scale contractors play an increasingly central role in both policy formation and service delivery) *from the very category of the political.*

This is not so much a relaxation of the liberal stance on state ownership (even less so a move away from it) as a *mutation* of it, one that allows preserving and reaffirming a clear-cut separation between the economic and the political under a new guise, and one that simultaneously (supposedly) establishes a clear distinction between 'good' and 'bad' state ownership, and between liberal and illiberal forms of state-capital hybrids. The KPMG report cited earlier points at the same process when it says: 'Over the long term, we expect the private and public sectors to continue to drive each other to achieve ever-higher levels of performance, regardless of the chosen implementation method. As a result, we expect to see fewer public and private decisions being made on *"ideological" grounds* in the future' (KPMG 2016, np; our emphasis). By presenting certain types of state-capital hybrids as post-ideological, depoliticized creatures, the new view can delineate a liberal role for the state as owner of capital in Development, legitimating some uses and forms of state-capital hybrids, while delegitimating others and negating their role in Development.

Second, and in relation to the previous point, the new vision reaffirms notions of progress and modernization as applied to state-capital hybrids. This is a key theme of the multiple OECD, World Bank, and IMF reports dedicated to the governance of SOEs and state-owned banks. The argument is simple: transforming the 'old', inefficient, corruption-prone state-capital hybrids into fully legit economic and development actors is presented as a process of *modernization*. Development, then, also consists in modernizing state-capital hybrids, by 'strengthening the quality of governance', 'professionalizing government ownership', 'strengthening commercial orientation', 'introducing independent boards of directors', 'improving firm-level financial incentives', adopting 'modern risk management practices', implementing 'effective governance frameworks', and the like. With the emerging vision, the notion of modernization of state-capital hybrids has experienced a mutation too: throughout the 1990s, modernizing state-capital hybrids simply meant privatizing them (under almost any circumstance). By contrast, in the twenty-first century, modernizing state-capital hybrids means turning them into organizations that mimic the practices and organizational goals of comparable private-sector entities, adopt the techniques of liberal governance, and are broadly market-confirming (see again Chapter 6). Furthermore, as they articulate this new vision, multilaterals present themselves as centres of knowledge, technical expertise, and self-endorsed authority to assist in this process of modernization (see Alami and Taggart 2024 for a full elaboration of this argument). The OECD (2015, 5), for example, consistently repeats throughout its reports that 'it is the leading forum for standard setting and knowledge sharing in the areas of government ownership and corporate governance of SOEs'. Similarly, the World Bank presents the learning curriculum, teaching methodology, and certification programme that it offers in the context of the *Leadership Training Toolkit for State-Owned Enterprises* as based upon the Bank's 'perspectives, resources, and experience in working with the SOE sector and the state as an owner' (International Finance Corporation and World Bank 2021, viii).

Third, the emergence of this new vision is a *reactive* process. It is being articulated as an explicit response to the geopolitical reorganization of global capitalism analysed in Chapters 4 and 5, and in particular the combined expansion of muscular forms of statism and state-capital hybrids. Reports from multilaterals emphasize that there is a need for traditional Development actors 'to react', 'adapt', and 'draw lessons' from the current rise of state capitalism. This may be seen as explicit admissions that these actors are struggling to remain relevant in a rapidly changing world, and that they are facing multiple challenges to their established authority and expertise. Yet, at a deeper level, this must be interpreted considering the role that they play in the governance of global capitalism: these are liberal institutions fundamentally concerned with lifting barriers to the accumulation of capital and with facilitating its flow on a planetary scale. The point we made about the liberal anxieties generated by state capitalism is particularly relevant here. We see the articulation of this new vision of the state in Development as playing a fundamentally political role: it is an attempt at minimizing the multiple risks and dangers that are perceived to be associated with the current rise of state capitalism. This includes minimizing the potential for the political 'use' of state-capital hybrids, which would risk creating a further (geo)politicization of economic relations and a spiral of protectionism, particularly in the tense geopolitical context (Babic, Dixon, and Liu 2022). This also includes controlling the proliferation of state-capital hybrids and making sure that they assume liberal forms (especially in developing countries). Finally, this involves ensuring that their increasing cross-border activities create the least frictions possible in the global circuits of trade, production, and finance, and do not disrupt the competitive operations of the law of value. Put differently, we see the discursive re-legitimation of the state in Development, and its limited embrace of state-capital hybrids, as a *strategic ideological adjustment* to preserve and further enshrine the centrality of market regulation in Development in an age of rising state capitalism and turbulent geopolitical reordering.

Conclusion

Our analytical focus in this chapter has been on the current re-articulation of the Development project in relation to the global rise of state capitalism within global dynamics of uneven development. Drawing upon research papers, policy documents, and other forms of intellectual output released by key multilaterals since the early 2010s, we have identified a gradual yet fundamental reorientation of official agendas and discourses about the state, which now embrace a fuller (if highly circumscribed) role of the state in Development, including as promoter, supervisor, and owner of capital. Concisely put, the uneven and combined development of state capitalism within global Development landscapes is prompting traditional Development actors such as multilaterals to react to this new 'state capitalist normal'. Our key contention is that such reaction has taken the form of a *strategic discursive and ideological adjustment* (involving a certain re-legitimation of the state in Development, and a limited embrace of state-capital hybrids and statist modalities) which has been buttressed by a profound apprehension for the direction in which the political form of global capital accumulation is heading (i.e., runaway geoeconomic fragmentation).

Our analysis in this chapter invites three main conclusions. First, our approach and argument bring together several important claims that have been made concerning transformations in the global Development regime, albeit in relative isolation from each other. Recent scholarship has studied the mutations of the (post-)Washington Consensus (Sheppard and Leitner 2010; Güven 2018), the return of classical liberal notions and modernization principles (Mawdsley, Murray, Overton, et al. 2018), and the tendency to increasingly center the logic and objectives of national and international security in mainstream Development theory and practice (Mitchell 2010; Roy 2010; Essex 2013). A focus on the changing role of the state in relation to Hart's D/development dialectic, seems to us a particularly useful epistemic angle to tie these threads (and others) together in a comprehensive geographical political economy of the turbulent global Development regime. For instance, our analysis shows that the re-articulation of the place and role of the state is deeply entangled with other reform agendas and projects, such as the *Maximizing Finance for Development* agenda and the deepening of market-based finance in Development (Mawdsley 2018; Gabor 2021; Mawdsley and Taggart 2022; Schindler, Alami, and Jepson 2022).

Second, much recent scholarship on multilaterals tends to reflect on their place in the context of the current crisis of US-led international liberal order (e.g., Ikenberry 2018). Yet, these institutions are not only cornerstones of the international liberal order, they are also (and, perhaps, foremost) regulative agencies committed to the global imposition of disciplines central to capitalist reproduction. Cammack (2010) may well be right when he argues that they embody and enforce a universal class project centred on embedding global competitiveness. However, these institutions remain permeated by geopolitical forcefields. Our conclusions suggest that there is a need for more research into how they adapt their discourses and Development practices concerning the state in response to geographical capitalist restructuring and geopolitical reordering. We draw attention to the ideological dimension of this process, whereby intellectual production and discursive operations such as the championing of reform agendas are deeply implicated in the construction of a clear separation between the private and the public (Charnock 2008). The challenge, then, is not only to expose how maintaining this fetishized boundary (including by subtly shifting its parameters, or hollowing it out by bringing, for example, management consultants deeper into government) is so central to liberal governance and contributes to concealing and depoliticizing the contradictions of capitalism. The challenge is also to uncover how multilaterals aim at transforming these discourses about the public/private boundary into orthodoxies which legitimate some specific forms of state intervention and ownership and negate the political legitimacy of others.

Finally, future research may investigate how the process of redefinition of the role of the state in Development may be accelerating in the post-pandemic world, the extent to which it is the object of socio-political struggles between actors within and beyond multilaterals (including in developing countries), and the gaps that may exist between discourse and practice. Indeed, already in the early days of the pandemic, a series of reports found alarming evidence that where the IMF has provided financing, post-COVID-19, developing countries have had to drastically curtail public sectors and implement deep austerity cuts (Munevar 2020). As intimated earlier, there are reasons to believe that the ongoing ideological adjustment involving a certain re-legitimation of the state's role in Development may benefit large, deep-pocket state actors much more than others, thereby reproducing enduring lines of division in the world capitalist economy.

9

Conclusion

A Spectre Haunting Capitalism?

In an age of intensifying geoeconomic competition, resurgent imperialist ambitions, supply chain disruptions, backlash against 'globalization', pandemics and climate catastrophe, this much is now clear: global capitalism is currently experiencing a turbulent and polymorphous (geo)political reordering, encompassing multiple transformations in the landscapes of state intervention. Without discounting the power of critical events—such as the 2008 global financial crisis, the global spread of COVID-19, or Russia's war of aggression in Ukraine—in accelerating the movement of history, amplifying 'shocks', compounding crises, and often catalysing critical change, we have argued in this book that the ongoing process of state restructuring must be located within a longer historic arc, which has emerged at the turn of the twenty-first century and consolidated over the past decade. This arc has notably been characterized by a drastic reconfiguration—and in many cases, an enlargement—of the state's role as promoter, supervisor, investor, and owner of capital across the spaces of the world economy. States have centralized vast amounts of capital into their own hands and have experimented with a range of state-owned and state-controlled corporate entities, or what we called 'state-capital hybrids'. State-owned enterprises, sovereign funds, and policy banks of various stripes have vastly expanded their control over assets, resources, and markets, and in many cases, have developed into sophisticated and globally competitive corporate organizations deeply integrated into the global circuits of capital. Concurrently, states have also experimented with muscular and increasingly assertive modalities of statism, from techno-industrial policies and spatial development strategies to economic nationalism and trade and investment restrictions.

We argued in this book that the concept of state capitalism can aid us in grasping these transformations conceptually and throw fresh light on the world we live in. We proposed to use the concept neither to refer to a national (or regional) variety of capitalism, nor as an abnormal deviation

The Spectre of State Capitalism. Ilias Alami and Adam D. Dixon, Oxford University Press.
 DOI: 10.1093/9780198925224.003.0009

from liberal, market-based capitalism, but as a flexible means of problematizing this historic arc in the trajectories of state intervention and the role that it plays in the (geo)political re-organization of global capitalism. Making sense of these transformations requires seeing them as variegated, interactive, and as part of an evolving world-historical totality. We thus made the case for revitalizing systemic and macro-geographic forms of theorizing in state capitalism studies, rooted in theories of the capitalist state and uneven development.

We showed that the sources of these state transformations lie in the historical development and geographical remaking of global capitalism, notably two world-historical economic mutations rooted in changing forms of labour exploitation facilitated by technological innovation: on the one hand, the emergence of more complex constellations of 'old' and 'new' international divisions of labour; and on the other, deep-seated tendencies towards economic stagnation and industrial overcapacity. Present-day state capitalism must be understood as a process of self-transformation of capitalist states as they have politically mediated these global (but regionally uneven) secular mutations since the turn of the millennium. Put differently, the currently unfolding historic arc in the trajectories of state intervention must be seen as the *political form* of these determinate transformations of planetary capital accumulation.

This process of political mediation has involved significant changes in pre-existing landscapes of state intervention, a rearticulation of the relations between states and the circuits of capital, shifting boundaries between the state and civil society, and a dramatic aggregate expansion of their role as supervisor, regulator, guarantor, as investor-shareholder, and as direct owner of capital. More precisely, we identified four tendencies towards state capitalist impulses:

- a *productivist* impulse, geared towards increased direct state intervention in production arrangements and the competitive dynamics of productive and extractive capital;
- an *absorptive* impulse, oriented towards absorbing and recycling surpluses by putting them into motion as financial capital; and absorbing over-accumulated capital, 'toxic' assets, and socializing 'bad' debt and risks;
- a *stabilizing* impulse, aimed at mitigating crisis and economic volatility, propping up the value of financial assets, preventing the disorderly unfolding of crises, maintaining economic sovereignty, and preserving domestic political orders;

- a *disciplinary* impulse, including both increasingly coercive and repressive forms of political rule at home (often encompassing exclusionary notions of national identity and citizenship, and the brutal disciplining of workers and surplus populations), and aggressive attempts on the part of governments to shift the burden of economic adjustment to other states by actively mobilizing geoeconomic power; these two aspects of the disciplinary state capitalist impulse, the domestic and the geoeconomic one, are intimately connected, both on a material and ideological level.

As the wealth of examples and cases discussed throughout the book show, combinations of these four state capitalist impulses have been observable to various degrees across the world economy. Moreover, we argued that, in order to understand how these state capitalist impulses develop and concretely shape trajectories of state intervention at various scales, we must attend to the individual and collective agency of states and firms, notably in the realms of geopolitics and geoeconomics. We illustrated this argument by examining various types of relations between state actors, and between trajectories of state transformation, namely, *competitive emulation* in the context of geoeconomic and geopolitical rivalry; *peer group learning* and *mimetic behaviour*; and *enabling and mutual reinforcement*. These combinatorial mechanisms, dynamic interactions, and relational entanglements contribute to the cumulative expansion of state prerogatives, with cascading impacts across geographic space and policy domains (technology, geopolitics, industry, energy, money and finance, trade, foreign policy, security, infrastructure, investment, development, labour, and so on), both at home and abroad. They play a constitutive role in the aggregate expansion of the state's role as promoter, supervisor, and owner of capital, and its tendency to develop in spiral-like movements. Importantly, what obtains is not a clash of neatly distinct, rival models of capitalism, but multilinear, hybrid, recombinant landscapes of state intervention, which both shape and are shaped by world capitalist development.

As we made these arguments, we warned against tendencies to see the new state capitalism as an exclusively, or even a primarily, inward-looking dynamic. Much like the 1990s theorists of globalization tended to conflate the reconfiguration of the national scale of regulation with a withering of state power in the face of globalized market forces, many theorists today conflate the more visible role of the state in the regulation of intra- and cross-borders territorial flows with a 'return' to the nation in search for protection from market forces. Others interpret this as epitomizing a backlash against globalization, or as inaugurating de-financialization. In our view, this is a mistake. The uneven and combined development of state capitalism is best seen as a complex reconfiguration and rescaling of political authority, sovereignty, and territoriality, which is irreducible to a unidirectional movement, whether inside/out, or outside/in. We certainly can observe a certain 'hardening' of the nation alongside bellicose parameters (think, for instance, of the protection of particular national sectors and segments of capital, bans on foreign technologies, or the adoption of foreign investment screening mechanisms, and the more general 'securitization' of economic policy). Yet we can also, simultaneously, observe a clearly outward and transnationally oriented movement (with, for example, the increasingly global operations of marketized state-capital hybrids, which have become a major force of transnational capitalism). Our point is that if ongoing state transformations are indeed rooted in the multifaceted and geographically uneven mutations of capital accumulation mentioned earlier, then it follows that we would be hard-pressed to find a single, unifying logic or orientation to contemporary state capitalism. The search for a parsimonious characterization of state capitalism's general orientation is bound to be elusive. State capitalism studies would be best served to scrutinize how ongoing state restructuring concurrently entails both preserving and reconfiguring economic flows, notably by producing new scalar articulations of political authority, sovereignty, and territoriality.

We insisted throughout the book that this uneven and combined movement of state transformations catalyses struggles over the political legitimacy of emergent and reconstituted landscapes of state intervention, and over the definition of the relations between the state qua public and the private, in the process remaking the terrain of struggle itself. Indeed, at times where state capitalist impulses have ostensible implications for the circuits of capital, the balance of power between and within classes and segments of capital, and in terms of geoeconomic force fields (as it is the case at the current historical juncture), the prevailing norms establishing a clear separation between the state qua public and the private may appear to be suddenly crumbling, notably from the standpoint of state and business actors who either stand to lose from such reconfigurations, or who anxiously perceive that they are. For example, much ink has been recently spilled in (neo)liberal academic and policymaking circles, over the extent to which the increasingly transnational operations of sovereign funds and state enterprises are distorting markets, generating unfair competitive advantages over private firms, and even constituting a threat to global security and the liberal world order. The lesson for state capitalism studies is that no particular capitalist configuration or institutional form must be assumed to be politicized a priori, and distinct from allegedly non-politicized ones. On the contrary, our task is to analyse the dynamic and conflictual processes through which certain landscapes of state intervention and state–capital relations *become* politicized and the object of particular legitimacy struggles. We illustrated this argument by exploring the strategic discursive and ideological adjustment that is currently taking place in the realm of international Development.

We hope to have shown in this book that these material and ideological transformations, and the broader evolutionary dynamic we called uneven and combined state capitalism, are profoundly consequential. We can confidently say, and many readers will presumably agree with us, that they will play an increasingly central role in world politics and planetary capital accumulation in the years to come. So, the question as we see it, is not if, but *how*, state capitalism will shape our near future. The remainder of this concluding chapter is dedicated to this core question. Needless to say, what follows are not fully formed answers, but rather tentative thoughts, provisional arguments, and speculative hypotheses. We draw upon a long tradition of dialectical thinking which emphasizes the idea that a particular process, or set of social relations, contains not only its pre-conditions, history and genesis, but also possible futures (see, for instance, Ollman 2003). Put differently, it contains the seeds of likely or potential future transformations. The point of our exercise is not to forecast the future. Rather, reflecting on possible futures can help enhance our understanding of the present.

What, then, can we say of the new state capitalism and its futures, based on the relational-processual analysis conducted in this book? Importantly, none of the potential futures and developmental paths discussed below are pre-ordained or pre-determined. Our thinking here is non-deterministic: there is nothing inevitable about the patterns and trends we analyse. These will be resolved in the outcome of concrete class-political and geoeconomic conflicts. With all this in mind, in what follows we identify possible future transformations contained within our state capitalist present, which we discuss with respect to neoliberalism, climate change, the future of capitalism as a mode of production, and progressive politics.

State Capitalism and Neoliberal Futures

Let us start by asking: what does the rise of state capitalism mean for the hegemony of neoliberalism? While acknowledging that things are very much in flux and moving fast, we can formulate a few provisional thoughts. It is clear that many of the modalities of state intervention discussed in this book have involved a significant degree of departure from what we have come to see throughout the 1990s as 'orthodox' neoliberal theory and practice. Modalities of state intervention deviating from such orthodoxy include a greater embrace of state ownership, the relegitimization of assertive and visible forms of techno-industrial policy, or the implementation of trade and investment restrictions. However, many of these modalities of state intervention have been deployed alongside, and sometimes in tandem with, more conventional neoliberal policies, such as those that we often associate with the post-Washington Consensus (liberalization, deregulation, tax reforms, harsh fiscal austerity, etc.), particularly in the Global East and South. For instance, capital controls have proliferated, but have not challenged commitments to long-term capital account liberalization. In addition, many of the institutional and organizational forms that we commonly associate with the new state capitalism, such as state enterprises, sovereign wealth funds, and other state-capital hybrids, have displayed clear affinities with neoliberal logics. This is particularly evident when they explicitly embrace the institutional, cultural, and social norms of global finance (including shareholder value orientation, depoliticized discourses of economic efficiency and public value creation, and other neoliberal narratives and practices). Even when the adoption of neoliberal logics and corporate practices is less explicit, the operations of state-capital hybrids tend to deepen and reinforce the centrality of market rule and regulation across societies.

A similar observation can be made about the muscular forms of statism we have recently witnessed, including ramped up techno-industrial policies and state-led infrastructural development: while these deviate from the post-Washington Consensus narrowly defined and other neoliberal orthodoxies, they nonetheless aim to aggressively produce and support competitive and powerful firms and territories, which is a quintessentially neoliberal objective. Indeed, Davies (2020) argues that the neoliberal paradigm always contains the contradictory imperatives of 'upholding the market as a legally-mandated universal norm of social organization, while nurturing the *most* innovative, competitive and powerful firms and territories' (whether national territories, city-regions, or other polities) (see also Davies 2014).

There is, therefore, evidently no clean break with neoliberalism as a shape-shifting class-political project fundamentally concerned with depoliticizing market rule and establishing a competitive market order maintained and enforced by an impartial and authoritative 'strong state' (Biebricher 2019, 26–27, 34). Rather, future research should address the role and place of the new state capitalism *alongside*, and *within*, mutations in neoliberal experimental statecraft. Does the rise of state capitalism signal a sort of *third moment* of neoliberalization (complementing, but not replacing, the 'roll-back' and 'roll-out' moments)? If yes, this begs the question of the sort of tensions that may develop between these three moments of neoliberal restructuring. Alternatively, is state capitalism about the development of forms of statecraft which are distinct from neoliberalism, if not necessarily incompatible with it? In which case, what are the terms upon which the two trends interact and shape each other is an important research topic worth exploring. For instance, to what extent are state capitalist instruments and practices constrained by the path-dependencies (institutional or otherwise) of neoliberalism? To what extent are emerging institutional forms and modalities of intervention and ownership absorbed by neoliberalism? And to what extent is state capitalism papering over, or adding to, the tensions, instabilities, and antagonisms generated by neoliberalism over the past three decades?

A more sustained conversation between studies of state capitalism and neoliberalization, then, would not only help specify how the two trends are influencing ongoing patterns of state transformation, regulatory experimentation, and economic restructuring, it would also help outline the various forms of continuity and gradual change in the reproduction of the existing neoliberal order (see Peck and Theodore 2019; Arsel, Adaman, and Saad-Filho 2021; Davies and Gane 2021). Here we find the notion of 'mutant neoliberalism' articulated by Callison and Manfredi (2020) particularly productive. 'The figure of the "mutant"', Callison and Mandredi argue, 'offers an adept analytics for conceptualizing the transformation of contemporary neoliberalism(s). For within the "species" of neoliberalism, new variants are emerging that are distinct but nevertheless members of the same cast' (2020, 3). 'Mutants are new life forms seeking to survive within changing environments' (2020, 4). We see the global process of state restructuring analysed in this book as a turbulent catalyser of political economic transformations (both material and ideational), prompting neoliberalism to adapt. To be sure, adaptation is not guaranteed. It is likely to be protracted, contradictory, precarious, and conflict ridden. It will require the conscious design of strategies on the part of a variety of actors and institutions, such as the emergent strategies of adaptation of multilateral Development institutions documented in the preceding chapter. Another example is that of the architecture of global governance, which, as a whole, is also experimenting with difficult transformations to adapt to the new state capitalism (see Alami and Taggart 2024). The fact that global governance institutions are themselves the terrain of power struggles between competing states is nevertheless posing a formidable obstacle to transformation.

While the future of mutant species of neoliberal is very much open, we can already identify three features. First, it seems clear that neoliberalism is gradually seeking to incorporate state ownership into its mainframe. The version of state ownership that is seen as compatible and absorbable within neoliberalism is, of course, one that is restricted to very specific parameters, which include commercial orientation, profit maximization, depoliticization, and subjection to tight market or market-like discipline. Second, ongoing mutations in neoliberalism appear to be reflecting a search for new ways to conciliate the two contradictory neoliberal imperatives mentioned earlier, namely, on the one hand, 'upholding the market as a legally-mandated universal norm of social organization', and on the other, 'nurturing the most innovative, competitive and powerful firms and territories' (Davies 2014, 2020). States have undoubtedly been leaning more and more heavily into the latter pole of this contradictory unity. Yet this does not necessarily signal an abandonment of the former pole (at least there is little evidence that this is the case so far). What this suggests, however, is that the tensions between these two imperatives are rapidly intensifying. We can speculate that this is likely to lead to the search for new institutional, legal, and political mediations to conciliate and find a new precarious balance between these two imperatives. Again, there is no guarantee that such 'fix' can be found, but we would argue that this dialectical tension will act as an animating force of mutating neoliberalism in the near future.

Third, and relatedly, we submit that future mutant variants of neoliberalism will be shaped by its potential loss of hegemony. To our mind, while talks of post-neoliberalism are premature (insofar as neoliberalism is displaying remarkable signs of resilience, has survived many of its predicted deaths, and continues to manifest across policy domains and social spheres), we can nonetheless envisage a scenario where neoliberalism loses its hegemony but remains dominant. It may therefore rely more on the use of force. We can only hypothesize that this may push neoliberalism to develop mutants which even more aggressively mobilize and embrace the coercive powers of the state, at the service of both disciplining domestic social relations and geoeconomic competitors. If this happens, neoliberalism may itself be a future determinant of state capitalist impulses, particularly of the *disciplinary* kind.

In sum, the task of future research on state capitalism and neoliberalism will be to specify the contours of emergent species of mutant neoliberalism, their interrelations with state capitalist transformations, and identify strategies of resistance and openings for progressive social change (more on this below).

State Capitalism in an Age of Accelerating Climate Change

What of the future of state capitalism in an age of accelerating climate crisis and environmental breakdown? Civilizational transformation and collapse are likely to co-occur in the context of catastrophic climate heating (Paterson 2021). States may well react to this combination of transformation and collapse with renewed activism and a further extension of state prerogatives. There are indeed reasons to think that climate change will profoundly bear upon the four state capitalist impulses, and in all likelihood, will heighten their salience.

Consider, for instance, the probable impacts of climate change on financial and economic stability. It is now widely recognized that more frequent and severe natural disasters (heatwaves, wildfires, rains and floods, hurricanes, pandemics, etc.) will affect systemic financial stability. This is due to the exposure of a wide range of financial and non-financial actors to 'physical' risks, that is, risks of abrupt operational or value losses in climate risk-sensitive geographical areas, which can lead to the erosion of collateral and asset values for a large number of financial institutions, and rapid changes in the cost and availability of liquidity and credit (Giuzio, Krušec, Levels, et al. 2019; Brunetti, Dennis, Gates, et al. 2021). There are also 'transition' risks, which 'materialize when mitigation policies, technological advances or changes in public sentiment lead to value reassessments by financial market participants, possibly in an abrupt manner' and therefore leading to sudden asset price devaluations (Giuzio, Krušec, Levels, et al. 2019, np). These risks are of course particularly salient for fossil capital, carbon-intensive firms, and oil-rich economies, but a much wider range of corporate and sovereign actors are also exposed to them, albeit unevenly. Climate change will also likely result in supply chains disruptions, crop failures, energy market fluctuations, failing public infrastructure, shocks to housing markets, and other disruptions which will likely induce recurrent disproportionalities between supply and demand, and, in turn, monetary instabilities (as we saw with the recent bout of inflation). Moreover, direct or indirect climate related risks to economic activity (collapse of business operations, destruction of assets, rise of unemployment, fall in profitability rates, etc.) can also create or add to financial instability. In short, there are multiple feedback loop mechanisms between all these climate change-induced physical, economic, monetary, financial risks and vulnerabilities, which tend to amplify shocks through economic and financial systems, and we are fast moving to a much more unstable macro-financial environment, as a result of collapsing socio-ecological metabolic relations.

Countries in the Global South will be disproportionately exposed to these deflagrations, in a vicious cycle where vulnerability to climate change translates into higher external financial fragility, deteriorating sovereign credit ratings, and pressures to generate foreign exchange to service external debt. These pressures tend to intensify the extraction of mining, energy, and other raw materials for exports, which then further expose developing and emerging economies to ecological degradation, and in turn increase financial risks (Althouse and Svartzman 2022; Franz and McNelly 2023). In the more vulnerable countries, this may lead to further constrains on policy space, reproducing enduring global inequalities in state capacities to address crises (Löscher and Kaltenbrunner 2023). However, broadly speaking, it is highly likely that these instabilities and the violent crises they will trigger will give a major boost to the *stabilizing* and *absorptive* state capitalist impulses. This will manifest as increasingly muscular modalities of central banking intervention, and the large-scale mobilization of other state-capital hybrids to manage, mitigate, and absorb local, regional and systemic financial risks. We thus foresee an increasing presence of state ownership and intervention in global financial networks as a result of accelerating climate change.

Insofar as high technologies such as next-generation semiconductors, artificial intelligence and machine learning, electric batteries and storage, carbon capture technologies, new materials, and the like, are central to green transitions and renewable energy (let alone rather disturbing developments such as geoengineering), states will likely develop further modalities of techno-industrial policy to support the development of advanced manufacturing in these sectors, in a context of intensifying competition. The green subsidies race that we have commented upon in previous chapters may well deepen and accelerate, potentially constituting a boon for the firms and sectors which manage to leverage interstate competition and capture subsidies, tax breaks, state contracts, abatements and deferrals, loan guarantees, public grants and funding supports, discount schemes, debt write-offs, public–private partnerships, and so on. With the further expansion of these various modalities of support to business, the looming risk of 'corporate welfarism' will magnify, if states fail to enforce conditionalities in order to align business behaviour with their own green-developmental goals (Bulfone, Ergen, and Kalaitzake 2023). Given the critical need for investment in low-carbon production systems, green transportation, clean energy infrastructure, in all likelihood states will increasingly boost the firepower of municipal, national, and multilateral policy banks to either directly offer loans or co-invest with the private sector.

It is also likely that climate change will increasingly disturb regional, national, and global production networks, therefore prompting a partial reorganization of the geographic structure of the world economy, in the form of reshoring and 'friend-shoring' critical supply chains. Here again, this would require significant state activism in the form of state-led investment in infrastructure as well as various modalities of territorial planning. Furthermore, we will likely witness the further development of green industrial plans in resource-rich economies. States who own vast quantities of fossil capital will aim to plan for a transition to a post-hydrocarbon world, which will involve mobilizing sovereign funds and state enterprises to manage oil and gas rents and invest in low-carbon industrial sectors and activities, both at home and abroad. States who own critical transition minerals will most probably expand the scope of industrial strategies based on green extractivism. Whether any of these green strategies will be successful or not in setting economies on more sustainable pathways, we argue that climate change will further stimulate *productivist* state capitalist impulses in multifaceted ways.

Finally, both the domestic and the geoeconomic dimensions of the *disciplinary* state capitalist impulse will most probably experience a major acceleration. Starting with the latter, we can see already that the COVID-19 pandemic and Russian invasion of Ukraine have hastened the convergence of climate and geoeconomic imperatives. This convergence is now well already under way and is catalysing renewed state interventionism. Examples include the heightened competition between states to secure critical transition materials such as rare earth metals (Kalantzakos 2021). Competition in this area as well as other conflicts over resources are likely to intensify in the future, prompting states to intervene more actively, including via beggar-thy-neighbour measures and other explicit attempts to leverage their economic positions to favour themselves over others. We can foresee, for example, a much more systematic use of trade and investment restrictions to protect strategic green resources, technologies and assets, but also to engage in green protectionism. It is also likely that 'net zero' strategies will become increasingly integrated into national security principles and foreign policies, and that states will be tempted to weaponize control over access to green energy resources and technologies. In short, we may see deepening forms of what Charbonnier calls 'war ecology' (2022), all of which will arguably involve the development of aggressive statist modalities and an expansion of state-capital hybrids. The Innovation Fund recently created by the NATO military alliance offers an early example of the latter. The NATO Innovation Fund is the world's first multi-sovereign venture capital fund, with a mandate to invest EUR 1 billion in start-ups developing cutting-edge technological solutions addressing critical defence and security challenges, including green tech and renewable energy (NATO 2023). State-capital hybrids may well become privileged instruments for bringing together and combining security and green imperatives.

Similarly, it is likely that we will continue to see a proliferation of domestic disciplinary state capitalist impulses as a result of environmental breakdown. As temperatures increase, global sea level rises, ecosystems collapse, rivers and groundwater dry up, and extreme weather events multiply, millions of people will lose their livelihoods and means of survival, and will be on the move, predominantly in the Global South, amplifying other forms of conflicts, displacement and dispossession, and bloating the ranks of surplus populations (Bernards and Soederberg 2021). The world could see as many as 1.2 billion climate-related refugees by 2050 (TNI 2021). So far, states have tended to react to this trend with violent repression and the development of an authoritarian migration and border regime. The clearest manifestation of this is the proliferation, reinforcement, and fortification of borders. While there were only a dozen border walls at the end of the Cold War, there are now at least seventy-four across the globe, most erected over the last two decades; with another fifteen in some stage of planning (Vallett 2022). These walls are ineffective in preventing illegal immigration (insofar as they often re-route migrants to other, more dangerous paths), but are part of a system of control and surveillance of population flows, which entails the dehumanization of racialized bodies, and routinely results in mass death. Border walls are often planned, financed, constructed, and managed by complex state-capital entanglements involving a range of state and private actors (on the Canadian border, see, Bhagat and Phillips forthcoming). The trend shows no sign of abating and will likely prompt states to deploy even more resources to the monitoring, policing, and control of populations, with the border and migration regimes consolidating their position as a key locus of experimentation for both authoritarian politics, tech-powered surveillance, and state capitalist accumulation.

Climate change will likely exacerbate the fraught class politics that structure capitalist societies. As carbon emissions continue to increase while manufacturing as a share of total employment continues to decrease (notably as a result of the general economic stagnation discussed earlier in this book and the growing difficulties of capitalism to produce sustained demand for stable wage labour), the phenomenon of 'noxious deindustrialization' intensifies (Feltrin, Mah, and Brown 2022). This consists in many places and communities, in both the Global North and South, experiencing a combination of rapid loss of employment with continued environmental degradation. In a context of low economic growth and enduring austerity, states are rarely compensating these dwindling labour market opportunities with an expansion of economic rights, social benefits, or other redistributive policies to these populations. On the contrary, states' overwhelming response has been a combination or 'organized abandonment' (Gilmore 2022) and repression when protests and dissent happen. Despite the now omnipresent jargon of 'leaving no place or community behind' and of 'just green transitions',[1] green policies have so far had highly unequal impacts along class and spatial lines (as well as other lines of division, such as race), and states have responded to resulting opposition with criminalization and repression of protests (as evidenced by the *Gilet Jaunes* uprising, which was originally triggered by gas and diesel tax increases). While we acknowledge that the recent wave of green industrial plans (such as the Inflation Reduction Act, the EU Green Deal, and other recent state-led green initiatives) display a certain sensitivity to regional disparities and, to some extent, to class inequalities, it remains to be seen if they will deliver on their stated objectives of (simultaneously) fostering economic growth and reindustrialization, creating decent and well-paying jobs, and accelerating the low-carbon transition. That *multiple* states are simultaneously engaging in these efforts in the context of a highly competitive world economy is complicating things, insofar as relative success in one place of the world economy is largely contingent on failure elsewhere. In addition to this zero-sum game scenario, there is also the looming prospect of aggravated and generalized overcapacity, as these green industrial plans duplicate productive capacities across the world economy at an accelerated pace.

More fundamentally, these objectives (economic growth, reindustrialization, employment creation, and environmental transition) may not be so easy to reconcile, even for individual states. The intersecting crises of economic growth, employment, and nature are presenting states with difficult policy challenges and trade-offs. The dynamics inherent to each one of these crises significantly constrain the state's room for manoeuvre to address the others. Managing any single one of these crises has unpredictable consequences and impacts on the management of the other two, rendering the task of state governance fraught and contradictory. Thus, rather than presenting a set of compatible and complementary objectives which can align state-led policy efforts, these crises constitute a 'wicked trinity' of governance, which pulls the state in opposite directions (Alami, Copley, and Moraitis

[1] See for instance, 'A green transition that leaves no one behind', an open letter signed by world leaders on the occasion of the Paris Summit for a new global financial pact in June 2023. Available at: https://ec.europa.eu/commission/presscorner/detail/en/ac_23_3426 (last accessed 13 September 2023).

2023). This concentrates and compounds the class tensions at the heart of the capitalist state, rather than attenuates them. As capitalism develops and the 'wicked trinity' of governance becomes more acute, states may arguably turn to increasingly illiberal means and repression to contain its fallouts (Alami, Copley, and Moraitis 2023). Put differently, the trends so far suggest that accelerating climate change may deepen and intensify *disciplinary* state capitalist impulses in the area of governing working classes and populations rendered surplus.

In sum, in an age of catastrophic climate heating and environmental breakdown, we will most likely see a ramp up of all four state capitalist impulses. Add to this the power of combinatorial and cumulative ripple effects, which have played such an important role in the proliferation of state capitalist transformations across geographic space and policy domains over the past two decades. This suggests that the new state capitalism is not only here to stay, but its presence (whether in the form of state-capital hybrids or muscular modalities of statism) might be felt throughout the world economy like never before in recent capitalist history. Landscapes of state capitalism will arguably become more complex and polymorphous, more integrated into the planetary circuits of capital accumulation, but also more contested.

A Permanent, Foundational Shift in Capitalism?

If these projections are correct, what would this mean for the future of capitalism as a mode of production and social order determined by economic compulsions and structural imperatives? Our first tentative response here is that the phenomenon of state capitalism denotes fragility and instability rather than robustness and balanced expansion, both for capitalism as a mode of production, and for the state as the political form of this mode of production. The story told in this book is not one of an all-powerful state experiencing smooth transformations in order to accompany the relentless development of capitalism and consistently contain its tensions. For us, state capitalist impulses are best understood as messy, crisis-driven, always incomplete, and vulnerable to rollback. State capitalism is not a Polanyian counter-movement where states redress capitalism's excesses or rationally aim to set capitalist economies on more stable paths. Rather, state capitalist impulses are signs of the state stumbling and failing forward, under the weight of capitalism's political, economic, and environmental contradictions, and in a context of geopolitical crispation. This is not a prediction of terminal crisis or imminent collapse, but to emphasize the frailty rather than vigour of the state capitalist moment. This is also to express scepticism as to the possibility of states successfully containing ongoing and future crises and class conflicts, and engineering a new broad-based, dynamic cycle or regime of accumulation.

Whether we do see an uptick in capital accumulation and economic growth or not, it seems clear that the growing significance of the new state capitalism signals a 'geohistorical inflection point' (Peck 2023b; Dixon, Peck, Alami, and Whiteside 2023). Might future state capitalist impulses trigger an epochal transformation of capitalism? Our provisional response to this question is this: state capitalist impulses may indeed deepen and shape the trajectories of capital accumulation in such a consequential way that a tipping point is reached, after which state capitalism *could* become epoch-defining. The reader will have noticed a tension here between this claim about the potentially epoch-defining character of state capitalism, and the argument made earlier in this book about state capitalist impulses springing out of the ordinary (meaning, form-determined) operations of the capitalist state. We also repeatedly warned against the pitfalls of neat periodizations of capitalism, with discrete stages of history succeeding each other (such as liberal, Keynesian, developmental, neoliberal, or financialized capitalisms, each corresponding to paradigmatic modalities of state intervention and institutional forms).

We propose to tentatively resolve this tension as follows. To understand the present state of affairs requires that we conceive of state capitalism as a *quantitative* development (an enlargement of the state's role as promoter, supervisor, and owner of capital and an extension of its prerogatives). This quantitative development, as argued throughout the book, does not herald a fundamental mutation of the capitalist state into something else. The potentiality of state capitalist impulses is indeed contained in the form of the capitalist state and built into its DNA. Yet we must be open to the idea that further quantitative expansion, of the type we forecast, may lead to *qualitative* change, that is, a deeper mutation in the form of the state and its relation to capital. This may in turn imprint the future of capitalism with a distinctly new flavour. This (hypothetical) dialectical inversion of quantity into quality is precisely what we call the *spectre* of state capitalism. The metaphor of the spectre suggests that this tipping point, (that is, a point after which qualitative change happens), while not here just yet, somehow already inhabits and haunts our present. It also suggests that qualitative change may happen without a moment of total rupture or upheaval. In short, the spectre of state capitalism is the hypothesis that the cumulative combination of resurgent state ownership and ramped up statism, while not aimed at transforming the social property relations of capitalist society, may inadvertently end up doing so, with consequences for the nature of global capitalism.

What would this new configuration, or, dare we say it, *period* of capitalist development, look like? Again, we can only speculate here, but it seems to us that at least two elements are worth reflecting upon. The first one concerns the growing significance of state-capital hybrids and the increasing concentration of capital in the hands of states. To be sure, such process does not entail the abolition of capital. State-owned capital is still subjected to the imperatives of self-valorization. The state can partially or temporarily suspend these imperatives (for instance, by accepting a lower-than-average rate of profit, or by institutionalizing other social and political goals alongside profit maximization), but if it does so over the long term, the risk is that the capital becomes devalued. State-owned capital must therefore continue to valorize not to be destroyed, and with it, the social wealth that it represents. However, one can wonder what would be the consequences of the growing fusion of private and state capital and of the further development of flexible and liquid forms of property that collapse the distinction between state and private ownership, control and management.

We can foresee here a potential transformation in the nature of the socialization of capital, production, and private labour. We know from Marx that the expanded reproduction of capital contains an immanent contradiction between private property and the need for capital to assume the form of a directly collective property, that is, a socialized form of capital (Marx 1894/1991, 1867/1991; Starosta 2015). Marx argued that this contradictory tendency has historically been mediated by the emergence of joint stock companies and the modern financial system, which allowed for the socialization of production, social product, and private labour under the contradictory form of 'appropriation of social property by a few' (Marx 1894/1991). As Blumenfeld (2023) notes, for Marx and subsequent revolutionary thinkers, this immanent development of new forms of social production and social property 'could facilitate a transition away from a capitalist society of private ownership and private production toward a communist society of associated producers owning social wealth in common' (Blumenfeld 2023, 437). This could only be possible 'if the expropriated class are able to finish the project of expropriation that capital started, that is, to release the means of production from the ownership of anyone whatsoever' by means of state (2023, 437). The interesting thing here is that what is currently happening is indeed a form of socialization of capital and private labour that no one anticipated: it unfolds neither fully under the aegis of the state, nor is it confined solely to capitalist classes. The forms of social production and social property emerging from such hybrid processes of socialization could significantly alter patterns of class formation and recomposition. They could also lead to transformations in how capital is allocated, insofar as capital allocation would not be strictly the aggregate outcome of the decisions of private and independent producers and capital holders. Consequently, while this would still remain firmly within the confines of the capitalist mode of production, this could significantly transform how capital is invested as well as how its movement enforces value-disciplines on economic agents. This should prompt us to reflect on how the disciplinary power of capital would expresses itself in a world of increasing fusion of private and state capital, particularly if such hybrids become the dominant actors within the global total social capital (the sum of all individual capitals). How financial markets would develop under such conditions is also a question worth exploring.

Now, turning our gaze to the second modality of state capitalism, which is what we have referred to throughout the book as muscular forms of statism. Here, too, there are interesting reflections to be had if such modalities of interventionism continue to deepen and become ever more present in the circuits of capital. A key issue is that of the formal separation between the economic (the sphere of private market activity) and the political (the public sphere of the state). We know that the capitalist state-form is predicated on the formal separation of these mutually constituted spheres (mirrored in the separation of the state from civil society). This separation is important because it allows presenting the capitalist market economy as an autonomous and apolitical entity which allocates resources solely according to criteria of efficiency and optimization. This allows 'emptying' the capitalist economy of its social and political content, isolating it from broad-based democratic decisions, and portraying it as immutable (Meiksins Wood 1995). In other words, this separation is key to depoliticizing the capitalist economy, and it is functional to its reproduction. That said, we know from the history of capitalism that there can be considerable variation in terms of *how* this separation is constructed. We may wonder, then, how would this separation be reconstructed, institutionally mediated, and enforced, in a world of extensive and intensive state intervention in the circuits of capital and widespread state-capital hybridization? This immediately raises three important additional questions: what are the limits to state power set by its subsumption into capitalist social relations based upon private property? And how *far* can states go without subverting them? Finally, what will class-political and geopolitical struggles look like under such conditions, including resistance from below?

Avowedly, our reflections so far raised many more questions than they offered answers. Our hope is that they will foster creative re-explorations, and perhaps even reconstructions, of state theory (cf. Alami 2021; Whiteside, Alami, Dixon, and Peck 2023). In particular, the topic of state ownership and its mutations must be re-centred in state-theoretical debates, as well as the core question of the form-determinations of the capitalist state, with a focus on both conjunctural transformations and the more abstract features of the form and class character of the state. Relatedly, we also foresee potential productive conversations to be had between state capitalism studies and debates on other (potentially) epochal transformations in global capitalism, such as those happening under the headings of 'techno/neo-feudalism' (e.g., Durand 2020; Dean 2022; Morozov 2022; Rikap 2023) and 'political capitalism' (e.g., Riley and Brenner 2022; Barker 2023; Seaton 2023).

Progressive Openings?

Thinking through these questions (and others) about ongoing and possible future state capitalist transformations is important because it can help us identify potential openings for progressive and emancipatory politics. As should be clear to the reader by now, there is nothing inherently progressive about states concentrating and centralizing vast amounts of capital in their own hands, or about states acting as market agents, investors, or shareholders. State-owned or state-controlled capital can be, and often is, as environmentally destructive as privately owned capital. Consider, for instance, the vast quantities of fossil capital and non-renewable resources owned by states, in the form of national oil and gas companies, sovereign funds fuelled by oil and gas wealth, or majority and minority stakes in carbon-intensive assets, industries, firms, and factors of production (de Graaff 2012; Babić and Dixon 2023). Moreover, as mentioned earlier, state-owned capital is subjected to the imperatives of capital valorization and associated compulsions to increase market shares, profit margins, economic performance, and labour productivity. It is not rare, then, for processes of labour exploitation to be as intense within state-capital hybrids as they are in privately owned firms. More broadly, the multifaceted processes of state transformation studied in this book, which manifest as an aggregate expansion of the state's role as supervisor, regulator, guarantor, as investor-shareholder, and as direct owner of capital, overwhelmingly aimed at maximizing capital accumulation, shoring up profits, taming crises, and disciplining working classes, in order to stabilize economic and political relations, in the context of an increasingly competitive and geopolitically charged world capitalist economy. This is hardly, then, a 'return' of the state as a protective figure, even less so as a force for progressive social change. Our analysis should be sobering to anyone still convinced that increased state interventionism is a virtue in itself, or that governments' expanded roles would necessarily deliver desirable outcomes.

Is there, however, scope to influence what states will do with their newfound capabilities, powers, and resources? Finding bold and creative strategic answers to this question is a pressing task, given the urgency of the climate crisis and that of social reproduction (see Fraser 2016). We know from both the history of capitalist states and state theory that states are caught up in, and significantly determined by, the dynamic of valorization of capital. But we also know that, as the political form of antagonistic capitalist social relations, they are fields of social struggles. The latter perspective opens up space for analysis and identification of sites and strategies for political intervention, in other words, for conjunctural analysis (see inter alia Grayson and Little 2017; Gilbert 2019; Leitner and Sheppard 2020; Peck 2023a).

With this in mind, what sorts of opportunities and constraints does the new state capitalism offer for emancipatory politics and progressive social change? Our response is that the new state capitalism, as a geohistorical moment and inflection point, generates openings for at least two types of strategies and political engagement with (and against) the state, a reformist and a transformative one, which we discuss in the remaining pages of this book. To be sure, the line between the two is not always clear cut, and the former would no doubt have a role in enabling the latter, as the well-known notion of 'non-reformist reforms' suggests. The distinction is nonetheless useful for heuristic purposes. We address our strategic reflections to a collective 'us', by which we mean anyone concerned with a liveable future *for all* on this planet.

Democratizing and Greening State Capitalism?

We can call the reformist strategy 'democratizing and greening state capitalism'. The logic of this strategy is that the state capitalist conjuncture offers a window of opportunity, in both ideological and material terms. States are indeed extensively intervening across economies and societies, in ever more explicit and visible ways. Ideologically, this makes it much harder for free-market ideologues to claim that states are incapable of doing meaningful things besides protecting private property rights, maintaining sound money, and waging war. This is also an opportunity to redefine what are considered appropriate and legitimate modalities and purposes of intervention. The (partial) crisis of legitimacy of neoliberalism is also contributing to this greater space for legitimacy struggles. Orthodoxies are much more difficult to defend and police in an area of remarkable regulatory experimentation and state restructuring. The new state capitalism also offers a material window of opportunity for pushing states to use their newfound capacities and resources in directions that are, at a minimum, less socially and environmentally destructive, and, going a step further, in ways that (1) immediately address the worsening crisis of social reproduction in both the Global North and South; and (2) alter the balance of class forces in favour of the greater majority in the short to medium term. In addition, given the climate emergency, the new state capitalism shows that states can, and indeed must, do more for us, notably in terms of redressing inequalities and leading decarbonization transitions. Let us illustrate this argument with a few examples.

Central banks have demonstrated that they can mobilize incredibly powerful resources to maintain financial stability, prop up the value of financial assets, and influence the terms according to which states and firms fund themselves. This opens the possibility that such financial and regulatory power can be harnessed for altering financing conditions in ways that encourage the channelling of credit and financial capital away from fossil-fuel based and carbon-intensive industries and towards green and low-carbon sectors, industries, infrastructure, and technologies. Beyond existing and narrow responses such as mandatory climate risk disclosure, repurposed central banks could also contribute to offering low-cost finance to states, as they did after the 2008 global financial crisis and during the COVID-19 pandemic, only this time to massively augment their firepower to invest in low-carbon production systems, green transportation and mobilities, ecosystem and biodiversity restoration, electrification, agroecology, renewable energy infrastructure, climate mitigation and adaptation. Strategic coordination with treasury departments and industry, energy, housing, transport, and other ministries could maximize the effectiveness of central bank climate activity (Best, Paterson, Alami, Bracking, et al. 2023). Similarly, state-owned policy and development banks have become again major economic actors, with a proven track record in supporting firms, sectors, and industries deemed strategic. Why not drastically scale up their lending capacities to steer rapid decarbonization pathways, as well as to facilitate vast transfers of financial resources from richer to poorer countries?

States also now directly or indirectly own vast amounts of capital and assets, via their state enterprises and sovereign wealth funds, which are themselves invested in a wide range of firms and sectors. Here, too, there is potential for leveraging this increased state presence in the circuits of capital. Where relevant, this could mean forcing states to divest from carbon-intensive and extractive industries, or, on the contrary, forcing them to keep fossil fuels in the ground (Malm 2020; Pellegrini and Arsel 2022; Babić and Dixon 2023). This could also mean making state asset management companies, state enterprises, and sovereign funds behave as 'activist shareholders', that is, putting pressure on the firms where they hold equity to transform their activities and operations towards less environmentally destructive ones. If state enterprises can be turned into modern corporations which efficiently manage complex transnational operations, then they could also, or rather, alternatively, be transformed into agile public energy companies, tasked with coordinating public investment into electrification (rather than simply de-risk projects for the private sector) and delivering cheap, clean energy (Brusseler 2023).

Moreover, if muscular forms of statism can be mobilized to penalize foreign states and firms, then surely these coercive capabilities can be redirected towards enforcing strict regulations and robust tax systems to discipline carbon-intensive capital and drive accelerated decarbonization strategies. These coercive powers could be used to discipline private bond holders and solve the looming debt crisis in the developing world in ways that afford states the resources to address the climate crisis. The massive subsidies that fossil capital continues to benefit from could be redirected to green sectors. Techno-industrial policies and national innovation systems could be repurposed to serve the development and global transfer of low carbon technologies rather than the ongoing race for digital tech supremacy. We could use dozens of other examples of how state capitalist impulses could be re-channelled towards better ends, but the broader point is the new state capitalism offers *objective* opportunities (which does not mean that these opportunities would be easy to seize, as discussed below) to struggle over the shape and direction of state transformations.

Importantly, efforts to green state capitalism would arguably only work in ways that benefit and empower the greater majority if they are pursued in conjunction with strategies of broad-based economic democratization. This could include pressuring state-owned and state-controlled corporate entities to internalize public goals and values, such as strengthening democratic control, empowering local communities, enhancing public accountability, and favouring labour participation. In addition, putting powerful and democratically controlled and accountable economic institutions at the centre of our economic systems could help reduce the influence of purely profit-maximizing financial actors, and could help build working-class power and mass popular support for decarbonization pathways (see for instance McCarthy 2022 and the excellent work of the UK-based think tank Common Wealth). That progressive labour and civil society organizations are increasingly calling for vast democratic public ownership, social wealth funds, and the like, as a means to complement or gradually substitute for private capital allocation at national and municipal levels is indeed a sign of the grasp of the spectre of state capitalism on our political imaginations.

Overall, 'democratizing and greening state capitalism' as a reformist project thus aims at achieving a form of capitalism safer for humans and non-human natures, beyond neoliberalism. Yet such a project also faces major potential obstacles and limitations. One is of course the fierce political opposition of various segments of capital who stand to lose most from its realization, not least firms and states owning fossil fuel resources and carbon-intensive assets. Another major obstacle is the *disciplinary* state capitalist impulse, in both its geoeconomic and domestic dimension. Indeed, there is the risk that competition and interstate rivalry undermine the potential positive effects of this project at the aggregate, planetary level (for instance, if gains for workers and citizens in one country are made at the expense of populations and non-human natures elsewhere, strengthening ongoing patterns of eco-apartheid and green imperialism) (Ajl 2021). Moreover, the liberal-democratic channels and mechanisms of parliamentary representation through which progressive forces have pushed for reformist projects in the past (such as trade unions and the broader labour movement, social democratic parties, collective bargaining institutions, etc.) have been structurally eroded over the past decades. Restoring these channels would be a long and difficult task. Furthermore, as we have seen, states in both the under- and the overdeveloped world have generally turned towards more coercive and authoritarian forms of rule, empowering repressive apparatuses to suppress dissent and quell various forms of mobilization, protests, and demonstrations. These trends of domestic and geoeconomic state capitalist *disciplinary* impulses are not easily separable from, say, the *productive* and *absorptive* state capitalist impulses. To put it bluntly, the strategic terrain constituted by the new state capitalism offers objective opportunities for progressive forces and coalitions of workers and populations rendered surplus to shape the future of state transformations, yet it also produces considerable obstacles and constraints to do so in ways that benefit the greater majority.

Towards Democratic Planning and Alternative Forms of Ownership?

As we have just seen, from the perspective of reformist strategies, expansive state ownership and muscular modalities of statism offer a material and ideological opportunity to leverage for improving our world in its current (capitalist) form. But from the perspective of a transformative project, that is, one that aims to radically transform existing social relations in order to bring another world into existence (beyond capital and the state), the contemporary advent of state capitalism offers something altogether different. It reveals fault lines and cracks in capitalist society. As we peer into these fissures, we can get a glimpse of what a radically different future society might look like. We can identify the seeds of progressive future societal transformations, including alternative forms of *planning* and *ownership* of our productive activities.

Consider the formal separation between the economic and political spheres, which, as explained earlier, plays a central role in depoliticizing economic and market relations under capitalism. An unintentional, yet particularly potent, effect of the enhanced and more visible role of the state, whether in the form of resurgent state ownership or muscular statism, is that it contributes to the re-politicization of economic relations: all of a sudden, the capitalist economy appears in plain sight for what it is, that is, an irreducibly political construct that is fundamentally (and perhaps increasingly) underpinned by political power and public authority in the form of the state. What this fissure reveals is the very possibility of politically reconstructing relations of production and exchange, so that we do not experience them as an external, impersonal, semi-autonomous force (in the form of the movement of prices, markets, money, and other economic abstractions), as we currently do. By contrast, they could be reconstructed in such a way that they are directly subordinated to our collective decisions. This is not simply about delegating to the state more roles and responsibilities for planning the economy, regulating exchange, or governing markets. This crack offers us a glance at a much more radical prospect of politicization of economic relations: that of directly and consciously organizing our productive activities and regulating our metabolic relation with nature, following principles of voluntary association and cooperation, based on our capacities and on our collective identification of needs and desires to be fulfilled, while balancing goals of efficiency, justice, democracy, and equality (Arboleda 2021; Sorg 2023).

Relatedly, the new state capitalism reveals another fissure in contemporary capitalist society, this time concerning questions of ownership and control. Capitalism is based on a particular set of social property relations, where the greater majority of us are dispossessed of the means of reproducing ourselves. The means of production are owned or controlled by a small group of firms and individuals, who also own or control vast amounts of wealth, resources, and assets. With this comes tremendous power, that of deciding how the social product is allocated, and where and how labour and non-human natures are put to work, left to die, or destroyed. In short, this is the power to invest, withhold, or withdraw capital across sectors and geographies. Now, as argued earlier, there is no reason to assume that state ownership of capital is necessarily better than private ownership (although it can be). Rather, from the perspective of a radical project of transformation, what the new state capitalism shows, in however partial, lop-sided, and ephemeral way, is that social property relations are not natural or eternal, and the very power to allocate social wealth can be wrested away from the owners of capital and assets. In other words, this crack reveals the potential for radical democratic experiments with alternative forms of public ownership, through which communities can own, manage, and socialize the wealth they produce in ways that do not prioritize profits over social life and non-human natures, but rather favour objectives of human flourishing, sustainable nature-society relations, planetary solidarity, and the self-development of individuals (cf. Buller and Lawrence 2022). Alongside the spectre of state capitalism, we catch a fleeting glimpse of how we could reclaim power and control over our collective future.

References

Adler, P. 2009. Marx and organization studies today. In P. Adler (ed.), *The Oxford Handbook of Sociology and Organization Studies: Classical Foundations* (62–91). Oxford: Oxford University Press.

Agnew, J. 1994. The territorial trap: the geographical assumptions of international relations theory. *Review of International Political Economy* 1 (1): 53–80.

Agnew, J. 2017. *Globalization and Sovereignty: Beyond the Territorial Trap.* London: Rowman & Littlefield.

Agnoli, J., and P. Brückner. 1968. *Die Transformation der Demokratie.* Frankfurt a. M.,: Europäische Verlagsanstalt.

Aguilera, R. V., J. Capapé, and J. Santiso. 2016. Sovereign wealth funds: A strategic governance view. *Academy of Management Perspectives* 30 (1): 5–23.

Aharoni, Y. 2018. The evolution of state-owned multinational enterprise theory. In A. Cuervo-Cazurra (ed.), *State-Owned Multinationals: Governments in Global Business* (9–44). Cham: Springer International Publishing.

Aiyar, M. S., M. J. Chen, C. Ebeke, M. C. H. Ebeke, M. R. Garcia-Saltos, T. Gudmundsson, M. A. Ilyina, M. A. Kangur, T. Kunaratskul, and M. S. L. Rodriguez. 2023. *Geo-economic Fragmentation and the Future of Multilateralism.* International Monetary Fund.

Ajl, M. 2021. *A People's Green New Deal.* London: Pluto Press.

Alami, I. 2019. *Money Power and Financial Capital in Emerging Markets.* London: Routledge.

Alami, I. 2021. State theory in the age of state capitalism 3.0? *Science & Society* 85 (2): 162–170.

Alami, I. 2023. The spiral of state capitalism: labour transformations or the 'whip of external necessity'? *Global Political Economy* 2 (1): 17–36.

Alami, I. 2024. *Foreign investment screening mechanisms and emergent geographies of (post)globalization.* Denver: AAG Keynote Lecture in Economic Geography.

Alami, I., and A. Dixon. 2022. 'Expropriation of capitalist by state capitalist': Organizational change and the centralization of capital as state property. *Economic Geography* 98 (4): 303–326.

Alami, I., and A. D. Dixon. 2023. Uneven and combined state capitalism. *Environment and Planning A: Economy and Space* 55 (1): 72–99.

Alami, I., A. D. Dixon, and E. Mawdsley. 2021. State capitalism and the new global D/development regime. *Antipode* 53 (5): 1294–1318.

Alami, I., A. D. Dixon, R. Gonzalez-Vicente, M. Babic, L. Seung-Ook, I. A. Medby, and N. D. Graaff. 2022. Geopolitics and the 'new' state capitalism. *Geopolitics* 27 (3): 995–1023.

Alami, I., and J. Taggart. 2024. A partial conversion: How the 'unholy trinity' of global economic governance adapts to state capitalism. *European Journal of International Relations.* online first.

Alami, I., J. Copley, and A. Moraitis. 2023. The 'wicked trinity' of late capitalism: governing in an era of stagnation, surplus humanity, and environmental breakdown. *Geoforum.* Online first.

Allan, B., J. I. Lewis, and T. Oatley. 2021. Green industrial policy and the global transformation of climate politics. *Global Environmental Politics* 21 (4): 1–19.

Allen, G. 2023. China is striking back in the tech war with the U.S. *Time.*

Allenbach-Ammann, J. 2023. EU Commission's Vestager proposes change to state aid rules. *Euractiv* (13 January). https://www.euractiv.com/section/economy-jobs/news/eu-commissions-vestager-proposes-change-to-state-aid-rules/.

Al-Sadiq, A., and Gutiérrez, D. A. 2023. Do sovereign wealth funds reduce fiscal policy pro-cyclicality? New evidence using a non-parametric approach. IMF Working Paper 23/133.

Alsweilem, K., and M. Rietveld. 2018. *Sovereign Wealth Funds in Resource Economies: Institutional and Fiscal Foundations.* New York: Columbia University Press.

Althouse, J., and R. Svartzman. 2022. Bringing subordinated financialisation down to earth: The political ecology of finance-dominated capitalism. *Cambridge Journal of Economics* 46 (4): 679–702.

Altınörs, G., and Ü. Akçay. 2022. Authoritarian neoliberalism, crisis, and consolidation: The political economy of regime change in Turkey. *Globalizations* 19 (7): 1029–1053.

Anderlini, J. 2020. China is escalating its punishment diplomacy. *Financial Times*, 23 September.

Andreoni, A., and H.-J. Chang. 2019. The political economy of industrial policy: Structural interdependencies, policy alignment and conflict management. *Structural Change and Economic Dynamics* 48: 136–150.

Anguelov, D. 2021. Banking 'development': The geopolitical–economy of infrastructure financing. *Area Development and Policy* 6 (3): 271–295.

Arboleda, M. 2020. *Planetary Mine: Territories of Extraction under Late Capitalism.* London: Verso.

Arboleda, M. 2021. *Gobernar la utopía: sobre la planificación y el poder popular.* Buenos Aires: Caja Negra.

Arha, K. 2022. Pursuing freedom and openness in the Indo-Pacific. *East Asia Forum* (13 August). https://eastasiaforum.org/2022/08/13/pursuing-freedom-and-openness-in-the-indo-pacific/.

Aronoff, K., A. Battistoni, D. A. Cohen, T. N. Riofrancos, and N. Klein. 2019. *A Planet to Win: Why We Need a Green New Deal.* London: Verso.

Arsel, M., F. Adaman, and A. Saad-Filho. 2021. Authoritarian developmentalism: The latest stage of neoliberalism? *Geoforum* 124: 261–266.

Arrighi, G. 1994. *The Long Twentieth Century: Money, Power and the Origins of Our Times.* London: Verso.

Ashman, S. 2009. Capitalism, uneven and combined development and the transhistoric. *Cambridge Review of International Affairs* 22 (1): 29–46.

Åslund, A. 2019. *Russia's Crony Capitalism: The Path from Market Economy to Kleptocracy.* New Haven: Yale University Press.

Asmelash, E., and R. Gorini. 2021. *International oil companies and the energy transition.* Abu Dhabi: International Renewable Energy Agency.

Antunes de Oliveira, F., J. Germann, and S. Rolf. 2023. A system of mutual dependence and antagonism: Exploring the potential of uneven and combined development within Global Political Economy. *Global Political Economy* 2 (1): 2–16.

Babic, M. 2023. State capital in a geoeconomic world: mapping state-led foreign investment in the global political economy. *Review of International Political Economy* 30 (1): 201–228.

Babić, M., and A. D. Dixon. 2023. Decarbonising states as owners. *New Political Economy* 28 (4): 608–627.

Babic, M., A. D. Dixon, and I. Liu eds. 2022. *The Political Economy of Geoeconomics: Europe in a Changing World.* New York; London: Palgrave Macmillan.

Babic, M., J. Fichtner, and E. M. Heemskerk. 2017. States versus corporations: Rethinking the power of business in international politics. *The International Spectator* 52 (4): 20–43.

Babic, M., J. Garcia-Bernardo, and E. M. Heemskerk. 2020. The rise of transnational state capital: State-led foreign investment in the 21st century. *Review of International Political Economy* 27 (3): 433–475.

Bachher, J. S., A. D. Dixon, and A. H. B. Monk. 2016. *The New Frontier Investors: How Pension Funds, Sovereign Funds, and Endowments are Changing the Business of Asset Management and Long-term Investing.* London: Palgrave Macmillan.

Baglioni, E., L. Campling, and G. Hanlon. 2023. Beyond rentiership: Standardisation, intangibles and value capture in global production. *Environment and Planning A: Economy and Space* 55 (6): 1528–1547.

Bair, J., S. Ponte, L. Seabrooke, and D. Wigan. 2023. Entangled chains of global value and wealth. *Review of International Political Economy* 30 (6): 2423–2439.

Baldwin, E., S. Carley, and S. Nicholson-Crotty. 2019. Why do countries emulate each others' policies? A global study of renewable energy policy diffusion. *World Development* 120: 29–45.

Baldwin, R., and C. Teulings eds. 2014. *Secular Stagnation: Facts, Causes, and Cures.* London: CEPR Press.

Baltz, M. 2022. What lies beneath the 'Tariff Man'? The Trump administration's response to China's 'state capitalism'. *Contemporary Politics* 28 (3): 328–346.

Banerjee, R., and B. Hofman. 2018. The rise of zombie firms: Causes and consequences. *BIS Quarterly Review* (September). https://www.bis.org/publ/qtrpdf/r_qt1809g.pdf.

Barkan, J. 2013. *Corporate Sovereignty: Law and Government under Capitalism.* Minneapolis: University of Minnesota Press.

Barker, T. 2023. Some questions about political capitalism. *New Left Review* (140/141): 35–51.

Barrow, C. 1993. *Critical Theories of the State: Marxist, Neomarxist, Postmarxist.* Madison: University of Wisconsin Press.

Baum, A., P. Medas, A. Soler, and M. Sy. 2021. How to assess fiscal risks from state-owned enterprises: Benchmarking and stress testing. *IMF How to Notes* 2021/009. https://www.imf.org/en/Publications/Fiscal-Affairs-Department-How-To-Notes/Issues/2021/08/18/How-to-Assess-Fiscal-Risks-from-State-Owned-Enterprises-463616.

Baybeck, B., W. Berry, and D. Siegel. 2011. A strategic theory of policy diffusion via intergovernmental competition. *The Journal of Politics* 73 (1): 232–247.

Becker, U. 2014. *The BRICs and Emerging Economies in Comparative Perspective: Political Economy, Liberalization and Institutional Change.* London: Routledge.

Behuria, P. 2018. Learning from role models in Rwanda: Incoherent emulation in the construction of a neoliberal developmental state. *New Political Economy* 23 (4): 422–440.

Belesky, P., and G. Lawrence. 2019. Chinese state capitalism and neomercantilism in the contemporary food regime: Contradictions, continuity and change. *The Journal of Peasant Studies* 46 (6): 1119–1141.

Benanav, A. 2020. *Automation and the Future of Work.* London; New York: Verso.

Bernards, N. 2023. Undoing democratic social citizenship? The digitalization of G2p payments and the making of private digital authoritarianism. In Z. Bhorat and M. Rauchbauer (eds), *Decoding Digital Authoritarianism* (66–71). Los Angeles: Berggruen Institute.

Bernards, N., and S. Soederberg. 2021. Relative surplus populations and the crises of contemporary capitalism: Reviving, revisiting, recasting. *Geoforum* 126: 412–419.

Bernes, J. 2013. Logistics, counterlogistics and the communist prospect. *Endnotes* 3. Available at: https://endnotes.org.uk/issues/3/en/jasper-bernes-logistics-counterlogistics-and-the-communist-prospect (last accessed 9 January 2023).

Berry, C., J. Froud, and T. Barker. 2021. *The political economy of industrial strategy in the UK: From productivity problems to development dilemmas.* London: Agenda.

Best, J., M. Paterson, I. Alami, S. Bracking, D. Bailey, J. Green, E. Helleiner, J. Jackson, J. van't Klooster, P. Langley, S. Maechler, J. Morris, A. Roberts, S. Quorning, R. Watt, and S. Wilshire. 2023. Climate change governance by central banks in an era of interlocking crises. Working paper.

Bhagat, A., and R. Phillips. 2023. The techfare state: Debt, discipline, and accelerated neoliberalism. *New Political Economy* 28 (4): 526–538.

Bhagat, A., and R. Phillips. forthcoming. Financing the border: Practices of the Canadian racial state. *Review of International Political Economy.*

Bhorat, Z., and M. Rauchbauer eds. 2023. *Decoding Digital Authoritarianism.* Los Angeles: Berggruen Institute.

Biebricher, T. 2019. *The Political Theory of Neoliberalism.* Stanford: Stanford University Press.

Bieler, A., and A. D. Morton. 2018. *Global Capitalism, Global War, Global Crisis.* New York, NY: Cambridge University Press.

Birch, K., C. Ward, and E. Tretter. 2022. Introduction: New frontiers of techno-economic rentiership. *Competition & Change* 26 (3–4): 407–414.

Blanchette, J. 2021. Confronting the challenge of Chinese state capitalism. *Center for Strategic and International Studies.* Available at: https://www.csis.org/analysis/confronting-challenge-chinese-state-capitalism (last accessed 20 August 2023).

Blinken, A. and R. Kagan 2019. 'America First' is only making the world worse. Here's a better approach. Brookings Institute. Available at: https://www.brookings.edu/articles/america-first-is-only-making-the-world-worse-heres-a-better-approach/ (last accessed 22 August 2023).

Block, F. 2008. Swimming against the current: The rise of a hidden developmental state in the United States. *Politics & Society* 36 (2): 169–206.

Block, F. L., and M. R. Keller. 2011. *State of Innovation: the U.S. Government's Role in Technology Development.* Boulder, CO: Paradigm Publishers.

Blumenfeld, J. 2023. Expropriation of the expropriators. *Philosophy & Social Criticism* 49 (4): 431–447.

Boito, A., and A. Saad-Filho. 2016. State, state institutions, and political power in Brazil. *Latin American Perspectives* 43 (2): 190–206.

Bok, R. 2019. 'By our metaphors you shall know us': The 'fix' of geographical political economy. *Progress in Human Geography* 43 (6): 1087–1108.

Bonefeld, W. 2010. Free economy and the strong state: Some notes on the state. *Capital & Class* 34 (1): 15–24.

Bonefeld, W. 2014. *Critical Theory and the Critique of Political Economy.* New York: Bloomsbury Academic.

Bonefeld, W. 2017. *The Strong State and the Free Economy.* London; New York: Rowman & Littlefield International.

Bonizzi, B., A. Kaltenbrunner, and J. Powell. 2020. Subordinate financialization in emerging capitalist economies. In P. Mader, D. Mertens, and N. Van der Zwan (eds), *The Routledge International Handbook of Financialization* (177–187). Abingdon: Routledge.

Bougrea, A., J. Orbie, and M. Vermeiren. 2022. The new European financial architecture for development: Change or continuity? *European Foreign Affairs Review* 27 (3): 337–360.

Bourgery-Gonse, T. 2023. EU's Breton wants sovereignty fund to buy out firms of systemic importance. *Euractiv.* 1 July. https://www.euractiv.com/section/economy-jobs/news/eus-breton-wants-sovereignty-fund-to-buy-out-firms-of-systemic-importance/.

Boyer, R. 2020. Les Capitalismes à L'épreuve de la Pandémie. Paris: La Découverte.

Branstetter, L. 2018. China's forced technology problem—and what to do about it. In *Peterson Institute for International Economics Policy Brief* (18-13).

Braun, B., and D. Gabor. 2020. Central banking, shadow banking, and infrastructural power 1. In P. Mader, D. Mertens, and N. Van der Zwan (eds), *The Routledge International Handbook of Financialization* (241–252). Abingdon: Routledge.
Braunstein, J. 2014. The novelty of sovereign wealth funds: The emperor's new clothes? *Global Policy* 5 (2): 169–180.
Braunstein, J. 2019. *Capital Choices: Sectoral Politics and the Variation of Sovereign Wealth.* Ann Arbor: University of Michigan Press.
Brautigam, D. 2020. A critical look at Chinese 'debt-trap diplomacy': The rise of a meme. Area Development and Policy 5 (1): 1–14.
Bremmer, I. 2009. State capitalism comes of age: The end of the free market. *Foreign Affairs* 88: 40.
Bremmer, I. 2010. *The End of the Free Market: Who Wins the War between States and Corporations?* New York: Portfolio.
Brennan, E. 2021. Mapping Logistical Capitalism. *Theory, Culture & Society* 38 (4): 135–146.
Brenner, N. 2009. Open questions on state rescaling. *Cambridge Journal of Regions, Economy and Society* 2 (1): 123–139.
Brenner, N. ed. 2014. *Implosions / Explosions: Towards a Study of Planetary Urbanization.* Berlin: Jovis.
Brenner, N., B. Jessop, M. Jones, and G. MacLeod eds. 2003. *State/Space: A Reader.* Malden, Mass.; Oxford: Blackwell.
Brenner, N., J. Peck, and N. Theodore. 2010. Variegated neoliberalization: Geographies, modalities, pathways. *Global Networks* 10 (2): 182–222.
Brenner, R. 2006. *The Economics of Global Turbulence: The Advanced Capitalist Economies from Long Boom to Long Downturn, 1945–2005.* London; New York: Verso.
Bridge, G., and M. Bradshaw. 2017. Making a global gas market: Territoriality and production networks in liquefied natural gas. *Economic Geography* 93 (3): 215–240.
Brooks, S. M. 2005. Interdependent and domestic foundations of policy change: The diffusion of pension privatization around the world. *International Studies Quarterly* 49 (2): 273–294.
Brooks, S. M., and M. J. Kurtz. 2012. Paths to financial policy diffusion: Statist legacies in Latin America's globalization. *International Organization* 66 (1): 95–128.
Brophy, D. 2019. Good and bad Muslims in Xinjiang. *Made in China Journal* 4 (2): 44–53.
Bruff, I., and C. B. Tansel. 2019. Authoritarian neoliberalism: Trajectories of knowledge production and praxis. *Globalizations* 16 (3): 233–244.
Brunetti, C., B. Dennis, D. Gates, D. Hancock, D. Ignell, E. Kiser, G. Kotta, A. Kovner, R. Rosen, and N. Tabor. 2021. Climate change and financial stability. *FEDS Notes.*
De Brunhoff, S. 1981. *Etat et Capital. Recherches sur la Politique Economique.* Paris: François Maspero.
Brusseler, M. 2023. *Coordinating the Green Prosperity Plan.* London: Commonwealth.
Bruton, G. D., M. W. Peng, D. Ahlstrom, C. Stan, and K. Xu. 2015. State-owned enterprises around the world as hybrid organizations. *Academy of Management Perspectives* 29 (1): 92–114.
Bulfone, F. 2023. Industrial policy and comparative political economy: A literature review and research agenda. *Competition & Change* 0 (0): 10245294221076225.
Bulfone, F., T. Ergen, and M. Kalaitzake. 2023. No strings attached: Corporate welfare, state intervention, and the issue of conditionality. *Competition & Change* 27 (2): 253–276.
Buller, A., and M. Lawrence. 2022. *Owning the Future: Power and Property in an Age of Crisis.* London: Verso.
Burnham, P. 1996. Capital, crisis and the international state system. In W. Bonefeld and J. Holloway (eds), *Global Capital, National State and the Politics of Money* (92–115). London: Palgrave Macmillan.

Burnham, P. 2011. Towards a political theory of crisis: Policy and resistance across Europe. *New Political Science* 33 (4): 493–507.
Butzbach, O., D. B. Fuller, G. Schnyder, and L. Svystunova. 2022. State-owned enterprises as institutional actors: A hybrid historical institutionalist and institutional work framework. *Management and Organization Review* 18 (6): 1032–1076.
Byler, D. 2019. Preventative policing as community detention in northwest China. *Made in China Journal* 4 (3): 88–94.
Byler, D. 2020. The Global Implications of 'Re-education' Technologies in Northwest China. *New Lines Institute.* July 8, 2020. https://newlinesinstitute.org/rules-based-international-order/the-global-implications-of-re-education-technologies-in-northwest-china/.
Callison, W., and Z. Manfredi eds. 2020. *Mutant Neoliberalism: Market Rule and Political Rupture.* First edition. ed. New York: Fordham University Press.
Cammack, P. 2010. The shape of capitalism to come. *Antipode* 41 (s1): 262–280.
Carmody, P. 2020. Dependence not debt-trap diplomacy. *Area Development and Policy* 5 (1): 23–31.
Carmody, P. R., and J. T. Murphy. 2022. Chinese neoglobalization in East Africa: Logics, couplings and impacts. *Space and Polity* 26 (1): 20–43.
Carmody, P., P. Kragelund, and R. Reboredo. 2020. *Africa's Shadow Rise: China and the Mirage of African Economic Development.* London: Zed.
Carney, R. W. 2015. The stabilizing state: State capitalism as a response to financial globalization in one-party regimes. *Review of International Political Economy* 22 (4): 838–873.
Carney, R. W. 2018. *Authoritarian Capitalism: Sovereign Wealth Funds and State-Owned Enterprises in East Asia and Beyond.* New York: Cambridge University Press.
Carney, R. W., and M. A. Witt. 2014. The role of the state in Asian business systems. In M. Witt and G. Redding (eds), *The Oxford Handbook of Asian Business Systems* (538–560). Oxford: Oxford University Press.
Chacko, P., and K. Jayasuriya. 2018. A capitalising foreign policy: Regulatory geographies and transnationalised state projects. *European Journal of International Relations* 24 (1): 82–105.
Chan, Z. T., and S. Meunier. 2022. Behind the screen: Understanding national support for a foreign investment screening mechanism in the European Union. *The Review of International Organizations* 17 (3): 513–541.
Charbonnier, P. 2022. The birth of war ecology. *GREEN* 2 (1): 70–76.
Charnock, G. 2008. Competitiveness and critique: The value of a new-materialist research project. *Historical Materialism* 16 (2): 117–141.
Charnock, G., and G. Starosta. 2016. Introduction: The new international division of labour and the critique of political economy today. In G. Charnock and G. Starosta (eds), *The New International Division of Labour: Global Transformation and Uneven Development* (1–22). London: Palgrave Macmillan UK.
Charnock, G., and G. Starosta. 2018. Towards a 'unified field theory' of uneven development: Human productive subjectivity, capital and the international. *Global Society* 32 (3): 324–343.
Chazan, G., S. Fleming, and K. Inagaki. 2023. A global subsidy war? Keeping up with the Americans. *Financial Times*, 13 July.
Chen, M. 2021. Infrastructure finance, late development, and China's reshaping of international credit governance. *European Journal of International Relations* 27 (3): 830–857.
Cherif, R., and F. Hasanov. 2019. The return of the policy that shall not be named: Principles of industrial policy. *IMF Working Papers* (74).
Cherif, R., F. Hasanov, N. Spatafora, R. Giri, D. Milkov, S. N. Quayyum, G. Salinas, and A. M. Warner. 2022. Industrial policy for growth and diversification: A conceptual framework. *Departmental Papers* 2022 (017): A001.

Chimhowu, A. O., D. Hulme, and L. T. Munro. 2019. The 'New' national development planning and global development goals: Processes and partnerships. *World Development* 120: 76–89.

Chiyemura, F., E. Gambino, and T. Zajontz. 2023. Infrastructure and the politics of African state agency: Shaping the Belt and Road Initiative in East Africa. *Chinese Political Science Review* 8 (1): 105–131.

Christophers, B. 2012. Anaemic geographies of financialisation. *New Political Economy* 17 (3): 271–291.

Christophers, B. 2016. *The Great Leveler: Capitalism and Competition in the Court of law.* Cambridge, Massachusetts: Harvard University Press.

Christophers, B. 2020. *Rentier Capitalism: Who Owns the Economy, and Who Pays for It?* London; New York: Verso.

Chua, C., M. Danyluk, D. Cowen, and L. Khalili. 2018. Introduction: Turbulent circulation: Building a critical engagement with logistics. *Environment and Planning D: Society and Space* 36 (4): 617–629.

Chwieroth, J. M. 2014. Fashions and fads in finance: The political foundations of sovereign wealth fund creation. *International Studies Quarterly* 58 (4): 752–763.

Ciută, F., and I. Klinke. 2010. Lost in conceptualization: Reading the 'new Cold War' with critical geopolitics. *Political Geography* 29 (6): 323–332.

Clark, G. L., and M. J. Dear. 1984. *State Apparatus: Structures and Language of Legitimacy.* Boston; London: Allen & Unwin.

Clark, G. L., and A. D. Dixon. 2017. Sovereign wealth funds and the global political economy of trust and legitimacy. In Clark, G. L., A. D. Dixon, and A. H. B. Monk (eds), *The Oxford Handbook of Sovereign Wealth Funds* (2013). *Sovereign Wealth Funds: Legitimacy, Governance, and Global Power.* Princeton and Oxford: Princeton University Press.

Clark, G. L., and A. H. B. Monk. 2017. *Institutional Investors in Global Markets.* Oxford: Oxford University Press.

Clarke, S. ed. 1991. *The State Debate.* London: Macmillan.

Clarke, S. 1992. The global accumulation of capital and the periodisation of the capitalist state form. In W. Bonefeld, R. Gunn, and K. Psychopedis (eds), *Open Marxism, vol. I: Dialectics and History* (133–150). London: Pluto Press.

Clarke, S. 1994. *Marx's Theory of Crisis.* London: St Martin's Press.

Clover, J. 2016. *Riot. Strike. Riot: The New Era of Uprisings.* London: New York: Verso.

Coe, N. M. a., and H. W.-C. a. Yeung. 2015. *Global Production Networks: Theorizing Economic Development in an Interconnected World.* First edition. Oxford: Oxford University Press.

Copley, J. 2022. *Governing Financialization: The Tangled Politics of Financial Liberalization in Britain.* First edition. Oxford: Oxford University Press.

Copley, J., and A. Moraitis. 2021. Beyond the mutual constitution of states and markets: On the governance of alienation. *New Political Economy* 26 (3): 490–508.

Coppola, F. 2019. *The Case for People's Quantitative Easing.* Medford, MA: Polity.

Cowen, D. 2014. *The Deadly Life of Logistics: Mapping Violence in Global Trade.* Minneapolis: University of Minnesota Press.

Criscuolo, C., L. Díaz, G. Lalanne, L. Guillouet, C.-É. v. d. Put, C. Weder, and H. Z. Deutsch. 2023. Quantifying industrial strategies across nine OECD countries. *OECD Science, Technology and Industry Policy Papers* (150).

Cuervo-Cazurra, A. 2018. State-owned multinationals: An introduction. In A. Cuervo-Cazurra (ed.), *State-owned Multinationals: Governments in Global Business* (1–6). Basingstoke: Palgrave Macmillan.

Cumming, D. J., G. Wood, I. Filatotchev, and J. Reinecke, 145–158. Oxford: Oxford University Press.

da Silva, P. P. 2022. The reregulation of capital flows in Latin America: Assessing the impact of post-neoliberal governments. *Review of International Political Economy* 29 (5): 1497–1524.

Danyluk, M. 2018. Capital's logistical fix: Accumulation, globalization, and the survival of capitalism. *Environment and Planning D: Society and Space* 36 (4): 630–647.

Davies, W. 2014. *The Limits of Neoliberalism: Authority, Sovereignty and the Logic of Competition.* London: SAGE Publications Ltd.

Davies, W. 2020. Nationalism and neoliberal governance. *Law and Political Economy Project.* 27 April. https://lpeproject.org/blog/nationalism-and-neoliberal-governance/.

Davies, W., and N. Gane. 2021. Post-neoliberalism? An Introduction. *Theory, Culture & Society* 38 (6): 3–28.

Davis, M. 2006. *Planet of Slums.* London; New York: Verso.

de Graaff, N. 2012. The hybridization of the state–capital nexus in the global energy order. *Globalizations* 9 (4): 531–545.

De Graaff, N., and B. Van Apeldoorn. 2018. US–China relations and the liberal world order: Contending elites, colliding visions? *International Affairs* 94 (1): 113–131.

De Ville, F. 2019. 'Naïve no longer'? The hardening of EU trade policy discourse and practice towards China and its limits. Conference paper *Politicologenetmaal June 2019.* Antwerp.

Dean, J. 2022. Same as it ever was? *NLR Sidecar.* 6 May. https://newleftreview.org/sidecar/posts/same-as-it-ever-was.

Deng, P., A. Delios, and M. W. Peng. 2020. A geographic relational perspective on the internationalization of emerging market firms. *Journal of International Business Studies* 51 (1): 50–71.

Di Carlo, J., and S. Schindler eds. 2022. *The Rise of the Infrastructure State: How US–China Rivalry Shapes Politics and Place Worldwide.* Bristol: Bristol University Press.

Dicken, P., and A. Malmberg. 2001. Firms in territories: a relational perspective. *Economic Geography* 77 (4): 345–363.

DiMaggio, P. J., and W. W. Powell. 1983. The iron cage revisited: Institutional isomorphism and collective rationality in organizational fields. *American Sociological Review* 48 (2): 147–160.

Dixon, A. D. 2014. *The New Geography of Capitalism: Firms, Finance, and Society.* Oxford: Oxford University Press.

Dixon, A. D. 2017. The state as institutional investor: unpacking the geographical political economy of sovereign wealth funds. In R. Martin and J. Pollard (eds), *Handbook of the Geographies of Money and Finance* (279–297). Cheltenham: Edward Elgar.

Dixon, A. D. 2022. The strategic logics of state investment funds in Asia: Beyond financialisation. *Journal of Contemporary Asia* 52 (1): 127–151.

Dixon, A. D., and A. H. B. Monk. 2012. Rethinking the sovereign in sovereign wealth funds. *Transactions of the Institute of British Geographers* 37 (1): 104–117.

Dixon, A. D., J. Peck, I. Alami, and H. Whiteside. 2023. Making space for the new state capitalism, part III: Thinking conjuncturally. *Environment and Planning A: Economy and Space* 0 (0): 0308518X231185587.

Dodds, K. 2005. *Global Geopolitics: A Critical Introduction.* Harlow; New York: Pearson Prentice Hall.

Dolfsma, W., and A. Grosman. 2019. State capitalism revisited: A review of emergent forms and developments. *Journal of Economic Issues* 53 (2): 579–586.

Doucette, J., and B.-G. Park. 2018. Urban developmentalism in East Asia: Geopolitical economies, spaces of exception, and networks of expertise. *Critical Sociology* 44 (3): 395–403.

Dunford, M., and W. Liu. 2017. Uneven and combined development. *Regional Studies* 51 (1): 69–85.

Durand, C. 2017. *Fictitious Capital: How Finance Is Appropriating Our Future.* London; New York: Verso.
Durand, C. 2020. *Technoféodalisme: Critique de l'économie numérique.* Paris: Zones.
Durand, C., and W. Milberg. 2020. Intellectual monopoly in global value chains. *Review of International Political Economy* 27 (2): 404–429.
Economist. 2012. The rise of state capitalism. *The Economist.* 21 January.
Economist. 2019. A new kind of cold war: How to manage the growing rivalry between America and a rising China. *The Economist.*
Edel, C., and H. Brands. 2019. The real origins of the U.S.–China Cold War. *Foreign Policy.* 2 June. https://foreignpolicy.com/2019/06/02/the-real-origins-of-the-u-s-china-cold-war-big-think-communism/.
Engel, J., D. Kokas, G. Lopez-Acevedo, and M. Maliszewska. 2021. *The Distributional Impacts of Trade: Empirical Innovations, Analytical Tools, and Policy Responses. Trade and Development.* Washington, DC: World Bank Group.
Essex, J. 2013. *Development, Security, and Aid: Geopolitics and Geoeconomics at the U.S. Agency for International Development.* Athens: University of Georgia Press.
Estrin, S., J. Hanousek, E. Kocenda, and J. Svejnar. 2009. The effects of privatization and ownership in transition economies. *Journal of Economic Literature* 47 (3): 699–728.
European Commission. 2021a. The EU's capacity and freedom to act. 2021 Strategic Foresight Report. *Communication from the Commission to the European Parliament and the Council.* Available at: https://eur-lex.europa.eu/legal-content/EN/TXT/PDF/?uri=CELEX:52021DC0750 (last accessed 21 August 2023).
European Commission. 2021b. Commission staff working document impact assessment accompanying the Proposal for a Regulation of the European Parliament and of the Council on foreign subsidies distorting the internal market. Available at: https://ec.europa.eu/competition/international/overview/impact_assessment_report.pdf (last accessed 21 August 2023).
European Commission. 2021c. Trade Policy Review—an open, sustainable and assertive trade policy. *Communication from the Commission to the European Parliament.* Available at: https://eur-lex.europa.eu/legal-content/EN/TXT/HTML/?uri=CELEX:52021DC0066&rid=7 (last accessed 21 August 2023).
Fainshmidt, S., W. Q. Judge, R. V. Aguilera, and A. Smith. 2018. Varieties of institutional systems: A contextual taxonomy of understudied countries. *Journal of World Business* 53 (3): 307–322.
Fajgelbaum, P., P. Goldberg, P. Kennedy, A. Khandelwal, and D. Taglioni. 2023. The US–China Trade War and Global Reallocations. *NBER Working Papers* (29562).
Farrell, H., and A. L. Newman. 2019. Weaponized interdependence: How global economic networks shape state coercion. *International Security* 44 (1): 42–79.
Feltrin, L., A. Mah, and D. Brown. 2022. Noxious deindustrialization: Experiences of precarity and pollution in Scotland's petrochemical capital. *Environment and Planning C: Politics and Space* 40 (4): 950–969.
Florio, M., M. Ferraris, and D. Vandone. 2018. Motives of mergers and acquisitions by state-owned enterprises. *International Journal of Public Sector Management* 31 (2): 142–166.
Fortin, C., J. Heine, and C. Ominami. 2021. *El no alineamiento activo y América Latina: Una doctrina para el nuevo siglo.* Stanttiago de Chile: Catalonia.
Fourie, E. 2014. Model students: Policy emulation, modernization, and Kenya's Vision 2030. *African Affairs* 113 (453): 540–562.
Franceschini, I., and N. Loubere. 2022. *Global China as Method.* Cambridge: Cambridge University Press.

Franz, T., and A. McNelly. 2023. The 'Finance-Extraction-Transitions Nexus': Towards A Critical Research Agenda Exploring the Scramble for Transition Minerals. *SOAS Department of Economics Working Papers* (257).

Fraser, N. 2016. Contradictions of capital and care. *New Left Review* (100): 99–117. https://newleftreview.org/issues/ii100/articles/nancy-fraser-contradictions-of-capital-and-care.

Fröbel, F., J. Heinrichs, and O. Kreye. 1978. The world market for labor and the world market for industrial sites. *Journal of Economic Issues* 12 (4): 843–858.

Fukuyama, F. 1992. *The End of History and the Last Man*. London: Penguin.

Gabor, D. 2021. The Wall Street consensus. *Development and Change* 52 (3): 429–459.

Gabor, D., and N. S. Sylla. 2023. Derisking developmentalism: A tale of green hydrogen. *Development and Change* 54 (5): 1169–1196.

Gagliardone, I. 2019. *China, Africa, and the Future of the Internet*. London: Zed Books.

Gallagher, K. P. 2015. Countervailing monetary power: Re-regulating capital flows in Brazil and South Korea. *Review of International Political Economy* 22 (1): 77–102.

Gelb, A., S. Tordo, H. Halland, N. Arfaa, and G. Smith. 2014. Sovereign wealth funds and long-term development finance: risks and opportunities. *World Bank Policy Research Working Paper* (6776).

Gerbaudo, P. 2021. *The Great Recoil: Politics After Populism and Pandemic*. London: Verso.

Gergieva, K., and N. Okonjo-Iweala. 2023. World trade can still drive prosperity, but the international architecture must adapt to a fast-changing world. *Finance & Development* 60 (2): 10–11.

Germann, J. 2023. Global rivalries, corporate interests and Germany's 'National Industrial Strategy 2030'. *Review of International Political Economy* 30 (5): 1749–1775.

Gertz, G., and M. M. Evers. 2020. Geoeconomic competition: Will state capitalism win? *The Washington Quarterly* 43 (2): 117–136.

Gilbert, J. 2019. This Conjuncture: For Stuart Hall. *New Formations* 96 (96–97): 5–37.

Gilmore, R. W. 2022. *Abolition Geography: Essays towards Liberation*. London; New York: Verso.

Giuzio, M., D. Krušec, A. Levels, A. S. Melo, K. Mikkonen, and P. Radulova. 2019. Climate change and financial stability. In *Financial Stability Review, May 2019*. Frankfurt: European Central Bank. https://www.ecb.europa.eu/pub/financial-stability/fsr/special/html/ecb.fsrart201905_1~47cf778cc1.en.html.

Glasius, M. 2018. What authoritarianism is ... and is not:∗ a practice perspective. *International Affairs* 94 (3): 515–533.

Goldberg, P. 2023. Building trade policy on contemporary science. Paper presented at 2023 Heckscher-Ohlin Conference 'Building Trade Policy on Contemporary Science', Stockholm School of Economics, 11 May.

Goldberg, P. K., and T. Reed. 2023. Is the global economy deglobalizing? And if so, why? And what is next? *National Bureau of Economic Research Working Paper Series* 31115.

Gonzalez-Vicente, R. 2017. South–South relations under world market capitalism: the state and the elusive promise of national development in the China–Ecuador resource-development nexus. *Review of International Political Economy* 24 (5): 881–903.

Gough, J. 2004. Changing scale as changing class relations: variety and contradiction in the politics of scale. *Political Geography* 23 (2): 185–211.

Goulding, R., A. Leaver, and J. Silver. 2023. When the Abu Dhabi United Group Came to Town: Constructing an Organisational Fix for State Capitalism through the Manchester Life Partnership. *Antipode*.

Grayson, D., and B. Little. 2017. Conjunctural analysis and the crisis of ideas. *Soundings* 65 (65): 59–75.

Green, J., and J. Gruin. 2020. RMB transnationalization and the infrastructural power of international financial centres. *Review of International Political Economy* 28 (4): 1028–1054.
Griffith-Jones, S. 2022. *The Role Public National Development Banks Play in the Structural Transformation of Developing Countries.* New York and Geneva: UNCTAD.
Griffith-Jones, S., and J. A. Ocampo. 2018. *The Future of National Development Banks.* Oxford: Oxford University Press.
Grosman, A., I. Okhmatovskiy, and M. Wright. 2016. State control and corporate governance in transition economies: 25 years on from 1989. *Corporate Governance: An International Review* 24 (3): 200–221.
Gu, J., C. Zhang, A. Vaz, and L. Mukwereza. 2016. Chinese state capitalism? Rethinking the role of the state and business in Chinese development cooperation in Africa. *World Development* 81: 24–34.
Gurol, J., A. Jenss, F. Rodríguez, B. Schuetze, and C. Wetterich. 2023. Authoritarian power and contestation beyond the state. *Globalizations.* Online first. https://www.tandfonline.com/doi/full/10.1080/14747731.2022.2162290.
Gurol, J., T. Zumbrägel, and T. Demmelhuber. 2023. Elite networks and the transregional dimension of authoritarianism: Sino-Emirati relations in times of a global pandemic. *Journal of Contemporary China* 32 (139): 138–151.
Güven, A. B. 2018. Whither the post-Washington consensus? International financial institutions and development policy before and after the crisis. *Review of International Political Economy* 25 (3): 392–417.
Güven, A. B. 2022. Towards a new political economy of Turkish capitalism: Three Worlds. *Turkish Studies* 24 (1): 177–196.
Haberly, D. 2011. Strategic sovereign wealth fund investment and the new alliance capitalism: a network mapping investigation. *Environment and Planning A* 43 (8): 1833–1852.
Haberly, D. 2014. White knights from the Gulf: sovereign wealth fund investment and the evolution of German industrial finance. *Economic Geography* 90 (3): 293–320.
Haberly, D. 2017. From financialization to vulture developmentalism: South–North strategic sovereign wealth fund investment and the politics of the 'Quadruple Bottom Line'. In D. J. Cumming, G. Wood, I. Filatotchev and J. Reinecke (eds), *The Oxford Handbook of Sovereign Wealth Funds* (87–122). Oxford: Oxford University Press.
Haberly, D., and D. Wójcik. 2017. Earth incorporated: Centralization and variegation in the global company network. *Economic Geography* 93 (3): 241–266.
Habermas, J. r. 1988. *Legitimation Crisis.* Cambridge, UK: Polity Press.
Hall, S. 2021. *Respatialising Finance: Power, Politics and Offshore Renminbi Market Making in London.* Hoboken: John Wiley & Sons.
Hameiri, S., L. Jones, and J. Heathershaw. 2019. Reframing the rising powers debate: State transformation and foreign policy. *Third World Quarterly* 40 (8): 1397–1414.
Hancké, B., M. Rhodes, and M. Thatcher. 2007. *Beyond Varieties of Capitalism: Conflict, Contradictions, and Complementarities in the European Economy.* Oxford: Oxford University Press.
Hanieh, A. 2018. *Money, Markets, and Monarchies: The Gulf Cooperation Council and the Political Economy of the Contemporary Middle East.* Cambridge, United Kingdom; New York: Cambridge University Press.
Hart, G. 2010. D/developments after the Meltdown. *Antipode* 41 (s1): 117–141.
Hart, G. 2018. Relational comparison revisited: Marxist postcolonial geographies in practice∗. *Progress in Human Geography* 42 (3): 371–394.
Harvey, D. 2006. Neo-liberalism as creative destruction. *Geografiska Annaler: Series B, Human Geography* 88 (2): 145–158.
Harvey, D. 2006[1982]. *The Limits to Capital.* London: Verso.

Helleiner, E. 2021. *The Neomercantilists: A Global Intellectual History.* Ithaca, New York: Cornell University Press.

Helleiner, E., and A. Pickel. 2005. *Economic Nationalism in a Globalizing World.* Ithaca, New York: Cornell University Press.

Hendrikse, R. 2018. Neo-illiberalism. *Geoforum* 95: 169–172.

Hendrikse, R. 2021. The rise of neo-illiberalism. *Krisis | Journal for Contemporary Philosophy* 41 (1): 65–93.

Henow, A. 2022. Helpless victim of financialisation? Financial liberalisation, crisis and taking back control in South Korea. *Cambridge Journal of Economics* 46 (5): 1161–1182.

Hillier, B. 2022. A régulationist response to the new state capitalism: Views from the U.S. Federal Reserve. In B. Hillier, R. Phillips, and J. Peck (eds), *Regulation Theory, Space, and Uneven Development: Conversations and Challenges* (115–130). Vancouver: 1984 Press.

Hirsch, J., and J. Viertel. 1977. Elements of a materialist theory of the state. *International Journal of Politics* 7 (2): 9–82.

Holloway, J. 1991. The state and everyday struggle. In S. Clarke (ed.), *The State Debate.* (225–259). London: Palgrave.

Holloway, J. 1994. Global Capital and the National state. *Capital & Class* 18 (1): 23–49.

Ho, P. 2018. Institutional function versus form: The evolutionary credibility of land, housing and natural resources. *Land Use Policy* 75: 642–650.

Ho, S., and T. Marois. 2019. China's asset management companies as state spatial–temporal strategy. *The China Quarterly* 239: 728–751.

Hoffmann, C., and C. Ergenc. 2023. A greening dragon in the desert? China's role in the geopolitical ecology of decarbonisation in the eastern Mediterranean. *Journal of Balkan and Near Eastern Studies* 25 (1): 82–101.

Horner, R., and M. Alford. 2019. The roles of the state in global value chains. In S. Ponte, G. Gereffi, and G. Raj-Reichert (eds), *Handbook on Global Value Chains* (555–569). Cheltenham: Edward Elgar Publishing.

Huat, C. B. 2016. State-owned enterprises, state capitalism and social distribution in Singapore. *The Pacific Review* 29 (4): 499–521.

Hudson, R. 2016. Rising powers and the drivers of uneven global development. *Area Development and Policy* 1 (3): 279–294.

Hung, H.-f. 2016. *The China Boom: Why China Will Not Rule the World.* New York: Columbia University Press.

Ikenberry, G. J. 2018. The end of liberal international order? *International Affairs* 94 (1): 7–23.

IMF. 2020. *Fiscal Monitor: Policies Support People during the COVID-19 Pandemic.* Washington, DC: International Monetary Funds.

IMF. 2021. *External Sector Report: Divergent Recoveries and Global Imbalances.*

IMF. 2023. *World Economic Outlook: A Rocky Recovery.* Washington, DC: International Monetary Fund.

IMF/World Bank. 2015. *From Billions to Trillions: Transforming Development Finance Post-2015 Financing for Development: Multilateral Development Finance.* Washington, DC: IMF and World Bank.

IMF/World Bank/OECD/WTO 2022. *Subsidies, Trade, and International Cooperation.* Washington DC: International Monetary Fund, Organisation for Economic Co-operation and Development, World Bank, and World Trade Organization

Independent Evaluation Group. 2016. *Industry Competitiveness and Jobs: An Evaluation of World Bank Group Industry-Specific Support to Promote Industry Competitiveness and Its Implications for Jobs.* Washington, DC: World Bank Group.

Iñigo Carrera, J. 2008. *El capital: razón histórica, sujeto revolucionario y conciencia.* Buenos Aires: Imago Mundi.

Inoue, C. F. K. V., S. G. Lazzarini, and A. Musacchio. 2013. Leviathan as a minority shareholder: Firm-level implications of state equity purchases. *Academy of Management Journal* 56 (6): 1775–1801.

International Finance Corporation and World Bank. 2021. *Leadership Training Toolkit for State-Owned Enterprises (SOEs)*. Washington, DC: World Bank Group.

İpek, A. M. 2019. *Sovereign Wealth Funds in the Context of Subordinate Financialisation: The Turkey Wealth Fund in a Comparative Perspective*. Middle East Technical University.

Irwin, D. 2023. The return of industrial policy. *Finance & Development* June: 12–14.

Jayasuriya, K. 2022. The age of political disincorporation: Geo-capitalist conflict and the politics of authoritarian statism. *Journal of Contemporary Asia* 53 (1): 165–178.

Jensen, F. 2023. State capitalism and Spanish port development along the Maritime Silk Road. *Environment and Planning A: Economy and Space* 55 (3): 636–654.

Jenss, A., and B. Schuetze. 2021. Rethinking authoritarian power: The logistics space and authoritarian practices in and between secondary port cities of the Global South. *International Studies Quarterly* 65 (1): 82–94.

Jepson, N. 2020. *In China's Wake: How the Commodity Boom Transformed Development Strategies in the Global South*. New York: Columbia University Press.

Jessop, B. 2002. *The Future of the Capitalist State*. Cambridge: Polity.

Jili, B. 2023. Africa's demand for and adoption of Chinese surveillance technology. *Cyber Statecraft Initiative*. Issue Brief May 2023. Washington, DC: Atlantic Council DFRLab. https://dfrlab.org/wp-content/uploads/sites/3/2023/05/Africas-Demand-for-an-Adoption-of-Chinese-Surveillance-Technology.pdf.

Jones, L., and S. Hameiri. 2021. *Fractured China: How State Transformation Is Shaping China's Rise*. Cambridge: Cambridge University Press.

Jones, L., and Y. Zou. 2017. Rethinking the role of state-owned enterprises in China's rise. *New Political Economy* 22 (6): 743–760.

Jones, P. 2021. *Work without the worker: Labour in the age of platform capitalism*. London: Verso Books.

Juhász, R., N. J. Lane, and D. Rodrik. 2023. The New Economics of Industrial Policy. *National Bureau of Economic Research Working Paper Series* 31538.

Kalantzakos, S. 2021. Rare earths, the climate crisis, and tech imperium. In *LSE Blog*. London. 24 March. https://blogs.lse.ac.uk/cff/2021/03/24/rare-earths-the-climate-crisis-and-tech-imperium/.

Kanai, J. M., and S. Schindler. 2019. Peri-urban promises of connectivity: Linking project-led polycentrism to the infrastructure scramble. *Environment and Planning A: Economy and Space* 51 (2): 302–322.

Kaplan, R. D. 2019. A new cold war has begun. *Foreign Policy*. 7 January.

Kaplan, S. B. 2021. *Globalizing Patient Capital: The Political Economy of Chinese Finance in the Americas*, 1 online resource. Cambridge; New York: Cambridge University Press.

Karas, D. 2022. Financialization and state capitalism in Hungary after the Global Financial Crisis. *Competition & Change* 26 (1): 29–52.

Kavalski, E. 2018. China's Belt and Road Initiative in Central and Eastern Europe. *Asian International Studies Review* 19 (2): 13–31.

Kenney, M., and J. Zysman. 2016. The rise of the platform economy. *Issues in Science and Technology* 32 (3): 61–69.

Kiely, R. 2012. Spatial hierarchy and/or contemporary geopolitics: What can and can't uneven and combined development explain? *Cambridge Review of International Affairs* 25 (2): 231–248.

Kim, I., J. Lee, and H. Kim. 2022. Public-private battery alliance launched to source critical minerals. *The Korea Economic Daily*, 2 November.

Kim, K. 2019a. Indonesia's restrained state capitalism: Development and policy challenges. *Journal of Contemporary Asia* 51 (3): 419–446.

Kim, K. 2019b. Using partially state-owned enterprises for development in Indonesia. *Asia Pacific Business Review* 25 (3): 317–337.

Kim, K. 2020. State-owned entities as development policy tools: Political economy of state activism in Indonesia. London: King's College London.

Kim, K. 2021. Indonesia's modest new sovereign wealth fund. *East Asia Forum*. 12 February.

Kim, K. 2022. Locating new 'state capitalism' in advanced economies: an international comparison of government ownership in economic entities. *Contemporary Politics* 28 (3): 285–305.

Kim, K., and A. Sumner. 2019. *De-industrialization, Re-industrialization, and the Resurgence of State Capitalism: The Case of Indonesia*. World Institute for Development Economic Research (UNU-WIDER).

Klein, M. C., and M. Pettis. 2020. *Trade Wars Are Class Wars: How Rising Inequality Distorts the Global Economy and Threatens International Peace*. New Haven; London: Yale University Press.

Klingler-Vidra, R. 2018. *The Venture Capital State: The Silicon Valley Model in East Asia*. Ithaca: Cornell University Press.

Koelemaij, J. 2022. The world's number 1 real estate development exporter? Assessing announced transnational projects from the United Arab Emirates between 2003–2014. *Environment and Planning A: Economy and Space* 54 (2): 226–246.

Komachi, H., S. Neilson, and M. Voss. 2023. *Japan Unveils Green Subsidy Programme—Can It Compete with the U.S.* Inflation Reduction Act?. Allen & Overy.

KPMG. 2016. 10 Emerging trends in 2016. *KPMG Foresight*, January.

Kring, W. N., and K. P. Gallagher. 2019. Strengthening the foundations? Alternative Institutions for Finance and Development. *Development and Change* 50 (1): 3–23.

Krippner, G. R. 2011. *Capitalizing on Crisis: The Political Origins of the Rise of Finance*. Cambridge, Mass.; London: Harvard University Press.

Kuik, C.-C. 2016. How do weaker states hedge? Unpacking ASEAN states' alignment behavior towards China. *Journal of Contemporary China* 25 (100): 500–514.

Kurlantzick, J. 2016. *State Capitalism: How the Return of Statism Is Transforming the World*. New York: Oxford University Press.

Kutlay, M. 2020. The politics of state capitalism in a post-liberal international order: the case of Turkey. *Third World Quarterly* 41 (4): 683–706.

Labban, M. 2008. Contradiction of space, centralization of capital, and the hybrid state oil company: The case of Russia. *Human Geography* 1 (2): 59–71.

Lavery, S., McDaniel, S., & Schmid, D. 2022. European strategic autonomy: New agenda, old constraints. In Babic, M, Dixon, A., Liu, I. (eds), *The Political Economy of Geoeconomics: Europe in a Changing World* (57–80). Cham: Springer International Publishing.

Lavinas, L. 2017. *Takeover of social policy by financialization*. London: Palgrave Macmillan US.

Lawrence, M., and T. Hanna. 2020. *Ownership Futures towards Democratic Public Ownership in the 21st Century*. London: Common Wealth.

Lebdioui, A. 2022. The political economy of moving up in global value chains: how Malaysia added value to its natural resources through industrial policy. *Review of International Political Economy* 29 (3):870–903.

Lee, H. 2023. Yoon says competition in semiconductor sector is 'industrial war'. *Yonhap News Agency*. 8 June. https://en.yna.co.kr/view/AEN20230608004600315.

Lee, R. 2011. Acts of theory and violence: Can the world of economic geography be left intact. In J. Pollard, C. McEwan, and A. Hughes (eds), *Postcolonial Economies* (63–80). London: Zed Books.

Lee, S.-O., J. Wainwright, and J. Glassman. 2018. Geopolitical economy and the production of territory: The case of US–China geopolitical-economic competition in Asia. *Environment and Planning A: Economy and Space* 50 (2): 416–436.

Leitner, H., and E. Sheppard. 2020. Towards an epistemology for conjunctural inter-urban comparison. *Cambridge Journal of Regions, Economy and Society* 13 (3): 491–508.

Leonard, M., J. Pisani-Ferry, E. Ribakova, J. Shapiro, and G. Wolff. 2019. Redefining Europe's economic sovereignty. In M. Leonard and J. Shapiro (eds), *Strategic Sovereignty: How Europe Can Regain the Capacity to Act* (19–48). London: European Council on Foreign Relations.

Leung, E. M.-T. 2021. Developmentalisms: The forgotten ancestors of East Asian developmentalism. *Phenomenal World* 18 September. https://www.phenomenalworld.org/analysis/developmentalisms/.

Lewis, L. 2023. Japan arms itself for global chip wars with $6.4bn state-backed deal. *Financial Times*, 3 July.

Li, M. H., L. Cui, and J. Lu. 2017. Marketized state ownership and foreign expansion of emerging market multinationals: Leveraging institutional competitive advantages. *Asia Pacific Journal of Management* 34 (1): 19–46.

Lim, K. F. 2018. Strategic coupling, state capitalism, and the shifting dynamics of global production networks. *Geography Compass* 12 (11): e12406.

Lim, K. F. 2019. *On shifting foundations: State rescaling, policy experimentation and economic restructuring in post-1949 China. RGS-IBG book series.* Hoboken, NJ: Wiley.

Lin, J. Y. 2011. New Structural Economics: A Framework for Rethinking Development1. *The World Bank Research Observer* 26 (2): 193–221.

Lin, L.-W., and C. J. Milhaupt. 2013. We are the (national) champions: Understanding the mechanisms of state capitalism in China. *Stanford Law Review* 65 (4): 697–759.

Lipsky, J. 2008. Sovereign wealth funds: Their role and significance. A Speech by John Lipsky, First Deputy Managing Director, International Monetary Fund.

Liu, I. T. 2023. Beyond the spatial fix: Towards a finance-sensitive reading of the Belt and Road in Serbia. *Area Development and Policy*. Online first.

Liu, I. T., and A. D. Dixon. 2021. Legitimating state capital: The global financial professions and the transnationalization of Chinese sovereign wealth. *Development and Change* 52 (5): 1251–1273.

Liu, I. T., and A. D. Dixon. 2022. What does the state do in China's state-led infrastructure financialisation? *Journal of Economic Geography* 22 (5): 963–988.

Liu, Z., M. Dunford, and W. Liu. 2021. Coupling national geo-political economic strategies and the Belt and Road Initiative: The China-Belarus Great Stone Industrial Park. *Political Geography* 84: 102296.

Löscher, A., and A. Kaltenbrunner. 2023. Climate change and macroeconomic policy space in developing and emerging economies. *Journal of Post Keynesian Economics* 46 (1): 113–141.

Luger, J. 2020. Planetary illiberalism and the cybercity-state: In and beyond territory. *Territory, Politics, Governance* 8 (1): 77–94.

Lyons, G. 2007. State capitalism: The rise of sovereign wealth funds. *Journal of Management Research* 7 (3): 119–146.

MacDonald, S. B., and J. Lemco. 2015. *State Capitalism's Uncertain Future.* Santa Barbara: ABC-CLIO.

MacKenzie, R., J. Eckhardt, and A. Widyati Prastyani. 2017. Japan Tobacco International: To 'be the most successful and respected tobacco company in the world'. *Global Public Health* 12 (3): 281–299.

MacLeod, G. 2001. Beyond soft institutionalism: accumulation, regulation, and their geographical fixes. *Environment and Planning A* 33 (7):1145–1167.

Mader, P., D. Mertens, and N. van der Zwan eds. 2021. *The Routledge International Handbook of Financialization.* 1st ed: Routledge.

Maggor, E. 2021. The politics of innovation policy: Building Israel's 'neo-developmental' state. *Politics & Society* 49 (4): 451–487.

Malm, A. 2020. *Corona, Climate, Chronic Emergency: War Communism in the Twenty-first Century.* London; New York: Verso.

Maloney, W. F., and G. Nayyar. 2018. Industrial policy, information, and government capacity. *World Bank Research Observer* 33 (2): 189–217.

Mamadouh, V., and G. Dijkink. 2006. Geopolitics, international relations and political geography: The politics of geopolitical discourse. *Geopolitics* 11 (3): 349–366.

Mann, G. 2017. *In the Long Run We Are All Dead: Keynesianism, Political Economy, and Revolution.* London; New York: Verso.

Marois, T. 2012. *States, Banks and Crisis: Emerging Finance Capitalism in Mexico and Turkey.* Cheltenham, UK: Edward Elgar.

Marois, T. 2021. *Public Banks: Decarbonisation, Definancialisation and Democratisation.* 1 Edition. ed. New York: Cambridge University Press.

Marx, K. 1867/1991. *Capital: A Critique of Political Economy (Vol.I, B. Fowkes, trans.).* London: Penguin Classics.

Marx, K. 1894/1991. *Capital: A Critique of Political Economy (Vol.III, D. Fernbach, Trans.).* London: Penguin Classics.

Maskell, P. 2001. The firm in economic geography. *Economic Geography* 77 (4): 329–344.

Massey, D. 1995. *Spatial Divisions of Labour: Social Structures and the Geography of Production.* 2nd ed. London: Macmillan.

Mawdsley, E. 2018. Development geography II: Financialization. *Progress in Human Geography* 42 (2): 264–274.

Mawdsley, E., and J. Taggart. 2022. Rethinking d/Development. *Progress in Human Geography* 46 (1): 3–20.

Mawdsley, E., W. E. Murray, J. Overton, R. Scheyvens, and G. Banks. 2018. Exporting stimulus and 'shared prosperity': Reinventing foreign aid for a retroliberal era. *Development Policy Review* 36 (S1): O25–O43.

Mazzucato, M. 2011. *The Entrepreneurial State.* London: Demos.

McCarthy, M. 2022. Three modes of democratic participation. In F. Bloch and R. Hockett (eds), *Democratizing Finance* (159–186). London: Verso.

McGregor, N., and N. M. Coe. 2023. Hybrid governance and extraterritoriality: Understanding Singapore's state capitalism in the context of oil global production networks. *Environment and Planning A: Economy and Space* 55 (3): 716–741.

McNally, C. A. 2012. Sino-capitalism: China's reemergence and the international political economy. *World Politics* 64 (4): 741–776.

McNally, C. A. 2013. The challenge of refurbished state capitalism: Implications for the global political economic order. *dms–der moderne staat–Zeitschrift für Public Policy, Recht und Management* 6 (1): 9–10.

Meckling, J., B. Kong, and T. Madan. 2015. Oil and state capitalism: government-firm coopetition in China and India. *Review of International Political Economy* 22 (6): 1159–1187.

Medby, I. A. 2020. Political geography and language: A reappraisal for a diverse discipline. *Area* 52 (1): 148–155.

Megginson, W. L. 2017. Privatization, state capitalism, and state ownership of business in the 21st century. *Foundations and Trends® in Finance* 11 (1–2): 1–153.

Megginson, W. L., and J. M. Netter. 2001. From state to market: A survey of empirical studies on privatization. *Journal of Economic Literature* 39 (2): 321–389.

Meiksins Wood, E. 1995. *Democracy against Capitalism: Renewing Historical Materialism.* Cambridge; New York: Cambridge University Press.

Mertens, D., and M. Thiemann. 2018. Market-based but state-led: The role of public development banks in shaping market-based finance in the European Union. *Competition & Change* 22 (2): 184–204.

Mertens, D., and M. Thiemann. 2019. Building a hidden investment state? The European Investment Bank, national development banks and European economic governance. *Journal of European Public Policy* 26 (1): 23–43.

Mertens, D., M. Thiemann, and P. Volberding eds. 2021. *The Reinvention of Development Banking in the European Union: Industrial Policy in the Single Market and the Emergence of a Field.* Oxford: Oxford University Press.

Meulbroek, C. 2023. Gillian Hart in Beijing: Negotiating capitalist models at the World Bank–China nexus. *Environment and Planning A: Economy and Space* 55 (5): 1218–1238.

Meyer, K. E., and M. W. Peng. 2016. Theoretical foundations of emerging economy business research. *Journal of International Business Studies* 47 (1): 3–22.

Mezzadra, S., and B. Neilson. 2019. *The Politics of Operations: Excavating Contemporary Capitalism.* Durham: Duke University Press.

Milanović, B. 2019. *Capitalism, Alone: The Future of the System that Rules the World.* Cambridge, Massachusetts: The Belknap Press of Harvard University Press.

Milberg, W. 2008. Shifting sources and uses of profits: Sustaining US financialization with global value chains. *Economy and Society* 37 (3): 420–451.

Milhaupt, C. J. 2020. The state as owner—China's experience. *Oxford Review of Economic Policy* 36 (2): 362–379.

Milhaupt, C. J., and M. Pargendler. 2017. Governance challenges of listed state-owned enterprises around the world: National experiences and a framework for reform. *Cornell International Law Journal* 50 (3): 473–542.

Miliband, R. 1969. *The State in Capitalist Society.* London: Weidenfeld & Nicolson.

Miller, C. 2023. The West's de-risking strategy towards China will fail. The Economist, 4 August.

Miron, J. 2015. *Should China's Meltdown Be Surprising?* Cato Institute.

Mishura, A., and S. Ageeva. 2022. Financialisation and the authoritarian state: The case of Russia. *Cambridge Journal of Economics* 46 (5): 1109–1140.

Mitchell, K. 2010. Ungoverned space: Global security and the geopolitics of broken windows. *Political Geography* 29 (5): 289–297.

Mocanu, D., and M. Thiemann. 2023. Breeding 'Unicorns': Tracing the Rise of the European Investor State in the Venture Capital Market. *Competition & Change.* Online first.

Monk, A. H. B. 2009. The emerging market for intellectual property: Drivers, restrainers, and implications. *Journal of Economic Geography* 9 (4): 469–491.

Monopolkommission. 2020. *Chinese State Capitalism: A Challenge for the European Market Economy.* Bonn: Monopolkommission.

Montambault Trudelle, A. 2023. The public investment fund and Salman's state: The political drivers of sovereign wealth management in Saudi Arabia. *Review of International Political Economy* 30 (2): 747–771.

Moraitis, A. 2022. From the post-industrial prophecy to the de-industrial nightmare: Stagnation, the manufacturing fetish and the limits of capitalist wealth. *Competition & Change* 26 (5): 513–532.

Morozov, E. 2022. Critique of techno-feudal reason. *New Left Review* (133): 89–126.

Munevar, D. 2020. *Arrested Development: International Monetary Fund Lending and Austerity Post Covid-19.* Brussels: European Network on Debt and Development (EURODAD).

Musacchio, A., and S. Lazzarini. 2014. *Reinventing State Capitalism: Leviathan in Business, Brazil and Beyond.* Cambridge: Harvard University Press.

Musacchio, A., S. G. Lazzarini, and R. V. Aguilera. 2015. New varieties of state capitalism: Strategic and governance implications. *Academy of Management Perspectives* 29 (1): 115–131.

Musthaq, F. 2023. Unconventional central banking and the politics of liquidity. *Review of International Political Economy* 30 (1): 281–306.

Naczyk, M. 2022. Taking back control: Comprador bankers and managerial developmentalism in Poland. *Review of International Political Economy* 29 (5): 1650–1674.

Naqvi, N. 2021. Renationalizing finance for development: policy space and public economic control in Bolivia. *Review of International Political Economy* 28 (3): 447–478.

NATO. 2023. NATO Innovation Fund closes on EUR 1bn flagship fund. NATO website. 1 August.

Negreiro, M., and T. Madiega. 2019. *Digital Transformation.* Brussels: European Parliamentary Research Service.

Nem Singh, J., and G. C. Chen. 2018. State-owned enterprises and the political economy of state–state relations in the developing world. *Third World Quarterly* 39 (6): 1077–1097.

Newman, S. 2022. Global value chains and global value transfer. In Z. Cope and I. Ness (eds), *The Oxford Handbook of Economic Imperialism* (213–229). Oxford: Oxford University Press.

Nölke, A. ed. 2014. *Multinational Corporations from Emerging Markets: State Capitalism 3.0.* Berlin: Springer.

Nölke, A. (2022). *Post-Corona capitalism: The alternatives ahead.* Bristol: Bristol University Press.

Nölke, A., T. Ten Brink, C. May, and S. Claar. 2019. *State-permeated Capitalism in Large Emerging Economies.* 1st Edition. ed. New York: Routledge.

Nölke, A., T. ten Brink, S. Claar, and C. May. 2015. Domestic structures, foreign economic policies and global economic order: Implications from the rise of large emerging economies. *European Journal of International Relations* 21 (3): 538–567.

Ó Tuathail, G. 1997. Emerging markets and other simulations: Mexico, the Chiapas revolt and the geofinancial panopticon. *Ecumene* 4 (3): 300–317.

Ó Tuathail, G. 2005. *Critical Geopolitics: The Politics of Writing Global Space.* London: Routledge.

Ó Tuathail, G. 2018. *The Affective Geopolitics of the New Cold War.* Presentation given at The UCL Global Governance Institute Event series, 24.04.2018.

Ó Tuathail, G., and S. Dalby. 1998/2002. *Rethinking Geopolitics.* London and New York: Routledge.

OECD. 2015. *State-Owned Enterprises in the Development Process.* Paris: OECD Publishing.

OECD. 2017. *The Size and Sectoral Distribution of State-Owned Enterprises.* Paris: OECD Publishing.

OECD. 2020. *The Role of Sovereign and Strategic Investment Funds in the Low-carbon Transition.* Paris: OECD Publishing.

Offe, C. 1972. *Strukturprobleme des kapitalistischen Staates; Aufsätze zur politischen Soziologie.* 1. Aufl. ed. Frankfurt am Main: Suhrkamp.

Ollman, B. 2003. *Dance of the Dialectic: Steps in Marx's Method.* Urbana, Ill.: University of Illinois Press.

Öniş, Z. 2019. Turkey under the challenge of state capitalism: the political economy of the late AKP era. *Southeast European and Black Sea Studies* 19 (2): 201–225.

Öniş, Z., and M. Kutlay. 2021. The anatomy of Turkey's new heterodox crisis: The interplay of domestic politics and global dynamics. *Turkish Studies* 22 (4): 499–529.

Ornston, D. 2012. *When Small States Make Big Leaps*. Ithaca, NY: Cornell University Press.

O'Sullivan, L., and L. Rethel. 2023. Financial globalization, local debt markets and new state financial activism in middle-income countries. *Development and Change* 54 (2): 304–330.

Parenti, C. 2015. The 2013 ANTIPODE AAG lecture the environment making state: Territory, nature, and value. *Antipode* 47 (4): 829–848.

Paterson, M. 2021. Climate change and international political economy: Between collapse and transformation. *Review of International Political Economy* 28 (2): 394–405.

Paul, F. C., and A. Cumbers. 2023. The return of the local state? Failing neoliberalism, remunicipalisation, and the role of the state in advanced capitalism. *Environment and Planning A: Economy and Space* 55 (1): 165–183.

Pearson, M. M., Rithmire, M., & Tsai, K. S. 2022. China's party-state capitalism and international backlash: From interdependence to insecurity. *International Security* 47 (2): 135–176.

Peck, J. 2004. Geography and public policy: Constructions of neoliberalism. *Progress in Human Geography* 28 (3): 392–405.

Peck, J. 2010. Zombie neoliberalism and the ambidextrous state. *Theoretical Criminology* 14 (1): 104–110.

Peck, J. 2013. Explaining (with) neoliberalism. *Territory, Politics, Governance* 1 (2): 132–157.

Peck, J. 2019a. Combination. In T. Jazeel, A. Kent, K. McKittrick, N. Theodore, S. Chari, P. Chatterton, V. Gidwani, N. Heynen, W. Larner, J. Peck, J. Pickerill, M. Werner and M. W. Wright (eds), *Keywords in Radical Geography: Antipode at 50* (50–56). Hoboken; Oxford: John Wiley & Sons.

Peck, J. 2019b. Problematizing capitalism(s): Big difference? *Environment and Planning A: Economy and Space* 51 (5): 1190–1196.

Peck, J. 2021. On capitalism's cusp. *Area Development and Policy* 6 (1): 1–30.

Peck, J. 2023a. *Variegated Economies*. Oxford: Oxford University Press.

Peck, J. 2023b. Wrestling with 'the new' state capitalism. *Environment and Planning A: Economy and Space* 55 (3): 760–763.

Peck, J., and N. Theodore. 2015. *Fast Policy: Experimental Statecraft at the Thresholds of Neoliberalism*. Minneapolis: University of Minnesota Press.

Peck, J., and N. Theodore. 2019. Still Neoliberalism? *South Atlantic Quarterly* 118 (2): 245–265.

Pellegrini, L., and M. Arsel. 2022. The supply side of climate policies: Keeping unburnable fossil fuels in the ground. *Global Environmental Politics* 22 (4): 1–14.

Peng, M. W., G. D. Bruton, C. V. Stan, and Y. Huang. 2016. Theories of the (state-owned) firm. *Asia Pacific Journal of Management* 33 (2): 293–317.

Petry, J. 2020. Financialization with Chinese characteristics? Exchanges, control and capital markets in authoritarian capitalism. *Economy and Society* 49 (2): 213–238.

Petry, J., K. Koddenbrock, and A. Nölke. 2023. State capitalism and capital markets: Comparing securities exchanges in emerging markets. *Environment and Planning A: Economy and Space* 55 (1): 143–164.

Phillips, A., and J. C. Sharman. 2020. *Outsourcing Empire: How Company-States Made the Modern World*. 1st ed. Princeton: Princeton University Press.

Piroska, D. 2022. Financial nationalism and democracy. In A. Pickel (ed.), *Handbook of Economic Nationalism* (256–274). Cheltenham: Edward Elgar.

Piroska, D., and B. Schlett. 2024. Mandate management: A field theory approach to the EBRD's adaptive practice in Egypt. *Review of International Political Economy* 31 (1): 47–73.

Pollard, J., and M. Samers. 2007. Islamic banking and finance: Postcolonial political economy and the decentring of economic geography. *Transactions of the Institute of British Geographers* 32 (3): 313–330.

Pollard, J., C. McEwan, N. Laurie, and A. Stenning. 2009. Economic geography under postcolonial scrutiny. *Transactions of the Institute of British Geographers* 34 (2): 137–142.

Pompeo, M. 2020. Communist China and the free world's future. Speech on China policy at the Richard Nixon Presidential Library. Available at: https://2017-2021.state.gov/communist-china-and-the-free-worlds-future-2/ (last accessed 21 August 2023).

Pop, G., and D. Connon. 2020. *Industrial Policy Effects and the Case for Competition.* Washington, DC: World Bank Group.

Poulantzas, N. A. 1973. *Political Power and Social Classes.* London: NLB; Sheed and Ward.

Power, M. 2010. Geopolitics and 'development': An introduction. *Geopolitics* 15 (3): 433–440.

Prates, D. M., and B. Fritz. 2016. Más allá de los controles de capital: Regulación de los mercados de derivados en moneda extranjera en la República de Corea y el Brasil después de la crisis financiera mundial. *Revista de la CEPAL* 2016 (118): 193–213.

Reboredo, R., and E. Gambino. 2023. Connectivity and competition: The emerging geographies of Africa's 'Ports Race'. *Area Development and Policy* 8 (2): 142–161.

Reynolds, M., and M. Goodman. 2022. *China's Economic Coercion: Lessons from Lithuania.* Washington, DC: Center for Strategic and International Studies.

Rikap, C. 2021. *Capitalism, power and innovation: Intellectual monopoly capitalism uncovered.* Abingdon, Oxon; New York, NY: Routledge.

Rikap, C. 2023. Capitalism as usual? Implications of digital intellectual monopolies. *New Left Review* (139): 145–160.

Rikap, C., and B. Lundavll. 2021. *The Digital Innovation Race: Conceptualizing the Emerging New World Order* Cham: Palgrave Macmillan.

Riley, D., and R. Brenner. 2022. Seven theses on American politics. *New Left Review* (138): 21–27.

Rioux, S. 2015. Mind the (theoretical) gap: On the poverty of international relations theorising of uneven and combined development. *Global Society* 29 (4): 481–509.

Roberts, A., H. Choer Moraes, and V. Ferguson. 2019. Toward a geoeconomic order in international trade and investment. *Journal of International Economic Law* 22 (4): 655–676.

Robinson, W. 2020. *The Global Police State.* London: Pluto Press.

Rodrik, D. 2016. Premature deindustrialization. *Journal of Economic Growth* 21 (1): 1–33.

Rodrik, D., R. Juhász, and N. J. Lane. 2023. *Economists Reconsider Industrial Policy. Project Syndicate.*

Rogers, S. 2022. Illiberal capitalist development: Chinese state-owned capital investment in Serbia. *Contemporary Politics* 28 (3): 347–364.

Rolf, S. 2021. *China's Uneven and Combined Development.* London: Palgrave Macmillan.

Rolf, S., and S. Schindler. 2023. The US–China rivalry and the emergence of state platform capitalism. *Environment and Planning A: Economy and Space* 55 (5): 1255–1280.

Rosenberg, J. 2013. Kenneth Waltz and Leon Trotsky: Anarchy in the mirror of uneven and combined development. *International Politics* 50 (2): 183–230.

Rosenberg, J. 2022. Uneven and combined development: a defense of the general abstraction. *Cambridge Review of International Affairs* 35 (3): 267–290.

Rosenberg, J., A. Zarakol, D. Blagden, O. Rutazibwa, K. Gray, O. Corry, K. Matin, F. Antunes de Oliveira, and L. Cooper. 2022. Debating uneven and combined development/debating international relations: A forum. *Millennium* 50 (2): 291–327.

Roy, A. 2010. *Poverty Capital: Microfinance and the Making of Development.* London: Routledge.

Said, E. W. 1978. *Orientalism.* 1st ed. New York: Pantheon Books.

Samruk-Kazyna. 2014. *Transformation Program for Sovereign Wealth Fund 'Samruk-Kazyna'.* JSC. Astana.

Scheinert, C. 2023. EU's response to the US Inflation Reduction Act (IRA). Brussels: European Parliament.
Scheiring, G. 2020. *The Retreat of Liberal Democracy: Authoritarian Capitalism and the Accumulative State in Hungary*. Cham: Palgrave Macmillan.
Schindler, S. 2018. The coming infrastructure arms race between the U.S. and China. *Global Policy*. 28 September. https://www.globalpolicyjournal.com/blog/28/09/2018/coming-infrastructure-arms-race-between-us-and-china.
Schindler, S., and J. M. Kanai. 2021. Getting the territory right: Infrastructure-led development and the re-emergence of spatial planning strategies. *Regional Studies* 55 (1): 40–51.
Schindler, S., I. Alami, and N. Jepson. 2023. Goodbye Washington confusion, hello Wall Street consensus: Contemporary state capitalism and the spatialisation of industrial strategy. *New Political Economy* 28 (2): 223–240.
Schindler, S., I. Alami, J. DiCarlo, N. Jepson, S. Rolf, M. K. Bayırbağ, L. Cyuzuzo, M. DeBoom, A. F. Farahani, I. T. Liu, H. McNicol, J. T. Miao, P. Nock, G. Teri, M. F. Vila Seoane, K. Ward, T. Zajontz, and Y. Zhao. 2024. The second cold war: US–China competition for centrality in infrastructure, digital, production, and finance networks. *Geopolitics*. Online first.
Schindler, S., J. DiCarlo, and D. Paudel. 2022. The new cold war and the rise of the 21st-century infrastructure state. *Transactions of the Institute of British Geographers* 47 (2): 331–346.
Schmidt, V. A. 2002. *The Futures of European Capitalism*. Oxford: Oxford University Press.
Schmidt, V.A. 2003. French capitalism transformed, but still a third variety of capitalism. *Economy and Society* 32 (4): 526–554.
Schmidt, V. A. 2009. Putting the political back into political economy by bringing the state back in yet again. *World Politics* 61 (3): 516–546.
Schoenberger, E. 1999. The firm in the region and the region in the firm. In T. J. Barnes and M. S. Gertler (eds), *The New Industrial Geography: Regions, Regulation and Institutions* (205–224). London: Routledge.
Schoenberger, E. 2000. The management of time and space. In G. L. Clark, M. Gertler, and M. Feldman (eds), *The Oxford Handbook of Economic Geography* (317–332). Oxford: Oxford University Press.
Schwartz, H. M. 2022. Intellectual property, technorents and the labour share of production. *Competition & Change* 26 (3–4): 415–435.
Seaton, L. 2023. Reflections on political capitalism. *New Left Review* (142): 5–27.
Sevastopoulo, D., and G. Long. 2021. US development bank strikes deal to help Ecuador pay China loans. *Financial Times*, 14 January.
Sheppard, E., and H. Leitner. 2010. Quo vadis neoliberalism? The remaking of global capitalist governance after the Washington Consensus. *Geoforum* 41 (2): 185–194.
Shields, S. 2012. *The International Political Economy of Transition: Neoliberal Hegemony and Eastern Central Europe's Transformation*. London; New York: Routledge.
Shields, S. 2021. Domesticating neoliberalism: 'Domification' and the contradictions of the populist countermovement in Poland. *Europe-Asia Studies* 73 (9): 1622–1640.
Shih, V. 2009. Tools of survival: Sovereign wealth funds in Singapore and China. *Geopolitics* 14 (2): 328–344.
Shilov, A. 2023. China's subsidies expand legacy chip production, stoking US and EU Fears. *Tom's Hardware*. 1 August.
Shipan, C. R., and C. Volden. 2008. The mechanisms of policy diffusion. *American Journal of Political Science* 52 (4): 840–857.
Shipan, C. R., and C. Volden. 2012. Policy diffusion: Seven lessons for scholars and practitioners. *Public Administration Review* 72 (6): 788–796.

Shivakumar, S., C. Wessner, and T. Howell. 2023. *The Strategic Importance of Legacy Chips.* Washington, DC: Center for International and Strategic Studies.

Sidaway, J. D. 2000. Postcolonial geographies: an exploratory essay. *Progress in Human Geography* 24 (4): 591–612.

Sidaway, J. D. 2003. Sovereign excesses? Portraying postcolonial sovereigntyscapes. *Political Geography* 22: 157–178.

Sidaway, J. D. 2012. Geographies of development: new maps, new visions? *The Professional Geographer* 64 (1): 49–62.

Sidaway, J. D., and M. Pryke. 2000. The strange geographies of 'emerging markets'. *Transactions of the Institute of British Geographers* 25 (2): 187–201.

Skalamera Groce, M., and S. Köstem. 2023. The dual transformation in development finance: Western multilateral development banks and China in post-Soviet energy. *Review of International Political Economy* 30 (1): 176–200.

Slater, D. 2004. *Geopolitics and the Post-colonial: Rethinking North–South Relations.* Malden, Mass.; Oxford: Blackwell.

Smith, J. E. 2020. *Smart machines and service work: Automation in an age of stagnation.* New York: Reaktion Books.

Smith, N. 1984/2008. *Uneven Development: Nature, Capital and the Production of Space.* Athens: University of Georgia Press.

Smith, T. 2017. *Beyond Liberal Egalitarianism: Marx and Normative Social Theory in the Twenty-first Century.* Leiden, The Netherlands: Brill.

Sokol, M. 2023. Financialisation, Central banks and 'new' state capitalism: The case of the US Federal Reserve, the European Central Bank and the Bank of England. *Environment and Planning A: Economy and Space* 55 (5): 1305–1324.

Sorg, C. 2023. Failing to plan is planning to fail: Toward an expanded notion of democratically planned postcapitalism. *Critical Sociology* 49 (3): 475–493.

Sparke, M. 2020. Comparing and connecting territories of illiberal politics and neoliberal governance. *Territory, Politics, Governance* 8 (1): 95–99.

Spechler, M. C., J. Ahrens, and H. W. Hoen. 2017. *State Capitalism in Eurasia.* London: World Scientific.

Sperber, N. 2019a. The many lives of state capitalism: From classical Marxism to free-market advocacy. *History of the Human Sciences* 32 (3): 100–124.

Sperber, N. 2019b. State capitalism and the state–class nexus. *Science & Society* 83 (3): 381–407.

Starosta, G. 2015. *Marx's Capital, Method and Revolutionary Subjectivity.* Leiden: Brill.

Steinfeld, E. S. 2010. *Playing Our Game: Why China's Economic Rise Doesn't Threaten the West.* Oxford; New York: Oxford University Press.

Stern, P. J. 2011. *The Company-State: Corporate Sovereignty and the Early Modern Foundation of the British Empire in India.* New York: Oxford University Press.

Stiglitz, J. E., J. Y. Lin, and C. Monga. 2013. *The Rejuvenation of Industrial Policy*: The World Bank.

Strauss, K. 2020. Labour geography III: Precarity, racial capitalisms and infrastructure. *Progress in Human Geography* 44 (6): 1212–1224.

Su, X., and K. F. Lim. 2023. Capital accumulation, territoriality, and the reproduction of state sovereignty in China: Is this 'new' state capitalism? *Environment and Planning A: Economy and Space* 55 (3): 697–715.

Sullivan, J. 2023. Remarks by national security advisor Jake Sullivan on renewing American economic leadership at the Brookings Institution. Available at: https://www.whitehouse.gov/briefing-room/speeches-remarks/2023/04/27/remarks-by-national-security-advisor-jake-sullivan-on-renewing-american-economic-leadership-at-the-brookings-institution/ (last accessed 21 August 2023).

Sum, N.-L., and B. Jessop. 2013. *Towards a Cultural Political Economy: Putting Culture in Its Place in Political Economy*. Cheltenham, UK: Edward Elgar.

Swyngedouw, E. 1992. The mammon quest: 'Glocalization', interspatial competition and the monetary order: The construction of new scales. In M. Dunford and G. Kafkalis (eds), *Cities and Regions in the New Europe. The Global-Local Interplay and Spatial Development Strategies* (39–67). London: Belhaven Press.

Szabó, L., and C. Jelinek. 2023. State, capitalism and infrastructure-led development: A multi-scalar analysis of the Belgrade-Budapest railway construction. *Environment and Planning A: Economy and Space* 55 (5): 1281–1304.

Taylor, I. 2014. Emerging powers, state capitalism and the oil sector in Africa. *Review of African Political Economy* 41 (141): 341–357.

Taylor, I., and T. Zajontz. 2020. In a fix: Africa's place in the Belt and Road Initiative and the reproduction of dependency. *South African Journal of International Affairs* 27 (3): 277–295.

Taylor, M., and B. Asheim. 2001. The concept of the firm in economic geography. *Economic Geography* 77 (4): 315–328.

Taylor, M., and P. Oinas eds. 2006. *Understanding the Firm: Spatial and Organizational Dimensions*. Oxford: Oxford University Press.

Ten Brink, T. 2013. Paradoxes of Prosperity in China's New Capitalism. *Journal of Current Chinese Affairs* 42 (4): 17–44.

Thatcher, M., and T. Vlandas. 2016. Overseas state outsiders as new sources of patient capital: Government policies to welcome Sovereign Wealth Fund investment in France and Germany. *Socio-Economic Review* 14 (4): 647–668.

Thatcher, M., and T. Vlandas. 2022. *Foreign States in Domestic Markets: Sovereign Wealth Funds and the West*. First edition. ed. New York; Oxford: Oxford University Press.

Thurbon, E. 2016. *Developmental Mindset: The Revival of Financial Activism in South Korea*. Ithaca: Cornell University Press.

Thurbon, E., and L. Weiss. 2021. Economic statecraft at the frontier: Korea's drive for intelligent robotics. *Review of International Political Economy* 28 (1): 103–127.

Thurbon, E., S.-Y. Kim, H. Tan, and J. Mathews. 2023. *Developmental Environmentalism: State Ambition and Creative Destruction in East Asia's Green Energy Transition*. 1. ed. New York: Oxford University Press.

Tilley, L. 2015. Decolonizing the study of capitalist diversity: epistemic disruption and the varied geographies of coloniality. In M. Ebenau, I. Bruff, and C. May (eds), *Directions in Comparative Capitalisms Research* (207–223). London: Palgrave Macmillan.

Tjia, L. Y.-n. 2022. Kazakhstan's leverage and economic diversification amid Chinese connectivity dreams. *Third World Quarterly* 43 (4): 797–822.

TNI. 2021. Global Climate Wall: How the world's wealthiest nations prioritise borders over climate action. Amsterdam: Transnational Institute.

Tooze, A. 2018. Tempestuous seasons. Review of *In the Long Run We Are All Dead: Keynesianism, Political Economy and Revolution* by Mann, G. *London Review of Books* 40 (17): 19–21.

Tyler, H. 2022. The increasing use of artificial intelligence in border zones prompts privacy questions. *Migration Information Source*, 2 February. https://www.migrationpolicy.org/article/artificial-intelligence-border-zones-privacy.

UNCTAD. 2015. Trade and Development Report, 2015. Geneva: United Nations Conference on Trade and Development. Geneva: UNCTAD.

UNCTAD. 2016. Trade and Development Report, 2016. Geneva: United Nations Conference on Trade and Development. Geneva: UNCTAD.

UNCTAD. 2017. *The Role of Development Banks in Promoting Growth and Sustainable Development in the South.* Geneva: UNCTAD.

UNCTAD. 2018. World Investment Report, 2018. Geneva: United Nations Conference on Trade and Development. Geneva: UNCTAD.

UNCTAD. 2019a. National Security-related screening mechanisms for foreign investment: An analysis of recent policy developments. *Investment Policy Monitor Special Issue.* Geneva: UNCTAD.

UNCTAD. 2019b. World Investment Report: Special Economic Zones. Geneva: UNCTAD.

UNCTAD. 2020. World Investment Report 2020: International Production beyond the Pandemic. Geneva: UNCTAD.

UNCTAD. 2021. Trade and Development Report 2021: From recovery to resilience: the development dimension. Geneva: UNCTAD.

UNCTAD. 2022a. Trade and Development Report: Development Prospects in a Fractured World. Geneva: UNCTAD.

UNCTAD. 2022b. World Investment Report: International Tax Reforms and Sustainable Development. Geneva: UNCTAD.

UNCTAD. 2023. The evolution of FDI screening mechanisms: Key trends and features *Investment Policy Monitor No 25.* Geneva: UNCTAD.

Vallett, E. 2022. *The World Is Witnessing a Rapid Proliferation of Border Walls.* Migration Policy Institute.

van Apeldoorn, B., and N. de Graaff. 2022. The state in global capitalism before and after the COVID-19 crisis. *Contemporary Politics* 28 (3): 306–327.

van Apeldoorn, B., N. de Graaff, and H. Overbeek. 2012. The reconfiguration of the global state–capital nexus. *Globalizations* 9 (4): 471–486.

Vasileva-Dienes, A., and V. A. Schmidt. 2019. Conceptualising capitalism in the twenty-first century: The BRICs and the European periphery. *Contemporary Politics* 25 (3): 255–275.

Veselinovič, J. 2022. European foreign policy think tanks and 'strategic autonomy': Making sense of the EU's role in the world of geoeconomics. In Babic, M, Dixon, A., Liu, I. (eds), *The Political Economy of Geoeconomics: Europe in a Changing World* (81–106). Cham: Springer International Publishing.

Victor, D. G., D. R. Hults, and M. C. Thurber eds. 2012. *Oil and Governance: State-owned Enterprises and the World Energy Supply.* Cambridge, UK; New York: Cambridge University Press.

Viktorov, I., and A. Abramov. 2020. The 2014–15 financial crisis in Russia and the foundations of weak monetary power autonomy in the international political economy. *New Political Economy* 25 (4): 487–510.

Viktorov, I., and A. Abramov. 2022. The rise of collateral-based finance under state capitalism in Russia. *Post-Communist Economies* 34 (1): 15–51.

von der Leyen, U. 2023. Speech by President von der Leyen on EU-China relations to the Mercator Institute for China Studies and the European Policy Centre. Available at: https://ec.europa.eu/commission/presscorner/detail/en/speech_23_2063 (last accessed 21 August 2023).

Wade, R. H. 2012. Return of industrial policy? *International Review of Applied Economics* 26 (2): 223–239.

Walter, A., and X. Zhang. 2012. Understanding variations and changes in East Asian capitalism. In A. Walter and X. Zhang (eds), *East Asian Capitalism: Diversity, Continuity, and Change* (247–280). Oxford: Oxford University Press.

Wang, Y. 2015. The rise of the 'shareholding state': financialization of economic management in China. *Socio-Economic Review* 13 (3): 603–625.

Warburton, E. 2018. A New Developmentalism in Indonesia? *Journal of Southeast Asian Economies* 35 (3): 355–368.

Ward, C., F. Brill, and M. Raco. 2023. State capitalism, capitalist statism: Sovereign wealth funds and the geopolitics of London's real estate market. *Environment and Planning A: Economy and Space* 55 (3): 742–759.

Wehr, I. 2015. Entangled modernity and the study of variegated capitalism: Some suggestions for a postcolonial research agenda. In M. Ebenau, I. Bruff and C. May (eds), *New Directions in Comparative Capitalisms Research* (134–151). London: Palgrave Macmillan.

Weiss, L. 2014. *America Inc.?: Innovation and Enterprise in the National Security State.* Ithaca; London: Cornell University Press.

Werner, M. 2021. Geographies of production II: Thinking through the state. *Progress in Human Geography* 45 (1): 178–189.

Werner, M., J. Bair, and V. R. Fernández. 2014. Linking up to development? Global value chains and the making of a post-Washington consensus. *Development and Change* 45 (6): 1219–1247.

Whiteside, H. 2022. State capitalism is capitalism in Canada. In M. Wright, G. Wood, A. Cuervo-Cazurra, P. Sun, I. Okhmatovskiy, and A. Grosman (eds), *Oxford Handbook on State Capitalism and the Firm* (659–676). Oxford: Oxford University Press.

Whiteside, H., I. Alami, A. D. Dixon, and J. Peck. 2023. Making space for the new state capitalism, part I: Working with a troublesome category. *Environment and Planning A: Economy and Space* 55 (1): 63–71.

Whitley, R. 1999. *Divergent capitalisms: the social structuring and change of business systems.* Oxford: Oxford University Press.

Whitley, R. 2000. The institutional structuring of innovation strategies: Business systems, firm types and patterns of technical change in different market economies. *Organization Studies* 21 (5): 855–886.

Wigger, A. 2023. The new EU industrial policy and deepening structural asymmetries: Smart specialisation not so smart. *JCMS: Journal of Common Market Studies* 61 (1): 20–37.

Wiig, A., and J. Silver. 2019. Turbulent presents, precarious futures: urbanization and the deployment of global infrastructure. *Regional Studies* 53 (6): 912–923.

Wilkinson, A., G. Wood, and R. Deeg eds. 2014. *The Oxford Handbook of Employment Relations: Comparative Employment Systems.* Oxford: Oxford University Press.

Williams, R. D. 2020. Beyond Huawei and TikTok: Untangling US concerns over Chinese tech companies and digital security. Working paper: *The Penn Project on the Future of US-China Relations. University of Pennsylvania: Philadelphia, PA, USA.*

Witt, M. A., and G. Redding. 2013. Asian business systems: Institutional comparison, clusters and implications for varieties of capitalism and business systems theory. *Socio-Economic Review* 11 (2): 265–300.

Witt, M. A., L. R. Kabbach de Castro, K. Amaeshi, S. Mahroum, D. Bohle, and L. Saez. 2018. Mapping the business systems of 61 major economies: a taxonomy and implications for varieties of capitalism and business systems research. *Socio-Economic Review* 16 (1): 5–38.

Wong, S. 2018. The State of Governance at State-Owned Enterprises. *IFC Governance Knowledge Publication* 40.

Wood, G. T., E. Onali, A. Grosman, and Z. A. Haider. 2023. A very British state capitalism: Variegation, political connections and bailouts during the COVID-19 crisis. *Environment and Planning A: Economy and Space* 55 (3): 673–696.

World Bank. 2013. *Global Financial Development Report 2013.* Washington, DC: World Bank Group.

World Bank. 2014. *Corporate Governance of State-Owned Enterprises: A Toolkit.* Washington, DC: World Bank Group.

World Bank. 2017. Survey of National Development Banks. Washington, DC: World Bank Group. Available at: http://documents1.worldbank.org/curated/en/977821525438071799/pdf/2017-Survey-of-National-development-banks.pdf (last accessed 27 August 2023).

World Bank. 2018. *Maximizing Finance for Development.* Washington, DC: World Bank Group.

World Bank. 2023. *Global Economic Prospects.* Washington, DC: World Bank Group.

World Bank-PPIAF. 2017. *Who Sponsors Infrastructure Projects? Disentangling Public and Private Contributions.* Washington, DC: The World Bank and the Public-Private Infrastructure Advisory Facility.

Wright, M., G. Wood, A. Musacchio, I. Okhmatovskiy, A. Grosman, and J. P. Doh. 2021. State capitalism in international context: Varieties and variations. *Journal of World Business* 56 (2): 101160.

Wullweber, J. 2021. The politics of shadow money: Security structures, money creation and unconventional central banking. *New Political Economy* 26 (1): 69–85.

Yeung, H. W.-c. 2016. *Strategic Coupling: East Asian Industrial Transformation in the New Global Economy.* Ithaca; London: Cornell University Press.

Yeung, H. W.-c. 2017. Corporations and the nation-state. In D. Richardson, N. Castree, M.F. Goodchild, A. Kobayashi, W. Liu and R.A. Marston (eds) *International Encyclopedia of Geography.* https://doi.org/10.1002/9781118786352.wbieg0647.

Youngs, R., and S. Ülgen. 2022. The European Union's competitive globalism. In S. Ülgen (ed.), *Rewiring Globalization* (51–62). Washington, DC: Carnegie Europe.

Zajontz, T. 2022. Debt, distress, dispossession: Towards a critical political economy of Africa's financial dependency. *Review of African Political Economy* 49 (171): 173–183.

Zenglein, M. J. 2018. Europe needs to stand up to China's state capitalist model. *Financial Times.* Available at: https://www.ft.com/content/cacd1e7c-803f-11e8-8e67-1e1a0846c475 (last accessed 22 August 2023).

Zettelmeyer, J. 2019. The return of economic nationalism in Germany. *Peterson Institute for International Economics Policy Brief* 19-4.

Zhang, J. 2017. Firms. In D. Richardson, N. Castree, M. F. Goodchild, A. Kobayashi, W. Liu, and R. A. Marston (eds), *International Encyclopedia of Geography.* https://onlinelibrary.wiley.com/doi/10.1002/9781118786352.wbieg0735.

Zhang, J., and J. Peck. 2016. Variegated capitalism, Chinese style: Regional models, multi-scalar constructions. *Regional Studies* 50 (1): 52–78.

Zhang, L., and T. Lan. 2023. The new whole state system: Reinventing the Chinese state to promote innovation. *Environment and Planning A: Economy and Space* 55 (1): 201–221.

Zhang, X., and R. Whitley. 2013. Changing macro-structural varieties of East Asian capitalism. *Socio-Economic Review* 11 (2): 301–336.

Index

For the benefit of digital users, indexed terms that span two pages (e.g., 52–53) may, on occasion, appear on only one of those pages.

abnormality of state capitalism 172
absorptive impulse 18, 78, 95–99, 108*t*, 138, 176–177, 231, 239, 251
Abu Dhabi 130–131, 136
Afghanistan 104
Africa 11–12, 34, 96, 125, 128–129, 175–176, 221
Africa Green Hydrogen Alliance 135–136
agency and centralization 141–170
  centralization of capital and organizational change 157–158
  explanatory model of organizational change 156*f*
  historical-geographical perspective on organizational change 153–157
  institutional change 148–149, 151*t*
  marketized hybrids 143–144, 146–153, 157, 168
  marketized hybrids as organizational fix 158–168
    financial system, role of as 'lever' of centralization 164–168
    social and spatial patterns of centralization 159–164
  Polanyian double movements 150–153, 151*t*
  political authority 149–150, 151*t*
  rise of 145–153
  social and spatial patterns 159–164
  strategic decisions at firm-level 146–148, 151*t*
  theorizing firms and organizational change 153–158
Aguilera, R.V. 25–26, 29–30, 185
Algeria 11–12
alterity of state capitalism 172
alternative conceptual framework and research agenda 74*t*
Altmaier, P. 193–194
Amaeshi, K. 32–33
ambivalences 3–6
Amsterdam School of critical IPE 35
Anglo-American geopolitics 183
Angola 101
anti-globalization 223
Argentina 29–30
Arrighi, G. 84
Asia 1–2, 175–176
  Central 11–12
  comparative capitalism 28–30
  policy emulation, uncontrolled 218
  sovereign wealth funds (SWFs) 34
  techno-industrial policies and national development plans 210–211
  territorial and geographical factors 45
  see also East and Southeast Asia
Asian financial crisis (1997-98) 100
Asian Infrastructure Investment Bank 174, 205–206
AUKUS (US, UK and Australia) 189
Australia 1–2, 196, 222–223
authoritarianism 20–21, 37, 99, 198, 251
  digital 127–129
  migration and border regime 241
Avions de Transport Régional (EU) 160

Babic, M. 28
backstopping 98–99
Bangladesh 29–30
Bank for International Settlements 122
Bank of England 103
Bank of Japan 103
bank recapitalizations 103
Becker, U. 184–185
beggar-thy-neighbour measures 240–241
Behuria, P. 125–126
Belarus 29–30, 132
best practices 166
Biden, J. 1–2, 180, 189, 191

'big D' Development and 'little d' capitalist development 21–22 n.11, 199 n.1, 199–200, 223–224, 228
Blackstone (USA) 162
Blanchette, J. 180
Blinken, A. 183, 189, 192
Blumenfeld, J. 245–246
Bok, R. 155
Bolivia 11–12, 102
Bolivia Fund for Productive Industrial Revolution 142
Bonefeld, W. 57–59
Botswana 101
Boyer, R. 44–45
Bpifrance 94, 97–98
Brands, H. 187–188
Brazil 11–12, 93–94
  comparative capitalism 31
  democratic state capitalism 37
  national development and policy banks 206
  peer-group learning and mimetic behaviour 122–123
  uneven development 102
  Workers' Party 47–48
Bremmer, I. 37, 172
Brenner, N. 64
Brenner, R. 84
Breton, T. 117
Bretton Woods institutions 101
BRICS 9, 172, 174, 203
British Energy 161
Bruton, G.D. 25–26
Bulgaria 208
Burnham, P. 57
Byler, D. 128–129

Callison, W. 236
Cammack, P. 228–229
capital
  controls 100–101, 234–235
  patient 94
  redeployment 161
  transfers 94
  valorization 247–248
  see also capital accumulation
capital accumulation 1, 18, 21–22, 112, 134–135, 174, 231–234, 247–248
  agency and centralization 144–145, 153, 155, 169–170
  climate change/crisis 243
  foundational shift 243–244, 246
  global political economy 35
  ideological and discursive changes 200–201, 223–224, 228
  'missing link' 40
  problèmatique of state capitalism 50–51, 55–59, 61–62, 65, 68–69, 73
  strategic management 27
  territorial and geographical considerations 47–48
  uneven development 77–78, 82–83, 87–89, 99–100
Carney, R.W. 29–30, 34–35, 99
catch-up 43
Central Asia 11–12
central banks 53–54, 98–99, 113–114
  capitalist impulses 61–62
  democratizing and greening state capitalism 249
  global development 201
  interventions 41–42
  peer-group learning and mimetic behaviour 122–123
  stabilizing role 103
  weaponization of new state capitalism 176–177
Central and Eastern Europe 11–12, 28–29, 132–133
centralization *see* agency and centralization
changing role of the state 6–7
Charbonnier, P. 240–241
Charnock, G. 66–67
ChemChina 159–160
Chen, G.C. 34–35, 46, 148–149
Chiang Mai Initiative (East Asia) 205–206
Chile 101, 122–123
China 3, 9, 11–12
  authoritarian state capitalism 37
  Belt and Road Initiative (BRI) 92–93, 119–120, 132–133
  capitalist impulses 63–64
  comparative capitalism 29–32
  competitive emulation 114–115, 118–121
  Digital Silk Road 128–129
  diplomacy and foreign policy 187–189
  geopoliticization, protectionism and fragmentation 222–223
  global political economy (GPE) 34, 36–38
  government investment model 1–2

China (*Continued*)
Made in China 2025 11, 71–72, 90–91, 192–193
managing state capitalism 28
market distortion and unfair competition 221
marketized hybrids 160, 162, 167
mutually reinforcing trajectories 130–134
National Development and Reform Commission 119–120
National Integrated Circuit Industry Investment Fund ('Big Fund') 94
party-state capitalism 58–59 n.1
peer-group learning and mimetic behaviour 122–123
policy emulation, uncontrolled 218, 220
preventative policing system and coercive internment camp system 128–129
rogue state capitalism 4
Silk Road Fund 119–120
sovereign wealth funds (SWFs) 7–8, 202–203
state-controlled investments 47–48
state-led green developmentalism 116–117
state-owned enterprises (SOEs) 48, 148–149, 209
territorial and geographical factors 45
trade, technology, competition and investment screening 192–197
uneven and combined development (U&CD) 68–69, 93–94, 106–107
and USA National Defense Strategy (2018) 185
weaponization of new state capitalism 171–172, 174–176, 180, 183–184, 198
see also 'Second Cold War' between China and United States
China Africa Development Fund 119–120
China Communist Party 189, 191
China Development Bank 119–120, 206
China Import-Export Bank 119–120
China Investment Corporation 96, 142
China Machinery Engineering Company 119–120
China Railway International 119–120
China State-Owned Assets Supervision and Administration Commission (SASAC) 161–162
Christophers, B. 46–47 n.2
Chwieroth, J.M. 121–122
Cinda (China) 98
Citigroup (USA) 162
Ciută, F. 181–182
Claar, S. 37–38, 185–186
Clarke, S. 57, 84
class politics 241–242
clientelism 172, 181, 183–185
climate change/crisis 1–2, 15, 22, 107, 136, 203, 205, 208, 210, 215–216, 230, 234, 238–243, 248–250
Clover, J. 6–7
CNOOC (China) 160
co-constitutive movement 13, 19, 113
co-dependence and competition 37–38
co-development 53–54
Coe, N.M. 147–148, 154
co-expansion 77
co-governed variety of capitalism 30–31
Cold War narrative 20–21, 171–172, 175–176, 178–179, 181–182, 187–188, 198, 241
see also 'Second Cold War' between China and United States
Colombia 122–123
combinatorial mechanisms 19, 62, 68–69, 72–73, 135–136, 138, 176–177, 243
commodity super-cycle 68–69, 81–82
company-states 5, 145–146
comparative capitalism 16, 39*t*, 23–24, 28–34, 172, 184–186
critical assessment 31–34
competition 37–38, 86, 173, 191–197
competitive emulation 19, 70–71, 113–121, 138, 210, 218, 232
competitive escalation 115
competitive neutrality 220
Comprehensive Agreement on Investment (CAI) (EU and China) 190
concentration 157–158
conceptual development *see problématique* of state capitalism
contemporary state capitalism 15–19, 21–22, 216–217, 232–233
agency and centralization 141, 145, 150
combination and political multiplicity 112–114, 121–122, 138–139
ideological dimensions 21–22, 171
material determination of 88*f*
periodization 44–45

problèmatique of state capitalism 54–57, 64–65, 67–68, 70–76, 74*t*
territorial and geographical considerations 47–49
uneven development 72–73, 87–89, 88*f*, 105, 107–110, 112, 138–139
weaponization of state capitalism 171
contextuality, geographical 173–179
convergence 139–140
coordinated-market economy (CME) 28–29
Copley, J. 59
core competencies 85
Cornyn, J. 191
corporate welfarism 239
corporatized hybrids *see* marketized and corporatized hybrids
corruption 172, 181, 183–185, 198, 218–219
COSCO (China) 132
COVID-19 pandemic 1–2, 15, 162, 205, 206, 208, 230, 240–241, 249
credit, subsidized 94
critical transition materials 240–241
Croatia 208
cronyism 184–185
cross-listing 165–166
cross-ownership to expand control 161–162
cumulative causation 19, 114, 137, 139, 243

Dalby, S. 174, 178–180
Danske Commodities 161
Davies, W. 235
decarbonization strategies 250
decentralization 25–26, 148, 157–159
defensive measures 104–105
de Graaff, N. 36–38, 42
deindustrialization 81–82, 212, 241–242
noxious 241–242
premature 81–82
democratic planning and alternative forms of ownership 252–253
democratic state capitalism 20–21, 37, 248–251
Denmark 90
de-risking policy 203, 205
Deutsche Bank 2–3, 161
developmentalism 1, 29–30, 43
developmental regionalism, open 213–214
development banks 9, 41–42, 102, 119–120
see also multilateral development banks; policy and development banks
development funds *see* sovereign wealth funds (SWFs)
development plans
long-term 58–59
national 9–10, 210–213
development studies 16
digital economy 118–119
Dijkink, G. 174, 181
diplomacy and foreign policy 173, 187–191
disciplinary impulse 18, 78, 104–107, 108*t*, 121, 126–127, 138, 176–177, 231, 251
discursive dimensions 21–22, 171, 200, 228
divergence 139–140
diversity
institutional 25–27, 30–33, 47–48, 51, 69–70, 74*t*, 113–114, 120–121
organizational 25–26
political 69–70
division of labour
international 105, 121–122
see also new international division of labour
Dodds, K. 183, 186–187
Dolfsma, W. 44–45, 150–151
double movements (Polanyian) 150–153, 151*t*
Dunford, M. 65
'Dutch disease' ('resource curse') 101
Dutch East India Company 5, 145–146
dynamic development 19, 176–177

East and Southeast Asia 210, 219
classical developmental states 58–59 n.1
comparative capitalism 30–32
competitive emulation 115–116
developmentalism 43
peer-group learning and mimetic behaviour 125–126
uneven development 71–72, 78–79, 81, 90–91, 96–98
eco-apartheid and green imperialism 251
economic geographies of firm 144–145, 168–169
economic governance 30–31
economic nationalism 10–13, 53–54, 61–62, 113–114, 230
global development 213–217
techno-industrial policies and national development plans 210
uneven development 69–70, 104–105

economic performance at firm level 25
economic stagnation 83–85, 158, 168–169, 231
economic stimulus packages 84–85
economisation of strategic policy 104
Ecuador 11–12, 91–92, 120
Edel, C. 187–188
EDF 161
Egypt 11–12, 37, 136
emerging markets crises (early 2000s) 100
enabling and mutual reinforcement 19, 138, 232
ENI 161
environmental destruction 247–248
E.On 161
Equinor (Norway) 161
equity investment 35–36, 94
Erdoğan, R.T. 101–102
Ethiopia 11–12
Eurasian Development Bank 205–206
Eurofighter 160
Europe 1–2, 5, 11–12, 28–29
  see also Central and Eastern Europe; European Union
European Bank for Reconstruction and Development 119–120, 136, 208
European Central Bank 103
European Investment Bank 94, 118–120, 136
European Renewal 195–196
European Union 20–21
  and China relations 190–191
  Chips Act 11, 71–72, 90, 115–116
  competitive emulation 117
  competitive globalism 106
  Europe fit for the Digital Age, A programme 118–119
  framework on foreign investment screening 193
  geopoliticization, protectionism and fragmentation 222–223
  Global Gateway 92–93, 119
  Green Deal 71–72, 90, 117, 241–242
  Industrial Strategy 2020 90
  Inflation Reduction Act 241–242
  material interests and strategic policy adjustments 186–187
  mutually reinforcing trajectories 130, 135–136
  NextGenerationEU programme 117
  Open Strategic Autonomy 190
  Open, Sustainable and Assertive Trade Strategy 194–195
  peer-group learning and mimetic behaviour 128–129
  policy emulation, uncontrolled 220
  Regulation 2019/425 71–72, 195
  REPowerEU 90
  Smart Specialization 90
  Sovereignty Fund 117
  State Aid rules 117
  state-owned enterprises (SOEs) 209
  strategic autonomy framework 106
  trade, technology, competition and investment screening 192–195
expansion
  of capital as state property 158
  geographical 11–12, 159–161, 163
  joint and concurrent 13–14
  of new state capitalism 200
  of state ownership 158
explanatory model of organizational change 156*f*
external integration in global political economy 31

Fainshmidt, S. 29–30, 185
Fichtner, J. 28
financial globalization 34–35, 99, 149–150
financialization 34–35, 85–89, 94, 97, 150
financial system, role of as 'lever' of centralization 164–168
Finland 90
firm-state nexus 169
FONSIS (Senegal) 96–97
Ford, C. 188
foreign direct investment (FDI) 8–9, 35–36, 89–91, 146–147, 213–214, 219, 232–233
foreign policy and diplomacy 187–191
form-determined operations 61–62
Fortune Global 500 141–142
fragmentation
  geoeconomic 21–22, 48, 157–158, 200–201, 214, 222–224, 228
  working class 80–81
France 127, 134
  dirigisme d'état 28–29, 58–59 n.1
  Electronique 2030 11
  France 2020 90
  managing state capitalism 28

marketized hybrids 162
sovereign wealth funds (SWFs) 34, 47–48
free-market capitalism 46, 180
Fund Corporation for the Overseas Development of Japan's Information and Communication Technology 119–120

G-7 - *Build Back Better World* 92–93, 119
G-20 9, 21–22, 174, 199, 209, 221–223
Gabor, D. 136–137, 203
Gallaher (UK) 159–160
Gambia 208
Gazprom (Russia) 160
geo-capitalist engagement 106–107
geo-category state capitalism 179–181, 186–189, 193, 197–198
geoeconomic changes 186–187
geoeconomic conditions 64
geoeconomic fragmentation 21–22, 48, 157–158, 200–201, 214, 222–224, 228
geoeconomic goals, market mechanisms for 23
geoeconomic statecraft 10–11
geoeconomic terrain 197–198
geographical 'anaemia' 46–51, 67–68
geographical approach 16, 45–49
geographical contextuality 173–179
geographical dispersion 157
geographical expansion 11–12, 159–161, 163
geographical imaginaries 180, 186–187, 191, 193, 196–198
geographical reconstruction of contemporary advent of state capitalism 18
geographical remaking of global capitalism 44, 77, 110, 112
geographical remaking of late capitalism 18
geographical reorientation 16–18
geographical scale 66
geographies of extraction, production and consumption 83–84
geographies of state capitalism 28, 32, 48–49, 67–68
geo-institutional differentiation 70, 110
geopolitical category 172–173
geopolitical changes 186–187
geopolitical conditions 64
geopolitical discourse 4, 20–21
geopolitical goals, market mechanisms for 23
geopolitical interests 35–36
geopolitical objectives 192–193
geopolitical re-organization 53–54, 73, 227, 230–231
geopolitical rivalries *see in particular* United States and China
geopolitical terrain 197–198
geopolitics 200–201, 222–224, 232
Anglo-American 183
critical 173, 197–198
Georgieva, K. 223–224
Germany 127
Industrial Strategy 2030 11, 90
Industrie 4.0 90
managing state capitalism 28
marketized hybrids 160, 162
Monopolkommission - *Chinese state capitalism: A challgenge for the European Market economy* 194–195
National Industrial Strategy (2030) 193–194
periodization 43
sovereign wealth funds (SWFs) 34
state-driven modernization 58–59 n.1
trade, technology, competition and investment screening 193–194
uneven development 106–107
Gershenkron theory of late development 31
Ghana 101
Ghana Heritage Fund 142
global capitalism 5, 9, 11, 16–18, 35, 231
agency and centralization 143–146, 158
geographical remaking of 44, 77, 110, 112
marketized hybrids 168
'missing link' 41–42
permanent, foundational shift 247
problématique of capitalism 53–55
territorial and geographical factors 48–49
uneven development 103
global development: liberal anxieties and ideological adjustment 199–229
economic nationalism and trade and investment restrictions 213–217
geo-politicization, protection backlash, and geoeconomic fragmentation risks 200–201, 222–224
market distortion and unfair competition risks 220–222

global development (*Continued*)
national development and policy banks 204–206
new vision of state in development 224–227
sovereign wealth funds (SWFs) 202–204
state-owned enterprises (SOEs) 206–209
techno-industrial policies and national development plans 210–213
uncontrolled policy emulation, risks of 218–220
global distribution of surplus 176
global financial crisis (2008) 44–45, 84–85, 95, 100, 102, 162, 205–206, 211–212, 230, 249
Global Financial Development Report 224–225
global governance 236
global green subsidies race 116–117
global imbalances 95
Global Infrastructure Hub 209, 221–223
globalization 3–4, 230, 232–233
capitalist 181–182
comparative state capitalism 28–29, 31–33
financial 34–35, 99, 149–150
ideological and discursive changes 214–215
increasing 24–25
managing state capitalism 27
neoliberal 44–45, 106
of production 85
rhetorical weaponization of new state capitalism 178–179, 190
global political economy (GPE) 16, 23–24, 34–38, 39*t*, 48
global and regional production networks 89–90
global state-capital nexus 23
global value chains (GVCs) 11, 210, 215, 219, 221, 224–225
Goldberg, P. 215
Gonzalez-Vicente, R. 34, 167
good governance 123–124, 166–167, 204
Goulding, R. 130–131
governance networks, effective 220
government procurement policies 104–105
government-sponsored entities 10
Great Wall (asset company China) 98
Green Deal (EU) 71–72, 90, 117, 241–242
green industrial plans 240–242
green protectionism 240–241
Grosman, A. 44–45, 150–151
Gulf States 11–12, 78–79, 223

Haberly, D. 28, 34–35
Habermas, J. 55–56
Hall, S. 131–132
Hanieh, A. 130–131 n.3
Hart, G. 21–22 n.11, 199 n.1, 199–200, 224, 228
Harvey, D. 153
Hausmann, R. 220
hedging 133–134
Heemskerk, E.M. 28
Heine, J. 175–176
historical development 18, 44, 77, 110, 112
historical-geographical factors
capitalist transformations 16–18
context 43, 54–55, 57
development of social relations 58
fullness 68
materialism 144–145, 168–169
perspective on organizational change 153–157
transformations 64–65, 67
historical materialist tradition 42, 52–53
historic arc in trajectories of state intervention 6–7
Holloway, J. 57
Huarong (China) 98
Huat, C.B. 34–35
Huawei (China) 104–105, 193
5G networks 114–115
Safe City 128–129
Hudson's Bay Company 145–146
Hungary 3, 11–12, 102–103, 132–133

ideological adjustment *see* global development: liberal anxieties and ideological adjustment
ideological dimensions of contemporary state capitalism 21–22, 171
impulses of state capitalism 44–45, 55–65, 87–89
synchronicity 68–69
see also absorptive impulse; disciplinary impulse; productivist impulse; stabilizing impulse
Independent Evaluation Group (IEG) 212
India 29–31, 36, 122–123, 133

Indonesia 3, 11–12, 29–30, 37, 91–94, 102
Indonesia Investment Authority 98
Industrial Development Bank of India 206
industrial overcapacity 158, 168–169, 231
industrial policy 13, 27, 53–54, 61–62, 69–70
industry bailouts 103
informal politics 172
infrastructure investment and project implementation 10–11, 60–61, 119–121, 209, 235
institutional change 30–31, 148–149, 151*t*
institutional contours 45–46
intellectual labour, valorization of 79–80
intellectual monopoly capitalism 86–87
intellectual property law 104–105
International Development Finance Corporation (IDFC) 120
international division of labour 105, 121–122
  old 158–159, 168–169, 231
International Finance Corporation 206–207
International Forum of Sovereign Wealth Funds 123–124, 204
internationalization 35–37, 147–148
International Monetary Fund (IMF) 9, 21–22, 95, 167, 199, 200–201
  economic nationalism and trade and investment restrictions 214
  Finance and Development magazine 220
  Fiscal Monitor 206–207, 220–221
  geopoliticization, protectionism and fragmentation 222–223
  global development 229
  How to Note 206–207
  Industrial Policy for Growth and Diversification 210–211
  market distortion and unfair competition 221–222
  national development and policy banks 205
  new vision of state in development 226–227
  peer-group learning and mimetic behaviour 122
  policy emulation, uncontrolled 219–220
  Return of the Policy that Shall Not Be Named, The 210–211
  sovereign wealth funds (SWFs) 203–204
  State-owned enterprises: the other government 206–207
  state-owned enterprises (SOEs) 209
  Subsidies, Trade and International Cooperation 215–216
international political economy (IPE) *see* global political economy (GPE)
international portfolio investment 163–164
inter-referential form of state capitalism 19, 176–177
investment
  equity 35–36, 94
  funds, state 47–48
  international portfolio 163–164
  opportunistic behaviour 177–178
  screening 173, 191–197, 213
  see also infrastructure investment and project implementation; trade and investment restrictions
Ireland 47–48, 90
  Strategic Investment Fund 97–98
Irwin, D. 220
Israel 11–12, 127–129
Italy 43, 47–48, 127
  Cassa Depositi e Prestiti Equity 97–98

Japan 11, 115
  comparative capitalism 28–31
  Green Transformation Act 117
  managing state capitalism 28
  Ministry of Economy, Trade and Industry 115–116
  periodization 43
  policy emulation, uncontrolled 218
  Policy Program for Promotion of Overseas Infrastructure Systems (2025) 119
  state-led industrialization 58–59 n.1
  trade, technology, competition and investment screening 193–194
  weaponization of new state capitalism 174–175
Japan International Cooperation Agency 119–120
Japan Investment Corporation 115–116
Japan Overseas Infrastructure Investment Corporation for Transport and Urban Development 119–120
Japan Tobacco 159–160, 162
Jayasuriya, K. 106
Jelinek, C. 132–133
Jensen, F. 132

Jessop, B. 55–56, 64
joint ventures 85–86, 127–128, 130–131, 136, 160, 163, 164, 245–246
Jokowi administration 102
Jones, L. 36–37
Jones, M. 64
Jordan 11–12
Judge, W.Q. 29–30, 185
Juhász, R. 211

Kabbach de Castro, L.R. 32–33
Kanai, M. 92–93
Kaplan, R.D. 187–188
Kaplan, S.B. 34
Kazakhstan 11–12, 125–126
Kazakhstan 2050 Strategy 124–125
Kenya 91–92
Kenya Vision 2020 125
Khazanah (Malaysia) 96–97, 124–125
Kirgizstan 208
Klinke, I. 181–182
Koelemaij, J. 130–131 n.4
Kong, B. 35–36
Korea 90–91, 122–123, 174–175, 202–203, 218
  K-Chips Act 11, 115–116
Korea Development Bank 94, 206
Korea Export-Import Bank 117
Korea Investment Corporation 96
Korea Trade Insurance Corp. 117
KPMG 209, 221–223, 226
Kurlantzick, J. 37, 42, 45–47, 172
Kuwait 202–203

Labban, M. 143, 165–166
labour process transformations under large-scale industry 78–81
Lane, N.J. 211
Laos 29–30, 133
late capitalism, geographical remaking of 18
late development theory (Gershenkron) 31
Latin America 11–12, 175–176
  classical developmental states 58–59 n.1
  comparative capitalism 28–29
  global political economy (GPE) 34
  peer-group learning and mimetic behaviour 125
  uneven development 78–79, 82–83, 96
Latin America Reserve Fund 205–206
Laurie, N. 185–186
Lazzarini, G. 25–27, 43
Leaver, A. 130–131
legitimacy struggles 63–64, 178–179, 248–249
Lemco, J. 177–178
Leonardo (Italy) 160
LG Energy Solutions (Korea) 117
liberal anxieties *see* global development: liberal anxieties and ideological adjustment
liberal capitalism 52
liberal democracy 99
liberal economic order 37
liberalism 1–2
  see also neoliberalism
liberal-market economy (LME) 28–29, 51
Lin, J.Y. 211–212
Lipsky, J. 202
Liu, W. 65
locating state capitalism 38–40
  see also territorial and geographical considerations
logistics 11, 85–90
Luger, J. 128–129
Lukoil (Russia) 160

McCaul, M.T. 189
MacDonald, S.B. 176–177
McEwan, C. 185–186
MacLeod, G. 64
McNally, C.A. 37–38
Macron, E. 195–196
Madan, T. 35–36
Malaysia 11–12, 29–31, 37, 93–94
Mamadouh, V. 174, 181
managing state capitalism 24–28
  critical assessment 26–28
Manfredi, Z. 236
Mann, G. 1
Mansour bin Zayed Al Nahyan, Sheikh 130–131
mapping state capitalism literature 39*t*
market-conforming, financial-return oriented state capitalist paradigm 34–35
market distortion, risk of 220–222
market failures, fixing 27
marketized and corporatized hybrids 5, 24–25
  see also under agency and centralization

market power 85–86
Marx, K. 67, 153, 157, 162–165, 245–246
Maskell, P. 147–148
Massey, D. 70–71
material interests and strategic policy adjustments 186–197
materialist state theory 50–51, 55–56, 73
Mauritania 136
Maximizing Finance for Development report 203, 228
May, C. 37–38, 185–186
Meckling, J. 35–36
Medby, I.A. 181–182
mergers and acquisitions (M&A) 35–36, 162–164
Merrill Lynch (USA) 162
Mexico 101
Meyer, K.E. 25–26
Mezzadra, S. 99–100
Micron (China) 114–115
Middle East 11–12, 97–98, 136
  peer-group learning and mimetic behaviour 125
  sovereign wealth funds (SWFs) 34
  state-controlled investments 47–48
  territorial and geographical factors 45
  uneven development 96
Miliband, R. 55–56
Miron, J. 172
'missing link': robust theory of the state 40–42, 49
modernization 96–97, 146–147, 226–228
Mohamed Bin Salman 101–102
Mongolia 29–30
monopolistic positions 4, 11, 29–30, 52–53, 60–61, 85–86, 89–90, 185
Moraitis, A. 59
Morocco 91–92
  Ithmar Capital 96–97
multilateral development actors/institutions 21–22, 174, 236
  ideological and discursive changes 199–207, 209–211, 213, 216–218, 220–229
multilateral development banks 9, 97, 167, 174, 239
multilateralism 205–206, 213–214, 223
multi-level governance 48
multinational enterprises (MNEs) 141–142, 176
multiplier effect 72–73, 112, 138–139
Murdoch School 55–56
Musacchio, A.A. 25–27, 43
muscular forms of statism 11–15, 113–114, 138–139, 230, 246
  climate change 243
  co-development 53–54
  democratic planning and alternative forms of ownership 252
  democratizing and greening state capitalism 250
  global development 201
  neoliberal futures 235
  new vision of state in development 227
  periodization 44
  problématique of state capitalism 73
  techno-industrial policies and national development plans 210
  uneven development 66–71, 77, 87–89, 93–94
  weaponization of new state capitalism 176–177
  see also economic nationalism; industrial policy; spatial development; trade and investment restriction
mutually reinforcing trajectories 129–137

Namibia 136–137
'national champions' 35–36, 104–105, 148–149, 193–194
national development plans 9–10, 210–213
national innovation systems 250
nationalism
  economic 10–13, 53–54, 61–62, 113–114, 230
  methodological 46–48
  resource 3, 11–12
  techno 11–12
national policy and development banks 9, 204–206
national security 10–11, 105, 215
nature and extent of state intervention 29, 46–47
Neilson, B. 99–100
Nem Singh, J. 34–35, 46, 148–149
neoliberalism 1, 23, 52, 150, 248–249
  futures 234–237
  global hegemony of 37
  logics 234–235
  market capitalism 37–38

neoliberalism (*Continued*)
mutant variants 236–237
periodization 43
neo-mercantilism 3, 10–11
Nepal 133
Netherlands 115
net zero strategies 240–241
New Deal 43
New Development Bank 205–206
new geographies of extraction, production and consumption 95
'new global drama', searching for 178–186
new international division of labour 78–79, 81–84, 95, 126, 158–159, 168–169, 231
new state capitalism 5–12, 14*f*, 16–18, 23–24, 53–54, 232–233
capitalist impulses 55–56, 62
democratic planning and alternative forms of ownership 253
democratizing and greening state capitalism 248–249
neoliberal futures 236
as object of inquiry and analytical construct 54*f*
paradigmatic organizational forms 19–20
progressive openings 248
uneven development 77–78
see also weaponization of new state capitalism
new structural economics 211–212
new vision of state in development 224–227
Nexen (Canada) 160
Niger 208
Nippon Export and Investment Insurance 119–120
Nixon, R. 183
Nölke, A. 37–38, 43, 185–186
non-reformist reforms 248
North Africa 11–12, 136
North America 1–2, 28–29
see also United States
North Atlantic Treaty Organization (NATO) 175–176
Innovation Fund 240–241
Norway 7–8, 136
Government Pension Fund Global 142
Nvidia 162

Obama, B. 188–189
Offe, C. 55–56
offensive measures 104–105
oil and gas industry 35–36, 160
Okonjo-Iweala, N. 223–224
old international division of labour 158–159, 168–169, 231
oligopoly 159
opportunistic investment behaviour 177–178
organizational change *see under* agency and centralization
organizational fix 155–157
organizational and governance form 24
organizational isomorphism 143–144
Organization for Economic Cooperation and Development (OECD) 8–9, 21–22, 28, 141–142, 199, 202–203
geopoliticization, protectionism and fragmentation 222–223
Guidelines on Corporate Governance of State-Owned Enterprises 207–208
market distortion and unfair competition 221
Monitoring the Performance of State-Owned Enterprises 207–208
national development and policy banks 204–205
new vision of state in development 226–227
Ownership and Governance of State-Owned Enterprises 207–208
policy emulation, uncontrolled 218–219
sovereign wealth funds (SWFs) 204
State-Owned Enterprises in the Development Process 207–208
state-owned enterprises (SOEs) 209
Subsidies, Trade and International Cooperation 215–216
techno-industrial policies and national development plans 211
Orient (China) 98
Overbeek, H. 42
overcapacity and market saturation 160–161
ownership and control redistribution 85–86

Pakistan 29–30, 91–92
partial state ownership 8–9, 24–25, 99, 165–166
patrimonial forms of capitalism 11–12, 172, 184–185
Peck, J. 52, 72

peer group learning and mimetic behaviour 19, 113, 121–129, 138, 218, 232
Peng, M.W. 25–26
periodization 38–40, 42–45, 49, 68, 110, 244
permanent, foundational shift in capitalism 243–247
Petramina (Indonesia) 160
Petrobras 160
Petronas (Malaysia) 160
Philippines 29–30, 174–175
planning policies 69–70
plasticity 52
Poland 11–12, 91–92
  Development Fund 94
Polanyian double movements 150–153, 151*t*
policy and development 11–13, 53–54
policy and development banks 11–13, 61–62, 113–114, 201, 230, 249
  national 9, 204–206
political authority 232–233
  reinforcement of 149–150, 151*t*
political capitalism 3, 247
political economic transformation 3–4
political economy 1, 13–14, 57, 66, 148–149, 173, 186–187
  authoritarian 11–12
  geographical 155, 228
  global 16, 23–24, 31, 34–38, 41–42, 65, 139–140, 150, 174, 176, 186, 197–198
  international 22, 31, 144, 146, 148
  see also global political economy (GPE)
political multiplicity 19, 65, 68–69, 71–76, 112, 138
political relations, direct 71–72
politicization 62–64, 73
politics of governing alienation 59
politics of representation 155, 166–168
Pollard, J. 185–186
Pompeo, M. 183, 191
post-developmentalism 3
post-neoliberalism 3
Poulantzas, N. 55–56
Powergen 161
predatory state elements 29–30
privatization 25–26, 146–147, 206–207, 209
  neoliberal 148
  partial 124–125, 148
problématique of state capitalism 16–18, 50–76
  alternative conceptual framework and research agenda 74*t*
  rigid model to flexible *problématique* 51–55
  state capitalist impulses in form of capitalist state 55–65
  uneven and combined development (U&CD) 50–51, 65–76
productive potential 50–51
productivist impulse 18, 78, 89–94, 108*t*, 121, 138, 148–149, 176–177, 231, 251
progressive openings 247–253
protection backlash, risk of 222–224
protectionism 21–22, 31, 47, 105, 200–201, 213, 215, 217–218, 221–223, 227, 240–241
Proust, F. 195
PTT (Thailand) 160
public offerings 165–166
Public-Private Infrastructure Advisory Facility (PPIAF) 10, 209
public-private ownership 165–166, 209

Qatar 202–203
Quad alliance (USA, Japan, Australia, India) 189
qualitative change 244–245
quantitative development 244–245
quantitative easing 41–42, 98–99

Redding, R. 29–30
reformist strategy 248, 252
refurbished state capitalism 37–38
regional and transnational, relation between 48
reinvention 33, 42–43, 148–149
relational-comparative work 70–71, 73–76
relative surplus populations 80
renewal 33, 42, 252
rentiership 85–90
representational category 3–4, 40–41, 50–51, 73
re-primarization, economic 81–82
rescaling 57, 62, 232–233
reshoring and 'friend-shoring' critical supply chains 240
resource-nationalism 3, 11–12
resurgence 33, 42, 252
risk management by diversification 162–163
risks, 'physical' 238–239
RJ Reynolds (USA) 159–160
Rodrik, D. 211
Rogers, S. 132–133

rogue state capitalism 4
Rolf, S. 118
Royal African Company 145–146
rule of law 42, 57, 107, 120–121, 171–172, 180, 184–185
Russia 3, 29–30, 101–103, 133–134
  authoritarian state capitalism 37
  diplomacy and foreign policy 188–189
  Direct Investment Fund 162
  oil and gas exports 11–12
  rogue state capitalism 4
  weaponization of new state capitalism 175–176, 183–184
Russian war of aggression in Ukraine 10–11, 104, 162, 230, 240–241
Rwanda 11–12
Rwanda Development Board 125–126
Rwanda Social Security Board 125–126

Samers, M. 185–186
Samruk-Kazyna (Kazakhstan) 96–97, 124–125, 133–134
Samsung (Korea) 117
Santiago Principles 123–124, 166–167, 204, 225
Saudi Arabia 162, 202–203
  Public Investment Fund 101–102, 162
Saudi Aramco 8–9
Scatec Solar 161
Schindler, S. 92–93, 118
Schmidt, V.A. 28–29, 172
'Second Cold War' between China and United States 10–12, 20–21, 71–72, 175–176, 180–182, 187–189, 200, 223
securitisation of economic policy 10–11, 104
self-transformation 87–89
semiconductor chip industry 114–116
Senegal 91–92, 125, 134–135
Serbia 11–12, 132–133
service-oriented economies 82
Shih, V. 99
Sidaway, J.D. 179–180, 185
Silver, J. 130–131
Singapore 3, 37, 125–126, 128, 202–203, 218
  Economic Development Board 125–126
  Smart Nation 90–91
Singapore Economy 2030 90–91
Sinochem 159–160
Slater, D. 183–184
Smith, A. 29–30, 185
Smith, T. 58
SNCF (France) 161
social dimension 66, 245–246
social and economic processes 16–18
social goods, providing 27
socio-technical conditions 67–68
SoftBank Vision Fund 162
South Africa Reserve Bank 122–123
sovereignty 232–233
Sovereign Wealth Fund Institute 7–8, 124–125
sovereign wealth funds (SWFs) 5, 7–9, 11–13, 19–20, 23, 113–114, 230, 233–235
  agency and centralization 142–144, 147, 149–150
  capitalist impulses 61–63
  democratizing and greening state capitalism 250
  global development 201–204
  global political economy (GPE) 34–36
  marketized hybrids 162, 168–170
  'missing link' 41–42
  mutually reinforcing trajectories 130
  peer-group learning and mimetic behaviour 123–125
  problématique of capitalism 53–54
  progressive openings 247–248
  stabilization 5, 101–102
  territorial and geographical factors 45–46
  trade, technology, competition and investment screening 192–193
  uneven development 69–70, 96–99
  weaponization of new state capitalism 176
spatial development strategies 13, 53–54, 61–62, 113–114, 210, 230
spatialities 16, 20–21, 50–51, 57–58, 64–65, 67–68, 73–76, 74*t*
spatialized social relations 71–72
spatial parameters 5, 16–18
spatial planning 11–12
Spechler, M.C. 46
Sperber, N. 3–4, 52–53, 59–60
Sri Lanka 29–30
stabilization sovereign funds 5, 101–102
stabilizing impulse 18, 78, 99–103, 108*t*, 138, 176–177, 231, 239
stagnation
  economic 83–85, 158, 168–169, 231
  secular 83–84

Stalinism 43
Starosta, G. 66–67
state activism 47–49, 63, 68–69, 113
state asset management companies 35–36, 98
state-business relations 23, 29
state capitalism 3.0 43
state capitalism and capitalist state distinction 40–41, 54–55, 62
state-capital nexus 15
statecraft 10–11, 235–236
state investment funds 47–48
stateness, liabilities of 25
state-organized business system 28–29
state-owned banks 94, 102–103, 120–121, 199, 204–206, 224–227
state-owned enterprises (SOEs) 8–13, 19–20, 23, 113–114, 230, 233–235
 agency and centralization 141–144, 146–149
 capitalist impulses 61–62
 centrality and longevity of 25
 China 48, 148–149, 209
 democratizing and greening state capitalism 250
 global development 201, 206–209
 global political economy (GPE) 35–36
 internationalization and upgrading 34–35, 221
 managing state capitalism 24–28
 marketized hybrids 159–163, 166–170
 'missing link' 41–42
 problématique of capitalism 53–54
 stock exchange listings 27
 territorial and geographical factors 45–47
 trade, technology, competition and investment screening 192–193
 uneven development 104–105
 see also transnational state-owned enterprises (TSOEs)
state-owned investment funds *see* sovereign wealth funds (SWFs)
state-permeated variety of capitalism 31
state-platform capitalism 118, 127–128
state as promoter, supervisor and owner of capital 6–7
statism 59–64, 176–177, 224–225
 see also muscular forms of statism
Stenning, A. 185–186
Stiglitz, J. 211–212
strategic alliances 163
strategic coupling 11, 130–131
strategic decisions at firm-level 146–148, 151*t*
strategic decoupling 214
strategic discursive and ideological adjustment 21–22, 200, 227–228
Strategic Foresight Report 2021 (EU) 190
strategic investment funds *see* sovereign wealth funds (SWFs)
strategic management 16, 39*t*, 23–24, 27, 56–57
strategic policy adjustments and material interests 186–197
Sullivan, J. 189
Sunak, R. 196
sustainable development 213
Sustainable Development Goals (SDGs) 97, 203
Sweden 115, 127
Swedish Model 43
Swyngedouw, E. 59
Sylla, N.S. 136–137
Syngenta (Switzerland) 159–160
system-wide attributes 52–53
Szabó, L. 132–133

tacit knowledge, codification of 79–80
Taiwan 11, 30–31, 122–123, 174–175, 189
Taylor, I. 34
technical revolution and computer-assisted automation of labour process 80–81
techno-industrial policy 3, 9–13, 113–114, 191, 230, 234–235
 climate change 239
 democratizing and greening state capitalism 250
 global development 210–213
technological innovation 89–90
technological and productivity frontier 82
technology 173, 191–197
techno-nationalism 11–12
techno-neo-feudalism 247
Telefónica 161
Temasek (Singapore) 96–97, 124–125

temporalities 5, 16–18, 50–51, 64–65, 68–69, 73–76, 74*t*
ten Brink, T. 37–38, 185–186
territorialities 45–49, 58, 232–233
Thailand 29–31, 91–92
Thalès (EU) 160
Thatcher, M. 34
theoretical reconstruction *see problématique* of state capitalism
theorizing firms and organizational change 153–158
Tilley, L. 184–186
time horizons *see* periodization; temporalities
Timor-Leste 101
Tooze, A. 187–188
trade 173, 191–197
trade and investment restrictions 11–12, 53–54, 61–62, 105, 113–114, 230, 234–235
  climate change 240–241
  global development 213–217
  techno-industrial policies and national development plans 210
trade-related dislocation 215
transformative strategy 248
'transition' risks 238–239
transnational capitalism 232–233
transnational embeddedness 31
transnationalization 45, 163
transnational state-owned enterprises (TSOEs) 28
transparency 166–167, 213, 220
Trotsky, L. 114
Trump, D. 114–115, 191
Turkey 3, 11–12, 101–103, 122–123
type of state 23, 29, 52

Ukraine *see* Russian war of aggression in Ukraine
uncontrolled policy emulation, risks of 218–220
uneven development 16–18, 50–51, 65–73, 77–112, 138, 234
  absorptive impulses 78, 95–99, 108*t*
  disciplinary impulses 78, 104–107, 108*t*
  economic stagnation 83–85
  labour process transformations under large-scale industry 78–81
  new international division of labour 78–79, 81–84, 95
  productivist impulses 78, 89–94, 108*t*
  rentiership, logistics, centralization and finance 85–90
  stabilizing impulses 78, 99–103, 108*t*
unfair competition, risk of 220–222, 233–234
United Arab Emirates 130–131, 162, 202–203
United Kingdom 127, 131–132, 160
  Build Back Better 90
  Global Britain 92–93, 119
  Industrial Strategy 90
  Infrastructure Bank 94
  National Security and Investment Act (2021) 196
  National Semiconductor Strategy 115–116
United Nations Conference on Trade and Development (UNCTAD) 9, 21–22, 105, 125–126, 141–142, 199
  Investment Policy Monitor 213
  liberal anxieties 217–218 n.4
  national development and policy banks 205–206
  policy emulation, uncontrolled 219
  sovereign wealth funds (SWFs) 203
  state-owned enterprises (SOEs) 209
  Trade and Development Report 203, 210, 213–214
  World Investment Report 9, 203, 206–207, 210, 213
United States
  Bipartisan Infrastructure Investment and Jobs Act 71–72
  CHIPS and Science Act (2022) 11, 71–72, 115–117
  competitive emulation 114–115, 118–119
  diplomacy and foreign policy 187–189
  'entity list' 114–115
  Federal Reserve 103
  Foreign Investment Risk Review Modernization Act 191
  geopoliticization, protectionism and fragmentation 222–223
  Hamiltonian developmentalism 58–59 n.1
  'hidden' industrial policy 41–42
  Inflation Reduction Act (2022) 71–72, 116–117

Infrastructure Investment and Jobs Act 116–117
international liberal order 228–229
material interests and strategic policy adjustments 186–187
military-industrial complex 41–42
mutually reinforcing trajectories 133
National Defense Strategy (2018) 185, 188–189
National Security Strategy 188–189
peer-group learning and mimetic behaviour 128–129
policy emulation, uncontrolled 220
trade, technology, competition and investment screening 191–196
treasury debt 37–38
uneven development 90–91, 106–107
weaponization of new state capitalism 176, 180
see also 'Second Cold War' between China and United States

van Apeldoorn, B. 36–38, 42
Vasileva-Dienes, A. 172
Vattenfall 161
Venezeula 11–12, 29–30
Vestager, M. 71–72, 117
vicissitudes in state capitalism studies 3–6
Vietnam 29–30, 37, 133
Vlandas, T. 34
von der Leyen 190–191

Walter, A. 29–30
Ward, C. 130
'war ecology' 240–241
Washington Consensus 37–38, 218
weaponization of cybersecurity 104–105
weaponization of economic interdependence and networks 104
weaponization of new state capitalism 20–21, 171–198
geographical contextuality 173–179
material interests and strategic policy adjustments 186–197
diplomacy and foreign policy 173, 187–191
trade, technology, competition and investment screening 173, 191–197
'new global drama', searching for 178–186
weaponized interdependence 10–11
Wehr, I. 184–186
Wento (Poland) 161
Western liberal capitalist model 38
'whip of external necessity' 114–116, 121, 139
Whitley, R. 28–31
Witt, M.A. 29–30, 32–33
Wójcik, D. 28, 34–35
'Wolf warrior diplomacy' 174–175
working class 79–81, 242–243, 247–248, 250–251
fragmentation 80–81
World Bank 9–10, 21–22, 134, 167, 199, 200
Corporate Governance of State-Owned Enterprises 208
Distributional Impacts of Trade 215
Global Financial Development Report 204–205, 219–220
Integrated State-Owned Enterprises Framework (iSOEF) 208, 225
Leadership Training Toolkit for State-Owned Enterprises 225–227
national development and policy banks 205
new vision of state in development 224–227
policy emulation, uncontrolled 219
Rethinking the role of the state in finance 204–205
sovereign wealth funds (SWFs) 203
state-owned enterprises (SOEs) 209
Subsidies, Trade and International Cooperation 215–216
techno-industrial policies and national development plans 211–213
world-historical totality 13
World Trade Organization 196–197, 215–216

Yellen, J. 189
Yeung, H.W.-C. 147–148, 154
Yoon Suk Yeol 115–116

Zambia 11–12
Zenglein, M. 192–193
Zettelmeyer, J. 193–194, 196–197
Zhang, X. 29–31
'zombie firms' 103
Zou, Y. 36–37
ZTE (China) 104–105
5G networks 114–115
SmartCity 128–129